# YEAR OF THE FIRES

BOOKS BY STEPHEN J. PYNE

*Cycle of Fire*

*The Story of Fire: An Introduction*

*World Fire: The Culture of Fire on Earth*

*Vestal Fire: An Environmental History, Told Through Fire, of Europe and Europe's Encounter with the World*

*Fire in America: A Cultural History of Wildland and Rural Fire*

*Burning Bush: A Fire History of Australia*

*The Ice: A Journey to Antarctica*

*How the Canyon Became Grand: A Short History*

*Grove Karl Gilbert*

*Fire on the Rim: A Firefighter's Season at the Grand Canyon*

*Introduction to Wildland Fire*

*America's Fires: Management in Wildlands and Forests*

# YEAR OF THE FIRES

*The Story of the Great Fires of 1910*

STEPHEN J. PYNE

•

VIKING

VIKING
Published by the Penguin Group
Penguin Putnam Inc., 375 Hudson Street,
New York, New York 10014, U.S.A.
Penguin Books Ltd, 27 Wrights Lane,
London W8 5TZ, England
Penguin Books Australia Ltd, Ringwood,
Victoria, Australia
Penguin Books Canada Ltd, 10 Alcorn Avenue,
Toronto, Ontario, Canada M4V 3B2
Penguin Books (N.Z.) Ltd, 182–190 Wairau Road,
Auckland 10, New Zealand

Penguin Books Ltd, Registered Offices:
Harmondsworth, Middlesex, England

First published in 2001 by Viking Penguin,
a member of Penguin Putnam Inc.

1 3 5 7 9 10 8 6 4 2



Maps by Mark Stein Studios

Library of Congress Cataloging in Publication Data
Pyne, Stephen J., 1949–
Year of the fires : the story of the great fires of 1910 / Stephen J. Pyne.
p. cm.
Includes bibliographical references (p. ) and index.
ISBN 0-670-89990-9 (alk. paper)
1. Forest fires—Montana—History. 2. Forest fires—Idaho—History.
3. Fires—Montana—History. 4. Fires—Idaho—History. I. Title.

SD421.32.M9 P96 2001
363.37'9—dc21 00-069337

This book is printed on acid-free paper. ♾

Printed in the United States of America
Set in Bembo
Designed by Jaye Zimet



INSERT CREDITS: Oregon Historical Society: p. 7, top right and bottom (negatives 4684 and 4681); Barbara Tokmakian, from the collection of Roscoe Haines: p. 9, top, and p. 12, bottom; reprinted from *American Forests* magazine: p. 9, middle and bottom, and p. 10, top; The Museum of Northern Idaho: p. 10, middle; Minnesota Historical Society: p. 12, top and middle; Fred Plummer, *Forest Fires*, Forest Service Bulletin 117 (1912): p. 16, bottom left and right. All others courtesy of the U.S. Forest Service.

*To Sonja*
*who stayed close to the heart*
*and the North Rim Longshots*
*who stayed on the line*

# CONTENTS

# DRAMATIS PERSONAE

*(their roles in 1910)*

*Politicians and Bureaucrats*

CHRISTOPHER COLUMBUS ANDREWS • Civil War general; later ambassador to Sweden and Brazil; active in public service. Most noted for work in establishing state-sponsored forestry in Minnesota.

RICHARD BALLINGER • Seattle lawyer, brought into public service by Roosevelt to overhaul the General Land Office and later elevated to secretary of the interior under Taft. His rivalry with Pinchot helped disrupt the Taft administration.

JOSEPH CANNON • Representative from Illinois; later Speaker of the House (1903–1911). Considered Powell, not Roosevelt, the originator of government conservation. Frequent foe of Progressive reformers.

LOUIS GLAVIS • An investigative agent for the General Land Office. His work on the leasing of Alaska coal lands led him to question Secretary Ballinger's integrity, erupting into the Ballinger-Pinchot controversy. Fired by Ballinger in 1909; later reinstated.

HENRY SOLON GRAVES • One of the founders of American forestry; first dean of Yale School of Forestry; succeeded Pinchot as chief forester (1910–1920); later returned to Yale. Highest-ranking forestry official involved in the 1910 fires.

WILLIS MOORE • Chief of the Weather Bureau. Sided with Lieutenant Colonel Hiram Chittenden in arguing that forests did not prevent floods and pleaded with Taft not to indulge in rainmaking schemes during the 1910 fires.

GIFFORD PINCHOT • Scion of a wealthy family; became interested in forestry and conservation; appointed chief of the Division of Forestry in 1898 and chief forester of the Forest Service after it received the reserves in 1905. His quarrel with Ballinger ended in his dismissal in 1910. Later elected twice as governor of Pennsylvania.

JOHN WESLEY POWELL • Explorer and early conservationist; second director of the U.S. Geological Survey and longtime administrator of Bureau of Ethnology; critic of federal forest reserve scheme and a skeptic of such conventional wisdom as the existence of a timber famine and the value of fire suppression.

THEODORE ROOSEVELT • President, 1901–1908. Put conservation on the national political agenda, transferred the forest reserves to the U.S. Forest Service in 1905, and sparked the political ambitions of Gifford Pinchot.

WILLIAM HOWARD TAFT • President, 1909–1912. Roosevelt's anointed successor, Taft was more cautious about reforms than Roosevelt and insisted on his own appointments. His administration ripped apart, helped by the Ballinger-Pinchot controversy.

JAMES WILSON • Onetime professor of agriculture and congressman from Iowa. Secretary of agriculture from 1897 to 1913. Helped rebuild the Forest Service after Pinchot's dismissal and supported the Service in its 1910 firefight.

## *The Scientists*

HERMAN HAUPT CHAPMAN • Forestry professor at Yale. His studies of fire in the southern pines forced a reevaluation of fire ecology and helped promote controlled burning in the South.

FREDERIC E. CLEMENTS • One of the founders of the American school of ecology; developed schemas for how communities changed following a disturbance. Author of a founding paper on forest fire ecology in 1910.

HENRY GANNETT • Chief cartographer of U.S. Geological Survey; later active in National Geographic Society. Oversaw the survey of the forest reserves from 1898 to 1900. Conservationist; like Powell, a skeptic of forestry's claims but, unlike him, supported fire protection.

CHARLES SARGENT • Botanist and director of Arnold Arboretum at Harvard. Surveyed forests and fires for the 1880 census. Served on several commissions influential in establishing government reserves, in both New York and the country at large, including the 1896 National Academy of Sciences' forest committee.

*The Foresters*

E. T. ALLEN • Forester who worked for California and the Forest Service before overseeing the Western Forest and Conservation Association, the umbrella group of private institutions with an interest in fire protection.

COERT DUBOIS • Young forester in California during 1910s. Published formative treatise on fire control, *Systematic Fire Protection in the California Forests,* in 1914.

WILLIAM BUCKOUT GREELEY • Graduate of Yale School of Forestry and admirer of Gifford Pinchot. Headed District One during the Great Fires. Later promoted cooperative fire protection as the foundation of American forestry. Chief forester, 1920–1928.

ROSCOE HAINES • Forest Service ranger active in the Great Fires; later transferred to the Coeur d'Alene, where he became largely responsible for handling the claims for compensation filed after the 1910 fires.

JOSEPH HALM • Former star athlete at Washington State College; ranger active on the Coeur d'Alene during the Great Fires. Made the Forest Service his career and attended the 1960 fire reunion.

ELERS KOCH • Montana native, graduate of Yale School of Forestry, supervisor of Lolo National Forest for almost forty years. First "published" the collected stories about the 1910 fires. Critic of Forest Service fire policy for backcountry.

WILLIAM WEST MORRIS • Forestry graduate of the University of Michigan; worked on Coeur d'Alene from 1909 to 1913. Wrote a series of letters and accounts that describe firefighting during the summer of 1910. Attended the 1960 fire reunion.

EDWARD PULASKI • Forest ranger for Wallace District, Coeur d'Alene National Forest. Famous for his exploits during the 1910 fires; stayed on the district and later devised the pulaski tool.

FERDINAND AUGUSTUS SILCOX • Assistant district forester of District One during the Great Fires, with responsibilities for logistics. Later headed the district and oversaw its efforts to contain large fires. Chief forester, 1933–1939.

ROBERT Y. STUART • Night shift supervisor in District One during the Great Fires. Later chief forester, 1928–1933.

ED THENON • Early forester on the Clearwater forest. Best known for his account of the firefight on Moose Creek in the Selways.

WILLIAM G. WEIGLE • Supervisor of the Coeur d'Alene forest during the Great Fires. After filing a summary report after the burns, he transferred to Alaska.

MEYER WOLFF • Fire guard on the Kaniksu forest during the Great Fires. Later supervisor of the Coeur d'Alene forest, who promoted memorials for the dead firefighters and the pulaski tool.

*The Soldiers*

LIEUTENANT COLONEL HIRAM CHITTENDEN • Officer in Army Corps of Engineers. Served two tours at Yellowstone and was busy with waterworks, including the Seattle canal. Became vigorous critic of forest-flood thesis.

LIEUTENANT E. E. LEWIS • Commander of Company G, Twenty-fifth Infantry, stationed at Avery, Idaho, during the Big Blowup.

MAJOR WILLIAM LOGAN • Former Army scout; assumed superintendency of Glacier National Park in May 1910 and led firefighting efforts there.

GENERAL LEONARD WOOD • Army chief of staff during Taft administration. Supported efforts to use the military to fight fires, but only as an emergency measure.

# THE TUNNEL

*Rockfall clogs the entry. Seepage through the loose rubble feeds a wild growth of mosses, bracken, woody saplings, and long-tendriled flowers. The West Fork of Placer Creek splashes a few feet below. This is not an easy place to find. The midsummer lushness practically blots the tunnel from view. One has to peer carefully, even when standing across the stream. Apart from the hum of gnats and mosquitoes and the low rustle of the creek, the scene is silent. It has the feel of some mythical grotto, the source of a sacred spring like Lourdes, a sepulcher, an oracle. It is, in truth, all these.*

•

PROBABLY THE SITE is as obscure as any on the National Register of Historic Places. (The identifying plaque is well away, conveniently planted alongside the paved portion of forest road 456 south of Wallace, Idaho.) The story the site tells is as buried by the shards of time and the rank growth of institutions as the tunnel's entrance. It is hard to find its plot now, amid the detritus and weediness, or to hear its lines above the larger din of engines, chain saws, and air tankers. But in the summer of 1910 it stood as a dark sanctuary, the moral axis of a vast maelstrom of flame.

What happened that astonishing summer was that American society and American nature collided with almost tectonic force. Spark, fuel, and wind merged violently and overran whatever mountains and people had placed in their way. The sparks came from locomotives, settlers, hobo floaters, and lightning. The fuel lay in heaps, like those alongside the newly hewn Milwaukee Railway over the Bitterroots and down the St. Joe Valley and across hillsides ripped by mines and logging and untouched woods primed by drought. The Rockies had experienced a wet winter but a dry spring that ratcheted, day by day, into a droughty summer, the worst in memory. Duff and canopies that normally wouldn't burn now could. The winds came with the passage of shallow cold fronts, rushing ahead from central Washington and the Palouse and the deserts of western Oregon, acting like an enormous bellows that turned valleys into furnaces and side canyons into chimneys.

The Great Fires began simply enough. Lightning sizzled down snags and kindled fire in the spiral tears it gouged out of the dead trees. Abandoned campfires and candle-size flames sparked by railroads crawled through scrub and slash. Fires smoldered in damp duff, and in litter compacted by winter's heavy snows, and tuffs of bunchgrass sending green shoots into a dry spring. But they did not go gently out. They remained aflame. They grew, and new fires added to the burden of burning. As the weeks wore on, the fires crept and swept, thickening during calms into smoke as dense as pea fog, then flaring into wild rushes through the crowns until they eventually scorched millions of acres across the middle tier of North America and, climbing to a summit in August, shattered vast patches of Washington, Oregon, and especially Idaho and Montana. It flung smoke to New England; its soot sank into Greenland ice. In its peak moment, the fires bore no more relation to burning snags than a creek's runoff to the Mississippi River in flood. Towering flames burned conifer stands like prairie grass and came over the ridges, as one survivor recalled, with the sound of a thousand trains rushing over a thousand steel trestles. One ranger said simply, the mountains roared.

There were people amid those flames. As the fires scaled up, the fledgling U.S. Forest Service, barely five years old, tried to match them. It rounded up whatever men it could beg, borrow, or buy and shipped them into the backcountry. The crews established camps, cut firelines along ridgetops, and backfired. Over and again, one refrain after another, the saga continued of fires contained, of fires escaping, of new trenches laid down. Then the Big Blowup of 20–21 August shredded it all. Farms, mining camps, trestles, hobo camps, and whole towns cracked and burned. Smoke billowed up in columns dense as volcanic blasts, while the fire's convection sucked in air from all sides, snapping mature cedar and white pine like toothpicks, spawning firewhirls like miniature tornadoes, flinging sparks like broadcast seed. Those on the lines heard that savage thunder and felt a heat that could melt iron and buffeted in winds that could scatter whole trees like leaves and stared, senseless, into smoke too dense to see their own hands before them. Crews dropped their saws and mattocks and fled. That day seventy-eight firefighters died.

The panorama is vast, the summer endless, the meaning of the Great Fires easily lost in streamers of flame and throbbing smoke. Yet an order exists. Consider the season as a vast nebula made of fires instead of stars, with flame swirling inward from a loosely herded periphery to a tightly bound core. Trace that narrative coil, ignoring the garden variety fires, even when lethal, and move, first, to the northwestern United States. Within that tangle of mountains and plateaus, tighten the focus to the Northern Rockies. Move still more closely to the crushing core with the Big Blowup, and trim the panorama to the rugged landscape between the Coeur d'Alene and St. Joe rivers. Narrow that vision further to a mine tunnel, grim and despairing, along the West Fork of Placer Creek. Finally, focus on the heart and mind of a ranger at its entrance, like the windless eye of a hurricane, standing between a cowering crew and the bellowing flames. Here geography and story merge, and a crazed, fatal firefight becomes one of the great tales of Americans and their lands.

Fires express their surroundings: The big fires of 1910 became Great Fires because they grew out of an extraordinary cultural context. Wind, drought, and woods collided with bureaucracies, railroads, political scandal, pioneering, ideas about nature, and reformist zeal, and because they compelled a reply, the fires became a moral force. In 1910 America's politics were as eruptive as its landscapes. It was a reformist era, an age that sought to act. The fires brought to a fast boil institutions, policies, beliefs, and land practices that might otherwise have simmered for decades. Controversy swirled, in particular, over the legacy of conservation as a popular movement. The Great Fires did what fires do best: They quickened, destroyed, fused. Within two years the Big Blowup was followed by a Big Breakup of the Republican party. Meanwhile the young U.S. Forest Service had the memory of the conflagrations spliced into its institutional genes, shaped as profoundly by the Great Fires as modern China by the Long March. Not for more than thirty years, until its founding generation had passed from the scene, would the trauma of the 1910 fires begin to heal and would the nation's leading agency for administering wildlands consider fire as anything but a hostile force to be fought to the death. Because of that link, probably no fire short of the holocausts that accompanied Earth's putative collision with an asteroid along the Cretaceous/Tertiary boundary has had such global ecological reach.

The Great Fires became America's ur-fire, the founding story of how Americans would relate to a natural phenomenon at once as common as sunflowers and as powerful as tornadoes, an ecological element only partly tamed and partly captive and, like a trained grizzly, ever ready to turn feral. The narrative of wildland fire in America remains a series of glosses on that primordial text. The Great Fires were unlike any American fire before them, and no wildland fire since has fundamentally differed from the pattern they inscribed. The choices faced in the summer of 2000, as fires once again, with eerie echoes, splattered across the West, remained those laid down in 1910. Yet to interpret that text properly requires a trip to the enigmatic grotto on the West Fork, for here, in the obscuring shadows, the old events utter their delphic meaning.

•

*The trek to the site is arduous, not because the way is long (it isn't), but because the primary trail, which used to trend to Striped Peak, is abandoned and overgrown, vanishing into a Northern Rockies hillside beneath boulders, talus, roots, forbs, and the slender shafts of willow and alder. A secondary path to the old mine is even dimmer. You won't find the tunnel without a reason to search for it.*

*Yet to understand the Great Fires, you need to reach that murky orifice. You'll need a text to guide you, and more than a translator's dictionary or a Rosetta stone to interpret the words, you may need practically, not merely figuratively, a tool. This story originated in deeds, not words. Its legacy survives in acts more than texts. You need something sharp to slash through the scrub. You need something durable to grub out steps through the loose rubble and root-clogged slopes. You need all these tools and a hand free besides. You need a pulaski.*

# BEFORE

For the 1880 census Charles S. Sargent of Harvard's Arnold Arboretum surveyed the state of America's forests and then performed the more astonishing task of mapping the nation's fires. Eighteen eighties America resembled 1980s Brazil, a fire-flushed agricultural country that was rapidly industrializing. Flame was everywhere.

Many places needed it; others could not avoid it; few evaded it altogether. Old farmers burned fallow. New settlers fired the woods to make fields. Herders torched stale pasture. The hard fact was, agriculture could not thrive without some regimen of burning, and folk culture not only accepted but celebrated that reality. Still, such fires at least flamed within contained spaces and designated seasons. What appalled educated observers was the spectacle beyond the field, the enormous litter of wanton, malicious, and accidental fires that marred every landscape. Critics likened the flaming scene to a landed equivalent of the conspicuous consumption, fraud, and waste that characterized industrial America's nouveau riche. Writing in the 1920s, V. L. Parrington aptly dubbed the era the Great Barbecue. True, industrialization promised, eventually, to replace open fire with internal combustion, to substitute fossil biomass for living fallow, to suppress free-burning flame, and to shed a field-based folklore for a technology-based science. But the present reality was that steam engines, and especially the locomotives they powered, threw sparks with lavish abandon. Like the demographic profile of an industrializing country, America's birthrate for fire shot up while its fire deaths diminished. The landscape swelled with flame.

Above all, fire—abusive fire—followed the ax. Flame fed on the extravagant wreckage left by logging and land clearing. Freshly recut New England had suffered through two devastating fire seasons, 1903 and 1908. The Lake States seemed, at times, like a portal to hell as forests and wooden towns like Peshtigo, Hinckley, and Metz burned with sickening regularity. Long-smoldering fires then stripped the soil down to sand; the lands, worthless for logging or farming, wasted into abandonment. Those ghost acres sprawled into the millions. In the South, where industrial logging next turned, the cutover pineries were annually fired until they thinned into savannas, apt for loose-herding by cracker cowboys. Then, as the ax migrated into the Northwest, the vast forests of the Coast Range, Cascades, and Northern Rockies began to burn in strikingly different ways from before. John Muir voiced common sentiment when he fumed that awful as wholesale logging was, the damage wrought by fires was ten times worse. Fire and ax were the searing breath and rough claws of what one outraged observer called "the dragon Devastation." Before them the American forest, and all that depended on it, seemed doomed.[1]

•

FOR ALL THE HORROR, however, public sentiment stood strangely silent. Smoke over the woods, like smokestacks over cities, was a badge of progress. "Whole communities," wrote Franklin Hough, "regard these fires with satisfaction, provided they escape personal damages. . . ." Most shrugged off the conflagrations as fleeting; most assumed they would vanish during the natural course of settlement. Once it was thoroughly burned, once converted to farms and towns, the land would be inoculated against further outbreaks. Besides, life was impossible without the torch. Writing from California in 1904, a forester observed that "the Indians were accustomed to burning the forest over long before the white man came. . . . The white man has come to think that fire is a part of the forest, and a beneficial part at that. All classes share in this view, and all set fires, sheepmen and cattlemen on the open range, miners, lumbermen, ranchmen, sportsmen, and campers." Still, ultimately, settlers believed the conflagrations would fade away or sink into the chained rhythms of burned fallow. Loggers veered toward greater fatalism. The fires would come, they knew. The trick was to cut fresh timber before the flames roared out of the slash and left nothing for them to mill. The promiscuous fires quickened the tempo of an industry already notorious for its migratory habits. To the pull of uncut timber was added the push of wildfire that made only a madman consider replanting the cutover.[2]

But America's emerging elite—its scientists, technocrats, political reformers, those who argued for Progressivism—were less willing to accept laissez-faire settlement with its wastage of soil, forests, waters, fields, and lives. They saw fire as cause, catalyst, and consequence of a frontier economy that an industrializing America could no longer tolerate. They believed that its weedy fires were corroding the country's natural wealth and that controlling fire had a significance that was both immensely practical and symbolic. In the 1890s Bernhard Fernow, the Prussian-trained forester who headed the Division of Forestry, had denounced America's ceaseless burning as a product of "bad habits and loose morals." Henry Gannett, overseeing a survey of the nation's fledgling forest reserves, declared that the country's fires were "a magnificent spectacle, but one too expensive to be indulged in even by Americans." Gifford Pinchot, replacing them both as guardian of the national woodlands, thundered with abolitionist zeal that "the question of forest fires, like the question of slavery, may be shelved for a time, at enormous cost in the end, but sooner or later it must be faced."[3]

•

BUT WHO WOULD do it? What agency of government would stand before the flames? What principles would guide its protecting hand? Who—what political knight errant—would lead the crusade against the "dragon Devastation"? These were questions not of ecology but of politics, and they were to shape the impact of the Great Fires as fully as the valleys and ridgelines of the Rockies.

When Sargent wrote, the answer seemed obvious: The U.S. Geological Survey, freshly minted a year before, would lead the charge for conservation. In particular Major John Wesley Powell, who assumed the directorship in 1881, had written a founding text from his field studies in the Far West that laid out ways the federal government could rationalize western settlement. *Report on the Lands of the Arid Region of the United States,* published in 1878, transported George Perkins Marsh's *Man and Nature* from European history to the American frontier. It focused on waters because agriculture could advance in a dry country only through engineered waterworks and those who controlled the source of the water controlled the land. But waters led to watersheds, and that meant forested mountains, and those burned. *Arid Lands* included a stunning map of Utah's burned landscapes and a candid account of what the fires meant.

To the universal burning Powell assigned the West's thinned woodlands, many of its vast prairies, and its general lack of forest cover. "Throughout the timber regions of all the arid lands," he observed, "fires annually destroy larger or smaller districts of timber, now here, now there, and this destruction is on a scale so vast that the amount taken from the lands for industrial purposes sinks by comparison into insignificance." The grander cause he attributed to climate, notably the West's aridity. It was climate (even if acting through fire) that controlled forests, not forests that shaped climate. Few woodlands escaped the ravages of either drought or fire. Against the first, one could do little save store waters and irrigate. But against fire, one could take active countermeasures. "A sufficiency of forests for the country depends," Powell concluded, "upon the control which can be obtained over that destructive agent."[4]

From its beginnings, then, conservation accepted the need for some sort of fire protection. Beyond that, ideas competed, and so did institutions founded on those ideas. Powell's vision favored locally controlled districts that would regulate the use of water, woods, and grass, thus avoiding both the monopolies threatened by industrial capitalism and the imperial bureaus that sprouted up in Europe's Asian and African colonies. Control, that is, rested with rural communities. The Geological Survey, or its bureaucratic cognates, could advise, could bring a measure of scientific rigor to actual practice, rather on the model of an agricultural extension service. The inference was that the government's technical bureaus could assist in the campaign to prevent or, where necessary, suppress free-burning fire, while political power rested with those living on the ground.

A rival strategy existed, however. It grew out of the broader experiences of European colonization and was part of the cosmopolitan culture of conservation. It was clear that contact had upheaved many biotas, that some ameliorative measures were essential, and that indigenous communities could not, by and large, be entrusted with the task. In particular, forest reserves served a nobler agenda than commerce. They stabilized climate and watersheds, preventing floods and droughts, advanced a program of public health, preserved stocks of vital timber, informed practice by scientific scholarship. Against the power of a globalizing economy, and amid the stubbornness of rural folkways and the narrowness of indigenous politics, local communities had proved incompetent to stop the wreckage, and ruling authorities were reluctant in any event to devolve important decisions to the subject masses. Only imperial institutions had the power and purpose to stanch the environmental ruin. Only they especially could end the relentless biotic erosion wrought by fire. Fire protection (or fire conservancy, as it was called) brought with it control over indigenes because without free access to fire much of the land remained inaccessible. Fire protection was, in effect, a form of land reservation. They would keep fire out by keeping fire-setting people out, and regulating those who could enter. The premier agencies were forestry bureaus like those devised by Britain for India and France for Algeria. In the late nineteenth century they offered the boldest experiments in wholesale conservation.

The United States wavered. Most thoughtful observers were uneasy with both approaches, laissez-faire folk burning or imperial fire control. Fire, however, did not wait; it obeyed a logic independent of people. It was indifferent to august commissions, ruling councils, and parliamentary deliberations. It would not result from political deliberation; it had the power to force deliberation. Sooner or later, as Gifford Pinchot had insisted, it had to be faced. And whoever controlled fire controlled one of the checkpoints of conservation.

The choice of agency meant also a choice of strategies. If local communities oversaw the reserved lands, they would likely favor fire's use. If national or imperial bureaus administered those lands, they would veer toward fire exclusion. Then in 1890, when Powell's standing was at its height, there occurred a notorious episode in which he challenged the presumption that fire had to go. Bernhard Fernow, then head of the humble Division of Forestry, recorded the scene. He had arranged a meeting with John Noble, the secretary of the interior, to argue for a stronger forestry program. Fernow wrote:

> Major Powell asked permission to be present, which, of course, was politely granted. Before we had an opportunity to state the object of our visit, Major Powell launched into a long dissertation to show that the claim of the favorable influence of forest cover on water flow or climate was untenable, that the best thing to do for the Rocky Mountain forests was to burn them down, and he related with great gusto how he himself had started a fire that swept over a thousand square miles. He had used up our time when our chance came to speak. We consumed not more than two minutes, stating that we had

> not come to argue any theories, but to impress the Secretary with the fact that it was under the law his business to protect public property against the vandalism of which the Major had just accused himself.

There was worse to come.[5]

Before his political career ended, Powell challenged much of the growing doctrine of forest conservation on the European model. He urged local, not national, control, thus questioning the premise behind carving vast federal forest reservations out of the public domain. He dismissed alarms over a "timber famine" as political hysteria. The West, in particular, had plenty of timber for the needs of settlement. What it needed more of was water, and if the forests were thinned still further, runoff would improve. Also, as he did before an outraged Fernow, he questioned the axiom that a land without fire was intrinsically better than one with it. It seems that his close study of the American Indian, notably the Paiute, had caused him to reevaluate his initial, categorical condemnation of fire. He became convinced that the practice of regularly burning over the West's forest steppes was a surer method of protecting the land from wildfire than attempting to abolish fire altogether; besides, the lightly burned watersheds would improve the flow of waters. In 1890 the smart money would have bet that Powell's conception of conservation would eventually triumph, and the U.S. Geological Survey with it.

That didn't happen. Perhaps inevitably Powell overstepped himself. Within a year his political ambitions were crushed, his beloved Irrigation Survey (nestled within the USGS) was abolished, and Congress, though without quite knowing what it was doing, passed a provision in its end-of-session rush as part of the Sundry Civil Appropriations Act that authorized the president, by simple proclamation, to set aside forest reserves from the public domain. Powell's ideas on matters such as forests and fires would not prevail any more than his conceptions of water and farming. Nor would the Geological Survey be the primary vehicle for carrying out those reforms.

•

YET POWELL BEQUEATHED a trenchant legacy. The USGS remained, by far, the most powerful scientific agency in the federal government and the one most committed to reform in how the country exploited its natural resources. Under his successor, Charles Doolittle

Walcott, the Geological Survey became the "Mother of Bureaus," hiving off scientifically animated agencies, the very model of Rooseveltian reform, of Progressive management by technical experts. Powell's crony, paleontologist-cum-sociologist Lester Frank Ward, had sketched principles for a welfare state, which could also be extended to nature; Powell's alter ego, W J McGee, became, in Pinchot's words, "the scientific brains behind the conservation movement." That exemplar of rational administration the Inland Waterways Commission can trace its pedigree directly to Powell.

So when the General Land Office within the Department of the Interior struggled, without much direction, to administer the proliferating forest reserves, Congress turned to the National Academy of Sciences for advice and then to the USGS to map their actual condition. The NAS forest committee's conclusions were predictable enough: "Fire and pasturage chiefly threaten the reserved forest lands of the public domain." While "no statistics show the area of forests destroyed annually," the committee noted that "nearly every summer their smoke obscures for months the sight of the sun over hundreds of square miles, and last summer your committee, traveling for six weeks through northern Montana, Idaho, and Washington, and through western Washington and Oregon, were almost constantly enveloped in the smoke of forest fires." One member, a young forester named Gifford Pinchot—added at the recommendation of Walcott—stated simply, "There was too much fire. Which nobody could deny."[6]

The Geological Survey's reconnaissance agreed. For three years explorers trekked through the Northwest, from temperate rain forest to pine steppe, and found fire almost everywhere, but almost everywhere organized according to different regimes. Along the Northwest coast, fires came in spasms, tied to drought and the forced drying of slash. Amid the Great Plains, fires surged routinely through grassy hills, worsening when deluge preceded drought, as the first nurtured new fuels and the second stacked them to burn. A spectrum of fire regimes spanned the landscapes between coast and plains. For western Washington, Gannett concluded that "anyone who has passed the late summer and early fall in this State realizes the enormous destruction which takes place annually at this season. There are fires everywhere, and the smoke from them lies as dense as the fog on the New England coast for weeks at a time." Along the Washington Forest Reserve that straddled the Cascades, there were obvious differences, east and west of the divide.

On the west, H. B. Ayres noted "the occurrence of severely burnt areas"; along the Skagit River "very little other than severely burnt land was seen." Along the east slope, Martin W. Gorman concluded that "the numerous burnt stumps, the bare slopes of the west and southwest faces of the hillsides, the charred and dead trees, the burnt areas of different ages, and the paucity of humus outside of the moist ravines and valleys all attest that the region has been burned over, not once, but many times." On the Priest River Reserve in northern Idaho, J. B. Leiberg summarized a scene in which

> one meets with burnt areas everywhere—in the old growth, in the second growth, in the young growth, and where the seedlings that are beginning to cover the deforested areas have just commenced to obtain a fair hold. The burnt tracts are in large blocks, thousands of acres in extent, and in small patches of 15 to 50 acres which extend in all directions through the forest, which at a distance is apparently green; sometimes they are in broad swaths, sometimes in narrow, tortuous windings just sufficient to open a lane for the destructive high winds to tear the living forest down. The burnt areas are scattered all over the reserve, but the largest amount of damage lies within the zone of the white pine, by reason of its greater extent and peculiar susceptibility to destructive fires.

On Montana's Bitterroot Reserve, Leiberg saw that "immense fires have ravaged the district both in the past and in recent times. The only areas containing any considerable quantities of old growth are the ones . . . existing northeast of the Grave Mountains and the yellow-pine tracts in the Lower Lochsa and Lolo basins." Valleys and basins were routinely swept by fires and hence swept clean of trees. In the Bitterroot basin he observed fires "as extensive as elsewhere in the west," but because grasses carried the fires rapidly through yellow pine, they did minor lasting damage save, as always, to the thinning of the forest. The worst damages came from stand-replacing burns where denser forests of Douglas-fir prevailed, often on north-facing slopes, normally wetter but during droughts more heavily stocked with combustibles. The same held on the Flathead Reserve, where Ayres found "evidence of severe and repeated fires" in "abundance," even "actual prairie-making." On the Bighorn Reserve, Wyoming, F. E. Town affirmed that "fire has been and is the greatest enemy of this forest." Half the reserve was prairie, and all that the outcome of regular burning. Syncopated on that near-annual rhythm were outbreaks when drought and spark blew up over vast areas. "There is abundant evidence from these appearances that every acre of these mountains has been burned over at some time, and probably many times successively in the past." Finally there were the Black Hills, a remote outlier of the Rockies, sporting an irregular, scrubby savanna of yellow pine. "For this condition forest fires are directly responsible," Henry Graves concluded, "and the present aspect of the forest is the result of long abuse and the struggle of the forest to reestablish itself. The broken condition of the forest, the large proportion of defective trees, the many wind breaks, the prairies, parks, and bald ridges, are due to the destructive forest fires which have swept the hills periodically for years and probably for centuries." Practically the whole forest "shows traces of forest fires."[7]

Their condemnation was universal. The surveyors understood the rough ecology of burning and found that fires were as pervasive as mosquitoes and denounced them as equally obnoxious. Leiberg's judgment on the Bitterroot Reserve echoed that of the whole corps. The aftereffects of the fires—those of contemporary no less than of ancient origin—were "various, but are always evil, without a single redeeming feature." The forest explorers were there to map and to help decide if these sites merited status as formal reserves. So rife was fire that burned area became a cartographic category, and so widespread were the patches of intense burning, of stand-replacing conflagrations, that those swatches added a visual logic to the message of the text. It said that such places ought to be reserved so that they could be protected from further fire. "Forest fires were allowed to burn," Pinchot observed, "long after the people had means to stop them."[8]

•

IF THE USGS would not stop them, some other agency would. The General Land Office was too enfeebled, too hamstrung with its founding charge to transfer land from the public domain to private hands, perhaps too overgrown with clerks and too politicized. Since he took over the Division of Forestry in 1898, Pinchot was rabid to do the job and had commenced his administration with a study of fire damages as a means to convince Congress and the public about the need for forestry overall. The division became a bureau in 1901, but it had no authority except to advise. Then in 1905, friend and fellow conservationist President Theodore Roosevelt gave him the means to end fire's sad, lascivious legacy by reassigning the forest reserves to Pinchot's charge. The Bureau of Forestry became the Forest Service, and the forest reserves the national forests. The Transfer Act brought fire protection under the aegis of Progressive Era reforms and subjected it to Pinchot's fierce brand of conservation.

Pinchot took his mission to the public, sought to argue his case directly to the people rather than indirectly through bureaus and Congress. Quickly he claimed for himself and his patron, Roosevelt, the mantle of conservation. Unlike the Geological Survey, which could research but had no lands to oversee, the Forest Service controlled an immense estate, which it sought to expand. It abrogated to itself the status of vanguard. Conservation would thrive or wither away according to the success of its peculiar mission. Under the charismatic Pinchot, it was determined to push outward.

One means was by presidential proclamation. But Congress had wearied of executive privilege and in early 1907 had placed before Roosevelt a bill that he had to sign, which, among other provisions, abolished his power to create reserves by fiat. The conservationist clique outflanked that maneuver by arranging for the president to add, with great fanfare, a further sixteen million acres to the western national forests just before signing the bill. The "midnight reserves" aroused a furor. The proclamation held, though, and the Forest Service adjusted its internal administration, opting for a relative decentralization of operations. The Washington office remained large, a hefty, taunting target for congressional critics with its mailing list of 670,000 names and a bevy of clerks to send out promotional publications. But the bulk of decisions would devolve to regional levels.[9]

The move also forced the issue of future expansion back into Congress. In 1901 Representative John Weeks of Massachusetts sponsored legislation that would allow the national forests to acquire land in the eastern United States by purchase. Specifically, conservationists targeted the White Mountains of New England and the Southern Appalachians as critical landscapes: vital watersheds, rough-handled by settlers, scalped by loggers, given to apparent flooding. Salvation would come by bringing them under the protection of the federal Forest Service. That they were watersheds mattered because the constitutional justification undergirding the scheme was that these lands affected the waters of navigable streams and thus fell under the auspices of the interstate commerce clause. But year after year the bill stalled. There were strong arguments that the states, not the federal government, should oversee reserved forests if any forests should be reserved at all. Western politicians resented any further enlargement of Forest Service power while easterners feared that the act could never pass constitutional muster when its inevitable court challenge followed. Then scientific controversies broke through the surface about whether forests had any significant influence over flooding or climate at all. The waters muddied.

•

OUTSIDE CONGRESS AND the courts, however, there existed another, more practical test than constitutional quibbling over water, and that was fire. No agency could administer the reserves without controlling fire; indeed, to control fire was a primary purpose behind creating the reserves. As 1907 ended, the geography of American fire divided into four rough regions. Each had a different political administration, each a different dynamic of fire. What they shared was a sense, at least among the emerging elite of political reformers, conservationists, and scientists, that public fire practices had become promiscuous and that some agency of government would have to police them.

The most visible region was the Northeast, roughly buffeted by the return of its forests on abandoned farmland, by the rude slashings left by loggers, and by reserved forests like those in the Catskills and "forever wild" Adirondacks. These were fires wholly under the control of people: this was no natural fire landscape in which lightning would move in if humans moved out. People created the fuels; people set the flame; people fought the fiery outbreaks. Because the fires appeared practically at the doorstep of major centers of learning and journalism, they became visible. Even modest burns in the White Mountains or Adirondacks spoke through a media megaphone. The big fires of 1903, in particular, had galvanized the literate public and spurred New York into model reforms.

The Lake States displayed a more violent version. Settlement had cracked open the old North Woods, which lay ripening under the sun until flames from locomotives, settlers, hunters, and others gorged on them. For forty years the scenario had replayed itself. Roads and rails opened new lands; ax and fire cleared them; farmers moved in, sometimes too soon, and suffered while conflagrations mowed down million-acre swaths of slash and fresh forest. In 1871 Wisconsin fires killed an estimated 383 settlers. In 1881 the blows fell primarily on Michigan, in 1894, on Wisconsin and Minnesota, but every year they seemed to fall somewhere. Until settlement converted the land into something less combustible, the fires would continue. The prevalent strategy was one of laissez-faire: that once the woods were tamed, the wildfires would vanish. That brought small comfort to those burned out and elicited only sarcasm from those who believed that here was a place in which government could apply a necessary counterforce.

The most prevalent fire region was the South, and for conservationists, the most insidious. Writing from Florida in 1910, Inman Eldredge observed with an almost Faulknerian blend of amazement and outrage that "the people right down on the ground, the settlers, the people who lived in the woods, the turpentine operators, and so forth, were completely uninformed and were the greatest, ablest, and most energetic set of woods burners that any forester had to contend with." Fire—some fire—burned throughout the year.

> The popular sentiment of the residents within the Forests, in common with nearly all of the South, is unqualifiedly in favor of the annual burning over of the pineries. The homesteader and the cattleman burn the woods to keep down the blackjack undergrowth and to better the cattle range. The turpentine operator burns over his woods annually, after raking around his boxed trees, and at a time when the burning will do the least harm, in order to protect his timber from all the burnings that are sure to occur. He burns also with the idea of keeping the turpentine orchards clear of undergrowth and free from snakes, in order that his negro laborers may gather the gum with ease and safety. The camp hunters, of whom there is a large number during the fall and winter months, set out fires in order to drive out game from the thickets. All of these different classes of people have for a great number of years been accustomed to burning the woods freely and without hindrance of any kind, and it is done without the knowledge or the feeling that they are breaking the laws or in any way doing damage. One the contrary, they all have the most positive belief that burning is necessary and best in the long run.
>
> The turpentine operator burns his woods and all other neighboring woods during the winter months, generally in December, January, or February. The cattlemen set fire during March, April, and May to such areas as the turpentine operator has left unburned. During the summer there are almost daily severe thunderstorms, and many forest fires are set by lightning. In the dry fall months hunters

set fire to such "rough" places as may harbor game. It is only by chance than any area of unenclosed land escapes burning at least once in two years.[10]

At times it was hard to see the woods for the flame. In 1898 a three-million-acre wildfire slashed through the Carolina coastal plains like a hurricane, yet passed almost unnoticed amid the annual sweep of flame. Those who viewed the South from outside found its combustible mix both perplexing and absurd. When William Greeley toured the region, he discovered to his dismay that "man-set forest fires were well nigh universal. They were part of the accepted order of things." Here the pioneering phase never evolved, as it seemed to elsewhere; fires wandered through the woods like open-range cattle and razorbacks. Moreover, because the subtropical South allowed for some kind of burning year-round, fires did not cluster into a "season" but were broadcast throughout the calendar.[11]

Forestry could not afford to segregate the South, however rowdy its claims for exceptionalism. Full of timber lust, the American logging industry was heading south after having exhausted the pineries of the Northeast and the Lake States. There, if anywhere, Americans would regrow their lost woods. The Southern Appalachians, particularly the patch across North Carolina, was the special concern of the Weeks bill. Control over the ax, however, meant little without equal control over the torch. But fire, which proved so useful as a common cause elsewhere, especially between foresters and loggers, here turned troublesome. Rural southerners thought of fire as they did their woods, as a diverse resource, adaptable to the needs of the moment. They found fire a malleable medium, setting many fires, at various seasons, for assorted purposes. Proper burning kept the whole scene habitable, open, attractive, safe from wildfire, and productive, as the South's rural economy understood productivity. Unburned sites were useless, ugly, dangerous, bristling with snakes and ticks, and prone to explosive conflagrations.

American forestry believed it could never actively suppress fire on the public lands of the West and leave it to burn freely in the South. Neither could forestry tolerate controlled burning on the public domain while condemning it on the open range of the southern pineries. The Forest Service and its allies in the conservation crusade could hardly insist that the Southern Appalachians be added to the national forests, in order to protect them adequately, if the mountains continued to burn as before or, more improbably, if foresters took up the torch and did the burning themselves. Instead they sought to extend to these benighted lands the kind of enlightened security that the national forests enjoyed. That shifted the burden of proof to the western reserves, the fourth great fire region, where early returns on Forest Service fire policies were encouraging. Burned acreage had dropped. The principles were right. It remained only to staff the reserves adequately and extend them more broadly across the country.

The specter of free-burning fire had served conservationists nicely as an argument for reform; it now endured as an index of reform's success. "I recall very well indeed," Pinchot lectured, "how, in the early days of forest fires, they were considered simply and solely as acts of God, against which any opposition was hopeless and any attempt to control them not merely hopeless but childish. It was assumed that they came in the natural order of things, as inevitably as the seasons or the rising and setting of the sun. To-day we understand that forest fires are wholly within the control of men." Modern, ardent, committed, the renamed Forest Service would show how. Speaking in 1907, Pinchot declared that "the measures adopted for detecting and extinguishing fires on the national forests are efficient." Here was a clear test of whether the agency could do the job, whether it understood the problem properly, whether it had the will and skill to make it happen on the ground.[12]

•

BY EARLY 1908, the *annus mirabilis* of the conservation crusade, all the pieces seemed to have jostled into place. Teddy Roosevelt crowned his conservation record by convening a conference of governors on the subject. Meanwhile Congress authorized the secretary of agriculture to pay the costs of actual firefighting with supplemental appropriations, which granted the Forest Service the fiscal flexibility it demanded to meet fire seasons that, unlike trail building or answering letters, could not be budgeted years in advance. With the new fiscal year, the Forest Service completed its reorganization and bulked up its field staff. Then the November elections confirmed Roosevelt's anointed successor, William Howard Taft, who assured all that Pinchot would remain as chief forester.

Not least, the year was also, or so it seemed at the time, a pivotal moment for forest fire protection, one that quickly established itself as a standard for the worst-case scenario. Major wildfires savaged the country's northern rim and flared fatally across the Canadian border. That so many of these fires broke out in the Northeast meant that they commanded considerable attention. A small fire in Connecticut was worth a gigantic one in Nevada. A fatal fire, especially one that contained a sentimental message, was worth millions of seared trees. All that, 1908 offered. It was the last major outbreak in the Northeast until 1947; almost the last of a wretched, lethal litany for the Lake States, alone exceeded in acreage by the 1910 season. Only in the West was it a mere foreshadowing; there the 1910 fires would obliterate its memory. But matters looked different as the year ended—as Roosevelt prepared to hand over the presidency to Taft and then journey to Africa to shoot elephants and zebras for the Smithsonian. Observers concluded that the swarm of autumn fires had finally and conclusively ended the argument over the value of active fire control.

The fires of 1908 burned in all the usual places, and then some. The year opened quirkily with a January prairie fire in Harlem, New York City, that threatened the Consolidated Gas Company until engineer Edward Rowland "thought of a Western fire-fighting trick" and set a backfire. The odd became sensational in August, when fires in California threatened the Calaveras Grove of sequoias until stopped "by the heroic efforts of 600 men" working alongside forest rangers. But it was one thing to check a fire, another to extinguish it. The fires revived and were joined by new starts. The Big Trees' best protection was the fact that little grew under them, that they had been so long scorched by routine surface fires that they stood like great megaliths on a deeply shaded lawn. Years of protection, however, had allowed some scrub to invade, so again rangers, settlers, and visitors were called back to fight the flames. For a while the tops of the General Grant and the Garfield trees caught fire, along with the "Mother of the Forest," seventy-eight feet in girth. The weird became farcical in October, when, with more than 5,000 men on firelines in upstate New York, lumber companies hired Carl E. Myers, self-promoting rainmaker, to launch a great balloon salted with gases that he would explode with an electrical spark and that would then, or so he advertised, set off a chain of storms from the Mohawk Valley to the mountains.[13]

For 1908 such escapades were sideshows, newsworthy because they attached themselves to celebrity landscapes. What mattered more was a vast, stubborn drought that gradually settled across the northern tier of the United States and over the Canadian border. In June fires ripped through three villages and the surrounding forests in Michigan and later, outside Wilbur, wiped out thousands of acres of berries. Farmers around Manora, Long Island, battled to save houses from a wildfire that scoured the nearby woodlands and destroyed "hundreds of foxes and rabbits which infested" them. Then the fires settled in for a long siege with a droughty Northeast. Serious outbreaks occurred outside Ogunquit, Maine, and Plymouth, Massachusetts. In New Jersey they spread into cranberry bogs until fire wardens, "reinforced by men, women, and children," fought them to a standstill. Eastern Long Island continued its siege, with the "devout" offering prayers and the profane offering $4 a day "to all volunteers to work in subduing the flames." Flames erupted around Lake George in the Adirondacks until a regional rainstorm dampened them and shifted national attention to the West and Canada.[14]

The ravenous flames moved to the Rocky Mountains. Large fires swept along the Bitterroots, mostly feeding on the fresh slashings of the Milwaukee Railway and tempering the raw staffs of the Lolo and the Coeur d'Alene national forests. The real terror, however, struck the Elk River valley of British Columbia, where an immense patch of long-smoldering fires, fanned by winds, wiped out the coal-mining towns of Fernie and Hosmer, killed more than seventy-five, including "many of the fire fighters," and burned out bridges and rolling stock of the Canadian Pacific and Great Northern railways. Owing to a strike, the Canadian Pacific was hamstrung to respond, and when the calmed fires, hit by fresh winds, revived and drove toward Banff, the community had to protect itself as best it could. Its primary hope was the aura of aspen that surrounded the village, the ghostly residue of previous burns.[15]

By then the fires that made 1908 notorious had begun. They had seemingly leaped from British Columbia to Minnesota and Michigan before continuing to New York and New England. On 5 September, after burning three days, widespread fires obliterated Chisholm, Minnesota, its residents fleeing in fifteen boxcars provided by the Great Northern, leaving the state militia to guard the smoking ruins against looters. A subsiding wind spared nearby towns like Buhl and Nashwauk. Other fires threatened Grand Marais and Hibbing; they destroyed the center of Peshtigo, Wisconsin, scene of the 1871 fire tragedy;

they spread into the Oneida Indian Reservation; they burned villages around Rhinelander and Escanaba; they raged over the Mesabi Range. A homesteader and his two sons, aged 12 and 14, died fighting the flames near the Otter River. By 11 September there were fires in Maine and a yellow haze had settled over New York State. From its Washington office the Forest Service announced that the year's burns would go down as "one of the worst in the last quarter century." Then the Adirondacks caught fire, and the Catskills, and woodlands in Massachusetts, and in Winchester, Connecticut, and across western Pennsylvania, where "Forest Wardens in Lycoming and Clinton Counties were ordered by the authorities to shoot persons discovered starting fires in the woods," and the lot of it, the smoke from conflagrations in the Lake States and Canada and from thousands of unquenchable fires throughout the Northeast, covered New York City in a "heavy gray pall." Smoke even wafted in from the vicinity of Atlantic City.[16]

The fires refused to go out. They burned through September; they burned through October. A rain shower might momentarily dampen the flames, but they would rekindle from the deep duff. A spat of snow could squelch them only to have them flare anew. By mid-October fires still raged over a hundred square miles of Michigan, and the awful toll of burned towns, ruined farms, and casualties mounted. Outside Metz a relief train derailed when ties burned out and the rails warped, and fifteen refugees were cremated in the wreckage. It was impossible, officials concluded, to "compile anything like an authentic list of the fire victims" throughout the region. But upper Michigan and northern Minnesota were still, after a fashion, the frontier. More galling was the incapacity of a brash American society, eager proclaiming its Great Power status, to control fires in the Berkshires, the Blue Mountains, the Hempstead Plains, and most bafflingly the Adirondacks. Over the course of two decades New York State had fashioned what many observers considered a model fire protection system, made mandatory by the Adirondacks Park, and it had an organization, so its officials believed, well tempered as a result of the 1903 fires. This year wardens had fought twice as many fires and held them to half the burned area, yet the flames continued to taunt. The fires burned on, and on, until only the long-delayed rains could hope to wash them away.[17]

A pall of editorials replaced the smoke. It was apparent that clearing by conflagration was not a civilized method of settlement, that volunteer brigades could not cope with sudden outbreaks that threatened whole counties, that government had an obligation to protect forests from fire as it did for cities, that reserving lands was useless without shielding them from stand-devouring flames. The Forest Service brought home the economic damage by estimating that 1908's lost timber values alone would "provide for a good-sized navy of first-class battleships." It trumpeted the belief that the horrendous season of fire had "started a widespread movement in many States for rational systems of fire protection." In addition, the Forest Service, flanked by its allies, quickly pointed out the difference between the relative success of the national forests with the ignoble failure of fire protection elsewhere. With "careful patrol" and methodical organization the Forest Service had broken even large fires in the Rockies.[18]

Never one to shy from publicity, Gifford Pinchot judged that "in many ways this year's forest fires have been the worst I have ever known." Nothing could have greater clarity than the fact that "the forest fire question resolves itself into one of the most important problems before the Nation in the care of its National resources." Whatever else reasonable citizens might disagree over, they could not dispute, after 1908, that a fire crisis existed and that a smattering of rural fire wardens was insufficient to meet it. "No firefighting system has shown itself really effective that did not provide for range patrol," the chief forester intoned. "The one secret of fighting fires is to discover your fire as soon as possible and fight it as hard as you can and refuse to leave it until the last ember is dead." That was how the Forest Service fought fire; that was why the Northern Rockies had not suffered as the North Woods and the Adirondacks had. Left unspoken was the obvious deduction, the premise of the Weeks bill, that the best way to protect the eastern forests was to bring to them the degree of protection afforded the western forests under the guardianship of the Forest Service.[19]

The lessons of 1908 had been branded specially into the brief memory of the Forest Service's District One, which spanned the Northern Rockies. During the great reorganization, the district had hired or acquired by transfer most of the staff that would face the 1910 outbreak. Bill Greeley had become district forester; Gus Silcox, his assistant. Among the forests hardest hit, Major F. A. Fenn oversaw the Clearwater; William G. Weigle, the Coeur d'Alene; and Elers Koch, the Lolo. The 1908 fires had seasoned a green staff; they had met the worst, and survived, and learned. Every measure showed that the hapless General

Land Office, while overwhelmed in 1902, had improved on the rough-and-ready methods of frontier fire protection and that the USFS had improved that much again with respect to the GLO. Cooperative programs promised to spur the charge against fire even faster. From Washington, D.C., to Wallace, Idaho, foresters were confident that they could cope with whatever storm and settler threw at them. It seemed that the great scourge of the American countryside, fire, was beginning to fade, that the men and means were at hand to help erase, at long last, its menacing presence from the national scene.[20]

In 1909 Clyde Leavitt informed the National Conservation Commission on behalf of professional foresters that they had triumphed over "the greatest enemy of the forest." Though "undermanned," the Forest Service could "justly pride itself" on its fire record. The national forests offered "the best example in the United States of an efficient system of fire prevention and control," one that "demonstrated the fact that destruction of forest property by fire may be almost entirely prevented" by suitable methods. No one knew better (or believed he knew better) than Pinchot's zealous Forest Service what those methods were or how to apply them, and perhaps no one so fully failed to appreciate how thoroughly nature did not care.[21]

# THE FIRES

## JANUARY

ON THE NIGHT of 7 January, while Chief Forester Gifford Pinchot was preparing to depart for a dinner engagement, a messenger arrived bearing a letter from President William Howard Taft. Pinchot read what he "half expected," then trooped upstairs to his mother with the announcement that Taft had fired him. "My Mother's eyes flashed, she threw back her head, flung one hand high above it, and answered with one word: 'Hurrah!'" No less emboldened, son Gifford then hustled on to his gathering, where he flourished the letter and jubilantly announced his dismissal. The guests sat shell-shocked. Pinchot claimed he was "happy as a clam."[1]

He had been fired for—had deliberately provoked a firing for—insubordination. Systematically Pinchot had hounded his rival Richard Ballinger, then the secretary of the interior, with charges of corruption and, more generally, with reluctance to promote the great program of Rooseveltian Conservation. It was a long-smoldering affair, and Pinchot had deliberately fanned it to the point that it exploded. Both recognized that Pinchot had forced the crisis. "By your own conduct," Taft, the former judge, explained where no explanation was necessary, "you have destroyed your usefulness as a helpful subordinate of the Government."[2]

Gifford Pinchot of course had no desire to be subordinate to anything, save perhaps the will of Teddy Roosevelt. He believed that the constitutionally cautious Taft was damming the flow of conservation, that by not granting Pinchot the more or less free access he had enjoyed under Roosevelt and the free hand Roosevelt's secretary of the interior,

James Garfield, had allotted him in such bureaus as that of Indian Affairs, Taft was secretly derailing the crusade to manage and preserve America's undeveloped lands. Ballinger was an old nemesis; he and Pinchot had sparred after TR had recruited Ballinger to clean up the General Land Office. Ballinger did, and then drew and defended bureaucratic lines in the sand to halt Pinchot's encroachments. While adamant that he too was a "Roosevelt conservationist," Ballinger had a different vision of what that meant, one much closer to the bone of frontier development. He took pride as a self-made westerner, a Seattle lawyer; public service meant, for him, real financial loss. The scion of a wealthy family, Pinchot could thrive without his salary, could play the role of grandee, could indulge in government in the spirit of noblesse oblige. More gratingly, Ballinger had a stricter sense of agency protocol, one that left each agency to do its own appointed work, not poach on one another's turfs or campaign for world-spanning causes.

Now Taft had appointed Ballinger secretary, not merely an agency chief. When accusations surfaced that Ballinger had illegally conspired to lease coal lands in Alaska—the charges murky, none of them claiming illegality, but all the more valuable because they were so confused—Pinchot pressed what he saw as a scandal to his advantage. Legality per se did not matter; he wanted Ballinger tried in the court of public opinion. What mattered were appearances. What would sway the public was the aura of sleaziness and innuendo. The campaign fed on the contorted findings of Louis Glavis, a claims inspector with Interior, who dug up what he regarded as "suspicious" dealings. *Collier's* obliged by editorializing in August 1909 that "Ballinger Should Go." No indictments followed because no legal charges were ever filed. In September Ballinger fired Glavis. In the months that followed, Pinchot hounded the politically naive Ballinger, throwing Forest Service employees into the fray, endlessly stirring the press, and demanding Ballinger's dismissal as the price Taft had to pay to submit to Roosevelt's legacy. He was right that someone had to go. In the end it was Pinchot himself.

The day after the announcement the press was in pandemonium, the Taft administration in tatters, and the Forest Service in shock. However triumphant Pinchot personally felt, however gallant his parting message to the ranks, his abrupt dismissal had thrown his beloved Forest Service into turmoil. His associate chief, Overton Price, had also been fired; his law officer, Philip Wells, had resigned; and others threatened to follow suit, perhaps to stampede in protest. It was not obvious how the agency would continue, or under whose direction, or how the cause it claimed as its own could proceed, or, not least, how the crisis would affect those actually in the woods.

•

THE APPOINTMENT LETTER from Associate Forester Overton Price had arrived in Chicago on 18 June 1909. It informed the waiting William West Morris that he was appointed a forest assistant, at a salary of $1,000 a year, effective 1 July. By that date he must present himself at Forest Service District One headquarters in Missoula, Montana. There he would receive "definite instructions as to the character" of his work. The letter culminated a long dream. Will Morris had always "loved the woods," but four years of office work had inflated vague affection into a determination to become a professional forester. That led to five years of hard study at the University of Michigan, not until the third of which did he encounter a "subject dealing directly with the subject of forestry." He left with a master's degree in 1909. Now, with the civil service exam behind him, he could tramp the woods while earning his living. Young Morris quickly arranged his affairs, bade his father, mother, and siblings good-bye, and left Chicago for the Northern Rockies.[3]

It was a great adventure; in that, Morris was typical of Forest Service hires. But there was no standard profile among that throng. Morris had been born in Chicago, the youngest of seven children, both parents immigrants from Nova Scotia. It was a tidy household. Before William only older brother Sidney (generally known as Cousin Sid) had left the nest. The rest remained, unmarried, a family aging together, eager for the letters that Will dutifully mailed from the remote Rockies. The churchgoing Will quickly found himself in a churning social environment as strange as the upthrust mountains. "I travel with a different class of people most of the time from that I am accustomed to," he noted, then added that "it always seems good . . . to get on your good clothes, and meet some people more like the home ones." Instead he rubbed shoulders with miners, railroad gangs, loggers, a miscellany of crusty homesteaders (including veterans of the Crimean and Spanish-American wars and what seemed to him a surprising number of women schoolteachers) and of course other rangers, themselves an extraordinary mob. "I think people live easier out in this country, than home. They sleep late, and are more or less lazy and independent and I can't say I like them as well as the Eastern people." But he quickly adjusted. Soon he was tramping through snowdrifts and "cruising" timber with the likes of William Weigle, supervisor of the Coeur d'Alene National Forest; Joe Halm, a former football star from Washington State College; and Big Ed Pulaski, a onetime miner, packer, and general handyman, and shaking hands with William B. Greeley, chief of District One and a young professional from the first graduating class of the Yale School of Forestry. They were a fairly typical ranger corps. Before long Will thought of Wallace, Idaho, administrative seat for his home district, as a pert little town and welcomed Sunday services in the basement of the Bijou Theater.[4]

With its medley of eastern youths out for adventure, Yalies, idealists, and hard-bitten frontiersmen, Pinchot's Forest Service was a bureaucratic analogue of Roosevelt's Rough Riders and thought of itself as such. Still, the agency fell under civil service rule. It gave exams, which cut down on outright political patronage and excluded the most unsuitable of the potential applicants. The exams "really were effective," Supervisor Elers Koch believed. In 1910 the exam he administered in Missoula included two days of field events and one day for a written portion. The field trials involved rifle and pistol shooting, horse riding, packing, simple compassing and pacing, axmanship, and timber cruising, skills that would ensure that rangers could "generally take care of themselves outdoors." (The mysteries of the packer's diamond hitch baffled many; one wrapped his load with the equivalent of a granny knot that he tried to bluff away as an "Oregon wind.") Not least, the written test meant that a ranger had to be literate, a skill as essential to surviving in a bureaucracy as riding was in the mountains. Inevitably, any forest exam included questions about fires. The ability to write an answer did not, however, mean that real answers existed in the field. To the query, How do you fight a crown fire?, one applicant replied that there was only one way: Pray for rain and run like hell.[5]

But what really distinguished the Forest Service was its fighting spirit: its zealotry for conservation and its fealty to Gifford Pinchot. They were, as they put it, "Little GPs." Inman Eldredge recalled how they thought Pinchot was a prophet, that he was all-knowing and far-seeing. On the Lolo National Forest, headquartered in Missoula, Koch marveled at what a wonderful thing it was to belong to an organization composed almost wholly of young men. Because it was so new, men rose quickly up the ranks. Pinchot himself was 40 when the national forests fell into his hands; Koch, head of the Lolo, was 25; Greeley, chief of the district, was 29, as was Will Morris. In fact, that was the average age of the entire Missoula office staff, including its elderly stenographers. The Great Firefight of 1910 was the work of a mighty will and, behind it, a mighty imagination. But even limitless zeal required that someone stand against the flames. That callow corps of rangers and forest guards did just that. The crews that stood with them lived.

In November young Will was dispatched to the Menominee Indian Reservation, which he understood lay near "the center of the fight between Pinchot and Ballinger." Under Roosevelt's interior secretary, James Garfield, Pinchot had had a relatively free hand in forestry affairs within Interior. The Forest Service proffered advice and shunted advisers especially to the Bureau of Indian Affairs. Will discovered that his predecessor had been "in charge of every thing here," until the Indian agency "made things so uncomfortable for him he had to get out, and now a Ballinger man is in charge of the logging part." Here, on the ground, was the real power play behind the Ballinger-Pinchot quarrel over Alaskan coal. Already three senators in a private car had visited the Menominee Reservation to inspect the character of the work. Meanwhile Will Morris happily pointed out trees for felling to Indian aides, who marked them. He was to stay for two months. He requested, and received, a long leave for Christmas in Chicago. Before he could return to the woods, Pinchot was fired, Ballinger banned USFS foresters from Interior's domain, and Morris rode back to Missoula. The January snow, he noted, was "very deep in the mountains. . . ."[6]

# FEBRUARY

FOR FIVE DAYS after Gifford Pinchot's dismissal, Albert Potter, formerly head of the Forest Service's Grazing Division, served as caretaker of the Service. Then, on 12 January 1910, Taft appointed Henry Solon Graves, a Pinchot protégé, the second American (after Pinchot) to become a professional forester, and at the time dean of the Yale School of Forestry. The selection delighted Pinchot's devotees. A week later Congress passed a joint resolution to investigate the Ballinger-Pinchot brouhaha. The hearings would drag on through May. At least, believed the Pinchot boosters, the USFS had inherited an ideal disciple to replace the prophet.

Harry Graves was less sure. He was content at Yale; the deanship suited him by temperament and training. The Forest Service—despite Pinchot's posturing, or perhaps because of it—faced daunting challenges that would hurl its chief, whoever he was, into a political maelstrom. Graves reviewed the matter with Pinchot, the man who had mesmerized him seventeen years before and converted him to forestry. They had known each other at Yale; the freshman Graves had even beaten the senior Pinchot out of the quarterback slot on the Yale Eleven. Pinchot knew Graves "to be absolutely straight and entirely fearless"; he was careful in details, steadfast in purpose, tenacious, a superb complement to the charismatic Pinchot. In 1893 he was teaching in Connecticut when Pinchot invited him to join his forest consulting business as an assistant. Gifford's glowing description of forestry "fascinated" the restless Harry. "The very idea of pioneering in an undertaking that would take me about the country and in deep forest regions gripped" him and never let go. Still, his instincts remained those of a schoolmaster, and he requested a year's leave of absence from Yale before accepting Pinchot's and the president's call. On 1 February he settled into a sabbatical role as chief forester. He remained for ten years.[1]

They were a matched set, forestry's odd couple: Graves the professor, Pinchot the politician. Pinchot had jumped into forestry with meager training, eager to get into the woods, impatient to push the conservationist cause into the political arena. "Action," he admitted, "was what I craved." His father had recommended forestry as a profession, which meant Gifford traveled to Europe for his apprenticeship. There he met Dietrich Brandis, the German who had organized the Forestry Department for British India. Brandis helped enroll Pinchot in the French forestry school at Nancy, then included him in the party of British forestry cadets whom he took on European tour. It was a cobbled-together education, some thirteen months in all, but what it lacked in book learning it acquired in the inspiration of Brandis as a forestry pathfinder, equally visionary and administrator, making "Forestry to be where there was none before. In a word," Pinchot wrote, "he had accomplished on the other side of the world what I might hope to have a hand in doing in America."[2]

Graves had followed Pinchot's tracks, but with more scholarly rigor. Schooling was in his blood; his father had taught physics and chemistry at Phillips Academy; after graduating from Yale, unable to afford graduate training in science, the younger Graves taught at King's School until Pinchot fired his imagination. So he did what he knew best: He prepared a program of study and followed it through, at Harvard (under Charles Sargent) and in Europe, under the tutelage of the redoubtable Brandis. Upon his return to the United States, he paired up with Pinchot as an assistant as the restless Gifford toured American woodlands. Graves spun off briefly to participate in the U.S. Geological Survey's forest reserve inventory, for which he scouted the Black Hills. He linked back up with Pinchot when the latter became chief of the Division of Forestry in 1898. For two years they shared a house on Rhode Island Avenue in Washington, and for two years they lamented the sorry state of forestry in the public mind and the absence of professionals to carry real expertise into the woods. In 1900 they joined five others, a Magnificent Seven, to found the Society of American Foresters. Then, ever the schoolmaster, Graves pushed Pinchot on the need for better education. They simply had to have more hands to do the job.[3]

They also had to educate Americans in America, not ship them to Europe or rely on European émigrés to do the job. A forestry school had briefly flourished at the Biltmore estate in western North Carolina under Carl Schenk, but the first to offer a four-year curriculum had just emerged at Cornell under the direction of Bernhard Fernow after he yielded the Division of Forestry to Pinchot. Neither Pinchot nor Graves was satisfied with the program. The Prussian mind, formal, stiff, often scornful of democracy's social sloppiness, did not suit their vision of forestry in America. Their thoughts turned naturally to Yale, and one evening Graves blurted out that if the Pinchot family "would give an endowment for a Forest School at Yale, I will go up and run it." The family did, and Graves found himself dean. "The University had to take me," he later insisted, "because there was no one else in the country except a couple of Germans who were in our judgment impossible." Offering a two-year graduate program, the school disgorged its first corps in 1904, just as the Transfer Act was about to place the national forests under Pinchot's regime.[4]

Portrait photos often show Harry Graves as a wide-eyed, almost owlish campus don thrust into an unwelcome public spotlight. He retained a schoolmaster's insistence on rigor and detail; his reports lacked flair and the figurative language of a Pinchot-style publicist. "He frowned on smoking in the Forest Service headquarters and forbade whistling." Yet, while scholarly, he was not bookish, and if at times the chief forester seemed more like a chief professor, Graves had every bit as much backbone as his dazzling mentor. Almost to a man, associates recalled Harry Graves's "piercing black eyes." One did not have to look hard to see the fire within them.[5]

In fact, fire had from the beginning, as perhaps it inevitably had to, occupied much of his field of vision. As assistant consulting forester he had coauthored his first publication, a study of forest fires in New Jersey; as assistant chief of the Division of Forestry he had collaborated with Pinchot on a survey of fire damages; as a forester with the Geological Survey he had found the Black Hills so infested with fires that he reported "actual prairie-making" in progress as a result. At Pinchot's urging, from November 1904 to May 1905, he had scrutinized America's new forestry program in the Philippines, where he observed that "great fires occur in every dry season," and he had toured India, also awash with fires, with a letter from Brandis that "opened all the doors of officialdom."[6]

As Graves settled into his office, the challenges to the Forest Service, to forestry, to conservation seemed crippling, and they were mounting. Systematically he laid out the issues. There was so much to do, so many threats, so few men to send to the front lines. Yet he never doubted what to his generation of American foresters seemed the most fundamental of precepts: Without fire control nothing else mattered. There was no point in reserving national forests if they burned to ash on a windy afternoon. It was senseless to invest in silviculture if fires swept away the seedlings and if fried soils poured into mountain torrents. It was quixotic to campaign for long-term perspectives if no logger (or government) could afford to invest in replanting for fear that it would all vanish into smoke.

So, pen in hand, he began to write his prefatory lecture as chief, a survey of fire control. "The first measure necessary for the successful practice of forestry," Dean Graves intoned, "is protection from forest fires." No single forest problem was so important; fire risk was the "great obstacle" to forestry, the principal reason why the national forests lagged in silviculture, the primary cause for the lack of sound forest practices by the private sector. Over the coming months *American Forestry* published the treatise in installments. The Forest Service eventually reprinted it whole as Bulletin 82, *Protection of Forests from Fire,* on 12 August 1910, exactly one week before the Big Blowup shattered the forests of the Northern Rockies.[7]

•

THE FOREST SERVICE, Graves confessed, was "badly demoralized." Its "political and personal enemies" smelled blood. They were "jubilant and looked forward to smashing the whole system of National Forests." There were those who wanted the reserves abolished, those who wanted them turned over to the states, those who sought to liberalize access for miners, loggers, and homesteaders, those who wanted revenge on Pinchot and his zealous minions. Even Secretary of Agriculture James Wilson imposed new restrictions on how the Forest Service would conduct itself and had arranged a personal inquiry that skirted the office of chief forester. Item by item Graves sorted through the bureaucratic slush. He forced Wilson into a "painful" meeting that broke down the rubble of suspicion Pinchot had left behind. But the deeper threat was intellectual, and it occurred as the House Committee on Agriculture released a long-awaited report that challenged the linkage between forests and floods. Ten days into the Graves administration, the forest reserve system suffered severe blows to its core justifications, both constitutional and scientific.[8]

To the public two great fears about the forests had loomed and fed the sense of crisis that gave urgency to the conservationist movement. One was that loggers would exhaust the lumber supply, an alarm conveyed in the phrase *timber famine.* The other was that deforestation would destabilize the watershed, prone to extremes of flooding and drying. The 1897 Organic Act for the national forests had targeted precisely those purposes. To question the tenets behind them would be like someone in the 1990s questioning biodiversity or global warming. It was wrong, and dangerous, and could cast the speaker as the environmental equivalent of a Holocaust denier. Both fears hinged on the unquestioned assumption that fires were intrinsically evil and on the ability to manipulate fire imagery to advance other ends.

Pinchot himself had relentlessly, recklessly exploited these perceptions. American logging peaked between 1907 and 1912. In 1909 the USFS had published a survey that announced the country was hauling out of its lands more than three and a half times more wood than new growth could put in. Like good Progressives obsessed with "efficiency," the Forest Service argued that it was "not use which destroys the forests" but rather "waste" and that it was "doubly wasteful" to lock up the woods and leave them to rot. Still, the wood was going. In 1910 Pinchot thundered that it was "certain that the United States has already crossed the verge of a timber famine so severe that its blighting effects will be felt in every household in the land." It was a matter of simple arithmetic. The country, he insisted, was already feeling its effects.[9]

The same held true for flooding, and Pinchot took his case to the public with similar flourish. Asked if the massive 1907 floods on the Ohio and Mississippi rivers could be traced to cutover lands in the Appalachians, Pinchot had told a congressional committee: "Directly; directly. . . . It is a perfectly clear cut proposition." For other audiences he poured water over an inclined table covered with sand and let the sand flow to the floor to demonstrate how cutover and burned-over lands prompted floods, or he had an associate do the same with the photograph of a denuded hillside. It was good political theater but lousy science. From the sidelines a bemused Fernow observed that a "good deal of buncombe" went into public presentations. Frustrated when House Speaker Joe Cannon of Illinois repeatedly stymied passage of vital forestry legislation, Pinchot argued for "a little rioting," an "outburst of public opinion such as can not be trifled with." Such outbursts demanded simplistic slogans rather than complex, perhaps compromised science.[10]

But the science came, regardless. The House Committee on Agriculture's report was the most damaging because it was the most public and because it held a political knife at the throat of the Weeks bill. Building on studies by Lieutenant Colonel Hiram M. Chittenden of the Army Corps of Engineers, Willis Moore, chief of the Weather Bureau, argued that forests exercised little influence over patterns of flooding. Moore confessed that it was Chittenden's earlier work, first published in 1908, that had prompted his conversion; others followed.

Chittenden was no crank. One of the great engineers of his generation, a keen student of the western landscape and its history, he was a man largely sympathetic to Progressive reforms. He had labored long over waterways and understood the commercial and hydrologic significance of canals, levees, reservoirs, harbor improvements, and irrigation works. He had even shared with Pinchot the platform of the 1900 Irrigation Congress. Moreover, Chittenden the engineer was also Chittenden the scholar. He thrilled to the saga of the frontiersman as Romantic hero, admired the epic histories of Francis Parkman, and, like him, came to suffer from debilitating health that ended in virtual paralysis. Chittenden studied with pride the Army engineers who had explored the Far West; he wrote the first scholarly study of the Rocky Mountain fur trade; he did two tours of duty to Yellowstone National Park, then under Army administration, during which he laid out the basic grid of roads that survives today and then wrote up the Yellowstone's early history. He defended the park against "legal vandalism," as he called it, and later served on a commission to enlarge Yosemite. He publicly favored the existing forest reserves and their expansion.[11]

But he was outraged at the hokum that advocates passed off as science and at the bureaucratic body blows that advocates of multipurpose, centrally planned waterways delivered to the corps. Both concerns focused, particularly, on Pinchot's Forest Service. Yellowstone was the epitome of pristine wilderness, yet there Chittenden had routinely witnessed flooding in a landscape that had never known the ax. His doubts about the forest-flood axiom grew until in 1908 he published in the *Proceedings* of the American Society of Civil Engineers a formidable essay, "Forests and Reservoirs in Their Relation to Stream Flow with Particular Reference to Navigable Rivers," that smashed many of the assumptions popularized by the forestry lobby. The paper led to Moore's conversion and the February 1910 findings of the Committee on Agriculture. Forestry, Chittenden concluded, "will be left to work out its own salvation without any reference to the rivers."[12]

On this whole matter, for which the public showed such conviction, the Forest Service stood almost alone among the science-based bureaus of Progressivism. Even the Geological Survey remained silent. It too found little evidence to support the assertion that thick forests stanched floods and stabilized climates. Yet like the other bureaus, the USGS worried that a chorus of criticism might cripple conservation overall. The compromise was to defer the matter for further study and to move the test into the field. Before the month ended the Forest Service and Weather Bureau agreed jointly to staff experimental plots in the Colorado Rockies to test quantitatively the relation between forests and floods. The Wagon Wheel Gap experiment would take time, even as its outcome remained, for foresters, doubtful.[13]

As Chittenden insisted, forestry would need another intellectual lifeline, something tougher than the weak reed of the forest-flood syllogism. Something stronger than water would have to propel the Weeks bill through the political mire: something that argued compellingly and publicly for state intervention and governmental stewardship of mountain forests; something that demanded an active presence on the ground, that argued unequivocally for a vigorous Forest Service. The answer lay not with flood but with fire.

•

THE GEOLOGICAL SURVEY'S silence mattered. Far more than the Forest Service, the USGS had brought the geography of the western forests into formal scholarship. Even in 1910 its staff knew more about the public domain and had more credibility than the starveling USFS. Yet while John Wesley Powell proved an inspirational, even patriarchal figure for the USGS, he had bred no Little JWPs as Pinchot had Little GPs. Powell's legatees went their own robust ways, accepting some of his ambitions and assertions while downplaying others. It was of immense significance to the Forest Service that two of those heirs, Henry Gannett and Charles Walcott, in particular, blunted Powell's vision of fire and refused to have the Geological Survey challenge the

Forest Service, as the Corps of Engineers did, as the prime agency for managing flame and woods.

The USGS had evidence to dispute both of Pinchot's strongest claims for a forest crisis. It broke the linkage of forests with flooding, and it questioned the imminence of a timber famine. Its concern with connecting mountain watersheds to lowland farms gave it considerable understanding in how water moved from one to the other, while its role in the grand reconnaissance of forest reserves had allowed it to trace the flaming facts on the ground with cartographic rigor. Thanks to Walcott, Gannett and Pinchot had met as members of the National Academy of Sciences' Committee on Forestry. They took to each other, Pinchot recalled, "from the first day." They were mirror images, both men of "decided opinions and strong antagonisms," but they worked together like "Damon and Pythias, if those worthies ever did any work." Gannett then directed the Geological Survey's extraordinary inventory of the public domain's forest estate.[14]

Among their "strong antagonisms," they disagreed over the value of forests and the means for their protection. Gannett scorned the usual pleas for forest protection as "almost a religion." He scotched the claim that forests retarded floods, and he dismissed the assertion that the West was exhausting its timber. There were far more woodlands in the West than critics allowed, he asserted, and if one wanted better runoff to support settlement by irrigation, "it is advisable to cut away as rapidly as possible all the forests, especially upon the mountains. . . ." In his opinion, "the forests in the arid region are thus disappearing with commendable rapidity." Yet he supported the reserves and on that probably spoke for the Geological Survey as a whole. The reserved forests' justification would have to lie elsewhere.[15]

Where he and Gifford agreed was the conviction that America's fire scene was appalling. In northern Idaho, Pinchot wrote that "the fire devastation of the old forest between the Priest Mountains to the east and the Pend Oreille range to the west was sickening. . . . [T]here is probably not a body of one thousand acres on the whole reserve which has not been more or less seriously injured by fire." Gannett concurred. Throughout the Rocky Mountains, in particular, he wrote, fires were "so prevalent that there are few old forests in the region; nearly all of the existing ones being less than a century old." He then wrote for the *Forum* that the "principal enemies of the forest are the axe and fire."

The ax, at least, put the woods to work for humans and "in all probability" was not destroying the forests any faster than they could regrow. "But where the axe has slain its thousands, fire has destroyed its tens of thousands; and here the destruction does not in any way conduce to man's welfare, but is a misfortune without one redeeming feature." Although fires were an "evil of the first magnitude," no existing agency was charged with their control; they seemed to be everybody's business and so "concerned no one in particular." Recently, however, New York State and Yellowstone National Park had shown conclusively that with public will, sound technique, and proper institutions fires could be "practically prevented."[16]

What was needed was a national agency charged with fire protection that could hold the others together in the force field of its purpose. What was needed was a bureau that was not merely scientific or advisory but ready to take to the field. That was not a mission Powell's successor, the extraordinary Charles Walcott, desired for the Geological Survey. So while he had long labored on behalf of forestry, inspired, he wrote, by his years in the Far West as a field paleontologist, he played Aesop's sun to Powell's blustering north wind. With the weight of the USGS behind him, Walcott had helped shape the 1897 Organic Act, fielded the forest reserve inventory, and, when requested by Agriculture Secretary Wilson, recommended Pinchot to replace Fernow as chief of the Division of Forestry. Yet it was what he declined to do that mattered as fully. He was content to fission off new agencies: The Geological Survey would not fight the Forest Service as the Corps of Engineers, the Weather Bureau, the General Land Office, and others would. The USGS mission was not to manage the land. Even as the forest-flood controversy was cresting in 1910, the august Survey remained quietly on the levee. By so doing, it broke the solidarity of Interior ranks and granted the Forest Service some breathing space.[17]

So, likewise, perhaps what mattered most in the Survey's multiyear inventory of the forest reserves was not its tally of woods and waters. Colleagues, even friends, could disagree vehemently about how much timber resided on the mountains, about whether removing it helped or hindered settlement, about whether floods and droughts were more frequent after settlement than before. But nearly everyone—everyone belonging to the educated elite, everyone in the burgeoning scientific establishment in the nation's capital—could agree that there was too much fire. Here lay the real logic and urgency behind the push for a forestry bureau: It could control those fires. In a real sense, the public argument was inverted. It was less about ethereal relationships between climate and forests than about the fiery facts on the ground. The issue was less that the public lands demanded fire protection than it was that fire protection required the public to set aside lands permanently and to entrust their administration to a cadre of professionals. While its rangering corps spoke of public crusades and the nurturing power of trees, the practical reality of the Forest Service's early years proclaimed another purpose. In a sense the Service did not fight fire as part of a larger mission. Rather, that larger mission was made possible because the USFS was willing—ardent—to fight fire.

•

ON ASH WEDNESDAY, 9 February, Will Morris and a recent Yale graduate named Wilfred Willey, also a forest assistant, packed into Big Grizzly Creek. It was a hard slog; the snow was four and a half feet deep and falling steadily. Yet the log cabin into which they settled was snug and full of evidence "of a good housekeeper"; there had been, Morris wrote home, "women here once upon a time." Outside he watched trappers gathering mink and lynx, which reminded him of stories he used to read from the *Youth's Companion.* The cabin, he mused, would make a fine place for the family to stay for a summer. He found himself enjoying the deep silence of a northern Idaho February. "The woods in the winter are not what they are in the summer and in some ways I like them better. The stillness of some places is very impressive." The cabin was comfortable, even free of mice. "Still," Morris confessed, "the snow comes down. I don't know whether we can get out of here tomorrow or not."[18]

A week later he set out from Wallace with the snow on the divide over nine feet high and more coming down "nearly every day now." This time he was trekking to Big Creek, west of Wallace. Along with Willey, the party included Supervisor Weigle and Joe Halm and Ed Pulaski and C. H. Gregory, "the lumberman." Pulaski had constructed a "toboggan," which Wallacites hooted the group would never haul over the mountains, a taunt that made them all the more determined to do just that.[19]

Will hastened to add what his previous letters had omitted: that Ed Pulaski, the ranger who oversaw the Wallace district, "had for his great grand father Count Pulaski, who you remember fought under Washington in the Revolutionary War." It was untrue, and it was a rumor Big Ed always officially denied. His was a collateral lineage, descended from the count's brother. That an aura of the heroic and the legendary would irresistibly attach itself to him would be, for good or ill, Pulaski's peculiar burden and blessing. But in the spring of 1910 he was neither heroic nor legendary, just a ranger older than most, doing his job, working with his hands, relishing the country.[20]

He'd been born in Seneca County, Ohio, either in 1866, as the census reported, or in 1868, as recorded in his Forest Service dossier. The particulars are dim; how he arrived in Wallace, only less murky; and in that he was altogether typical of that great surge of men that flowed westward in search of work, thrills, fortune, or escape. An adventuring uncle, Edwin Crockett, flush with gold fever, had dashed to California, then followed the stampeding prospectors to the Fraser River in British Columbia, to Washington Territory, and to Idaho; letters sent home during those years were among Ed Pulaski's dearest possessions. In 1863 Uncle Edwin enlisted in the Union army and fought through the Peninsular Campaign save for six months during which he was wounded and hospitalized. After the war he returned to Ohio before moving to Saline County, Missouri, in 1880. Soon afterward his family suffered the tragic loss of four members. It appears that Edward Pulaski, roughly fifteen years old, was sent to help him. He lasted through a year of high school when, likely inflamed by Edwin's stories, he ventured to Idaho. Pulaski claimed only that he had "quit school at about 15 years to make [a] living."[21]

He was at Murray for the gold rush of 1884, packing goods over the mountains. Soon after he labored at assorted hard-rock mining jobs in Butte and Anaconda, then worked in the woods making ties for the Northern Pacific Railway, before drifting into the Owyhee Mountains outside Silver City. Still full of adventuring, he prospected around the Salmon River and the Clearwater and was a ranch foreman for two years in southern Idaho. By 1889 he had settled into Coeur d'Alene. A tall, hardened, plainspoken but kindly man, deliberate, calm, gifted with his hands, he qualified as a "woodsman, prospector, miner, steam engineer, smelterman, plumber, carpenter, blacksmith, and quartz mill expert" and, one could add, scaler, packer, and eventually forester, "equally at home in a mine as in the heavily timbered" mountains. He had, it was said, "pride in the skill of his hands." In 1898 he tried, unsuccessfully, to enlist for the Spanish-American War. Somewhere he married. He married again in 1900, this time to Emma Dickinson, for whom this was also a second marriage. By then Pulaski was a mill hand in Wallace and had rented a home. He was "practical and thrifty," and those who knew him agreed that he had "no desire for the pleasures or responsibilities of material wealth." The couple had no children, but by the time of the 1910 census had adopted Elsie, age seven.[22]

In 1908, at the age of 40, Ed Pulaski joined the Forest Service. He gave no reasons; he wrote little and over a lifetime published nothing. Those who knew him pointed to his "instinctive" love of the mountains and a desire to halt their reckless wastage. Probably that is true, though his passion likely had more to do with the memory of boyhood pioneering than with aesthetics. The brutal labor violence that had struck northern Idaho a few years earlier, sufficient to mobilize the Army to suppress it, likely helped turn him away from the seething mines and mills. Mostly, his wanderlust had ended. He wanted a steady job, a regular home, a career that would put him in the woods often and leave him to work with his hands. Now he was pushing through drifts of February snow, towing a toboggan he had made himself, an "Uncle Ed" to young adventurers not unlike an early version of himself, save for their education and commitment to the cause of conservation.

Although the toboggan, as predicted, proved a disaster, they heaved it along just the same, damned if they would give satisfaction to the mocking townsfolk. The first night they camped in snow while a "big storm came up and blew great guns." When he drifted off, Will Morris was asleep in "over ten feet of snow." The next day they reached Big Creek, dug out their cabin, and settled in. Morris, Pulaski, Willey, and Gregory prepared to survey timber for sale the next summer.[23]

# MARCH

WINTER SHOWED NO signs of waning. Around Wallace, Will Morris noted that snow had fallen nearly every day. Much of it settled uneasily on the steep slopes, many of them scalped and burned from logging, mining, and railroading. On the last day of February the snow turned to rain in Wallace but fell as wet sleet on the peaks around the towns of Burke and Mace, deep in narrow canyons, at a rail junction seven miles away. That night Will awoke from the shrill blasts of a locomotive, and the next morning he learned that a great snowslide had sloughed off Tiger Peak and buried Burke shortly after midnight and that another had struck Mace early that morning. Will and Joe Halm grabbed a camera and rushed to the scene to assist with rescue efforts. Nineteen people died under the snow. The force of the avalanche had shattered windows at the high school 500 feet away. It took some time, Will admitted, "before we got over the effects of this calamity, and felt as if we cared to venture forth in the mountains."[1]

Yet the same storms shoved snow off mountain summits all across the Northwest. Along the Washington Cascades the late February storms had dumped snow at the rate of a foot an hour along the route of the Great Northern Railway while rotary plows struggled to clear the tracks. At Stevens Pass a hundred hours of continual snow and repeated sliding overcame the exhausted crews and broken plows. Two westbound trains, one of passengers, one of mail, found themselves stalled on a steep, unstable slope near the Wellington depot. Six days passed. Then in the early morning of 1 March the piled snows shuddered and plummeted down. The avalanche thundered across the sitting cars. Ninety-six people perished.[2]

In both cases two implacable forces had collided. Nature did what it had always done: It stacked snow on the mountains, then released it. This year differed only in scale. So too American society was doing exactly what it had excelled at for a century. It was moving west, and as it had for the past forty years, it traversed the western mountains by locomotive. It was a fluke of timing that snow and rail crossed lethally in the Cascades and the Northern Rockies. But it was no accident that the rails had upended swaths of the western landscape and clashed violently with nature. More commonly, that collision had occurred with fire.

Rail and steam did everything imaginable to spread fire. Locomotives threw sparks like a Roman candle chugging down tracks. Wood burners were worse than coal burners, which were worse than oil burners. In 1910, however, oil was rare. Railroads used it because, for the most part, laws demanded it, particularly through heavily wooded or hilly country under some kind of fire protection. Mostly, coal powered the pistons, and the search for a suitable spark arrester makes for one of the strangest and longest-running technological soap operas of American fire history. The harder a locomotive tugged, the more explosive was its exhaust. The more incompletely it burned its fuel, the more likely it was to disgorge embers. Then there were faulty brake shoes, tossing off sparks like a whetting stone spinning across an ax blade. Steel tracks became streams of fire. Internal combustion sent trains over the rails; free-burning fire flanked their passage along rights-of-way and scattered flame over the landscape.

The scene, however, was actually worse. Sparks could kindle only if they found suitable combustibles. These too the rails supplied. Railway construction broke open landscapes, littered their passage with fresh fuels, promoted fire-hungry weeds among the ballast. In thicker growth, railway workers burned early and annually along the right-of-way to remove the flashy fuels that could catch sparks and carry them to the countryside. In untamed terrain, they piled up heaps of slash like mounded earth around a plowed furrow. Rail invited logging, logging invited farming; each chopped the land into combustibles, each sprinkled sparks atop them. Railways through woods quickly became burned-out wastelands.

Those rails were only the beginning. Fire-driven engines spread to their flanks as log-pulling steam donkeys and narrow-gauge logging locomotives punched farther into the backcountry and blew embers over ridge and ravine. With rail and steam, hard-rock mining became possible in remote locales, sending prospectors out to burn off hillsides in their search for good-color outcrops. Towns sprang up to support the mines; farms, to feed the towns; logging, to buttress mine shafts, erect buildings, clear farmsteads, and supply balk timber for the ties and trestles of further railway construction. Rail created demand; rail met demand.

It also hauled in wholesale people with little ecological understanding of the opened lands. On its tracks floated a vast flotsam of westering folk, some frontiersmen, many immigrants, most with a poor appreciation for how fire and place had accommodated each other. What had thrived for centuries, if not for millennia, under one kind of fire regime found itself upended. Old fires were removed, old fuels left to hoard. New fires kindled, and whole landscapes were crunched to stoke whatever spark might spring from machine, torch, or lightning, from malice, play, purpose, or random bolt. Railway construction towns like Taft, Falcon, and Grand Forks burned repeatedly until the wave of wreckage had passed away. Rail and steam shook the landscape, not like a kaleidoscope turning its pieces into new patterns but like a puzzle, crumbled into shards and placed back in its box.

To the extent that the Northern Rockies had entered the larger economy of American capital, the railroads that crossed it were responsible for that linkage. Without navigable rivers, and before the advent of asphalt and autos, only steam and rail bound the region to the rest of the nation. Internally, rails joined the major centers of labor: the mines and smelters along the Coeur d'Alene River and, over the Bitterroots, their counterparts in Montana. Much of the timber cruising that Will Morris did the spring of 1910 was for sales to railroads or, as with the party that included lumberman Gregory, for land exchanges. "The Forest Service," Will explained to his parents, "is estimating all the timber on Northern Pacific land, and is going to give them other timber for it, so as to get all of their holdings out of the National Forests." It was all part of a vast jostling of ownership shards and biotic bits in an attempt to rationalize an oft spasmodic and eruptive process—there was no real pattern—of frontier settlement.[3]

Even as the Transfer Act hustled Pinchot's boys into the mountains, the directors of the Chicago, Milwaukee, and St. Paul Railway decided to extend their line to the West Coast and sent surveying parties to explore routes through the Rockies. They finally decided to cross the Bitterroots at St. Paul Pass, even though that meant a tunnel 8,771 feet long. All in all, crossing the Rockies required sixteen tunnels and innumerable trestles. The $60 million estimate for construction swelled into $234 million. When completed, rail had cracked open the whole St. Joe River valley, from the Taft Tunnel to St. Maries. Workers drove the last spike on 14 May 1909. The Milwaukee Road was flush with cut forests, torn hillsides, abandoned camps, wooden towns and depots, and, after 4 July, regular freight traffic.[4]

The outcome here, as everywhere, was predictable. Everything could burn: the forests, the slash, the towns with their wooden roofs and sidewalks, the smelters, the trestles. Taft promptly burned on 13 August 1908. The Forest Service hired forest guards to patrol the tracks with speeders, swatting out the litter of fires left behind each train. Major shocks were expected; fires would happen. But it became clear that the aftertremors along all the great routes through the Rockies would not fade away and that they might, over many years, become worse. The responsible agents realized that they needed to shield themselves from the forces they had naively unleashed. Rail and mill towns demanded some kind of fire brigade. Timberlands required protection, at least sufficient to get the logs out of the woods in a form other than smoke and ash. Even the railways could not function if every fire season saw their bridges burned out. A snowslide was inconvenient, a fatal avalanche like that at Wellington, expensive and bad publicity to boot, but fires worked equivalent damage every summer. The only solution was to organize for active fire control.

On 14 March 1910, Secretary of Agriculture Wilson signed a cooperative agreement with Howard Elliott, president of the Northern Pacific Railway Company, for the "extinguishment of fires on or near its right of way in the national forests." Whatever their differences—and they were many, often bitter—both sides realized that they had to pool efforts to contain fire or risk mutual immolation. The Forest Service knew it had to extend those arrangements as rapidly as possible. Of the 128 class A fires started through 15 August 1910 on the Coeur d'Alene National Forest, at least 102 kindled along the Milwaukee Road.[5]

•

COOPERATIVE FIRE PROTECTION might seem commonsensical and should have been. The frontier offered ample instances of scattered neighbors who banded together against a common danger and helped raise the barn of a newcomer. Even America's industrial order, often caricatured for its competitive extravagance, its cutthroat Social Darwinism, knew that real survival depended not on individual strength but on mergers, if not by collective agreement, then by collusion or outright compulsion. But cooperation by institutions against forest fires came as a relevation.

For starters, not everyone wanted fire protection other than to spare farm buildings or towns. Fire control in the backcountry was neither doable nor desirable, and certainly there was little point in pursuing fires that roamed over uninhabited mountains as freely as bears. The idea that one should fight fires in every forest was considered eccentric, if not worse. To argue further that often bitter rivals ought to pool their efforts seemed to move beyond illusion into outright delusion. Yet to Bill Greeley, the brash chief of District One, there was no alternative and no other he might prefer. Wildfire was the great commonality that everyone with an interest in the American woods confronted. No one could suppress it alone.

William Buckout Greeley was the son and grandson of Congregational ministers. Born in Oswego, New York, he grew up in California's Santa Clara Valley and attended Stanford University before graduating from the University of California at Berkeley in 1901. Like Graves, he tried his hand at schoolteaching, but a meeting with Bernhard Fernow led him to consider forestry instead. His "long legs," Fernow informed him, would take him "through the woods and help . . . scramble over logs." He enrolled at Yale, where he was graduated at the head of the first class of the School of Forestry in 1904. Graves wrote Overton Price that Greeley was the school's "special star," ready for "almost any work which may come along." The Forest Service promptly shipped him back to California as a timber inspector and a year later promoted him to supervisor of the Sierra South National Forest. A self-described "forest missionary," W. B. Greeley was very much the Little GP.[6]

That year he had the privilege of riding with Pinchot himself, who came out for an inspection tour. Greeley got to know him "as men can know each other only in camp and on the trail." Around evening campfires Pinchot the prophet wove his spell. Conservation was a "great crusade." Every mile emboldened Greeley in that belief and that his boss was very much "a man's man." Once, sighting a rattlesnake that slithered across the trail, he bet GP that he would not be able to shoot it should it reappear. GP accepted the wager, Greeley shooed the rattler out of the brush, and GP plugged it clean through the head with a Luger he always carried, while holding a "skittish roan" in his iron grip. Obviously the admiration was mutual. In the great reorganization of 1908, Pinchot assigned Greeley, then 29 years old, to head all of District One, the Northern Region that extended across the Northern Rockies and into the Montana plains.[7]

Yet Greeley had something many of the Little GPs lacked: a genuinely human touch, sympathy with those eking out livings from hard land. Often he recalled his grandfather and stories of wresting a New Hampshire farm out of rock-ribbed woodlands. In those days settlers had burned white oak and black walnut and rolled white pine into the Connecticut River simply to get rid of the clutter. The waste appalled Greeley; his Yankee frugality matched nicely with the conservationist mantra to improve efficiency, particularly in the use of woods and waters, and his ministerial heritage made him unforgiving of outright land and timber fraud. Yet he understood the hardscrabble conditions that often led to that frontier ethos, and more tellingly, he recollected rousing sessions of New Hampshire town meetings, where everyone had his say and his grandfather might be politely but firmly told to save his moral nitpicking for the pulpit.[8]

He could be tough where toughness was called for, and he was indefatigable. In the Sierra Nevada he confronted illicit herding by Basques and stood his ground, eventually seeing the Supreme Court agree with him in a landmark 1910 ruling that affirmed Forest Service rights to regulate grazing. But he made it a lifelong policy never to carry a gun while in uniform. He preferred persuasion to force. He wanted, like his forebears, to reform by preaching rather than policing. Also like them, he wanted to know his congregation. "I formed a liking and respect for these plain-speaking direct-acting lumbermen," he admitted, "with whom disagreements could usually be settled once you met them face to face." That became his lifelong style: to meet critics one-on-one, to influence through talk and reason, to seek out common ground, to forge alliances. Where Pinchot thought of "the people" in terms of public opinion ready to rally around a cause, Greeley imagined them as the cacophony of a town meeting in which all had their say. The contrast between Greeley's clash with loggers and Pinchot's handling of the Ballinger affair is striking. Where Pinchot saw rivals to leadership, Greeley saw allies in a firefight.[9]

William Greeley never wavered from his belief that "first and last, fire has been the greatest destroyer of American forests." An accord with the Northern Pacific—and with anyone else willing to sign on—was ideal. He was even ready to enlist loggers in the cause, convinced that they would join once they realized that together they could stamp out the fire menace. In fact, events had forced their hand; timber companies were already organizing among themselves. The 1902 fires had frightened westerners, the 1903 conflagrations easterners. Bit by bit, in Pennsylvania, Maine, California, Oregon, ranchers and loggers were patching together ad hoc timber protective associations. State legislatures spurred the issue by openly debating the logic of compulsory fire protection. Conveniently, the breakthrough came in Idaho.[10]

The "Idaho idea" was a start, and it added to the broth of institutions that were compelled to address fire protection. It was unlikely that the Forest Service could expand everywhere, although it seemed to demonstrate that systematic fire control was possible. In its first two years the area under USFS control had increased by two-thirds while the burned area had fallen by half. Those statistics, while true, bred false hopes, however, because these were mild years, whose gains the horrific 1908 fire season quickly obliterated. Even the federal government, it seemed, could not carry the burden alone. In 1909 all the interested parties reviewed their experiences in a meeting out of which emerged a collectivity of associations, the Pacific Northwest Forest Protection and Conservation Association. When the California Forest Protection Association also signed on, the name changed to the Western Forestry and Conservation Association (WFCA). The new umbrella group held its first public meeting in January 1909.[11]

Its director, E. T. Allen, was the son of a Yale chemistry professor who had fled the groves of academe for a forest homestead near Mount Rainier. He tutored young Ned, who initially took to journalism before becoming, in 1898, the GLO's first forest ranger in the Pacific Northwest. He soon transferred to Pinchot's Division of Forestry, developed strong bonds with the region's lumbermen, and finally skipped to Washington, D.C., to join Pinchot's "Old Guard" until California invited him, in 1905, to become its first state forester. He accepted, yet retained a role as inspector of California's national forests. While in California, he first met Bill Greeley. They were too different to take an instant liking to each other—Allen, nicknamed Heathen, often offended the minister's son—but they could agree emphatically on two points: that fire control was the foundation of forestry and that no one agency could handle the job alone.[12]

By 1909 Allen had jumped from California back to the Northwest by way of the Forest Service before finally landing in the directorship of the WFCA. Answering his uncertainties about how to proceed, George Long of Weyerhaeuser Timber famously instructed him: "We want you to find out what is the right thing to do and then go ahead and do it regardless of whose interest it may affect." Gifford Pinchot could not have put matters more directly. The association's unifying bond would be fire protection; that was what had brought the group together, what most directly menaced its lands, what threatened its political relationship with state legislatures, what etched its shared frontier with the Forest Service.[13]

When the WFCA invited Greeley to join it in Spokane, he leaped at the chance. Soon he and Allen were collaborating on drafting uniform fire laws, on proposing cooperative fire districts, on sharing costs for fire suppression. Trust built; other gatherings followed. Greeley suggested a standard policy for agreements with private associations, and after some doubts, Pinchot approved it. It was hard to quibble over details when he had himself written in the *Use Book,* the Service's field manual, that "officers of the Forest Service, especially Forest Rangers, have no more important duty than protecting the Reserves from forest fire." With every officer in District One responsible for 250,000 to 400,000 acres, collaboration was the only realistic option. By June 1909 all parties had signed formal pacts.[14]

Thus by March 1910 William B. Greeley, barely 30 years old and the overseer of a landmass four times the size of Switzerland, could look forward to the summer with only modest anxiety. After the 1908 crisis the district had reorganized to good effect. Cooperative agreements existed with major timber owners, the railroads, the Big Blackfoot Milling Company, and the state of Montana. The states had at least a skeletal fire organization and were prepared even to commit money; so, improbably, were some counties. Rangers had made grudging progress at reducing the raw wounds on the landscapes that otherwise became points of infection for frontier fire habits. Not least, the snows heaped high on the mountains.[15]

•

THERE WERE GOOD reasons to believe the brash claim that federal foresters could suppress fire. The basics of fire behavior and control are simple enough. Even *Homo erectus* understood them sufficiently to manipulate campfires.

A fire needs oxygen, something to oxidize, and enough heat to start and continue that reaction. The oxygen is everywhere, 21 percent of the atmosphere. If there isn't enough for fire, there isn't enough for people. The fuel is pretty universal as well. Hydrocarbons in the form of plants lather the surface of most lands, save the most barren deserts and ice sheets. Not all that fuel is available because some of it is too wet, or too big, or too high in canopies to ignite easily. The small stuff burns more rapidly than the large. Toss dry pine needles onto a campfire, and it will flare quickly. Dump a log (or green branch), and it will sputter and perhaps expire. The flaming front follows the fine fuels—the needles, the grasses, the tiny-branched scrub. Still, nothing will burn unless it receives a spark or, if it starts, unless the resulting fizz of oxidation releases more heat than the fresh fuel absorbs in order to ignite.

Remove any of those three elements, and the fire goes out. Since it is tough to smother fire of any size, in practice fire control means breaking up the gathered fuels or cooling the chain of rekindling. In a campfire you separate the burning logs, thus reducing the heat they blast at one another, and you quench the flames and coals with water or dirt. If you are careful, the campfire has a rocky ring around it or sits on bare ground so no flames can touch the woods beyond, and you would shield it from winds that might scatter embers far and wide. A free-burning fire complicates this scene because it burns unconfinedly, searching for ready fuels, soaring with the winds, racing up slopes with the rising smoke, and booming through narrow canyons like immense chimneys. But the principles remain the same.

A small forest fire is much like a big campfire. You extinguish it by similar means. Break up the fuels; douse the flame and hot spots with dirt and water; attack it directly. A larger fire forces one to hold to the flaming perimeter, however, the flank from which the fire can spread. Build the equivalent to that rocky ring and bare ground. Hold the fire along cliffs, roads, rivers, lakes. If none exists, construct an opening through the fuels that the flame cannot cross. Call it a fireline, or fuelbreak, and scrape it down to mineral soil. Pick the location for that line carefully. Find a site—on the lee of a ridge, for example—that will play against the wind and slope that drive fires up mountainsides. Allow enough time to construct the line that you can complete it before the wild flames arrive. All this involves a calculated gamble, a race between the spreading flames and the lengthening line. Likely, it means that unburned fuels will exist between the fireline and the fire.

These are a threat. The simplest way to remove them is by burning from the fireline inward (a technique called burning out or backfiring). The main fire then halts because there is nothing more for it to combust. At this point the fire is considered contained. But it could still leap the line with firebrands blown on the wind. The fire's perimeter, like a twisting campfire strung through the woods, must be systematically doused until all coals, embers, and flames are gone, so that nothing can rekindle a new start across the line. That means too that burning snags must be felled, and unburned snags shielded from contact with the flame. At this point the fire is considered controlled. It must still, however, be watched—patrolled—until every smoke has vanished. Only then is it out.

These simple facts have suggested two philosophies for fire protection. One focuses on ignition; the other, on fuels. The first accepts as an axiom that a fire prevented is a fire controlled. Eliminate careless burning—or better yet, abolish burning altogether—and you remove the need to fight fire because nothing ignites. Still, some starts will happen, and the proper response is to detect and attack them rapidly. The smaller the fire, the easier the problem of suppression. The sooner a fire is found, the smaller it is likely to be. Eventually such reasoning led the Forest Service to investigate means to suppress even lightning.

The alternative philosophy accepts the proposition that to control fuels is to control fire. If there is little to burn, then ignition hardly matters, because feeding on sparse combustibles, a fire will soon starve or be so weakened that it can be easily beaten out or halted with backfires. The best way to wrest fuels into such a state, particularly across whole landscapes, is to burn them under controlled conditions. In effect, one sets benign backfires over vast tracts well before any wildfire ignites.

Of course there is no intrinsic reason why both strategies can't coexist. Yet there are regional differences that shunt the strategy one way or the other. The Northeast has few lightning fires, leaving ignition in the hands of people, which suggests that fire control is largely a matter of social control. The Southeast, by contrast, tends to overflow with voluptuous annual growth unless beaten down, arguing for controlling fuels. The tendency was strong in national programs, however, for one philosophy or the other to dominate, however regionally inappropriate.

Thus it mattered that the crisis occurred in the raw backcountry of the Northern Rockies and that the decision fell to foresters. Foresters didn't want a thinned woodland; they wanted a much thickened one. Dense woods, humus thick as blubber, restocked savannas and prairies—these were professional obsessions, the announced goals of forest conservation. That those massing woods were also aggregating fuels meant that fire protection under forestry was driven to select ignition as its treatment of choice. The announced goal was to prevent fires from ever starting and, where accident, arson, or act of God kindled them regardless, to fight them as quickly as possible. As the 1910 fire season opened, that inclination took to the field, and by the time the season closed, doctrine was fast becoming dogma. Thanks to Greeley's instincts for collective action, government foresters had ample allies. The firefight the Forest Service yearned for, it seemed splendidly equipped to win.

•

STILL, THE NORTHERN ROCKIES, however vast their dominion, were remote from public consciousness. As fire regions, natural geography favored the South, and political geography the Northeast; those were the places where the nation's fire season traditionally broke out. That's where it began in the early spring of 1910.

As March lengthened, wildfires raged across western Pennsylvania and West Virginia. Flames burned through oil storage tanks, powerhouses, woods, and "brush." Volunteers, mostly farmers, fought the Pennsylvania fires through the night. Kinsley Courtney, age ten, died when a hose reel deployed by city firemen crushed him. At month's end the West Virginia burns, gorging on second-growth scrub, continued "practically unchecked."[16]

For New England overall, however, 1910 was a mild year. Much of what had been ripe for burning, fire had already claimed. The very specific—and hence rare—collusion of massive fuels, prolonged drought, and abundant spark that powered large fires was unraveling. But there were, inevitably, local exceptions. New Jersey was one of them. The state forester, Alfred Gaskill, admitted that his office was largely a "Forest Fire Service." This year it faced fires that had come early and hard. Apart from a few brief showers, "no rain fell in the greater part of the State between March 7 and April 17." Instead dry cold fronts raced like freight trains through the still-dormant woods. The winds caught whatever flame was present. Five fires became serious until a regional rain fell and a general greenup dampened the scene. July and August turned dry again and powered another large fire. A late-fall drought did the same. Still, Gaskill pointedly noted, "there is evidence on every hand that if the State of New Jersey had not had a moderately efficient fire service, the record for the year [1910] would have been one of disaster, as it was in most parts of the country." A scant 2 percent of reported fires accounted for almost all the burned area.[17]

Their causes were mixed. The largest category reported was simply "unknown." Railroads were prominent sources of ignition, so were brush burning and general agricultural cleanup, and so was "carelessness." A grumpy Gaskill listed some examples: "Time after time, a fire is caused by the man who builds a smudge to keep flies off his horse; by the man who gets cold while hunting and hastily leaves the fire he has made to warm him; by the man who chases a squirrel to its hole and proves the mighty hunter by firing the tree to smoke it out; by the man who sets fire to the brush in the woods merely to make it uncomfortable for a snake." The verdict was clear: Control people and, in this landscape, you control fire.[18]

"Not many States," Gaskill observed with just pride, "will report a lessened fire loss in this the worst fire year the country has known." New Jersey could. In May 1910 Gaskill had informed the *New York Times* that the solution to the state's forest problems, both the damages caused and the lack of revenue received, lay "in the control of forest fires. Hitherto these fires have been allowed to run almost unnoticed, and the harm done has been considered inevitable." It was just such a scene that had prompted the state in 1895 to hire Gifford Pinchot, then a consulting forester (assisted by Graves), to thunder against the unholy wreckage with abolitionist zeal. The means were at hand; the state simply had to assume responsibility for fire protection. So it had: By 1910 the era of laissez-faire fire was ending. The solution was the same as that applied by New York, an orderly system of fire surveillance and suppression grafted onto the rootstock of rural settlement. In such an environment this was sufficient. To New Jersey officials like Alfred Gaskill, the state's success in 1910 vindicated its (ever-understaffed) commitment to organized fire control. The era of blowup fires had ended forever in the East. The country's fire crises would happen elsewhere.[19]

•

THEY WERE HAPPENING, in fact, in the South, though no one was much intent on recording them. A partial exception was North Carolina, the first southern state to address forestry seriously, as it did, revealingly, within the context of its state Geological Survey, and whose western mountains were the object of the Weeks bill's southern strategy. Its fire exceptionalism was early apparent. Whereas colonial New England had passed laws to restrict burning, North Carolina had legislated that certain kinds of burning must be done and had regulated ways to do it. Indeed, its geography—spanning coastal plain, piedmont, and mountains; pocosins, longleaf savannas, unruly rough, bottomland and mountain hardwoods—made North Carolina a typical southern state, synecdoche for the South overall. Its state forester, J. S. Holmes, however, made it an atypically vocal place on matters of fire.[20]

Likely the sheer pervasiveness of burning kept surface fires from exploding. Statistics, never good, show only those burns that escaped, that required action, that fell under the jurisdiction of an official organ of the state. The mountain region escaped in 1910, but two "severe" droughts across the eastern reach of North Carolina ramped up the annual burned area by 43 percent. Yet this is an artifact of counting. It fails to include the routinely burned sites that didn't escape control, which of course remained the greatest source of fire. Timber owners in eastern North Carolina, for example, "burn to protect their timber from more destructive conflagrations," Holmes reported. Still, the fires were not wholly benevolent. In Cumberland County one woman died, and in Columbus County two others, all trying to protect their property. In the mountains two men, in separate incidents, perished fighting the flames.[21]

The specter remained deeply invisible. While foresters might consider southern woods burning the single greatest fire problem in America, the American public hardly cared. Southerners were hostile to fire control on the Forest Service model; the remainder of the country was largely indifferent. To nearly everyone the fires were practically veiled. The *New York Times* would run no Sunday supplement on the insidious horrors of chronic woods burning. No Senate resolution would thunder against the sly evils done to soils and the butts of slash pine by folk fire practices. The South was left to simmer. What the educated elite perceived as a national crisis of fire would have to find some other venue, some more starkly visible site, to promote their message and the morals behind it.

•

WINTER WAS SHEDDING its snowy coat. On the Coeur d'Alene reserve, rangers and forest guards marked timber, prepared for their annual inspections of homesteads, began in a desultory way to imagine the approach of fire season. Supervisor Weigle filed reports, Joe Halm no doubt tested his speeder, and Ed Pulaski, endlessly fidgeting with his hands, likely inspected tools and tinkered at his forge in after hours.

Their backcountry duties done, Will Morris and his long-wintered companions crossed over the passes into the valley of the St. Joe River, relieved to have the heavy snows at last behind them. Will noted with some surprise that there was "hardly any" along the St. Joe. They took the train to St. Maries, boated to Harrison, then hopped another train back to Wallace. "The snow has all gone here," Will observed on 20 March, "and it is quite Spring like."[22]

# APRIL

ALONG THE ST. REGIS RIVER timber cruisers hiked over four to six feet of snowpack, sufficiently dense that they could tread without snowshoes. Elsewhere, as Will Morris discovered, the melt had started. None of this was unusual. That April delivered no spring showers, however, was. No further snow fell; the sparse rains failed to spark a rapid greenup of grasses. For Idaho overall, March had been drier than any known to date; April and May had a deficit of 20 percent, worse up north; June was to break records for dryness; July had only half its usual rain, and that accompanied by dry lightning. Uneven rainfall is common in the West, month by month and year by year, but the drought that began to press down gently over the northern and especially the northwestern United States in the spring of 1910 was not. August would be the driest month ever, of *any* month, since the onset of reliable records in 1894.[1]

"In this region," Henry Gannett informed readers of the *Forum,* "there are only two seasons, a wet and a dry." For a geographer scrutinizing forests and fire, it was an astute observation, for fire's regimes cling closely to the rhythms of wetting and drying, the one needed to grow fuels, the other to ready them to burn. Places that are normally wet, and hence fluffed with combustibles, become available for burning during times of dryness; places that are normally dry require an outbreak of exceptional rains to sprout the grasses and forbs on which fire can feed. It was Powell's old argument—climate controlled forests, not vice versa—and for the West fire was a primary medium through which climate worked.[2]

But how, exactly, does this happen? A good rule for fire studies is: Follow the fuels. Recall that fuel is not the same as vegetation. A greater congestion of plants does not mean a greater likelihood of fire. Not all biomass can burn; only a fraction is actually available as fuel. What determines availability? Mostly the arrangement and moisture content of the particles on the site. Enough heat has to reach a particle that has to be in a form that can truly ignite and sustain combustion. Not much of a normal forest can do this. Much of its matter is too large to kindle; much is too scattered to carry flame from fuel particle to fuel particle, or too high above the ground, or too matted and buried beneath other debris. Much of it is simply too wet.

The parceling of moisture within a forest is complex. Sprinkling water within and around the woods strongly controls what fraction of a forest is available for burning. Before a pine needle or a grass stalk or a branch can burst into flame, heat must boil off its free water, which is the moisture that moves into and out of the particle from rain or atmospheric humidity. Since water has a high specific heat, purging it requires considerable energy. If the moisture content of dead woody material is greater than 24 percent, no combustion will result. The needle will wilt, the twig char; the nominal heat source will become a heat sink, absorbing more heat than it gives off. A somewhat different chemistry applies to living fuels. They can burn with moisture contents well over 100 percent of their oven-dry weight because they contain additional chemicals like terpenes and oils that volatilize at low temperatures yet combust with gusto. Still, there are limits. The trunk of a living tree is unlikely to burn at all; a canopy of flush fir needles, only when their internal moisture drops significantly.

In brief, moisture varies, and it varies by place, season, and year. In northern climes, winter is a time of long dormancy, filled with dry matter but typically blanketed with snow or chilled below the point of kindling. The summer growth season is lush with moisture, as trees and grasses pump water from their roots to their leaves and canopies. They are most flush in late spring—the time of greenup, as they surge back to life—and most drained as they edge into fall dormancy. That leaves two periods of vulnerability: spring, if the snows melt early and greenup comes late, and fall, if the snows are late and dormancy premature, perhaps because of drought. These annual events frame the living fuel cycle. The dead fuels, those on the ground, will wet and dry with storm and sun, and if they are large, they will surrender their interior moisture only after prolonged summer parching. The ideal times for burning come, then, in early spring and late summer. Fires seize whatever fuels may be present, here creeping through surface-dried needles, there flashing through pre-greenup shrubs, smoldering in logs, exploding through canopies.

Drought destroys this intricate almanac of moisture-laden fuels. Dead fuels parch completely. Living fuels drain and shrivel. The moisture mosaic between large and small particles, between litter under deep shade and grasses on an open hillside, between flush summer growth and the spring residue of last year's bloom, all dissolves into a common smear of dry combustibles. The more prolonged the drought, the more completely it wipes out every trace of difference. No longer do pockets of moisture baffle and buffer fire; no longer can water diffuse into green stalks and fresh needles cause them to absorb more heat than they blast out. Everything becomes available as fuel; everything burns. Big fire years are invariably drought years.

Yet drought cannot explain everything. A drought does not by itself cause fires and cannot by itself prompt surface fires to blow up into conflagrations. While drought can make almost all biomass available for burning, important distinctions still exist in physical arrangements that affect whether flame and fuel can connect. Places jackstrawed with wind-fallen lodgepole pine burn differently from grasslands sprinkled with aging ponderosa pine. Even within a place stocked with a common fuel, fires burn unequally. They typically burn better in the afternoon than in the morning, better in the day than at night. They race and blow up when triggered by short-term weather, such as the quickening and shifting of winds during the passage of a cold front. Typically, drought-sustained burns will creep and sweep, smolder and explode as local conditions permit. They can persist for weeks, even months. But that stubborn smoldering is what makes them difficult to extinguish and lethal if they escape.

More tellingly, the effects of drought can swell or quell with the actions of people, who can also make massive amounts of combustibles available, chopping even the huge boles of coastal Douglas-fir into kindling. Unlike drought, they can ignite those piles. They keep fire nearly constant on the landscape. By its nature, drought disconnects spark from fuel. The more pronounced the drought, the more fuel it can make available but the less likely it is to hurl lightning into those waiting combustibles. If thunderstorms become abundant, the drought will end. If the drought deepens, lightning-laded storms become more remote. From the perspective of fire, the ideal circumstance is to have just enough moisture for the mountains to spawn thunderstorms, but not enough for those clouds to end in a downpour. The ideal is a carefully choreographed mix, the dreaded dry lightning storm in which lightning reaches the ground, while rain does not.

But with people, there is no such check. Only law, custom, will, or whim dampens their capacity to kindle fire. They cast sparks wherever they go. Eliminate those sparks, and with or without drought, you eliminate fire, except for what lightning can replace. To almost every observer it was clear that the control of fire meant, first, the control of people, and that was precisely the point of creating forest reserves.

Before April ended, the Coeur d'Alene National Forest had its first fire.[3]

•

IT WAS AMONG their least favorite chores. Yet they dutifully trudged to every claim of every homesteader to verify that each was honoring the requirements of their patent, or legal claim. Morris had stopped by the claim of Mr. and Mrs. Corbin on his way back from the Little North Fork. "They are a nice old couple and the old man is an old soldier," he explained. "They have a nice place and cut all their wood, churn, turn the grindstone, and wash by means of water power." Last year Will had carried in some goods for them, so Mrs. Corbin greeted him warmly before presenting him with a letter from the General Land Office saying that the Forest Service "was holding up her patent, and wanted to know if I wouldn't see about it." Will agreed to inquire; Mr. Corbin told them if they were ever hungry "to come around, as he always had a few crusts left to eat." Gregory, the lumberman, was so incensed that he announced to Will that "if the Forest Service keeps them from getting their claim I would like to put a stick of giant powder under the whole d--- outfit," and "I agreed with him," Will wrote his family.[4]

There were scores of homesteaders much like the Corbins, some thirsting for a bit of pioneering, some fleeing love affairs gone bad, many just longing for a simpler life, not a few of them women. But the rash of filings often had nothing to do with a Little House in the Big Woods and a lot to do with a claim to Big Timber. The Timber and Stone Culture Act of 1878 had intended to assist farmers on the plains but invited fraud when applied to the heavily forested but uncultivatable mountains. Settlers filed, met patent, then sold to timber companies for hefty profits. Where there were not enough settlers, companies used vagrants or agents to file dummy claims or less scrupulously simply jumped claims or drove off residents. "Of course," Will Morris noted, "the service has to be very careful about each settler as their [*sic*] are a great many who have not lived up to the homestead laws, and most of them are staking the claims as an agricultural claim, when in reality they are looking for the timber."[5]

The forest reserves had, in principle, broken that chain of corruption. But the rhetoric of homesteading, its political capital, was as great as the hard currency of resales. Western politicians, particularly those in Idaho, Montana, and Washington, often resented the reservations and sought to turn them to their own ends. Thus, in 1906, shortly after the Transfer Act granted the Forest Service control over the reserves, Congress enacted the Forest Homestead Act, which hobbled its exercise of that power. Specifically, the act allowed for patents on national forests if the claimants could demonstrate that the land was best suited for agriculture—if, in practice, they could farm it. This invited a small number of legitimate filings and an avalanche of bogus ones.

The General Land Office remained the final judge of title. But the Forest Service had to submit reports of what was actually on the site. Patent required that claimants "improve" the land, that they inhabit it for a minimum of six months and a day each year, and that they persist for at least five years. "Improvements" generally meant a cabin and some kind of garden. In watered valleys this was possible, along with some grazing. In the mountains it was not. Legitimate homesteaders turned to trapping, packing, foraging, town work, whatever could supplement their meager foodstocks and income. Few remained on site year-round. With the coming of spring, they returned to their cabins, and so, to report that fact, forest officers made their rounds. They were seldom welcome. True homesteaders resented the inspections and the delays caused by the bureaucratic squabbling between the GLO and the Forest Service. The fraudulent even threatened violence. The work required discretion and diplomacy.

Yet it had to be done. The reserves would be a hollow shell if unregulated patents cored out the prime timber. Worse, frontiersmen were notoriously indifferent, or, worse still, partial, to fire. From the Priest River Forest Reserve, J. B. Leiberg recorded such comments as

"If the Government intends to guard and preserve the timber from fires and prevent unlimited cutting, we will try to burn up what is left as soon as possible." Such sentiments were common, he averred, "almost everywhere in the forested region in the West among those classes whose occupations bring them into closest touch with the living forest." They needed fire; they would have it, one way or another. Greeley, for one, understood perfectly the folk predilection for burning. Fire's "greatest wreakage has not come from the spectacular blazes that write headlines in the newspapers," he insisted. "It is the cumulative destruction, year after year, of thousands of little fires set by the woods-burning habits and carelessness of our people." Most pioneers were in fact "woods burners." Every new community had its "own unwritten code, based on good frontier logic, for burning the woods." The people assumed free access to fire as they did to woods and waters. Their legacy of burning, Greeley concluded, was "the greatest of all hazards to American forests." Just as forest reserves would regulate access to timber and forage, so also they must restrict untrammeled access to fire.[6]

One could muster sympathy for the true homesteaders; theirs was a hard, close-to-the-bone existence. Over an inland empire of forest reserves their isolated claims were little more than pinpricks. Because they stayed put, they were often more careful than passersby in how they handled fire; they would join fire crews if flame threatened their property. The real, the spreading infection came with the torrent of prospectors, loggers, rail camp workers, shepherds, hunters, vagrants, adventurers, and other wanderers and camp followers, who set fires freely but did not have to live with the aftermath of those burns. Even as the Forest Service hired gangs to suppress wildfire, others were setting fires, precisely to be hired to fight them. Crews burned off the slash stacked to the side of wagon roads. They walked away from campfires with hardly more than a kick of dirt. "The only precaution taken by the rancher," Martin Gorman lamented, "is to set out the fire to leeward of his buildings or fences, and then no effort whatever is made to prevent it from reaching the neighboring timber." Or the neighboring forest reserve; innumerable fires slammed into and crossed the boundaries from outside. What had really broken open the reserves, however, were the railroads. They inspired the bow wave of bogus land claims; they trailed logging slash in their wake; they shipped in the fiery "swarms" of the footloose and the fancy-free.[7]

The young Forest Service battled them all. The worst violence, though, spilled out of the saloons along the rails; the Forest Service proceeded to shut down those without a license, which meant all of them. The town of Grand Forks had pride of place. Ranger Joe Halm called it "a wild mushroom construction town," its center a hollow rectangle around which clustered a dozen or more saloons, behind which sprawled tents and shacks. Only toward evening did Grand Forks rouse itself to life. "Oil lamps began to glow, player pianos began their tinny din, an orchestra here and there began to tune up. Women daubed with rouge came from the cribs upstairs and sat at lunch counters or mingled with the ever-increasing throng of gamblers and rough laborers from the camps. As the hours wore on, the little town became a roaring, seething, riotous brawl of drinking, dancing, gambling and fighting humanity." Rangers repeatedly cited the saloonkeepers. Most ignored the fines or fled temporarily out of town. "I often think what a beautiful country it would be," Morris pondered, "if it wasn't defiled by man himself, but I think the Service will get the saloons out of there." The charade finally ceased when fires obliterated the towns themselves.[8]

At least those gangs moved on. Some of the most stubborn offenders, hermits and outcasts, hung on. In the Wallace district one such recluse, a naturalized German emigrant, caused endless trouble, staying civil only long enough to prove up his claim. Thereafter, C. K. McHarg recalled, "he was absolutely unapproachable and always went armed." It was inevitable that he and Ranger Ed Pulaski should clash. When that moment came, Pulaski beat him to the draw, then let him back down, which he did gracelessly. Unrepentant, he brewed more trouble that ended in more encounters. Pulaski later remarked, "I should have shot him when I could have done it in self defense. He would have killed me if he could that time. But I guess I feel better about it even if he is a lot of trouble."[9]

So as the spring melt began, the Coeur d'Alene corps made its reluctant rounds. It was, Morris lamented to his mother, "the most unpleasant work we have" since most of the homesteaders "have not complied with the land laws, and are holding the claims just for the timber. They are therefore very bitter towards the Service, who they think are trying to deprive them of their claims," though the ranger only gathered the "facts as to residence, etc" and handed them over to the GLO. Their bitterness, Morris thought, as he trudged to the Corbin homestead, was a likely cause for grudge fires.[10]

Ed Pulaski trekked once again, this time without the cumbersome toboggan, back to Big Creek to inspect the claim of Joseph Beauchamp. There he recorded the particulars of "improvement": a slatted fence, a two-acre clearing, a small garden, a root cellar for storing provisions, a cramped cabin. A homesteader himself, though of a bureaucratic stripe—settling into Wallace, putting down roots as a ranger—he expressed some sympathy. He entered the details into the proper forms, then photographed the scene for good measure. In the middle of the clearing stood the immense stump of a dead tree, a fire-hollowed snag. Fire, it seemed to say, was no respecter of patents.

•

AS THE NEWCOMERS rushed in, the natives continued to dribble away or to huddle onto the reserved remains of their homelands. The thirst for new country, for either its soil or its timber, that chipped and scored the forest reserves worked also on the Indian reserves. The equivalent of the "agricultural" lands in the national forests were the "surplus" lands on the Coeur d'Alene, Siletz, Flathead, and Spokane reservations, lands suitable for tillage or bristling with heavy timber yet exploited for neither purpose. An executive order readied that surplus for opening to patent on 1 April. It then found itself delayed until 2 May.

Conservationists could view the scene with mixed feelings, glad to see the land put to productive use, sorry to see it racked and burned, as it undoubtedly would be. Politically the episode offered a fearful specter for the forest reserves: If one reserve could be violated in the name of "homesteaders," so could another. While Indian reservations conveyed legal title to land, the status of the timber on them was unclear. One could be separated from the other, leaving the Indian forests vulnerable. Pinchot of course had tried to inject his own foresters into the scene, and a 1908 agreement with the Indian Service had allowed him to do so until his relationship with Ballinger became so toxic that Interior threw up bureaucratic fire walls. In 1909 Congress passed legislation that encouraged, for the first time, forest protection on Indian lands. In the spring of 1910 the Indian Service formally organized a "Forestry Unit" under its Lands Division, and by the end of June that callow corps had a charter. It also quickly found a massive fire problem.[11]

The issues were three. First, there was the question of how to cope with fire on the reserved lands. Foresters insisted that they knew best, that fire protection meant fire prevention. Revealingly, they attempted to project the same doctrines and practices onto Indian reservations that they applied to the forest reserves. The often bitter quarrel was whether a suitable forestry corps would reside in Interior or in the Forest Service. This was a fight over bureaucratic turf, not over the final goals.

More significant was the question of fire on the lands from which the Indians had gone. Foresters were only too well acquainted with the fiery onslaught that would inevitably commence. Fire would follow ax, pick, and plow; rail and steam would hack out new corridors of flame along lines of settlement; fire would pock the woods like the outcrops broken under prospectors' hammers. In fact, the scene was more complex because the more powerful story involved the biological aftershocks of *removing* Indian fire. Few observers understood that those fires had shaped the landscapes in profound ways and that their absence could trigger as much ecological pandemonium as the forecast onslaught of settler fires. Paradoxically, millennia of indigenous burning had left landscapes more prone to fire, yet these were often scenes at which fire could be more easily controlled and on which wildfires inflicted little damage. Fire protection might be better grounded in fire's calculated use rather than in fire's unwitting suppression.

Those were general theses. They became specific when one of the first foresters hired by the Indian Service, J. P. Kinney, toured the western states from mid-June to mid-September 1910. The 1910 onslaught burned more than three times as much Indian land as the next worst year on record. Yet "possibly the most striking conclusion" Kinney reached was "that the forests on Indian reservations had suffered less damage from fires than had forests on the public domain and on National Forests." He attributed the reason for this relative immunity to the infrequency of white contact, particularly the absence of prospectors. The welcome scene was certainly not the outcome of "more effective methods of fire prevention and control," as Kinney and other right-thinking foresters understood them. Kinney failed to appreciate how fully the erstwhile firing by the indigenes had substituted fires of choice for fires of chance. The more likely explanation for the surface scorching experienced by the Indian reserves is the simplest: that the Indian lands had suffered less severely because they had been lightly burned more often.[12]

That perception was, in truth, widely held throughout the frontier, and it raised the third and most important issue. In his *Arid Lands* report, John Wesley Powell had noted that most of the fires his crews had mapped in Utah were "set by Indians," a "fact well known to all mountaineers." He then spelled out the simplest solution: "The fires can, then, be very greatly curtailed by the removal of the Indian." His critique became more nuanced, however, apparently through his further studies, particularly of the Paiute. Probably Powell's outburst before Secretary of the Interior John Noble, which so offended Fernow, was an argument to rekindle some form of indigenous burning. Such a prospect was of course anathema to foresters, taunting not only their formal learning but their political ambitions.[13]

The "Indian way" of light burning appealed to many settlers who saw for themselves what happened once those fires ceased. They observed prairies, barrens, chains of openings, and annually burned valleys on the scale of the Willamette silt in with trees. They saw forests thicken into "jungles" with fresh saplings and poles; they saw (they believed) a worsening of pests; they watched fire control become more difficult, no longer a matter of beating out creeping surface fires with burlap sacks or simple backfiring. They pointed out that the magnificent forests for which loggers lusted had survived Indian burning and had perhaps resulted from it. They wanted those practices to continue. They wanted light burning to become the basis for forest protection. It was likely this perception, bubbling up from those close to the land, to which Powell had given political voice, lent scientific credence, and bestowed the prestige of his office.

Foresters feared and scorned the doctrine. On this matter, at least, Powell's successors in the Geological Survey deserted him. They followed the Powell of *Arid Lands,* who had argued for controlling fire, not the Powell of the Paiute, who evidently wanted to use it. They accepted the prevailing wisdom of the educated classes: that fire was an environmental evil. To a man the forest surveyors—Gannett, Leiberg, Ayres, Graves, Gorman, and the rest—denounced Indian burning, along with any other kind of fire. As chief forester, Graves had little good to say about its use, and Greeley nothing at all. Fire control was too important to compromise. Yet the memory of Powell's harangue likely lingered, and they were keen to exorcise it as mere "Paiute forestry."

What all this meant in the field was that the removal of Indian burning had further destabilized the old regimes, had, in particular, stirred more fuels into the cauldron. By 1910 routine burning by Indians in the greater Northwest was twenty to forty years in the past. For sites, like grasslands, that had experienced near-annual burning, woody scrub was invading the scene and locally overwhelming it. Spared the purging flame, sagebrush and juniper especially rooted and thrived. For forests like those of ponderosa pine that had known fire on a two- to eight-year rhythm, needles and windfall and clusters of young saplings crowded the land "thick as the hair on a dog's back." Forests more infrequently visited by fire absorbed the loss most easily; forty years meant less when fires had come every four hundred years than when they had arrived every five. The former might still be within the prevailing cycle of fire's return; the latter might have missed eight passes of the flame. While new lines and fields of fire had opened up, often violently, these only occasionally overlay ancient routes, and quartz outcrops and homestead plats did not reside where fire had previously helped harvest camas and huckleberries. The woods spread, as virtually every observer of the scene insisted they would. A century later the regrowth of fire-spared forests threatened to overwhelm not only meadows and berry patches but fire control itself.

# MAY

THE ENABLING LEGISLATION of 11 May took land from both forest and Indian reserves and melded them into Glacier National Park. For years the Great Northern Railway had campaigned for a major scenic park along its route, as the Northern Pacific had with Yellowstone and the Santa Fe with Grand Canyon. Glacier seemed ideal: monumental scenery, large game, lands that could be cheaply pried out of Forest Service District One and the Blackfeet Reservation, a stretch of rail not otherwise blessed with commercial traffic. But the Great Northern—or the American public that sought to celebrate North America's Alps—could promote only what it could protect.

Almost uniquely, the United States has never had any overarching national park law. Every new addition was the product of a singular act of Congress; every one can differ in its character and purpose. By being first, Yellowstone became in 1872, by default, the model. Not until 1916 did Congress create even a common agency, the National Park Service, to administer its spangled parklands. Until then Yellowstone again set the pattern. Its organic act stipulated that the land be spared from the ravages of "fire and axe." But while an underfinanced civilian staff could prevent logging, it stumbled trying to control vandalism, and it proved almost powerless against fire. Severed appropriations finally forced the inevitable. On 17 August 1886 the U.S. Army rode to the rescue when Captain Moses Harris of Troop M, U.S. First Cavalry, arrived at Mammoth Hot Springs. Before stepping down, Superintendent D. W. Wear had fired off two telegrams. One noted the general increase in "lawlessness" as the civilian force had faded, and the other, that "Three large fires [are] raging in the Park beyond my control." Captain Harris laid down regulations to corral the "class of old frontiersmen" responsible for the first crisis and then turned his attention to the second.[1]

The Army fought fires in Yellowstone all that inaugural summer. One large fire, "in full view from the Mammoth Hot Springs Hotel," started on 14 August and continued to burn on 4 October, when Captain Harris filed his first annual report. Others, some sixty in all, popped up. Their causes were various. Some resulted from the carelessness of tourists who abandoned their campfires; some were set by "unscrupulous hunters" trying to drive the game beyond the park borders; many were set for "malicious," if unspecified, reasons, including to embarrass the civilian administration. Two September fires resulted from hunting parties of Bannock Indians, who were "not particular whether they cross the line of the Park or not." A telegram to the Lemhi Indian Agency had them recalled. A snowstorm subsequently extinguished the fires.[2]

From the conclusion that the Yellowstone biota was a palimpsest of fire there were few dissenters. Like some ancient parchment, the forest had been written, roughly scraped off, overwritten, rudely erased again, overwritten atop the shadowy lettering in new ink, none of this completely. The landscape was a chronicle of its past burns. Investigating the Absaroka Range along its east border, Leiberg had concluded that "as far back as its history can be traced the forest has been more or less devastated by fires, its age and composition proving that these were very common and of wide extent during the Indian occupancy of the region." The park proper told the same story. Captain Harris's primary conclusion was that "the facility with which forest fires can be started, and the impossibility of extinguishing them, when once under way, by any available methods, render it extremely difficult in this high and wind-swept region to guard against them." Others, however, interpreted the outcome differently. They saw that the Army had driven off the primary sources of frontier fire, corralled the fires of errant tourists, and suppressed the residual flames that remained from lightning and accident.[3]

That late-summer campaign of 1886 marked the beginning of fire protection on the public domain. As Congress added natural monuments to the nation's crown jewels, it dispatched the Army to defend them against theft, defacement, and fire. Cavalry detachments went to

Yosemite and General Grant and were destined for Glacier under Major W. R. Logan, the park's superintendent. Logan was eager to have them. He had grown up with the Army, serving as a scout in the Sioux campaign (he was one of the first to see the massacre at the Little Bighorn), his father dying in the fight with the Nez Percé at Big Hole. He later oversaw the Fort Belknap Indian Agency. As he concocted grandiloquent plans for protecting and promoting Glacier, he could look covetously to Yellowstone for what he might accomplish. There the Corps of Engineers had laid down roads and erected facilities. Patrols had driven off trespassing herders and hunters, arrested vandalizing tourists, and fought fires. Their efforts impressed the eastern elite mightily and meshed with the colonial model, largely British, that lay behind the proposal to nationalize the forest reserves.[4]

The National Academy of Sciences' forestry committee naturally studied the experiment with a hopeful gaze. While no one seriously proposed an aggressive campaign of large-scale fire suppression—"no human agency can stop a Western forest fire when it has once obtained real headway"—it was still possible, as Yellowstone demonstrated, to avert the enormous losses owing to fire by means of prevention and prompt action. Since trespass and fire were the chief threats to the forest reserves, as they were to the parks, the committee members reasoned that the forests merited a similar solution. The duties, in brief, were "essentially military in character, and should be regulated for the present on military principles." The Army should, in effect, create a forestry corps equivalent to the Corps of Engineers. West Point should teach forestry. A special cadre of cadets should study at the great forestry schools of Europe. Without reform along these lines, the committee expressed its belief that it was "not possible to protect the forests on the public domain from fire and pillage." The Army would have to remain until a suitable civilian agency could assume those tasks. No one had the slightest idea how long that might take. Ultimately, the cavalry ran Yellowstone National Park for thirty years and might have remained had not the Great War found another use for the troopers.[5]

The proposal for a forestry corps died. The Spanish-American War intervened, and so did the reluctance of Americans to leave important institutions in the hands of the military even under the nominal direction of the secretary of the interior. The solution of course was to create a corps of civilian foresters who would embody the same esprit, the same level of training, the same discipline that the Army could ideally bring to bear. That was precisely what Gifford Pinchot achieved. Not West Point but Yale would instruct; not the cavalry but the Forest Service would field officers. When the civilian National Park Service arrived, it swept out the soldiers but kept their uniforms, their system of patrol, and their search-and-destroy strategy toward fire.

The chimera died slowly. So stark was the contrast between the fire-protected parks and the vulnerable lands around them that visionaries proposed to bring to all federal reserves the standard apparent in the parks, lands staffed with its frontier-toughened scouts and hard-riding rangers, firefighting conducted as a paramilitary pursuit. Forest officers could look with a certain longing, even of covetousness, as they compared their readiness for fire season with that of Yellowstone or Yosemite. The military model gave the federal government a charge that everyone could easily understand and a simple measure of its success: Either an area burned or it didn't. The true costs were more subtle, and they would surface only after the "temporary" assignments to fight fire had become permanent. Because the firefight never ceased; because the military model endured, a standing order to exclude, to fight, to contain, to suppress. For a while, through the medium of fire control, the military could intervene to separate the destructive collision of settlement with wildlands. For a spell, it could impose the ecological equivalent of martial law. The problem was what happened when that informing crisis passed. That query required another model, which no one foresaw, and it required that the fire crisis end, which it never did.

So when Major William R. Logan, ex-scout and veteran of the Indian Wars, assumed the superintendency of an inchoate Glacier National Park, he had potentially at his disposal what most observers considered the most suitable means for protecting a scenic wonder. He was understaffed; everyone was. But he had legal authority, he had the examples of Yellowstone and Yosemite, and he could call upon the Army for reinforcements. By a quirk of calendaring, however, Congress had allocated no moneys until the new fiscal year, 1 July. That would not seem to matter, save that this year fires burned according to their seasons, not sessions of Congress. Until then a mutual agreement negotiated by Bill Greeley allowed the Forest Service to patrol the park for fire. In a sense, Greeley was demonstrating on the ground what Pinchot had proposed in theory: that the Forest Service was the proper civilian alternative to military occupation. The USFS had not, however, been truly tested under fire, and as far as the national parks were concerned, no one could argue with the conclusion published thirteen years before, that "all efforts to manage . . . by civil officers of the Government had shown the futility of any attempts at control which did not rest on the moral and physical support of the Army."[6]

The first smoke in Glacier spiraled up in June.

•

WHATEVER SNOW THE Rocky Mountains still held, there was none that May amid the immense forests that framed the Great Lakes, and spring fires returned like migrating geese. Of the major fire regions, this was the most prone to explode. In particular, decades of land clearing and burning had pushed the fire frontier to the last major stocks of timber left in the region, a fire-prone triangle embracing northeastern Minnesota, northern Wisconsin, and the Upper Peninsula of Michigan. So far the early fires of 1910 had been subdued in the Northeast and had passed unobserved in the South. But they struck the Lake States with a howl. Before they ceased, flames scorched as much land as any year on record, and no year since then has approached their scale, not even that dark decade of drought the 1930s.[7]

Unlike fall fires, which gorge slowly on large logs and chew into deep organic soils, spring fires are shallow, fast, deadly. In late April a sudden snow shower stopped a Wisconsin fire that consumed half a million dollars' worth of timber in Bayfield County. On 10 May word arrived by wireless, hurriedly sent by an operator preparing to flee, that great fires were bearing down on Grand Marais. The fires splayed across 500 square miles; their smoke pall was the worst over Lake Superior in twenty years. Relief boats hurried to the scene. Wild animals were reportedly rushing into the lake to escape. Settlers thronged into streams and repeatedly submerged themselves to keep the heat from igniting their clothing. The village burned to the ground. Five children were hospitalized with burns.[8]

The fires—more fires—roared on. Trains poured into Duluth, itself threatened, full of terrified passengers who had passed between fires on both sides of the track with heat intense enough to blister the paint on the coaches. The citizens of Arnold rallied against "huge walls of flame" to save their pumping station. On 15 May word arrived of a firefight between a flaming front four miles wide and the town of Bemidji. The fire had smoldered for days in dry muskeg before worming into open timber and then, unfurled, sailing before the wind. The breakout occurred six miles south of the town and scattered the feeble ranger force arrayed against it. By 11 A.M. some 120 men and "several loads of blankets" had been rushed to the front; by noon, more than 500; and Governor A. O. Eberhart had called out the militia from Duluth and placed it under the control of Forestry Commissioner (and former Civil War general) Christopher Columbus Andrews. By 10 P.M. they had prepared a last stand along a state road a mile and a half south of the city. The fire front had slimmed to a width of only two miles, having slammed along its east flank into Lake Bemidji and otherwise narrowed as the wind drove it. All in all, 1,000 men faced the flames, with more farmers and neighboring townsfolk gathering to help, and the big timber companies, Weyerhaeuser and Shevlin, fielding crews to swat out firebrands that landed in their lumberyards on the outskirts of the town. The smoke, it was reported, "is nearly suffocating. It fills the churches where women and children are praying."[9]

Then the crisis passed. The fire sank back into the sands. The town failed to burn, so fire ceased to be news. Of the other conflagrations rambling untrammeled through the muskeg and boreal forest, nothing; they were too common for comment.

In truth, the Battle of Bemidji was little more than a skirmish in the grand saga of fire in the Lake States. Since rails first cracked open the North Woods in the decade after the Civil War, the region had become a second Burned-Over District, a more vicious echo of New England. Wildfire seasons that swept over half a million acres became normal, and this says nothing about the greater extents of land burned off to convert the slashed woods to fields and pastures. The wreckage was abysmal. Worse was the loss of life: Perhaps 383 people died in the Peshtigo fire of 1871, and another 750 in the Humboldt fire; between 138 and 200 in the Michigan fires of 1881; 418 in the Hinckley fire and 13 from the Phillips fire, both of 1894. There seemed to be no end to the carnage. The 1881 fires brought the American Red Cross into civilian disaster relief for the first time. The attrition went on, year after year, uncounted deaths singly and in handfuls. In comparison, the Battle of Bemidji was a triumph. The line held. Casualties were negligible.[10]

Yet it was against this dark and bloody background of fire—the forty-year assault on the North Woods, what seemed a caricature of Parrington's Great Barbecue—that conservationists in the late nineteenth century hammered out their forest and fire policies. The national discourse was shaped by the big fires of New York and New England, where the professional classes resided, and by the still larger and more lethal conflagrations of the Lake States, where American industry was relocating. Fires here were national news, in ways that fire busts in the Alabama hills or Arizona plateaus were not.

As the twentieth century opened, the Lake States ranged at midpoint in the national saga of fire. They stood geographically between New England, subject to fire only as people willed, and the Far West, where nature might well burn what people did not. Their holocausts offered, as even large fires out west did not, a powerful human drama, a set piece of fire literature and conservation politics full of fire-blasted lands and fire-terrorized refugees, hollow-eyed with ruin, huddling around makeshift tents, fleeing the wreckage, courageously rebuilding homesteads and villages. So too those horrific conflagrations composed a clear narrative, as the South could not, of fire as destruction. Here was unambiguous waste and folly and horror.

With the fires of May 1910, the Lake States straddled also the politics of fire. The spring burns came midway historically between the belief that only rapid conversion to agriculture could weed out the fire menace and the belief, made necessary by the creation of forest reserves, that some system of fire protection would have to be devised because the land would remain wild. Policy hung suspended between indifference and state intervention. Should fire control forces react only to major eruptions, as they did at Bemidji, or should they be on constant patrol, ready to attack every wisp of smoke? Should protection rely on the laissez-faire methods provided by settlement, with its planted fields, fire wardens, neighborly volunteers, or would it have to import, perhaps even invent, new state-sponsored methods, since settlement around the western reserves was either unstable or prohibited?

When the Great Barbecue began, the former ideas prevailed; by the time the Progressive Era ended, the latter. The transition came in 1910. When big fires broke out, especially in Minnesota, the region at last moved boldly to break down the prospects for their recurrence in the future. This was the last of the Lake States' million-acre fire years and the first to feature conferences dedicated to fire protection. The National Conservation Convention had scheduled its second meeting for St. Paul in September. A special Lake States Fire Conference, the first such convocation in American history, was to gather in St. Paul in December. What happened between May and December shaped not only the substance but the fervor of their agendas.

•

ONE OF THE virtues of the warden system was that it did not cost much. It relied on nearby communities as a first defense force. Mostly local people were the source of fires, and they were best positioned to suppress those that escaped. In long-settled communities, where agriculture had domesticated the biotas and commerce had laid down roads, the strategy worked reasonably well. It had evolved, side by side, with the land and its peoples. Custom as well as law guided both torch and shovel. But where the frontier crashed rudely into new lands or where statutes had in fact prohibited settlement, then fire protection stumbled from one crisis to another, always too late to prevent a blowup, never thorough enough to prevent rekindlings, endlessly chasing smokes and mopping up after the facts.

The issue vexed the national forests in particular. The Adirondacks Preserve had the skeleton of a warden system, however overextended. The national parks had the Army. The national forests had only their ranger staffs and whomever they could afford to hire as needed. Worsening the problem was the absence of a meaningful infrastructure. Without settlement, there was little push for roads, trails, telegraph and telephone wires. There was no resident population ready to sound the alarm if a fire sprang up, and none on hand to suppress it once begun. Excluding settlement had abolished a large fraction of the slash and spark that scarred the Lake States and New England; it had also banned the methods for control. There was no means to suppress wildfire and no strategy by which, over many years, the land would become more fire-free. If it wanted fire protection, the Forest Service would have to "settle" the backcountry for that purpose.

This took money, more than it could expect to raise. But at least the Service could look forward to steady improvement, year by year, each budgetary increment adding to the stock of trails and telephone lines and lookout towers. The more worrying dilemma was fielding patrolmen and staffing the firelines. Yet these, almost everyone agreed, were the necessary cost of doing business. An ounce of fire prevented was worth many pounds of fire fought. Stopping illicit fires was better than fighting them; controlling them while small was better than trying to contain them after they got big. These were truisms, obvious even to children, if not to Senator William Borah of Idaho and Speaker Joe ("Not-One-Cent-for-Scenery") Cannon of Illinois. Every serious observer of the 1908 season had argued for forest patrols.

The year's tolls seemed to agree. The Forest Service expended $30,000 protecting the entire national forest system, while New York alone had spent $138,000 struggling to beat down flames in the Adirondacks Preserve that only the rains finally extinguished and New Jersey had seen its costs swell from $12,000 in 1907 to $75,000 the next year. The Forest Service example was one the states would do well to emulate, the *New York Times* editorialized, and it was a model worth beefing up with more appropriations. The USFS had a summer force of 1,400 rangers, of whom about 400 formed the active fire patrol. On average each fire guard oversaw roughly 670 square miles. The Service deserved more funds.[11]

Nothing was more obvious, yet nothing proved more perplexing. The prospect of a dedicated fire brigade for wildlands came with a daunting price tag. It meant, in effect, a seasonal, standing army, which argued further to mobilize the regular Army, its troops already paid and in need of maneuvers. But the Army wanted nothing more than its existing tour with the national parks, and the larger task of administering the reserves seemed better suited to civilian agencies. But how much protection was enough? There was no means to value those public lands, save for the timber already sold. Where was the calculus to place a market value on wildlife, wilderness, watershed, humus, climatic stability, scenery, or wildlands squirreled away in mountain middens for future generations? Nor was there an objective way to judge the success of fire control. How does one count fires that don't happen? (There was no hint that eliminating fires might, over time, have a cost in itself.) There was no method by which to anticipate the severity of each fire season. How many fire guards would the 1908 season need in Montana? In California? How many fires might become large in Washington or Utah? Should the coming budget allocate more or less to firefighting? With which of the preceding five years of its tenure should the Forest Service compare the upcoming 1910 fire season? And what to do about that most disheartening of facts: that a single horrific season could obliterate in one fiery surge all the good work of decades? How could one anticipate such a year and move quickly to contain it?

One couldn't. But if one couldn't predict costs, one could pay for them after the season ended. In the Act of May 23 Congress had authorized just such a procedure as part of the general reforms of 1908. The Forest Fire Emergency provision allowed the Forest Service, with approval of the secretary of agriculture, to receive an advance on its general appropriations to pay for actual firefighting. The assumption was that the Service could make internal adjustments, shifting fire expenses from among its regions or borrowing against timber sales in progress or against future funds to cover the cost of the crisis. A bad season, however, could easily soak up every dollar allocated for every purpose, so the act became instead a means of seeking a deficiency appropriation after fire season ended. The Forest Service would tally its costs and submit its bills after the last smoke. While in principle there was constraint, in practice the temptation was tremendous for the unscrupulous or the slovenly to treat the forest fire fund (FFF) as a slush fund or, more accurately, to segregate the fight from the fund. Field officers spent what they thought necessary while Congress would make good the deficit before the fiscal year concluded. No one appreciated this was a glass mountain, that in 1994 the federal agencies slid down it to the tune of $965 million, and in 2000 more than $1.6 billion.

Finances were the slippery slope of fire protection. Emergency funding seemed the height of reasonableness, informed by both environmental and fiscal logic. One could not forecast droughts, dry lightning storms, social unrest, defective brake shoes, or the evolution of fire-prone biotas according to a budgetary calendar. In the broadest sense, one could not file so elusive a phenomenon as fire into the budgetary pigeonholes of a government bureaucracy. Not least, the act embodied noble truisms about patrolling and preparedness. Nothing since its passage had occurred to throw those presumptions into question. In 1908 the the Forest Service spent $30,000 (or $73,283, as recorded in its annual report; even then the figuring failed to agree), a pittance compared with the expenditures of those states who saw their landscapes crippled and their coffers emptied by conflagrations. In 1909 the Service expended $54,670. The FFF seemed the fiscal equivalent of the National Academy's call for military troops, a bureaucratic expedient for fire control until a more stable order could be secured. Already the sums promised to shrink.

# JUNE

THERE MIGHT BE disagreements, at the highest levels of government, over how to pay for fire suppression, but there was little dissent among the educated elite that fire protection was necessary and none over the belief that its costs were strictly financial. That fire damaged the woods and all they sustained was a professional and political axiom in 1910. That fire might serve some ecological purpose was irrelevant. That controlled burning might be a better basis for forest protection was inconceivable. Yet even as forest guards scanned the June horizon for smokes, a new Forest Service publication, Frederic E. Clements's classic *The Life History of Lodgepole Burn Forests,* arguably the origin of forest fire ecology, presented data that explained that fire did more than destroy trees.[1]

The Forest Service had long obsessed over fire—its damages, its difficulties to control, its value for publicity. In 1898 one of Gifford Pinchot's first acts as chief had been to initiate "a historical study of forest fires, with the purpose of ascertaining the amount of damage and the true place of fires in the economy of the forest." He quickly took those lessons to the public, lecturing about "The Relation of Forests and Forest Fires" for the readers of *National Geographic.* Almost every subsequent year prompted more "studies." In 1902 bureau foresters scrutinized fire "effects" in Maine, Vermont, Michigan, Maryland, the Appalachians, Wyoming, Utah, Idaho, California, New Mexico, and Arizona. A year later Pinchot proclaimed that the "object of the study of forest fires is to get the best information possible both on the immediate money loss by forest fires and on the indirect damage to the forest and to local interests of various kinds. The ultimate purpose," he assured readers, "is to find effectual methods of prevention and control." The USFS approached fire as the Army Medical Corps did yellow fever or the Rockefeller Foundation pellagra. Three regions came under special focus: the West, with its violent conflagrations; the South, with its chronic woods burning; and the Lake States, with their fiery collision between woods and settlement. The general reorganization of 1908 authorized some experimental forests, which became the site for "full field studies." In his 1910 treatise on protection, Henry Graves summarized the conclusions: Fire killed and injured trees, degraded soils, reduced growth, thinned woods.[2]

The Forest Service left to others the full-spectrum biology of burning. In particular the inquiry fell, in 1907, to two professors, both of whom quickly had to confront the near-universal presence of fire. For H. H. Chapman of the Yale School of Forestry, escorting students to Louisiana pineries for summer fieldwork, this meant the longleaf pine. For F. E. Clements, already one of the country's premier botanists and recently relocated from the University of Nebraska to the University of Minnesota, this meant elevating his study of community change from the prairies of the Great Plains to the lodgepole pine of Estes Park, Colorado.

Longleaf and lodgepole quickly established themselves as the twin enigmas of fire ecology. Research on both suggested a "creative" role for flame; the ecology of both argued for some silvicultural mix of fire applied and fire withheld. Chapman sparred with the Forest Service when he concluded that "fire always has and always will be an element in longleaf forests, and the problem is not how fire can be eliminated, but how it can be controlled so as, first, to secure reproduction; second, to prevent the accumulation of litter and reduce the danger of a really disastrous burn." Longleaf needed fire to prepare seedbeds, needed regular burns to reduce competition with grass and hold down fuels, needed a properly timed fire to inoculate it against blue spot fungus, needed fire to cull out competing hardwoods. The trick was getting the right recipe for applying and withholding fire. With the South submerged in a sea of woods burning, the Forest Service (and conservationists, at large) wanted nothing to sanction folk fire practices. Like his chosen topic, Chapman was both marginal and ultimately unavoidable. The Service could not ignore a forestry professor from Yale, yet he could be, and for decades was, institutionally isolated, almost quarantined. Not until the mid-1930s did the ecological story of southern fire become public, and not until 1943 did the Forest Service accept the evidence of its own research.[3]

Clements was both more visible and, because he was not a forester, more easily shunted aside. His 1910 monograph was the culmination of three years of research. The study showed him at his best: a close observer, ingenious at ferreting out precise measurements (like tree-ring scars), bold in his theoretical sweep. As a medley of grassy meadows and stratified woods, and a place of long human occupation, Estes Park was ideal for a study of fire, and as a fire-promoted species intermediate between the ponderosa pine savannas of the lower elevations and the dense spruce-fir forests of the summits, lodgepole pine was an ideal index. By analyzing fire-scarred trees, by sampling age classes, and by consulting written records, Clements reconstructed the history of the forest from its fires.

He discovered that while individual trees could shrug off some surface fires, the inevitable crown fire would sweep the scene clean. The key was seeding. Lodgepole had serotinous cones, close-sealed with wax until heated sufficiently to melt. Some cones, at some ambient temperatures, could open and fling forth their winged seeds. Most waited for flame to free them. The crown fire thus created the ideal conditions for reseeding, and lodgepole pine would saturate such sites. Additionally, a sweeping burn would drive off squirrels and chipmunks that otherwise feast on seeds, would prepare an ideal seedbed, would open the site to sun, and would, for a time, destroy competing species. As fires spread into the dominion of other species, the pioneering lodgepole would replace them. If fires ceased, then other, more shade-tolerant species, like white fir, would overgrow the lodgepole.

At Estes Park, Clements concluded that lodgepole was the key to the forests of the eastern Rockies, that fire was the key to lodgepole silviculture, that clear-cut logging differed from fire in "practically all" essential points, and that "by means of fire properly developed into a silvicultural method" the forest would be able "to extend or restrict lodgepole reproduction and lodgepole forests at will." In fact, the implications were vaster because, as Leiberg observed from the Yellowstone region, the "preponderance of lodgepole pine, is wholly the result of these fires." But where Clements saw the possibility of ecological engineering by fine-tuning fires applied and withdrawn, the Forest Service saw lodgepole as a trash species, the woody equivalent of fireweed, much as it saw jack pine in the Lake States and slash pine in the South, and foresters conceived their proper mission as one of abolishing fire to the fullest extent possible.[4]

Over time the successional patterns he worked out for Colorado, he elaborated for every imaginable landscape. The Clementsian schema of rigid evolutionism was deeply flawed, very much a creature of its time. As the years passed, it decayed into a caricature of jesuitical logic and neologisms, an ecological equivalent to the cumbersome cosmology of Ptolemy, full of biotic equants and epicycles. In 1910, however, Clementsian biology was still nuanced, close to its field data, and abuzz with insights. In 1910 Frederic Clements, one of the founders of the American school of ecology, could imagine fire as a lively and subtle ecological presence, the "creative force" to which Pinchot had alluded. But forester Progressives read that discovery differently. They saw what they wanted to see: They saw fire interrupting nature's drive to improvement; they saw fiery turmoil replacing quiescent stability; they saw waste instead of productive use. Free-burning fire was an index of unrest. When Pinchot asserted that "forest fires encourage a spirit of lawlessness and a disregard of property rights," he had centuries of European precedent behind him. So, likewise, fire defied nature's spirit of law and order. Fire control was thus of a piece with other conservation reforms of Progressivism: straightening stream channels; killing wolves and coyotes; fertilizing soils; draining swamps; damming rivers.[5]

Not least, the Forest Service was an agency committed to *doing.* The country was in crisis; it could not wait for decades while academics and meticulous scientists nudged their studies along. Fire, in particular, forced the agency into choice. The Service saw "studies" as a source of data useful for propaganda. Condemnatory photos of fire-scoured mountains and hollow-eyed refugees were the equivalent of pouring water on inclined sand tables. What would propel a great public outcry was a simple, self-evident message. There was no need for nuance, no urgency in elaborating ambiguous conclusions into public view, no reason to suggest that, in certain situations, some fire might be helpful. There was enough doubt circulating because of the whole wretched business over the relationship between forests and flooding; the Service could not tolerate a repetition with fire. To suggest that foresters had misread fire—had overblown its damages as they had apparently exaggerated forest influences—would drive a stake through the heart of forest protection as a popular movement. It was not enough to control fire; they had to control fire propaganda as well.

In June 1910, however, some slack still existed. The Service could publish Clements's study, while providing its own spin on what the research meant. It could debate with Chapman down the Gothic halls of Yale and through the piney woods of Urania, Louisiana. If the science was ambiguous, that was, after all, the way science often worked. More science would eventually prove what everyone knew to be true; no one doubted what the ultimate conclusion would be. Besides, the Forest Service exercised a virtual monopoly over forest research, especially fire research, in ways it did not control research on water or wildlife. The coarsening of curiosity, the bureaucratic toughening that would lead it to suppress unfavorable research, the grotesque simplification of its fire message: All that would come later. It would come after fires so big they burned away any tissue of subtlety and reduced the fine-textured relationship between humanity and flame to the simple question of whether foresters could hold the line against the flames or not. Before the Big Blowup, the Forest Service could confidently print Clements's study of fire and lodgepole. After the Great Fires, another thirty years would pass before it would grudgingly publish studies of equal sophistication regarding fire and longleaf.

•

SO THE SERVICE would fight fire, to the death, if necessary, and would rely on fire guards and fire patrols to accomplish that task. Greeley's assistant Gus Silcox told Supervisor William Weigle of the Coeur d'Alene that his was the region's most important forest. It had great reserves of white pine and had suffered bad fires in 1908 and again in 1909 along the border with the Coeur d'Alene Indian Reservation. The forest's value in the eyes of the district office was a nugget Weigle passed along to his staff, including Will Morris. But in early June fires were sparse, and Will joined three other rangers for a three-day mapping trip up the North Fork of the Coeur d'Alene River. Easy country, thought Will, though poling and towing their boat against the swift current were hard enough. They fished, admired the scenery, fished some more, watched their clothing turn grungy, fished further, grew full beards, fished "three times a day, and then some," and had hard work "to keep our supply [of fish] small enough." Later, when his brother Aubrey came for a visit, they relished a trip to Stevens Peak, where they tossed "great rocks" over the side and watched them "bound and leap like jack rabbits" down the flanks, hundreds of feet at a jump. Not a bad life.[6]

It was less winsome for supervisors. Elers Koch, native of Bozeman, Yale forester, for forty years a forest ranger, almost all of that tenure on the Lolo National Forest headquartered out of Missoula, described a forester's calendar as "divided into two parts—the forest fire season, and the rest of the year. In a bad fire season—from the first of July until the September rains—one lives, breathes, and thinks nothing but fire, and a good part of the balance of the year is spent in making plans and preparations for the next fire season." For administrators like Koch, there was no break to frolic and fish. For them, the worry was constant. There were never enough trails, never adequate communication, and, above all, never enough firefighters to send equipped to the backcountry on a moment's notice.[7]

Staffing was a revolving crisis. It was tough enough to keep the regular ranks filled, with pay poor and hours long, but rangers at least fell under civil service guidelines over who could be hired and fired. Behind that thin green line stood per diem fire guards, reliable men who could be hired for short bursts, just long enough to work a fire, then return to their farms or ranches. Those companies with use permits for the forests—herders, timber outfits, mines—found that the permit obligated them to send workers to fight fire when called. Cooperative agreements with the railways and with timber protective associations swelled the ranks further. But these call-ups could not continue day after day, week after week; big fires could. A major fire season demanded an enormous draft of men that could be filled only from the fluid reservoirs of migratory labor. The town of Avery, Idaho, was typical. Of those residing there during the April census, a third were born in the United States (more than thirty-one states); a third were from Bulgaria and Greece; the rest had emigrated, most of them recently, from Canada, Finland, Denmark, Belgium, Sweden, Holland, Germany, Ireland, England, Japan, Austria, Norway, Hungary, Turkey, India, and Scotland.

Rangers mustered that mob with whatever mixture of guile, threats, and enticements they could invent. They gathered the willing, the able, the enfeebled, the derelict, those fleeing from murky pasts and those fleeing to dim futures, those thirsty for adventure and those thirsty for anything this side of wood alcohol, whatever the labor markets in Butte, Spokane, and Missoula could flush out of saloons and flophouses. Many men signed under assumed names; most were unknown to those who worked beside them. As the summer drought worsened, crops failed and the railroads began sloughing off workers. By mid-July the Northern Pacific Railway had laid off 3,000 to 4,000 workers. By mid-August, Ranger Ashley Roche arranged to have a crew of 60 prisoners released from short-term sentences in the Missoula jail. Still, not enough footloose men were eager to fight fire, even for the extravagant wages offered, 25 cents per hour with board or 30 cents without. Professor J. E. Kirkwood, on a botanical tour of the Rockies, found himself drafted for the firelines at Graham Creek, swinging a mattock next to Will Morris. He immediately empathized with both sides: "Much difficulty was experienced by Weigle in getting men to fight fires. The rate paid was 25 cents per hour and board, yet considerable objection was heard to the work of fire-fighting, mainly on the grounds of its taking them away from other business, but largely also owing to apparent lack of interest in the work."[8]

No wonder. It was fatiguing, grunt labor, as hard on lungs and eyes as on hands and feet, particularly if done without the crusading zeal of the Little GPs. This was strong-back, weak-mind ditchdigging. The best crews were work gangs impressed from logging camps and railroads; the worst, mobs cobbled together of (more or less) warm bodies. Few such men came equipped; few had a taste for hard labor; fewer still understood fire behavior. In 1910, as Koch recalled,

> we had to gather together such men as we could get from the streets, the saloons, and off the freight train. As a result there was almost as much misery from handling the men as with fighting the forest fire. Such transients were almost like children—unreasonable, irresponsible, and acting purely on impulse. They had absolutely no feeling of obligation or responsibility to their employers, which was perhaps natural, since few employers of that time felt any responsibility toward them. Time and again a whole crew would walk out at a critical time for some trivial reason. If we were lucky there would be enough good lumberjacks in a crew to fill the axe and saw gangs, and the punks and stew bums would be given a shovel or mattock to get the best they could out of it.

He recalled an old ranger who phoned to report that a fire had broken away and needed some men promptly. "Send me ten men if they wear hats," he instructed Koch, and "if they wear caps, I'll need thirty." The distinction was that the "respectable lumberjack" never wore a cap in the summer, "always a felt hat, usually a black one, whereas the pool-hall boys and general stew bums, in those days, usually wore caps and shoved their hands deep in the pockets."[9]

So it went, and so it was that the Forest Service looked wistfully at the parks and their disciplined companies of the U.S. cavalry. The Army agreed. Watching the fitful civilians work on the Flathead Reservation, Lieutenant Horace F. Sykes stated flatly that "hoboes, or tramps, should not be engaged for this class of work. . . . They care nothing about the damage being done by the fires and have but one object in view and that is to secure the good wages and food with the least exertion possible and many of them have no desire to see the fires out or under control." Captain Charles Bates reported that Major Fred Morgan, the Indian agent, was "very much afraid of these men, and said he was going to get them out of the country just as soon as he could, although he did have some fear that they would set fires out of revenge as soon as they were discharged."[10]

Yet the fact remains that those polyglot mobs, mocked and maligned, bore the brunt of the fires. Led by rangers, their ranks stiffened by competent foremen and loggers, they built the trails, they slapped down flames with shovelfuls of dirt, they set backfires, they died. Of those who perished in flame that summer, not one was a soldier or a ranger.

•

HIRING WAS BUT one problem. Getting those hires to the firelines, equipping them for action, feeding and clothing them, even paying them were quite another. Worse, most rangers followed Greeley's example and led from the front. They stayed in the field, cycling the firelines and returning to offices only to round up more men, more mules, more rations and to fire off a flurry of telegrams before heading back to the lines. Someone had to remain at the head office and coordinate. Someone had to keep this swelling army of civilians—some 10,000 by mid-August—paid, fed, housed, tooled, and conscripted. That task, the role of quartermaster general, fell largely on the shoulders of Associate Regional Forester Silcox. Young generals, so the saying goes, talk strategy; old generals talk logistics. By the summer of

1910 Silcox was already an old general, one of the shrewdest in the Forest Service. Whatever might happen on the lines, he made it possible. He quietly established himself as the forgotten power behind the firefight.

Ferdinand Augustus Silcox was of a piece with those first-generation foresters, a young man inflamed with the cause of forestry, stamped by the personalities of Pinchot and Graves, an eager pioneer ready to head west. Yet he was an oddity, a southerner, an honors graduate of the College of Charleston in sociology, a woods lover, a man of immense personal charm. An article in the *Saturday Evening Post* inspired him to become a forester. He had exceptional intellectual gifts, a capacity to see squarely and freshly into subjects, a rare ability to organize, yet he had the instincts of a raconteur, an ability to meet people face-to-face and work through disputes, and an abiding feel for the downtrodden. In labor turmoil he generally sided with the workers. Quickly he passed up through the ranks. By 1908 he was associate district forester in Missoula. Two years later, heading the Forest Service's quartermaster corps, Gus Silcox made possible the Great Firefight that the Great Fires demanded.[11]

The numbers stagger. Individual crews ranged in number from twelve to twenty, each with a foreman, while over the foreman (or many foremen) stood a ranger or fire guard. They all needed tools to cut, scrape, and dig and received a ration of mattocks, axes, and shovels and a two-man crosscut saw, the exact mix adjusted to the character of the country, whether open or densely wooded. A crew of twenty could build roughly a mile of fireline a day. A large fire could easily soak up hundreds of men. They might be in the field for weeks. They would need bedding and boots, as well as rations. Koch got one batch to a fire at Frenchtown only to discover that contrary to assurances, the gang had only two bedrolls among the lot. "We fought fire all day," he explained, "and at night I had the men build up a good big campfire of logs. Of course they did not get much sleep, and most of them sat up all night by the fire, talking mostly about the relative merits of the different jails they had been in."[12]

Rails carried the gangs as close to the fires as possible. By 1910 Greeley was already a master at the game, too shrewd to hand out tickets to the motley crews he gathered, and instead he deposited them directly with the conductor. Give the men their own tickets, and many would clear out and convert them into something more potable. Koch related how he and Walt Derrick shipped out two crews from Missoula. They had counted them collectively, bought that number of tickets, and herded the lot into the cars, where "being mostly drunk," the men promptly fell asleep. When the conductor demanded a ticket tagged to each man, Koch and Derrick couldn't identify the gang or segregate them from regular passengers or workers. They couldn't ask their crews because "most of the men were asleep, and did not know where they were going anyhow." The conductor stormed off. The train arrived at Koch's fire first, so he rounded up the best fifty he could find and left the "worst drunks" for Derrick. From the stations, they still needed to reach the backcountry. Now the tough times started; the hike in could take one to five days. The only means of supply was by packtrain, so stock and packers were at a premium. Rangers scooped up almost anything with four legs that could take a diamond hitch. The desperate even hijacked pack strings from one another.[13]

Once on the line these crews had to be fed. Nothing soured a gang more than bad grub, and nothing sparked a camp like a splendid cook. A good cook could command whatever wage he wanted. He would build an outdoor stove and oven and even bake bread on the spot. The cook was the one man, outside the foreman or ranger, that men remembered. No written contract or voiced threat could hold together an inchoate mob of laborers like those in the Rockies. The best hook to remain was outstanding food, which most crews got. Compared with Army rations, the spread was lavish. Failure to furnish enough good chow was cause for desertion or mutiny. The *Daily Missoulian* published one protest from a group under guard Kenneth Robinson who listed as their principal charge that he had fed them "such a scanty supply of food" that they were "half-starved." One day they had for dinner only a small can of beans; another, two "cold soda biscuits and a 2 by 3-inch slice of ham." But most crews were fed, even stuffed with scandalously large portions, and for this they could thank chief cook Silcox.[14]

No one understood better than Gus Silcox the obstacles District One faced in an all-out firefight. Better than most he appreciated the challenges of an immense backcountry bloated with combustible conifers and starved for trails and telephone lines. He knew that the fireline was not the beginning of the fight but its climax; that no stockpile of fresh loaves could make up for the absence of good roads; that bold cheerleading could not break a crown fire; that a few smokechasers (a term he coined) to snuff out snag fires were worth thousands of men and mules after fires had sprung loose. This was what fire protection needed: more guards, more lookouts, more trails, more money to hit fires early when it mattered most.

Ferdinand Augustus Silcox never doubted that fire control was desirable, or that it was possible, or that, rightly done, it could smother potential blowups while they still nestled in punky logs and pine litter. Give me enough shovels and the men to wield them, he effectively declared, and great smokes will never again darken the skies of the Rockies. Of course there was never enough, but as June segued into July, he reckoned he could hold the line should nature choose to send out its lightning skirmishers and replay the 1908 season.

•

ON THE WESTERN fire front June was quiet. Across the country fires made their usual rounds and a little more. All over the South pastoral burning flourished, with a few outbreaks. The central grasslands burned but with reduced vigor; drought had made them fit for fire but had so starved growth that there was often less grass to burn. By mid-June the Southwest was the epicenter of major fires, yet there was little logging to heap fuels, almost thirty years of overgrazing had scraped pine savannas down to dirt, and the summer monsoons were still on the horizon. In the Northern Rockies rangers cruised timber and patrolled for smokes and fished. Fires popped up almost daily along the railways, but efficient patrol and railroad gangs swatted them out. Traditions of spring burning were weak; fire season would build from mid-July to the end of August. As Chief Forester Graves prepared for a swing through the western states, the dominant concerns were the usual political challenges to the reserves: homesteading, mining, reservoir sites.

The larger crisis concerned the aftershocks of the Ballinger-Pinchot brouhaha. Roosevelt had returned from Africa full of fight, querulous over Taft's possible desertion of conservation. Pinchot stormed across the country, continuing to stir the pot of the Ballinger scandal. Ballinger dug in, insisting that he was "not a quitter." Congress slogged along with debates over the Weeks bill to create forest reserves in the White Mountains and Southern Appalachians. Speaker Cannon at last had bowed to pressure, and a bill had passed the House. There seemed little hope in the Senate, which, according to the *New York Times,* had assumed "the dreary aspect of a filibuster." Even supporters like Senator Francis G. Newlands of Nevada, "while professing to approve the main idea of the bill," worked against it. The senator "aided in talking it to death from a natural fondness for speech that has made him notorious even when a filibuster is not in progress."[15]

Camping at the serene headwaters of the Coeur d'Alene River, Will Morris and his pals searched the evening horizon for evidence of Halley's comet. Shut out by the high summits, they saw nothing. But the comet had come, and the earth had passed through its tail, sopping up cold cosmic embers, now seemingly hidden in deep woods and mountains. As June ended, fires flared along the Canadian border from the Rainy River to Lake Superior. Ashes filled the air; navigation stalled; "the whole country seem[ed] to be burning." The burns spread into Wisconsin. Crown fires reportedly raced through canopies at a rate of four miles an hour.[16]

# JULY

THE IDYLL ENDED in July. Even the deepest duff and darkest woods were dry. Some of the thousands of sparks sown across the mountains took root and sprouted into flame. On the "glorious Fourth," while Will Morris was still floating on the North Fork and thinking of firecrackers, nature was preparing its own display of pyrotechnics. The next night he "got word of a big fire north of Murray" that threatened some mines. He and Williams hurried to it, a long fourteen miles away, on a railway speeder. "The whole mountain was afire, and looked like a big lawn party. Every once in a while a big tree would burst into flames." Fire season had come to the Northern Rockies.[1]

Morris hurried to Murray by speeder to round up a crew, while Williams raced to Prichard for tools. When they returned, a ranger named Hamilton was at work and miners were gathering around buildings and the magazine, full of dynamite. Guarding those structures became the highest priority. But the fire raged more ferociously on the other side of the mountain, and Morris's corps of rangers herded its crews to fight it. "We had it under control, about 4:30 A.M., and I went down the hill, when I heard some fellows shouting, and there the fire had jumped the divide, and was burning up fiercely with a heavy wind." Never had he been so tired; rarely had he been so disheartened. The millowner hitched his horses and readied to flee with the women and children. Morris never questioned his duty: "I had to climb straight up that steep hill again, and get every body at this point." Four men made it. Swathed in smoke, they knocked down the flanks and stopped the headfire with a trench. The next evening the fire "went down, and we kept a watch all night, and by the next night it was pretty well out." Returning to Wallace, he knew there would be more. "We are having very dry weather, and expect fires any day."[2]

The Murray firefight was more than a skirmish, yet far less than a campaign. How one fought fire depended on the number and caliber of firefighters one had, what tools were on hand, and what kind of burn one faced. Even fire guards knew the daily rhythms of fires: how they quieted at night as temperature dropped and humidity rose and winds spilled gently down hillsides and valley; how, by roughly ten on a July morning in the Northern Rockies, the sun heated the earth enough to break the evening inversion that pooled cold air in the valleys, so that fresh oxygen began to stir the embers and the humidity dropped and local winds began to churn up slopes and valleys, quickening as the afternoon warmed, until at last the sun ceased to drive them and the cycle reversed. They knew fires burned faster and more intensely upslope than down, that small combustibles like grasses and needles kindled more quickly than large branch wood and boles, that fires running with the wind burned hottest at their head. They distinguished among ground fires burning slowly in deep duff, surface fires crisply marching through needles, and brush and crown fires that soared like thunderheads through the canopies. They knew that the density and character of the vegetation shaped the intensity and speed of the fire, that flames were worse in scrub and thickly packed conifer crowns and easier in bunchgrass and hardwoods. They knew fires racing with the wind could be stopped only by more fire.

They adjusted their tactics accordingly. They worked hardest when the fire burned most slowly—at night, if the terrain allowed and there was sufficient firelight to see, or in the morning before the inversion cracked open. Sometimes they would sleep at midday, refusing to waste their strength against a freshening fire. Small fires they attacked directly with shovels of dirt or sand, or wetted sacks, or, if they had it, water carried in collapsible buckets. Mostly they tried to halt the flames by denying them combustibles. They cut swaths through the woods and bunchgrass, baring the ground down to mineral soil. A surface fire would burn out against such a barrier. To prevent logs and pinecones from rolling down slopes and starting fires below their line, they dug the sidehill lines deep and called them trenches. A fireline one and a half times as wide as the flames were high would prevent radiant heat from kindling fuels on the far side. They sited their trenches to conform to natural features, usually along or just over the top of a ridge, for example, never across the side of a mountain, where a fire heading upslope would simply spill over or debris tumble down. This took time. Trenching was slow, tedious work; lines had to be sited well in advance of the fire, or the labor would be lost as the fire outflanked them. Against most fires this strategy worked, particularly if the fires were patrolled until the flames had expired. The firelines, then, had to carry a lot of foot traffic, and when they did, the trenches became known as trails, which is what they were. Almost never did crews work inward from the fire-encircling trails to extinguish every flame and smoke.[3]

Overseeing a logging crew, Arthur Hogue described the practice:

> On the summit of the divide, for it was only a divide between two creeks, we struck the fire trail. In making a fire trail they work in as close to the fire as possible and always try to make the stop just after it has crossed the crest of a ridge, since it is almost impossible to check a fire running up hill. First a gang of axmen go along and cut all brush and small trees to a width of about 20 feet. They are followed by sawyers who fell all big trees that may touch branches across this trail, also any logs that may be down across it. They, in turn, are followed by shovel men who rake all leaves, leaf mold, grass, or dead wood to the opposite side of the trail from the fire. Thus a strip of bare ground about 16 feet wide, that under ordinary circumstances fire would not pass. If it does happen to cross, they cut a similar trail from the main trail, around the fire to join it to the main fire trail. This is called a "shoo fly."

Bosses, as Hogue bluntly put it, "herded" large gangs such as the Hungarian shovelmen or the Italians he worked with, many of whom had no experience on fires and little command of English.[4]

What such tactics could not stop was spotting, the tendency of embers to ride the wind and start new fires well in advance of the flaming front. The drier the landscape, the more easily spot fires could start; the stronger the winds, the farther the embers could sail. Torching trees shot brands upward like a catapult well beyond the slower, mixed flow along the surface; glowing debris caught by winds along mountain summits could travel for miles; a rolling crown fire could shower embers like snow—a scene observers likened to "fire flakes"—and saturate a site with new starts. Mass ignition led to mass burning, and if the flames captured a vortex, as was easy to do in rough terrain, then a true firestorm could emerge. Against such burning there was no possible defense, only a scramble for safety until the fury passed.

Although theorists pontificated that the best defense against fire was prevention, fieldmen knew that their truest weapon was fire itself. The safest place in a fire was where the flames had already passed; the strongest fireline was a black line, a trench that was widened by burning; the only hope against a crown fire was to set a backfire from a secure place and trust that it would consume the combustibles between it and the fire front. Ideally, the main fire, sucking air inward by gulps and streamers, would pull the backfire more briskly along and in the right direction. Like many theories, this one failed in the woods as often as it worked. But broadacre blacklining over a large area was, in more controlled form, the doctrine of light burning.

Clearly, success required that one reach the fire quickly. At its start, one smokechaser could extinguish a fire that, once blowing and going, could absorb hundreds. In populated areas this was possible, and settlers and millowners were keen to report or beat out flames themselves. But fires also began in the backcountry: lightning paid no heed to land patents. Forest guards could trek three, four, or five days to reach the scene, if they could even find the source amid a thickening fog of smoke. Messages could take one to three days, reinforcements another week; all the while the fire grew more robust. By this point a ranger could only pull back to some defensible locale and dig trenches, perhaps at the rate of a mile a day, and hope his ragged crews could complete the task in time to backfire. In such cases, the crews preferred to work regular ten-hour day shifts. One might think that it was possible, at a minimum, to forecast the high winds that could fan large, smoldering burns into blowups. Not so, and if the Weather Bureau could have issued warnings (as it began to do *after* 1910), there were no means to get the word to the men on the line. That required telephone lines, still probing timidly into the backcountry, and it required that fires had not yet severed them. Fire crews had to depend on the rangers directing them. These rangers were on their own.

What fire guards and rangers knew, they learned on the job, not in classrooms. Over and again, patrolmen were ordered to find and extinguish fires and told nothing about how to do it. A fire guard on the Coeur d'Alene recalled how "I had no previous training whatever in fighting forest fires and only instructions from Ranger Haun to put out any fires that might occur in my district. . . . About the only directive given me by Haun was that results were all that he was after, and that the guard the previous year had not gotten them so he had had to fire him." The story repeated itself endlessly. With respect to technical training, Yale graduates were often no better than the stewbums picked up off the streets of Spokane.[5]

Joe Halm had just stepped off the gridiron of Washington State College and was, in his words, "strong, active, full of enthusiasm, broke but happy." His parents had emigrated from Germany when he was two and raised him in Yakima County. The college accepted him in 1904, though he was deficient in basic skills and had to spend two years in a preparatory curriculum. He joined the football team in 1907 and commenced academics a year later, especially drawn to the forestry club. He starred in three sports, not only football but baseball (he pitched) and track (where he threw the hammer for a sixty-one-year record). Still, "Joe Bunch" never graduated. Instead he transferred his eligibility, as it were, to the college of the Coeur d'Alene. A forestry walk-on, he was untrained, ill clothed, and ignorant. Assigned to patrol twelve miles of rail on foot behind two daily passenger trains, he showed up for work in a cheap cloth hat, a silk dress shirt, khaki pants, and shoes that were too small. He was wet when it rained, blistered when the sun shone, and crippled from sore feet. Ed Pulaski had to teach him what a blazed tree looked like. As often as he could, he trudged to Stevens Peak, where he could scan the horizon for smokes. That first summer he sighted two, both already manned, both far removed from where he placed them. For Joe Halm, as for most rangers, firefighting was something he was to learn on the job.[6]

Fortunately, enough men in the Forest Service had grown up in the woods or on farms that the basics, which were easily enough understood, could diffuse through the agency. Trenching was no different from digging ditches, mop-up not unlike shoveling out a barn after a long winter, and most farmhands and loggers knew how to burn off a field or a pile of slash. What the Forest Service brought to the task was a larger vision, a sense of organization instinctive to a government bureaucracy, a zealotry that the discharged temporaries who picked up their fire pay as they left the line for the saloon could never match.

As Morris (and thousands of others) soon discovered, a solitary fire fought day and night was exhausting. But part of what distinguished the 1910 season was that the fires came in bunches, and they kept coming. One fire followed another; each fire stubbornly smoldered even when contained within its encircling trails; an immense swath of countryside combusted, insolently and unpredictably, from mid-July to the end of August. When Will Morris next wrote home, on 6 August, he had been twenty-four straight days on firelines and was still there, writing by firelight. He was to stay on the lines for another thirty-one.[7]

•

ON 11 JULY the fires left by settlers, cast by trains, and kindled by a smattering of dry lightning storms massed and ran. They popped up everywhere, from the Flathead Valley to the Lochsa River—indeed, all along the northern tier of the United States, from Washington State and British Columbia to Saskatchewan and the Black Hills to Michigan and Manitoba to New York and New Brunswick, where they obliterated Campbellton and Richardsville. Throughout Montana, towns like Whitefish found themselves surrounded by flame "licking up logging and tie camps." Fires broke out along the Milwaukee Railway around Grace, Alberton, and Huson, and the company sent out gangs to work under the direction of rangers. Fires flared wherever slash or lumber stockpiled like oily rags. Over the coming days, major fires boiled up in every national forest, along nearly every road and railway, even deep in the wild basins and peaks of the backcountry.[8]

On the 13th Will Morris, under instructions from Supervisor Weigle, was escorting Professor J. E. Kirkwood of the University of Montana, on a botanical survey for the Service, to the summit of Striped Peak. A lovely day, but very hot and dry, and while they unpacked their lunch, winds blew strongly from the southwest and carried smoke. Will took a compass bearing, but before he and the professor could return to lunch, they sighted a larger smoke to the southeast and then another to the southwest, even closer. "This was too much" for Assistant Forester Morris. He took compass bearings and, collecting the professor, hurriedly trekked to Wallace. "Little did I think," he recalled, that this would be his "last view of this beautiful panorama of green clad hills." Supervisor Weigle had already left for the fires, previously reported. The next day Morris and Professor Kirkwood headed for another, with the idea that they would continue their expedition after the flames had been controlled. They caught a train to the Graham Creek Ranger Station before hiking up two miles of road to the scene of some settler cabins, perhaps (Will speculated) the source of the fire from brush burning, now hurriedly evacuated as "some young ladies" visiting from Spokane had flung their suitcases into the creek in their haste to flee. They found a few men digging trenches with axes and mattocks and joined in, the professor proving "himself an expert with the mattock, as well as in the classification of plants." Two days later a gang of sixty roughshod men arrived. Will divided the lot into two groups whose lines eventually met and pinched off the head of the east slope fire. Next they started on the west slope burn until the wind rose and "scattered fire everywhere." They worked night and day to cut a line across the top of the divide and succeeded. By then most of the crew "had left or were unsatisfactory," so Will headed to Wallace for a fresh batch. Professor Kirkwood had long since departed.[9]

Once in Wallace, Morris discovered that however vast his battle had loomed while he stood next to the flames, it was a flyspeck in a regional panorama. Some 500 men were already on the lines in the Kootenai Forest; Major Fred Morgan, Indian agent for the Flathead Reservation, was reporting a large number of uncontrolled fires, and wildfires were raging over the Colville Reservation as well; a dozen fires had broken out on the Lolo Forest; flames still mocked the country's newest national park, Glacier. Like a firestorm sucking dry leaves and pine needles into its implacable column, the firefight drafted in loose men. Logging companies, railways, and mills rounded up all the stray workers they could find to send into the fight; 3,600 men were on the lines in Washington State alone. A fire south of Whitefish was reportedly sweeping through the forest "like an express train." Half a dozen logging towns were wiped out. Five persons died near Kalso, British Columbia, and two near Colville, Washington. Outside Detroit, Oregon, three loggers perished when, "against the advice of their foreman," they tried to save their tools. Hovey Polleys died on the Hilda Creek fire, then crowning, when a falling tree struck him. Large fires burned along the slopes of Mount Jefferson. Fires threatened West Seattle, burned between Lakes Washington and Sammamish, and pumped out a smoke pall that left the sky "a lead color." The Canadian Pacific reported twenty bridges burned out and countless lumberyards. Some 250 square miles of the Kootenai district were a mass of flame. Wildfires burned impervious to the international border and, to add to the confusion, burned down telegraph lines.[10]

But the storm fronts also fanned flames in the Lake States. Central Wisconsin burned, suffering even the loss of the Huntington Forest

Reserve. Large fires raged in northern Minnesota and Michigan. A homesteader near Negaunee stood in freezing waters up to his neck and watched his home incinerate. Two "little girls" in Ontario's Rainy River district wandered into the forest and "were burned to death." Outside Wausau, Wisconsin, H. H. Heinemann seized a St. Paul train "without waiting for permission" and engineered the evacuation of 100 villagers before "the track had been burned over." Around the 22nd rain began to fall, and by the 24th it had quelled the flames.[11]

Of this Will Morris had little news or need to know. Fires were everywhere he looked, Wallace was flooded with smoke; those in the woods had scant knowledge of what was happening beyond the next ridge. On the 20th county commissioners, for the first time, hired men to supplement the ranger force. Strenuous days in the field and sleepless nights had exhausted Supervisor Weigle. Still, he managed to rustle up twenty-nine new firefighters. The fires calmed. An old-timer told Morris that they would be all right so long as the winds didn't rise. But if they got a three-day Palouser, dry and howling from the southwest, they were lost.[12]

•

THE OLD-TIMER WAS right. The fate of fire season resided in the swirling dice rolls of the wind. The usual summer pattern was for cold fronts to ripple across the region every three to five days. In advance of each front, winds would freshen from the southwest, then shift to the northwest after passage. The frontal waves became a vast, slow bellows, drawing in warm, moist air from the south before driving it out with cooler, dry air from the north. Typically, high pressure over the center of the country sent wind in a great swirl out of the Gulf of Mexico, up through the center of Mexico, and into the American Southwest, the much-anticipated Mexican monsoon. How far north that roiling air moved depended on the pushes and pulls of the larger atmosphere. In droughty La Niña years such as this one, storm tracks shifted northward; the tug was weak, the storms feeble, the land dry. But gradually the track sank southward. The train of fronts that rattled through the Northwest beginning in early July captured this arc of moist air, gulping it in, then exhaling it out. The rhythm of the fronts set the rhythm of the burning.

Each surge of air would stir up old flames and trigger dry lightning storms that kindled new fires. The firefight would renew: new crews, new lines, new backfires. Then, as the winds shifted and died down, the fires would calm, the smoke settle in the valleys, the crews slacken with exhaustion. In the Northern Rockies the approaching fronts drew winds from the arid Columbia Plains and loess-capped Palouse—thus the Palousers of which the old-timer warned Morris. This was an ancient rhythm. But in 1910 the drought was worse, the storms held more lightning and less rain, the organization sagged from fatigue. The mid-July fire bust strained the Forest Service to its limits. Yet there was no real pause; climax followed climax: the big breakout of 23 July; the flare-ups of 1–2 August, 11–12 August, and 16–17 August; the Big Blowup of 20–21 August. Each built on the last, each fanned little fires into big ones and big ones into conflagrations, until at last a dusting of cold and wet began to dampen them out on 24 August.

It was the combination of lightning and wind that ultimately overwhelmed the firefight. The fire organization could cope with one but not both. Against the wind they could at least set backfires; against the lightning, they could do nothing, except try to spot and attack a kindled snag as quickly as possible. In 1910, however, that ambition was quixotic. The lightning came in thick busts, full of sound and fury and empty of rain. Worse, it struck according to its own ineffable logic, not that of miners, loggers, herders, railroaders, or rangers. Fires set by people clustered around settlements and routes of travel. It was possible, in principle, to prevent them, reduce them, attack them. At the least, people were present to sight them and fight them. In the uninhabited wilds of the Rockies, fires could burn unseen and untouched for days, even weeks.

There were some exceptions, of course. Homesteads, mines, and mills pocked the hills, and their inhabitants watched the horizon. From the Monarch mine outside Murray, Frances Eaton recorded the choreography of flame, smoke, and community. The wind would rise, the flames broach ridges, the men turn out to fight them, while families stood ready to evacuate. The winds would drop, the backfires abate, the smoke settle. For weeks household articles lined the rails, waiting to be loaded should a general flight become necessary. The winds were a mixed blessing: While they revived the fires, they blew away the cloying smoke. With each front, workers would leave the mines and battle the blazes. From the end of July families lived on a knife-edge of anxiety, unsure from day to day whether they could hold the flames at bay and remain or would be driven off. Small gangs of men moved up and down canyons. Pockets of heavy timber were especially worrisome. But the larger panorama remained obscure in its smoky shroud. "The sun rises in a bank of smoke," Mrs. Eaton wrote, "and sets in a bank of smoke," only "shining out clearly between times."[13]

The more the landscape became smoked in, the harder it was to find the burns. Fire patrolmen could tramp along trails—there weren't many—and climb peaks to scan for fresh smokes; but old smoke and new lay everywhere in a mingled dry fog. If the skies were calm, the pall thickened; if the winds rushed in and fanned the flames, massive convective columns rose to blot out the sun. Either way, the likelihood of sighting new smokes was slight. And if a new fire were found, days might pass before a crew could arrive to battle it. For a while the Forest Service reached a rough equilibrium, holding the line, doggedly suppressing enough old smokes to match the new ones being set. But in the end the firefighters could only hope to hold firm and wait for an early winter to extinguish the smokes. The season was too long and the fires too many.

•

INCREDIBLY, SOME CRITICS disputed the agency of lightning. Lightning started few fires in the East, where most educated observers and experts lived; even those from the West sometimes found it hard to accept lightning as a significant force because the vast bulk of burning came from people. Yet H. H. Chapman—the same Yale professor famous for his Louisiana studies—found himself in July and August on Montana's Flathead Forest, and on 3 July he witnessed the phenomenon for himself: Lightning sizzled down a dead larch and set it ablaze.

They could neither leave it nor fell it, so they waited for the tree to burn through, and then they trenched around it. Without water, thrown dirt was by itself ineffective. For two weeks the larch burned, "a constant menace." The fire even crept through the roots and escaped the trench. Had they not contained it again, with another two rainless months ahead, Chapman believed that it would have "swept the whole [Swan] valley." In another episode, he found a smoldering fire that lightning had kindled in the duff at the base of a scarred larch. For three days the "sleeper" had meandered through litter and needles until winds jolted it to life and Chapman's crew attacked it. Indifferent patrol, however, allowed it to escape three times. It was still burning when the rains of September finally arrived. Even so, "if allowed to run it could have burned over from 20 to 100 square miles."[14]

Chapman's experiences illustrated "in a small way" the "conditions which caused the larger conflagrations in Idaho." Remote fires were hard to reach, hard to hold, hard to flee in case of catastrophe. By the time a fire guard reached the smoke, several days might have passed, the fire had grown, and reinforcements were needed. The smokechaser had to hike to a telephone or station, from the office a ranger must assemble a crew and outfit, and "after a delay of from 3 to 7 days they reach the fire." Not infrequently, the relief crew was stalled further by fires they spotted along the route. By now the original fire had grown too large to control, only to check, likely smoldering over hundreds of acres. Whenever the winds stirred and struck, flame would leap beyond the lines in a great rush. Thus it was, Chapman concluded, that "largely through lightning, many fires were started that could not be reached. These fires, on the day of the great wind, swept down on the protected areas in solid fronts miles in extent and destroyed the work of weeks of fighting."[15]

So unorthodox in his insights into southern fire, Chapman accepted for the Northern Rockies the establishment argument that development would ultimately abolish wildfires. He concluded that with a complete network of trails, with an adequate patrol force, with "vast stretches of wilderness . . . populated as far as their resources will permit, the conditions that proceeded the great fires of 1910 will have been brought fully under control, and a repetition made impossible." But that scheme could not prevent lightning, only react to it. Of the 1,736 fires officially logged for the national forests of District One, lightning accounted for 223, or 13 percent. This was not an unusual bust. Between 1931 and 1973 lightning kindled 43,866 fires on the national forests of the Northern Rockies. From 1946 to 1973 the region witnessed 82 separate ten-day outbreaks of more than 100 fires. The monster of record remains 1940, when a ten-day bust resulted in 1,488 fires. Fire control would be busy.[16]

Besides, what had made lightning fire prominent was not nature alone but the creation of the reserves. Lightning loomed ever larger because it had little competition anymore from anthropogenic fires. The people who would have fought fires, or imposed their own fire regimes, were gone and had to be reinstated in the form of a protective fire force. Also, there was that most fundamental query of all: Why did fire control matter in such remote sites?

Professor Herman Haupt Chapman never answered that question

because busy fighting fires in the larch forests of the Flathead, he never asked it. Yet the proper reply was, again, people. People perceived the need for fire control; people demanded it; people paid for it. The shrewd insight that led Chapman to question knee-jerk fire exclusion in the South failed him during the long pack trip into the Swan Valley. It never occurred to him that crown fire in the Northern Rockies might be as ecologically sane as surface fires through longleaf savannas, that controlled burning might also apply here, that the abolition of fire in wildlands was a dangerous delusion. He could not see lightning's capacity to kindle as a creative force, could not envision the fires as anything but disastrous, could hardly contemplate amid the call to arms. Instead, sweaty and with shovel in hand, he argued for action and the money to make it happen.

•

MONEY WAS MUCH on everyone's minds as Secretary of Agriculture James Wilson arrived in Missoula on Saturday morning, 16 July. He looked tired, having come from a family funeral in Iowa. Like others, he had fled the sultry summer of the capital for publicity and fact-finding tours in the West. Henry Graves was on a western circuit, intending to end his swing at the National Conservation Congress in St. Paul. Teddy Roosevelt was on the rails, looking like a campaigner, growling over Taft's conduct. So was ex-Forester Gifford Pinchot; so was Speaker Joe Cannon; the two had met for an extemporaneous exchange over the meaning of conservation at the Knife and Fork Club in Kansas City. Cannon cited John Wesley Powell as the founder of the movement; Pinchot of course insisted the honor belonged to his political liege, TR. The purpose of Wilson's western tour was to inspect farms and forests, especially the nagging forest homesteader issue, now a chronic howl in the Flathead Valley. He had not looked into the forest fire situation, he claimed. Greeting him, Bill Greeley informed the secretary that the fires were "under fair control and would gradually be extinguished," barring some "unexpected" blow.[17]

But "Tama Jim" Wilson could hardly ignore the fires. The next day the Lolo recorded sixteen new starts and the Cabinet five, and Glacier Park, up the Flathead Valley, remained under virtual siege. Traveling with the secretary, Greeley was unlikely to equivocate. The Glacier crisis had galvanized Bill Greeley's usual blend of clarity and conviction. "We do not know whether there is any money appropriated in the national park funds for the purpose of fire fighting," he explained to the *Daily Missoulian* and no doubt to Wilson. But the fires were threatening two national forests and would not wait for long inquiries and exchanges of telegrams with the Washington office, so he had sent men to fight them. The act was instinctive for one who believed that no fire was safe and that fire protection was inherently cooperative. "The matter of meeting the expense will be settled afterwards."[18]

So it was, and Secretary Wilson was the jeweled bearing on which the door to the vault turned. "The entire forests of the northern Rocky Mountains," he later explained, though little explanation was needed, were at one time "threatened with destruction. Unless the fires had been checked, scores of towns and communities would have been wiped out and the lives and homes of thousands of people imperiled." He saw that for himself. "I was confronted," he continued, "with the problem of either putting out the fires or being directly responsible for what would have been one of the worst disasters in the history of the country. Without hesitation I called upon the forest officers to stop the fires and to make such expenditures as seemed absolutely necessary to accomplish this result." In effect, he declared an emergency, and the forest fire fund came into operation. Without that authorization the Forest Service could never have carried the fight beyond towns and railways. It would have had to recall its outposts in the backcountry, to fall back to the villages and roads, to abandon the mountains to the fiery hordes.[19]

While the money made it possible to hire more men, the men required their money quickly. The Service found it necessary to hire "special disbursing agents" to pay off the temporary laborers as soon as they left the fireline. Few of the men, Elers Koch recalled, "had a cent in their pockets when they came on a fire, nor did most of them have any permanent address to which a check could be sent." They demanded cash. "The ordinary routine of making vouchers, having them properly O.K.'d, sending checks and getting them cashed would consume so much time that many would hesitate to work with the prospect of having to wait for their pay." Accounting was a nightmare. Having pay on hand, moreover, tempted the laborers to leave suddenly and the rangers to let them go.[20]

Yet by 22 July both fires and funds had seemed to have reached a steady state. "For every fire we put out, a new one is reported," Koch told the *Missoulian*. He added, though: "[T]he rangers have been fighting fires steadily now for 10 days and they are about worn out." Everyone was ready for the long ordeal to end. Greeley thought the same, and paradoxically the specter worried him. This was no ordinary year; normal practices and routine bureaucratic procedures would not win the day. On 27 July he issued a circular letter to all forest supervisors urging them to beef up immediately their fire forces, to maintain patrol on smoldering burns to prevent breakouts, and "especially" to reduce "but slowly" the crews they already held. "Keep the best men and when they are no longer needed to guard a particular area, place them at some point where they will strengthen the patrol and be available when the next fire breaks out." He assured the supervisors that their temporary hires would be charged to the "Fire" account and not against their forest budget and that any new fire guards they hired as ad hoc Forest Service employees would be paid out of a national fund "as far as possible" and again not out of their appropriated moneys. The fire would go off budget. Readiness for the fight was the important thing. "I will be responsible for finding the necessary funds for putting [this plan] into effect."[21]

On 23 July the winds rose and rippled across the northern lands like a blustery tidal wave. Will Morris had retrieved ten more men and was on the line when the dreaded Palouser struck. "That night I was up all night and backfired along a new line we had made. I tried to get some sleep in the morning, but the wind started blowing hard and I went over to the fire. It fanned up quickly and pretty soon it was jumping our trail in all directions, the big trees burning like torches." He arrayed his crew around a cabin with water-filled buckets. "That night we backfired a whole mountain side, as the fire was coming down it rapidly. . . . That night the trees falling sounded like artillery fire."[22]

All over the Northwest and along the Rockies crews like Will's saw their fires blown over the landscape and heard trees crashing like cannons and found themselves setting fires they thought they could control as the only hope of stopping the ones they knew they couldn't. The fiery breakout had begun.

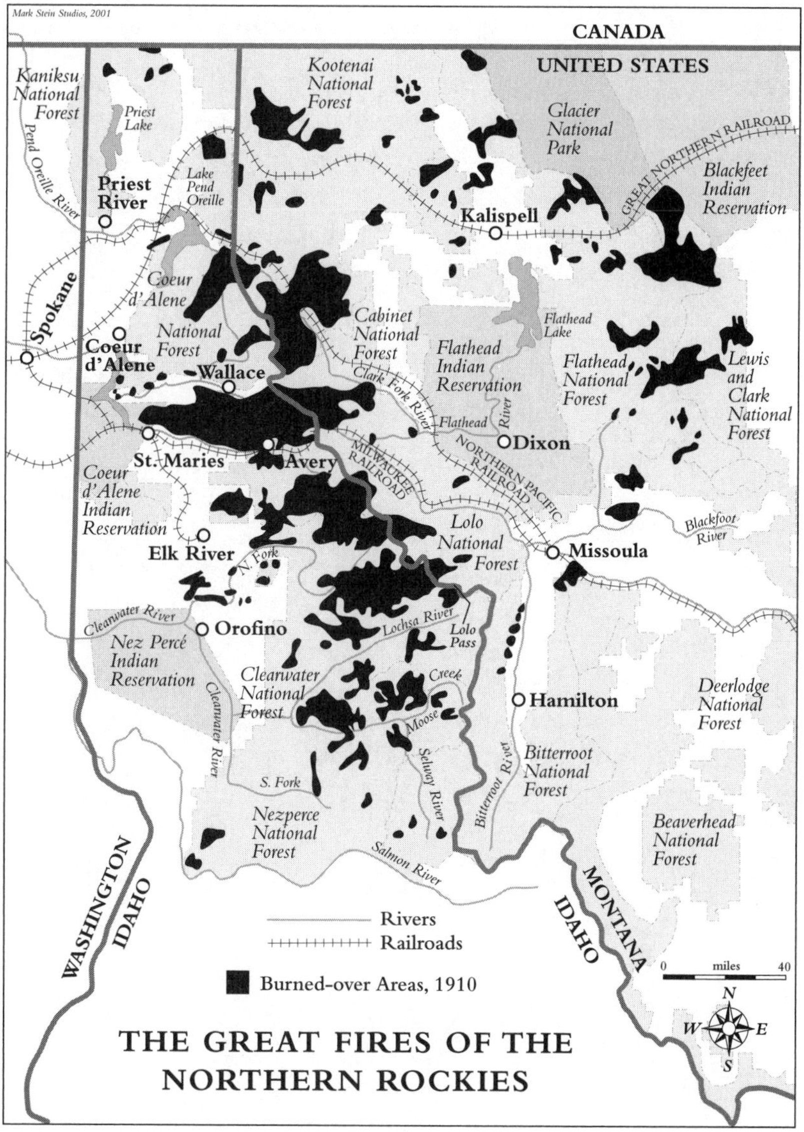
Mark Stein Studios, 2001
CANADA
UNITED STATES
Kaniksu National Forest
Priest Lake
Pend Oreille River
Priest River
Lake Pend Oreille
Kootenai National Forest
Glacier National Park
GREAT NORTHERN RAILROAD
Blackfeet Indian Reservation
Kalispell
Spokane
Coeur d'Alene National Forest
Coeur d'Alene
Wallace
Cabinet National Forest
Flathead Lake
Flathead Indian Reservation
Flathead National Forest
Lewis and Clark National Forest
Clark Fork River
Flathead River
Dixon
St. Maries
Avery
MILWAUKEE RAILROAD
NORTHERN PACIFIC RAILROAD
Coeur d'Alene Indian Reservation
Elk River
N. Fork
Lolo National Forest
Blackfoot River
Missoula
Clearwater River
Orofino
Nez Percé Indian Reservation
Lochsa River
Lolo Pass
Clearwater National Forest
Creek
Moose
Hamilton
Deerlodge National Forest
Clearwater River
Selway River
Bitterroot River
Bitterroot National Forest
S. Fork
Nezperce National Forest
Beaverhead National Forest
Salmon River
WASHINGTON
IDAHO
MONTANA
IDAHO
Rivers
Railroads
Burned-over Areas, 1910
0 miles 40
N
W
E
S
THE GREAT FIRES OF THE NORTHERN ROCKIES

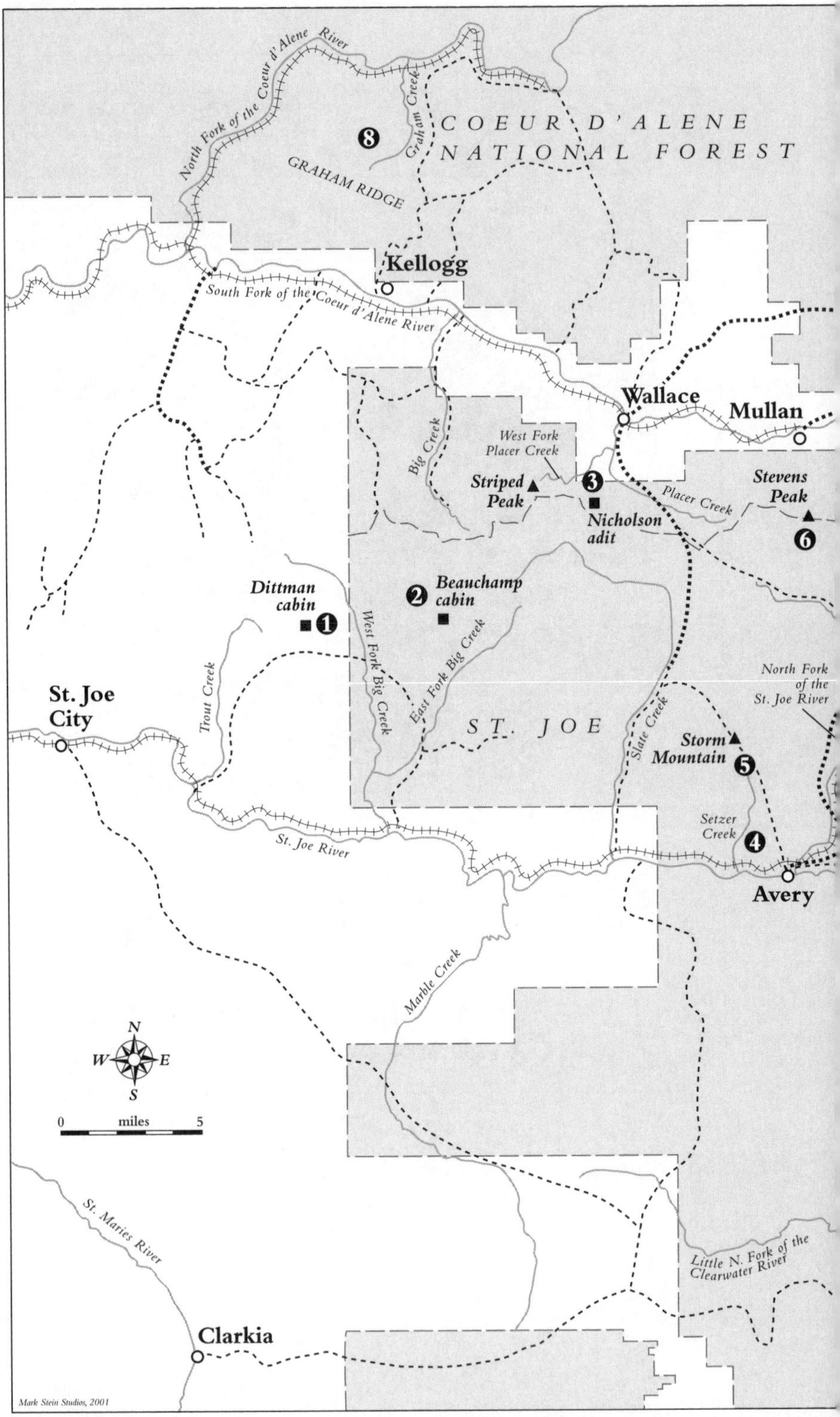

COEUR D'ALENE
NATIONAL FOREST
North Fork of the Coeur d'Alene River
Graham Creek
GRAHAM RIDGE
8
Kellogg
South Fork of the Coeur d'Alene River
Wallace
Mullan
Big Creek
West Fork
Placer Creek
Striped
Peak
3
Nicholson
adit
Placer Creek
Stevens
Peak
6
Dittman
cabin
1
2
Beauchamp
cabin
West Fork Big Creek
East Fork Big Creek
Trout Creek
St. Joe
City
ST. JOE
Slate Creek
North Fork
of the
St. Joe River
Storm
Mountain
5
Setzer
Creek
4
Avery
St. Joe River
Marble Creek
N
W
E
S
0
miles
5
St. Maries River
Little N. Fork of the
Clearwater River
Clarkia
Mark Stein Studios, 2001

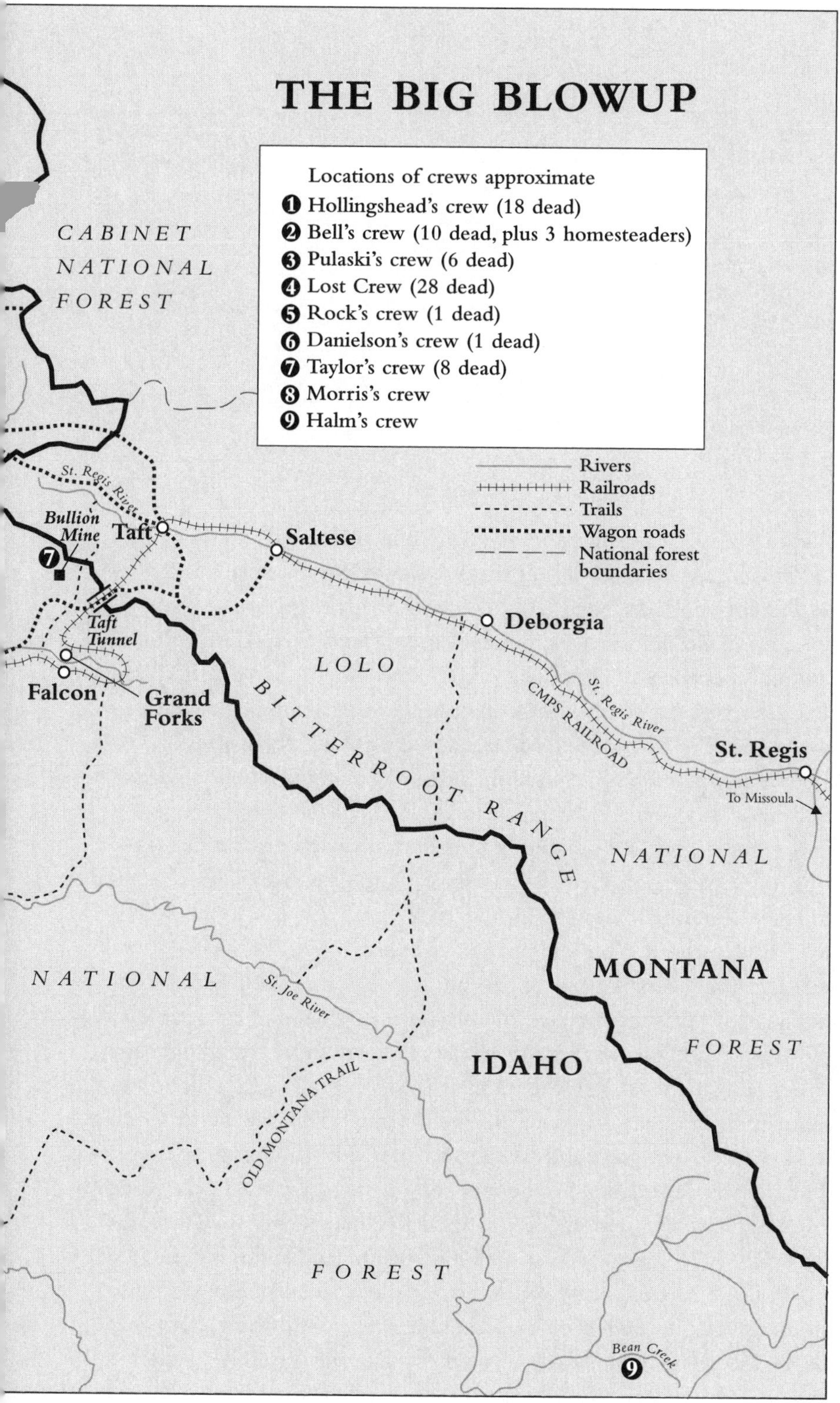

THE BIG BLOWUP
Locations of crews approximate
1 Hollingshead's crew (18 dead)
2 Bell's crew (10 dead, plus 3 homesteaders)
3 Pulaski's crew (6 dead)
4 Lost Crew (28 dead)
5 Rock's crew (1 dead)
6 Danielson's crew (1 dead)
7 Taylor's crew (8 dead)
8 Morris's crew
9 Halm's crew
Rivers
Railroads
Trails
Wagon roads
National forest boundaries
CABINET NATIONAL FOREST
St. Regis River
Bullion Mine
Taft
Saltese
Taft Tunnel
Deborgia
Falcon
Grand Forks
LOLO
BITTERROOT RANGE
CMPS RAILROAD
St. Regis River
St. Regis
To Missoula
NATIONAL
NATIONAL
St. Joe River
MONTANA
FOREST
IDAHO
OLD MONTANA TRAIL
FOREST
Bean Creek
9
7

# AUGUST

THE LASH OF storms worsened the scene, reviving dormant embers and rousing new starts. Veering winds whipped up old burns. Only the smallest of fires had been truly extinguished, or, given the extreme drought, could be; once surrounded, most were left to burn through duff and roots or gnaw into logs, subject only to a casual "patrol" along their trenches. A good puff of wind brought them to life and scattered glowing cinders like loose trash. Equally as perilous, the storms blasted the forests with lightning, so more snags flared and patches of needles smoldered and sparks flew, ready to catch the wind and kindle more fires. Lightning proved indifferent to the crews on the ground or the regional transportation system. The shaky equilibrium of fires kindled and fires controlled began to break down.

The Northern Rockies remained the hardest hit. Every category of land had fire, every agency of fire protection found itself badly overextended. There was not one fire, or even an extended tidal wave of flame, but hundreds of fires of various sizes, set over a period of many weeks, and they did not cluster in the Northern Rockies alone but spangled in a vast arc across the northern United States from the Coast Ranges of Washington and Oregon to the Minnesota and Michigan shores of the Great Lakes. At the onset of August, traditionally the worst fire month for the region, they formed five major clumps. The most celebrated were the complexes in the Idaho Panhandle around the Coeur d'Alene and Clearwater forests and those broadly arrayed around Glacier Park, in excess of two million acres. But major outbreaks plagued the Blue Mountains and southern Cascades of Oregon and the

Colville region of northern Washington. In fact, there were fires of some sort nearly every place that could burn. If the national forests and parks were holding their own, the states, counties, protective associations, and private landowners were not. What laborers the Forest Service sopped up were not available to others. The burned woods threatened a regional economy based on timber.

On 5 August the Western Pine Manufacturers Association and the Western Forestry and Conservation Association separately telegraphed a request to President Taft that federal troops cooperate with the Forest Service in California, Oregon, Washington, Idaho, and Montana. It was sent for review to Chief of Staff General Leonard Wood, who advised his commander in chief that "it is customary for Post Commanders to afford such relief as is requested upon application to them to extinguish fires occurring in the vicinity of their posts," but that in his opinion, it was "not practicable to make any general call of troops for this purpose; that there is no appropriation available to pay for the expense incident to it; that nearly all of the troops are now engaged in maneuvers, and in any event the section of the country referred to is very sparsely garrisoned, and therefore the number of troops that could be assembled would be inadequate for the purpose." Wood recommended that the states call out their organized militias and that individual posts assist their fire-threatened neighbors.[1]

Taft disagreed. These were, after all, federal lands. The Army was doing nothing that outweighed the political fallout of not ordering it into the fray; its numbers mattered less than its symbolism. On 7 August, from his summer White House in Beverly, Massachusetts, he telegraphed the acting secretary of war to "lend every assistance possible in the suppression of forest fires." That order went out to the four commands in the greater Northwest, the departments of California, Dakota, Columbia (Vancouver), and Missouri to hold troops in readiness and respond as requested by the Forest Service, which was also notified and which soon "bombarded" the Army with requests. The absurd rivalry between Interior and the Forest Service, however, spilled over even here, until Wood demanded they coordinate their appeals and actions.[2]

Still, response ever lagged behind crisis. The push to engage the military had followed a bout of bad burning; by the time the Army was ready to receive requests, the fires had quieted. Silcox wrote Captain James Hanson at Fort Harrison that "the fires are well in hand and are all practically under control" and that unless weather worsened, he would need no assistance. Hanson was pleased because "the maximum number of men that can be sent from this post is fourteen privates, two non-commissioned officers and a hospital corps man. No pack animals at all are on hand, and no wagon transportation can be furnished to go over ten miles or so from the post, and in that case only one four mule wagon." But other posts were better equipped, and other foresters knew the deep fatigue along their firelines, and within days, troops and packtrains headed to the Coeur d'Alene, the Lewis and Clark, the Wallowa, and the Colville national forests, as well as the Flathead Reservation and Glacier Park. (The return to Missoula of a battalion from maneuvers at American Lake kept Captain Hanson at his post.) Some troops, like the command at Fort Missoula, had foreseen the crisis and had previously requested training from the foresters in the tactics of firefighting. Most had not, and not all were keen to learn. Most manned coastal batteries.[3]

They apparently took their orders to "fight" the fires literally. The 60th and 147th companies, Coast Artillery Corps, under the command of Major A. W. Chase, set off for Colfax, California, with these instructions:

> Each company will have no less than seventy-five (75) men and will take their company tentage, field equipment, 1000 rounds of rifle ammunition, 1000 rounds of revolver ammunition and 10 days rations with them. Each man will be equipped with the following: Canteen, haversack, meatcan, cup, knife, fork, spoon, shelter tent complete, blanket, comb, housewife [sewing kit], soap, towel, 1 suit of fatigue clothing, 1 pair of leggins, 1 extra pair of stockings, 1 extra pair of shoes. Flannel shirts will be worn. In addition each non-commissioned officer will be equipped with a revolver and belt and one squad from each company will be equipped with magazine rifles and belts. Uniform blue with campaign hats.

The quartermaster somehow found room for a hundred axes, twenty-five pickaxes, and twenty-five shovels.[4]

That few specifics had come from the field, officials interpreted as evidence of the absolute seriousness of the situation. Meanwhile regional newspapers flooded the wires with a steady drumbeat of fire alarms, and not all the blazes of course were on the reserves. On 10 August, for example, the *Seattle Daily Times* quoted Fire Warden J. E.

Bowers: "Standing upon the top of Huckleberry Mountain, I could see nothing but a solid sea of flame. It seems as if several townships must be entirely burned over. I do not see how the fires can be stopped from spreading into Spokane county. I want men to fight the fire—any kind of men will do. I can use a thousand of them."[5]

In 1910 the standing Army of the United States held, on active duty, only 81,251 officers and men. This figure includes those troops stationed overseas, notably in the Philippines. General Wood, however, assured the *New York Times* that the Army would assist "to the limit of the number of soldiers available if necessary."[6] Eventually it committed thirty-three companies, perhaps 5 percent of that total, to the firefight.

•

AS WOOD'S TART recommendation hinted, nothing had dimmed interagency rivalries. Both sides still smarted from Pinchot's abortive crusade. Nothing would salve Forest Service honor so much as Ballinger's ignominious dismissal, and nothing would please Interior more than to expose Pinchot's agenda as little more than media bluster and bare-knuckle politics. Graves, Pinchot, Ballinger, Taft, Cannon, and endless others exchanged barbs over who should properly inherit the mantle of conservation. The charges against Ballinger were being tried, as Pinchot had wished, in the court of public opinion. Not surprisingly, conflicting theories of conservation soon found themselves being turned over a fire.

The matter of Glacier Park still festered. At the end of July, Ballinger dispatched a party of scientists and superintendents to make recommendations for the land's disposition. It was a miniature of the kind of survey Interior had fielded in the West decades ago: a geologist and topographer from the Geological Survey, a representative of the Great Northern Railway, a beetle specialist from the Bureau of Entomology, superintendents from the Blackfeet National Forest and Flathead Reservation, Major Logan, of course, and, as Ballinger's personal emissary, Chief Clerk Clements Ucker—fourteen horsemen in all and ten pack animals.

For a week they were "entirely cut off from communication with the world," unable to respond to frantic telegrams to arrange a meeting with Ballinger, then heading to Seattle, and to do whatever possible "to relieve conditions" in and around the park. On the twelfth Ucker arrived at Fort Yellowstone and replied with a lengthy letter to his "dear

Judge." While he had not departed with fire foremost in his mind, he so returned. Not only was the matter serious, but it might play into Interior's hands. "I am also anxious to handle the forestry side of the park in such a way as to demonstrate that there are different methods of handling the forestry proposition, and that the most successful one does not consist of newspaper notoriety." A slap against the Forest Service, but one Ucker was prepared to make: What the Forest Service had done prior to handing over Glacier as a park was little enough. The national forests, he sneered, "have been so blatant as to what they can and have accomplished, I think it is up to them to make a practical demonstration."[7]

Pinchot's strongest claim for the transfer of the forest reserves to his care had been that the GLO ranger staff consisted of political hacks, incompetent to practice forestry, and that, as he and every other forester endlessly trumpeted, fire protection was the cornerstone of scientific forestry. Ucker suggested that the Interior Department call their bluff. Foresters wanted to show they could control fire; let them do it. On the lands that became Glacier, they had made no effort to clear out "dead and down timber and underbrush, nor to log the ripe timber, nor in fact to do anything at all except to build a few ranger cabins, and to build one trail . . . which apparently followed the line of least resistance. It's going to be a gigantic task to clean this forest up, which will have to be done to make it a national park, else those who visit it will be in constant danger." The place, in brief, was "a veritable fire-trap." Now fires burned around and into the park itself.[8]

Still, the rangers were the only ones on the ground capable of controlling those fires. Not all the fires were serious, but Ucker "arranged with the forestry service to throw additional men in and do what they could to stop them." One new fire was particularly distressing because it savaged the land along the railroad and "will present an ugly appearance for some years to come," thus marring the park's scenic values. In response, he alerted Supervisor Roscoe Haines of the Blackfeet National Forest and requested that he personally take charge of the firefight; telegraphed James Jerome Hill of the Great Northern Railway to send "several hundred men"; and had Major Logan wire the Indian agent on the Blackfeet Indian Reservation "to bring up as many as possible of his people, including members of the Rockyboy band." Meanwhile Major Logan hurried to the scene, with instructions to request Army troops and have them remain throughout the duration of the season. Ucker justified operating "through the forestry service mainly for the reason that, they are presumed to know more about fighting forest fires" than anyone else he or Major Logan (then called out to fires at Yellowstone) could tap for duty. Besides, if Interior assumed full control, the park's $15,000 appropriation "would be used up in the course of a few days." The Forest Service was willing to carry the cost until Congress could make good the difference. That made it liable, if not eager, to accept the political cost for failure.[9]

His wager was a reasonable one. It was at least even money that the Forest Service might not survive the summer with its head high and hands unburned. Probably no agency could have coped with such a crisis without crashing, but no other claimed it could or made its campaign into a public trial of its larger mission. Pinchot himself had equated fire protection with abolitionism as a moral crusade, had insisted that "the means of control were fully within our reach," and that professional forestry, embodied in the Forest Service, was the proper agency of success. Yet when the summer ended, Elers Koch, whose veins flowed with forest green, called the 1910 campaign "a complete defeat for the newly organized Forest Service forces." Moreover, after the Big Blowup, eerily echoing Powell, his voice thickened with the sentiments of the rural West, Secretary Richard A. Ballinger informed a press conference in San Francisco: "We may find it necessary to revert to the old Indian method of burning over the forests annually at seasonable periods."[10]

•

PROBABLY NOTHING ELSE he could have said short of outright libel could have been calculated to inflame the Forest Service more. Worse, he was not alone. That very month—even as rangers staggered from one fireline to another, even as the Army marched whole companies to their defense as though to lift the siege of Beijing—the popular monthly magazine *Sunset* published an article asserting that the whole endeavor was misguided, that the "Indian way" was the only sane strategy for forest protection. The militarizing, firefighting Forest Service suddenly found that it had, as it were, a fifth column behind the lines. Again, as with the controversies over flooding, it faced a cadre of engineers not impressed with vague allusions to forest influences, fire's putative damages, and forestry's scientific credentials.

*Sunset* assured readers that measures to prevent wildfire were "vitally necessary." Yet it also insisted that the "prevention of fire may be made so complete as to menace the forests with greater danger than they now incur." George L. Hoxie, "C.E." (civil engineer) and "practical lumberman," challenged directly the "theoretical policy" of the Forest Service that fire prevention was the solution to fire protection. Rather, Hoxie brazenly proclaimed, "practical foresters contend and can demonstrate that from time immemorial fire has been the salvation and preservation of our California sugar and white pine forests." The very forests that the white man so coveted were the product of regular Indian burning, probably "at periods of about three years." Controlled burning makes fire a servant, Hoxie declared, while fire exclusion renders it a master.[11]

His arguments appealed to the commonsense logic of those on the ground. How was it that California had successfully grown magnificent pine forests before the era of active fire exclusion? Answer: Fires and forests had accommodated each other. Did not fire thin out the woods, leaving large old trees and little reproduction? Answer: Of course, and that pattern was exactly what the land and climate would sustain. How much of such forests had fire "destroyed"? Answer: Almost none. Freshly burned sites were in fact desirable: clean-floored and easy to work in, full of huge trees, fireproofed for a couple of years and thus less likely to spark into flame during logging operations. The conflagrations that horrified the public had resulted from coarse logging, reckless land clearing, and the expulsion of the old burning regime; those fires gorged on places that had allowed fuels to pile up like cordwood without routine fire to pare them back. "The practical realizes that nothing but a miracle will keep fire out of the forest areas, for, to accomplish this, even lightning must be eliminated; further, it is realized that if the theoretical continues for a few years longer there will be no hope of saving these areas from useless unnecessary and enormous damage" since more fuels will have built up during the fire-free interval. Beetles too were worsening under the forced abolition of burning. Firefighting alone would lead only to more firefighting until, ultimately, the "master fire" would control forestry, not vice versa. Even accidental summer burns, without suitable preparations, were preferable to the existing practices. Almost any controlled burn was better than none. "Better," Hoxie insisted, to "have fire at will than not at all and the periods of such burning should not exceed three to four years apart, oftener would be better."[12]

The article, in brief, completely inverted academic forestry's prevailing case for fire protection. What the "practical" wanted was to assist the good work of "servant fire"—to ignite the burns during the fall rather than the summer, to spread them along the summits and have them burn down slopes, to pull logs and large branches away from boles, to fill in fire-hollowed butt cavities, to trim limbs and thin thickets to encourage the right kind of burning. Publishing in *Sunset,* a popular magazine, rather than in a forestry journal, Hoxie was mirroring Pinchot's own political tactics, appealing directly to the public as a means to bypass the special interests bent on pursuing practices (to his mind) far removed from the public good. Reversing conservation's demand for public stewardship, Hoxie asked how private owners could protect themselves from the fire crisis that federal maladministration was creating on the reserves? In a startling rebuttal to the National Academy of Sciences, he suggested, "Would it not be well to put the whole management of the forestry system into the hands of the War Department and use the standing army . . . in preparing for and at the proper time of year using the servant fire, and by practising practical forestry insure perpetual forests and thus avoid conditions that now tend toward ultimate disastrous results?"[13]

Light burners, as Hoxie's colleagues became known, brought together an ungainly gaggle of critics. Among the most forceful were civil engineers, including William Hall, the state engineer for California. They were no more intimidated by forestry's credentials than Chittenden had been. But the novelist Stewart Edward White and the sentimentalist poet Joaquin Miller also signed on. So did large timber owners like T. B. Walker and the Southern Pacific Railway (which not coincidentally owned *Sunset*), keen to protect their holdings. On the rural frontier, the herders, the miners, the hunters and trappers, the farmers almost all agreed. This was in fact how they shielded themselves from wildfire. In the South such burning was so common that an alternative was almost unimaginable. For every argument that foresters advanced for fire exclusion Hoxie had a telling counterargument based on facts in the field.

Not every landscape could accept light surface burns, of course. A number of coniferous forests burned through their crowns or not at all; coastal Douglas-fir, high-elevation Engelmann spruce and white fir, lodgepole and jack pine, the lichens-laden spruce of the boreal forest belonged among them. While fire controlled their distribution, it did so under principles similar to those Clements had worked out at Estes Park. A period of fire exclusion might matter little. Yet most of the land, and nearly all the prime timber trees, did grow under the conditions Hoxie described, and in such places, fire exclusion for a decade or two mattered a good deal, for often the consequences of fire protection appeared quickly. But each side viewed these outcomes with dramatically different eyes. Where Hoxie saw more fuel added to a scene already fully stocked with trees, foresters saw a forest reclaiming its rightful inheritance from pilfering fires.

While their sparring had begun prior to August 1910, the *Sunset* salvo flushed the issue out of the scrub. The case for burning could not be dismissed as frontier sniping, crank whining, or the carping of incorrigible malcontents unhappy over the conservation crusade. If the light burners were right, then the Forest Service was wrong; its model administration of the forest reserves was a blunder, the triumph of ideology over fact; and the firefight in the Northern Rockies was an extravagant parody. By choice and chance, fire had become the core of the Service's public identity and its political justification. If it lost, it believed the fire damages in the woods would be nothing compared with those that would cascade throughout the conservation movement.

But it did not lose, and it is hard to explain its success and the intensity with which its foresters denounced light burning, save for the presence of the Great Fires. Their special fury forced a potential dialogue into a hardened dialectic. That the United States needed more fire, foresters denounced as insidious and absurd. In his treatise Graves had already addressed the matter and concluded that "merely setting fire to the woods without control" (a "practice in many parts of the South and West") was "nothing less than forest destruction." There were times and places where deliberate burning might be justified, but only where "absolute fire prevention can not be assured," when, in effect, protective burning was a means, no more than temporary, to help push the forest into a status of full protection. In particular, right-thinking conservationists could never sanction burning that damaged reproduction or humus.[14]

Clearly, Graves thought of fire as a mechanical force, something that uprooted seedlings, scarified soil, reduced slash, and gouged trees. It was a constant presence, like gravity, against which trees had to struggle. There was no sense that it might be a biological process, that some kind of mutual accommodation had evolved between certain kinds of fires and certain kinds of forests, that meddling with it might transform forestry into a sorcerer's apprentice. Rather, deleting fire would seem to remove a force against which the forest had to expend considerable effort to resist and from which, once liberated, like a seedling no longer crushed by a log, the forest would spring up all the better. There was no sense that like weightlessness, the condition was temporarily exhilarating and eventually debilitating. Under no circumstances could fire be left in the hands of laissez-faire folk practitioners. Even Chapman, convinced that the southern longleaf needed fire, could not imagine its extension to the North Woods. "Foresters who for any reason flirted publicly with fire as a silvicultural tool were severely and sincerely condemned," he wrote. There was no tolerance even for research on the subject since it would lead the public into "inevitable misunderstanding and misinterpretation."[15]

So the lines remained drawn. The Great Fires and fire control, light burning and fire use: Both went before the public simultaneously. One claimed academic authority, the other facts on the ground; one had a cause and a government podium, the other a case and popular sentiment. There is no doubt which claimed the headlines.

•

IN MID-AUGUST, PRACTICE continued to trump policy. The fires remained, real and menacing, with new ones puffing up as fast as old ones were snuffed out. In fact, while many fires were contained, few were truly extinguished. Small armies of men gathered, striking out into the backcountry and stringing along railways. The Forest Service had some 5,000 firefighters on the payroll. The Army had committed twenty companies, with more in reserve. No one in the ranks had died, and no one proposed that they return, respectively, to their barrooms and barracks. They had only to hold out for a few more weeks—the end of August, if the past was a guide—and the season would collapse in the first cold slush of winter storms. Then there might be time to reevaluate. A few timely licks, some reinforcements along the lines, and the fight would be over.

The call for troops scattered the Army throughout the greater Northwest. Some companies hurried to the hard-fought Northern Rockies, many to Washington and southern Oregon, and eventually a few companies marched to the California Sierras. As Wood informed Taft, most had gathered for annual maneuvers at American Lake, Washington, and had to be recalled to their home posts before accepting assignments for the foresters. Greeley placed his request on 10 August. The earliest companies pulled out on 13 August.

By then some 200 troops were battling an outbreak in Yellowstone Park. Two fires they corralled; one raced away, until a shift in wind and Yellowstone Lake helped contain it. Meanwhile the "sheets of flame" became a "magnificent night spectacle" for hundreds of tourists, and traffic continued unblocked. Dry lightning was the cause; the fires had blossomed because they kindled far from roads. Superintendent Major H. C. Benson, recently detailed to Glacier to help, returned to lead a campaign that lasted three weeks. What prevented a universal conflagration, he insisted, was a "careful and thorough patrol by soldiers twice daily of all roads and camp sites." Fire litter was common; four escaped to become wildfires. But without such close scrutiny, Major Benson believed, the "park would have been practically destroyed."[16]

The regional call-out rolled in two waves, one before 20 August and one after. From Fort George Wright two companies of the Twenty-fifth Infantry rode the rails to Kalispell and the fires on the Flathead Reservation; there they joined troops from Fort Missoula. Two companies headed to Wallace, two others to Glacier (though one was diverted to Kalispell), one to the Wallowa National Forest in the Blue Mountains, and two companies from the Vancouver Barracks headed to Republic, Washington. Quickly the troopers discovered that their field wagons were useless, that they would need packtrains and medical corpsmen, and placed orders for both.

Their experiences varied. Those first in the field found themselves with too little or too much to do, particularly since dispatching tended to come after crises, not before. The local forester decided on the course of action and informed the commanding officer, who then issued orders. The system worked well when it had something to work over.

•

NOT ALL DID. Companies C and D of the First Infantry arrived at Republic, Washington, on 15 August, after a heavy rain had passed over the district the evening before and bludgeoned the burns. The next day, accompanied by the forest supervisor, they marched twenty-five miles without seeing a single fire. The next morning Captain Alfred Aloe rode another ten miles and saw only old burns and very distant smoke, and "as there was absolutely nothing for us to do," the troops returned to Republic. They stayed through 23 August before decamping for the Colville Indian Reservation. There they found no agent. Captain Aloe got an "Indian Farmer" to guide them, and they went "looking for forest fires but found absolutely nothing." Whatever fires had blazed before, they were burned out now, and the troop, to its disgust, found only a few smoking stumps. They returned to Vancouver Barracks on 1 September, convinced that they had been smoke-chasing for snipes.[17]

Upon close questioning, Supervisor P. H. Leesh at Colville admitted that "he did not know why the troops had been asked for in that district as there was absolutely no use for them nor had there been any use for the troops at any time, and that he did not want the troops as he had absolute control over all the fires in that district." Who, then, had placed the order? Apparently a tavern owner named Le Roi. Aloe determined that most of the fires had been incendiary—which is to say, arson—that Leesh considered the burns had done more good than harm, and that in the future, "Forestry Officials [ought to] employ a proper amount of men, and properly equip them." If he were to be called again, he demanded a packtrain and he wanted his troops mounted. And, he did not need to add, he insisted there actually be fires to fight.[18]

•

COMPANY B, SENT to Union, Oregon, did eventually find fires, only to discover that it could do little to hold them. Two officers, fifty-two enlisted men, a civilian teamster, four mules, one horse, and an escort wagon, later joined by three members of the Medical Reserve Corps, arrived in Union on the evening of 14 August. The next morning half the company headed to a fire near Medical Springs. Accompanied by Ranger McLain, Lieutenant Ralph Lister "rode around the fire district that afternoon, but found very little fire." That did not matter much because the Forest Service could not get tools to the soldiers until the next day.[19]

Finally the winds rose on 18 August, and the entire detachment, now reunited, fought fire with "very little success." They would trench a line, backfire, and lose it as "heavy winds drove the fire repeatedly" over the trenches. They built five lines in all and lost each one. They stayed, fighting fire for fifteen and a half days. Two men took sick, and two replaced them. "The work was very hard and the men's clothing was completely worn out in many cases."[20]

•

TROOP L, FIRST CAVALRY had ridden from the Boise Barracks for sixteen miles the first day and seven the next until they arrived at Placerville, Idaho. Wisely the troop had decided to dispense with rifles and sabers in anticipation of rough duty. (The forty-two men did keep their revolvers and twenty rounds each.) There they met a 1,000-acre fire, all on the ground, on public land but not on the forest reserve. For three days, amid a calm sky, the troopers cut a "fire brake" around the perimeter. Then they patrolled it until the smokes expired. Not a settler passing by raised a finger to help them or to kick out the small fires that sprouted along the roadside like lupine.[21]

•

COMPANIES E AND H of the all-black Twenty-fifth Infantry departed Fort George Wright in Spokane on the afternoon of 14 August and arrived at 1:30 the next morning outside Dixon, Montana. There Major Fred Morgan, agent for the Flathead Reservation (and "the only civilian authority"), sent them to a fire district fifty by sixty miles in extent. Captain Charles Bates found the countryside "so thoroughly swept with fire that it was practically immune to any further conflagration," a charred scene that they "reconnoitered by small fire patrols" seeking out smoking stumps. They relocated to a gaggle of fires near tracks outside MacDonald. Overall, damages had been light: Fire had claimed a couple of haystacks and a rail fence, about 5 percent of the timber had suffered, and Bates considered that the "cattle interests" would welcome the flush of grass that would spring up now that flames had swept away the ungainly forest "rubbish."[22]

The "fire contagion," the captain concluded, had resulted from locomotives, prospectors, hunters, and possibly the feckless tramp firefighters whom Morgan both loathed and feared. A good posse of mounted fire guards, early in the season, would have eliminated the hundreds of men now called to the lines. The only defense against a running fire, once begun, was "an intelligently located and properly conducted back fire." This caused the one real threat to the troops. While working parallel to the tracks, a civilian fire gang set backfires in a side canyon that jutted into it and forced the company into a scrambled retreat.[23]

Meanwhile Companies L and M, with a total strength of 103 officers and men, detrained at Garry, Montana. Most of the land had already burned, and the troops patrolled until the winds of the Big Blowup fanned the scene back to life. Again, officers found much to admire in the local ranger ("enthusiastic in his work, indefatigable in his energy and very capable") and held little but scorn for the rabble under the rangers' nominal command ("poorly qualified for any kind of intelligent work"). Captain A. E. Lewis described the treatment given his men as "uniformly courteous," "very kind & considerate & thoughtful, necessities were supplied by them & reading matter furnished." They had had worse duties.[24]

•

THE TROOPS SENT to Glacier found themselves harder pressed. Colonel Maney and troops from Fort Assiniboine and Major Hasbrook from Fort Harrison were, in the words of Superintendent Logan, already "alive to the situation" and did "splendid work." But the "worst fire" fell to Lieutenant W. S. Mapes of K Company, Twenty-fifth Infantry, who reported to Major Logan on 15 August and went into camp on the North Fork of the Flathead River. The next morning they were joined by two gangs, one of thirty-seven lumbermen hired by Logan, the other of thirty-five Greek laborers "donated" by the Great Northern Railway. The local citizenry was indifferent to the fires, officials were alarmed, and the fire scene was, in Mapes's judgment, "very bad." The troops immediately plunged into work, though it went slowly until Logan rounded up a sufficient cache of tools.[25]

The work was "very fatiguing and dangerous." Smoke, falling trees, unfamiliar country, constant patrolling for escaped fires even at night, and tension between the troops, under orders, and the civilians, attuned only to their stomachs and paychecks, made for difficult times. On several evenings fires broke through the lines and Lieutenant Mapes rallied his troops, even forming a chain gang to haul buckets and kettles. But the civilians refused to aid. The lumberjacks were "excellent fire fighters" but would work only during regular hours, from 7:00 A.M. to 5:30 P.M. The others were interested in their pay and especially their "board which consisted of everything it was possible for money to buy." The Greeks were the worst. They were "worthless if sent out alone, on one occasion deserting their work and going fishing and on another throwing down their tools and watching the fire creep along and burn them with utter indifference." Finally Mapes sandwiched them between soldiers, and "their natural fear of the soldiers kept them well at work."[26]

The enormous disparity between disciplined troops and casual workers impressed officials mightily; not a single fire attacked by the soldiers rekindled. Yet the chasm between their poor pay and slim rations and the largesse lavished on lazy pickup laborers both stiffened and disheartened the troops themselves. Not least, they received no special uniform allowance for the clothes ripped and ruined in the trenches. Logan bubbled with praise and asked Secretary Ballinger to write the War Department for a commendation. "I doubt if I can say enough in praise of Lieutenant Mapes and his Negro troops. The work performed by them could not be improved upon by any class of men." Probably Mapes would have agreed. But extra rations and another uniform would have helped more than laudatory letters stuffed in the musty files of the adjutant general's office.[27]

•

TWO COMPANIES OF the Twenty-fifth Infantry, I and G, 103 officers and men plus 2 medical corpsmen, rolled into Wallace at 5 A.M. on 15 August. They camped in the ballpark. The next day G Company headed to Avery. On the 17th, I Company broke camp and marched to Placer Creek, where it recamped, divided into two detachments, and worked trails. One cut a path to the Placer Creek fire; the other cleared trails along the St. Joe road. The danger from falling trees was serious, and Lieutenant L. B. Chandler insisted that an experienced lumberjack go with each detachment. Wallace, now stripped of soldiers, was calm but apprehensive. As early as the 14th cinders had covered the streets, pine needles drifted downward, and awnings taken fire. Two days before the soldiers arrived, burning debris "as large as a man's hand" had fallen out of the sky and ignited more awnings. The nearest fire was then six miles distant.[28]

•

DESPITE AMPLE FIRE, even in the Northern Rockies, the situation was far below the exaggerated accounts floated by the press, and the disgrunted Captain Aloe was not alone in wondering why the

Army was there. Apart from political posturing, the reasons were that the fires, if smoldering, remained; that an exhausted ranger corps was near its breaking point; and that no one trusted the thousands of casual laborers, who, it was rumored, were busier setting fires than putting them out. More their moral authority than their labor was in the end cause enough for the troops' call-out.

The long siege had dampened the enthusiasms of even the most ardent forester. The August field diary of Ranger A. H. Abbott, a grazing specialist, shows why.

AUG. 1—Worked in office on grazing etc. Telegram from Silcox ordering me to Missoula. Left in afternoon for Billings. Left Billings 7:30. Graz. 9:00—

AUG. 2—Got Missoula at 8:30. Saw Silcox and was told to report to Mr Koch of the Lolo. Met Derrick of the Helena. Left Missoula at 4:30 and went to St. Regis where I reported to Asst. Ranger Beal. [Fire] Guard Armitage in camp. Fire [meaning his time was charged to the emergency fire fund].

AUG. 3—Worked all day fighting fire at 12 Mile Gulch. Fire. 7:00

AUG. 4—Fought fire all day at 12 Mile Gulch. F.F. [fire fund] 6:45 7:30

AUG. 5—Fought fire all day 12 Mile Gulch. Got it under control. Approx 3 mile fire line. F.F. 6:45

AUG. 6—Met Guard Spalding fought fire all day. Got meals and stayed at section house in even. F.F. 7:30 8:00

AUG. 7—Started out to fight fire. Sprained ankle. Sunday F.F.

AUG. 8—Went back to Beals. F.F.

AUG. 9—Piled lumber. Started back with a crew to tunnel 8 fire. F.F.

AUG. 10—Went with Crew up to fire. Went back for more men. F.F.

AUG. 11—Went to St. Regis for supplies and another crew. Went out for men and took a record crew to Tunnel 8 Fire. F.F.

AUG. 12—Got out to fire with men. Started building trails etc. F.F.

AUG. 13—Fought fire.

What did that cryptic phrase *fought fire* mean? For a boss like Ranger Abbott it meant close supervision of a labor gang that probably didn't know much about the job before them or cared to work too hard at it. He would have to teach and motivate; to hector, inspire, and threaten; and in the end to lead by showing. At some point he would have to share the grit and smoke and sweat. In truth, firefighting was something more eagerly discussed than done and more fondly remembered than lived. Paradoxically, big fires were more comfortable because one worked far from the smoke and heat; the point was to build, on favorable terms, a fireline from which one could backfire.

But small fires, which are what Abbott's crews apparently confronted, had to be attacked directly. The men would work as close to the fire as possible—hotline. They would knock down flames with shovelfuls of dirt, try to trench around the front faster than the fire could spread, attempt to halt its propagation by simply depriving it of fuel, which meant in practice, digging, cutting, chopping, scraping, over and again, through dense duff, brush, rock, and blowdown. If the fire front wound sinuously, advancing like the fingers of a groping hand, they might surround that fractal border with a straighter, more direct edge and burn out the intervening stringers of fuel. The closer they labored to the fire, the less room it had to make a run, the fewer sites remained to mop up, the more quickly they could end the ordeal. Yet the more they crowded that flaming front, the more heat assaulted them, until their clothes dripped with sweat; the more smoke they inhaled, until their raw throats ached and black mucus dribbled from their nostrils. They would be ravenously thirsty, chronically hungry, deadened with fatigue, and sometimes alarmed by falling trees, dislodged rocks, disoriented bears, and aroused flames. The first rush of adrenaline was enough for a day's firefight. But it passed quickly, and it was not uncommon, as Ranger Abbott discovered, to be on hotlines day after day after day.

AUG. 14—Fought fire.

AUG. 15—Fought fire.

AUG. 16—Fought fire.

AUG. 17—Fought fire.

AUG. 18—Fought fire and got it under control.

AUG. 19—Fought fire.[29]

•

OTHERS ALSO MOVED from fire post to fire post. On the Clearwater reserve, Ranger Ed Thenon had intended that summer to survey the Selway region for suitable ranger stations. Instead, with the onset of July's dry lightning, he had gone on continual fire patrol, and while he had fought many fires, he had "not yet fallen in love with one." But Thenon was, as Greeley described him, "a very fine type of frontiersman. The ideal type to put in charge of a bad situation." Throughout the forest, crews of five to twenty men scurried from one fire to another. Finally his survey party crossed the Bitterroots and was heading toward Missoula when Greeley met them in a buckboard and instructed them to hasten to the St. Joe region of the Coeur d'Alene forest. At Adair he met Pulaski, who led him and two other Clearwater rangers to the fireline that was to become home for fourteen days.[30]

But fires had boiled over on the Selway, his home district, and the forest supervisor, Major F. A. Fenn, had ordered his return. A veteran of the Nez Percé and Spanish-American wars, Fenn had 500 men on firelines, needed those rangers who could navigate the country even when smoked in, and, according to newspaper accounts on 10 August, gave "little hope of checking the flames unless rain comes." Assistant District Forester Gus Silcox, dapper in his bowler hat, arranged for them to meet a crew at Darby before crossing the Bitterroots and plunging on to Moose Creek through the smoke thick as dry fog. Before they reached camp, the packers had fled, spooked by what they thought was a nearby fire. The crew was typical of the times. There was "no telling how they would stand up under trouble." Besides, Thenon admitted, he "didn't know a man of them."[31]

•

THE HEAVIEST CONCENTRATION of fires and forces mustered on the Coeur d'Alene forest. Will Morris was on the lines when August broke. Fire had jumped their trench, a corridor of soil the width of a footpath. They had held the flames for a while along a road until the radiant heat became so intense it caused a snag across the break to burst into flame and scatter sparks everywhere. They made another stand along the creek. "Here for the first time we had a chance to use water," fire's "natural enemy." But it proved inadequate. An ember settled in a rotten stump and then spread until the west slope of Graham Creek became a "roaring furnace," a chimney shooting out billows of smoke. The little blowup threatened to cut the crew off, and in fact, the flames did isolate a handful of men, who had to flee over a ridge.[32]

They held on as long as they could. "The men worked like heroes that day." Will recalled specifically a lumberjack, Patsy, who had hired on drunk but now dashed into the fire with buckets of water or shovels of earth and did "everything that human power could do and much more than most human power." But they fell back, and finally the fire had simply overblown and outflanked them, and flame and wind combined into a continual roar and uprooted even the largest trees and in some places hurled the debris into whirls, "resembling the work of a tornado." The schoolhouse near Prichard Ranger Station collapsed in flame, its bell sounding a final clang as it fell. Still, the crews managed to bury boxes of black powder in the river before the explosives joined the sound and fury.[33]

They rested all night, then fought the fire that Saturday on the flatlands. Had it continued to soar, it would have threatened the whole upper river. Sunday they "built a long trail, but the fire got over it"—in fact, got over the Coeur d'Alene River. They dug several miles of fireline, "only to have the fire jump over it in spite of all efforts." They persevered and coldtrailing with a rockslide ran a trench to the summit. Here they stopped the front. "It is now about under control," Will wrote home, from the fireline. "The greatest danger from fire is not from the flames but from falling timber." The watershed, however, was "almost burned over." He was weary. "So much for the fire. I am tired of it, and talking about it."[34]

The fire did not care. It sat in the basin, sullen and smoldering. Will instructed his crew to trench along the high ridgeline and moved his camp there. It was a poor camp: no water, no access. But that was where the fire was, and it had jumped their line and menaced the Cedar Creek watershed thick with woods to the east. This is where they needed to be. They cut a shotgun trail to the ridge, so steep a packhorse could barely manage a moderate load over it, and they hauled in water themselves in five-gallon bags, and they ran supply trips every two or three days, and they beat back the flames. They made Indian-style tepees from young lodgepole pine, watched for bears (common amid the profuse huckleberry patches), and brooded over food.

"Bread of some kind is essential to the happiness of camp life," Will soon learned. For a while, though, they had none, and the packer, arriving late, told them with a shrug that he had none since the horse had slipped and rolled and scattered three dozen loaves down the rocky slope. Will promptly donned a rucksack and trudged off to retrieve them. It was an arduous task, like "picking up manna in the wilderness." But he salvaged most and returned to acclamation with a bulging pack of bread. Even better, he had found a man who claimed he could cook, had done so in the Army during the Spanish-American War. Despite doubts, he "proved to be a wonder and soon had order out of former chaos. He had a place for everything and built a fireplace with stone he found on the mountain top. He had the men line up for their meals and dished it out to them in a lordly manner as they passed in review. He could turn out some dishes that would make some of our fine hotel chefs take notice and with very little in the line of provisions or dishes to do it with and under the most trying circumstances."[35]

Thus the time passed—"days of most strenuous toil on the part of everyone but days which I can now look back to with some what a feeling of pleasure, for the fire at that time was under control and the life in the camp went along smoothly." It was a kind of manly idyll, an arduous campout. They set traps for bear, they ate in unburned patches of huckleberries, and they patrolled the firelines day and night "with a shovel instead of a gun." Will heard from Weigle that Slate Creek, where he had romped last summer, had gone up in flames. But along the ridge he and his bold crew had held the line, literally. "Our fires were smoldering," he noted, "but I felt they were under control." From the beginning the summer's ordeal had been "a fight against nature." Now, at long last, it looked to Will "as if we were getting the best of it."[36]

•

THERE, ON THE evening of 19 August, matters rested. Nearly everywhere flames had quieted. A hundred crews on a hundred fires felt as Morris did overlooking Cedar Creek.

They had waged a hard fight. In Washington and Oregon, Forest Service District Six, Acting District Forester George Cecil still considered the situation "so serious" that he elected to write "a special report rather than wait until the end of the month." For two months, no rain had fallen, save some "light" drizzles over the past week. Large fires burned on the Colville, the Wallowa, and especially the Crater national forests, near Butte Falls. Most of the fires skipped through open pine, little damaging the timber. Still, military assistance had come at an "extremely opportune" moment, not least because the call-out seemingly brought rain. From the Wallowa on 16 August, Supervisor Reid had telegraphed: "Eight hours rain. Two companies here now. Good prospects. Total fires to date twenty five." Elsewhere the Army dampened the enthusiasm of incendiaries or simply wandered in search of the rumored smokes. Cecil had a call for 500 more troops on the Crater and dreaded another "full month of the dangerous season" before him, while Washington fire wardens feared another Black Friday, like that of 1902. Even that perennial fire hazard and hotbed of light burning, California, had few fires, none by the 19th that could justify a military request. There were fires, as always; they were attacked, as usual. For once, though, California remained on the fringe of the firestorm rather than at its core. All in all, the foresters' fears proved far worse than the facts.[37]

The most serious alarms continued to ring out of District One. From Glacier, Chief Clerk Ucker telegraphed Acting Interior Secretary Franklin Pierce: "Fire situation thus, old fires practically under control, new ones constantly breaking out, looks to be incendiary. Troops can only keep under control." Still, everyone clamored for more troops: Logan wanted four companies, the supervisors of the adjacent Flathead and Blackfeet forests five, and all cooperated with one another. Eager to return to Washington, Ucker added, "Logan and Military officers can handle situation." Greeley was more cautious. He had personally dashed to the Blackfeet forest outside Glacier and had "got hold" of a Great Northern track crew and had "worked all night with the crew and got the fire stopped—night was the time to do it." On the evening of the 19th he headed for Kalispell. On the Kaniksu, on the Clearwater, on the Lolo, in Yellowstone Park, flames abated. Smoke, stale and stagnant, hung in the valleys. An edgy Elers Koch relaxed. "Things looked better. Many miles of fire line were held," he affirmed. The end of the season was in sight.[38]

Even the Coeur d'Alene, the hard kernel of burning, seemed, at last, to have sagged into a kind of pyric repose. On 19 August Supervisor Weigle "felt that everything was in good condition." He had 1,800 firefighters, two companies of soldiers, and trenches "practically around all of the fires." In any normal year—in almost all exceptional years—this would have justified his sweat-won satisfaction. Some rangers began to reduce crews; others, to restock. Joe Halm pared his fireline patrol from eighty-five to eighteen. Pulaski left his crew in camp near Lake Elsie and returned to Wallace for fresh supplies. Will Morris hiked to the Graham Creek Ranger Station to phone in a report to Weigle. That evening he wrote his mother: "Don't worry about me as there is no danger to speak of at present, and the newspapers exaggerate things."[39]

•

WHAT MAKES A fire big?

A big fire requires big dollops of all the things that make any fire. It needs lots of fuel. Often it needs lots of flame simultaneously burning over a large area. If it spreads through flashy fuels like western bunchgrass, it needs room to roam. If it burns amid dense forests of white pine or lodgepole, it likely needs a convective column to help draft in more air and gets it by burning under an unstable atmosphere where fire-lifted air can shoot skyward exactly like a thunderhead or by burning where furrowed terrain can channel the rising gases like a chimney. One exaggerated factor may compensate for weakness in the others. During World War II the Allied air forces, for example, managed to kindle firestorms at Hamburg and Dresden under near-calm conditions by the saturation firebombing of close-packed cities stuffed with combustibles. But almost always a big fire runs before a big wind.

Since the middle of July the rhythm of frontal winds had set the pattern of fire flare-ups and fire calms. The Big Blowup of 20 August outstripped the others because its winds were that much fiercer and because the area under fire had grown immensely with each prior surge. The Blowup occurred when wind, flame, terrain, and fuel combined in an especially explosive mix. Such eruptions had happened before. Dry lightning had kindled fires in drought-plagued forests for millennia, and wind had driven flame through their crowns. But it would be a mistake to regard the Big Blowup as a wholly natural event. The fires became huge because they timed perfectly the shift from a rural, frontier society to one that was industrializing, punching railways through wildlands, settling into cities, and committing to public lands. Humans had exaggerated every element of the mix, and then they had placed themselves into the cauldron.

Drought had prepared fuels; so had loggers, homesteaders, railways. Thunderstorms had kindled fires; so, far more plentifully, had hunters, campers, hoboes, locomotives, farmers, ranchers, Indians, loggers, prospectors, even (it was darkly rumored) job-hunting firefighters. Once started, fires moved where terrain and winds pushed and pulled them. Yet much of the land under fire burned because fire control efforts had laid down hundreds of miles of trenches and had backfired along them. Backfires, in brief, were a major source of burning. When the Big Blowup struck, the geography of fire in the Northern Rockies looked the way it did because, paradoxically, those fires were being fought.

But people could not stop or start wind. They could fear it, and they could fight the fires it whipped into whitecaps of flame or the fires long-traveling firebrands kindled miles from their source in torching trees. The great uncertainty, however, remained whether the winds would rise or fall. On 19 August they seemed to be ebbing. The synoptic weather map for the United States showed a large region of high pressure settled over Iowa, holding the northern tier of the country in deep drought. A smaller cell of high pressure hovered over Yellowstone. The gradients lessened toward the West Coast. Examining the scene years afterward, forecaster Edward Beals observed "no conditions sufficient to cause extraordinary winds, and the only conclusion that can be reached is that the fires themselves produced these furious gales, resembling as they did the wind rush attending a thunderstorm or the violent whirl characteristic of the tornado." Except for moisture, every other atmospheric condition necessary to produce those violent storms existed as well for the Blowup.[40]

Beals was right in his puzzlement over the winds' cause and likely wrong in his explanation. Every firsthand account insists that the rushing winds preceded the Blowup, that had the gale not fanned the surface fires the convective columns that blackened out the sun could not have powered upward. The winds pummeled the hills, washed over the flames, plucked mature white pines out by their roots, and generally fanned millions of embers to life. The wind-toppled trees were likely important in stoking the fire; the fire front could gorge on the freshly downed slash rather than depend on the awkward and rigid conditions that a true crown fire demanded. As the flames rose, their heated winds mixed with those already blowing, and the din blocked out sound as the smoke blocked out light. In Koch's words, "the mountains roared."

Where did that fateful rush come from? The synoptic maps for the days of the Blowup show a low-pressure cell brushing along the Canadian border, appearing on the 20th with its center on Saskatoon before skimming to Winnipeg on the 21st. At 8 A.M. on the 20th, winds blew from the north at Spokane, from the south near Walla Walla, and from the southwest at Helena. Clearly a front (and probably an upper-level trough) was passing through, rapidly, freshening surface winds and scrambling their higher profile so that the air mass became unstable. Likely a surface wind stream struck the higher mountains, yet above this splash layer, the winds blew less vigorously. Unlike a normal profile, where surface roughness slows the lower winds and lets the upper winds flow faster, here the profile inverted. There were lower winds powerful enough to fan flames even through dense forests and across rugged mountains, but once the fires renewed and began to pump their streamers of gas and flame upward, the higher winds were too weak to scatter those convective columns, which tightened and towered upward. Each column began to draw air into itself, and the fight between the two winds—one of tangled streams sucking into the convecting fires, the other flowing around those black-smoking columns—created vortices and picked up other whirls where the surging air churned and eddied over a jagged landscape of ridges and ravines like water splashing over boulders in a mountain stream. The firewhirls spun trees around like a lathe. In their concentrated funnels combustion strengthened, perhaps fivefold. Small fires became large, and large fires burned hugely, able both to spread and incinerate and to leap over mountains in a sandstorm of firebrands. Convective columns became the thunderheads of firestorms. The massed fires became a veritable "hurricane of flame." Their smoke eventually darkened Montreal and yellowed the skies over Massachusetts.[41]

The winds riled old burns all over the region. But their main force smashed with particular power along the Bitterroots between Pend Oreille in the north and the Selway River to the south. Four great blotches of fire scoured out the landscape in roughly east-west swaths. The swath between the Coeur d'Alene and St. Joe rivers became ground zero. Supervisor Weigle later reckoned that 15 percent of the fires had done the bulk of the damage. These he placed in the backcountry; these were the ones that were hardest to reach, that had crept and swept for up to two months, that most resisted extinguishment and encouraged far-removed backfiring, that commanded the greatest number of crews. Of the acres scorched in the Northern Rockies that summer, perhaps up to 75 percent burned during the Big Blowup. On the morning of 20 August, as the wind stirred the valley smoke, probably 400 men and two companies of soldiers labored on their trails and trenches amid the St. Joe Mountains between Wallace and Avery.

They were what made a big fire into an important one. The Big Blowup became a Great Fire not because of the millions of acres scorched but because there were people in its path, and there were people next to those flames because in defiance of natural logic, they were trying to fight them. They were there because the U.S. Forest Service had determined here to draw a line in the duff. Because the Service was young, brash, flush with emergency money, threatened by bureaucratic rivals, barely able to comprehend the real risks it faced. Because like William Greeley, they were part of a crusade; because like Elers Koch, they were foresters, and fire control was the most elementary thing foresters did; because like Joe Halm, they found rangering more adventurous than football and firefighting a more thrilling team sport; because like Will Morris, they loved the outdoors and wanted a job that would put them in the woods; because like Lieutenant L. B. Chandler, they had been ordered there; because like Ed Pulaski, they took pride in what they could do with their hands, and it was their job.

The Great Fires swept over the Canadian Rockies with hardly a whisper, but they smashed against the American Rockies because here the hammering flames struck an institutional anvil with a clang that still rings through America's wildlands.

•

ON THE MORNING of 20 August, Will Morris had started back to his ridgetop camp with Ranger Schneider when the dreaded Palouser struck. As the day brightened, the wind freshened, and by the time Will arrived at the camp, it was a gale, howling at a good sixty miles an hour. The wind fanned embers into flame, flame into conflagration, and the Great Fires into a holocaust.

The revived fire surged over the ridge and with a "mighty roar" cleaned out the watershed they had labored for so long to protect. Worse, it threatened camp and crew. The men hurriedly cleared a spot and dumped their provisions into it. While they cut a fireline through a lodgepole thicket on the ridgeline beneath them, hoping to hold the flame there, the fire crowned, and their "head axman" almost suffocated. They abandoned the line, retreated to the ridge above their camp, and waited, helplessly, for the winds to die with the ending day.[42]

But this was no ordinary day; it obeyed a deeper logic. The winds howled and the flames thundered, and together they plucked out trees like dandelions and sent flame upward in a towering burnt offering through the sky itself. The surging fire overran the upper ridge from where the crew huddled, leaving the ridgeline above and below them burned out. They were, Will admitted, "in a somewhat serious predicament." Trees crashed and burned continually. Sand and dirt and soot covered their food, but they gathered together and ate what they could and watched.[43]

Never had any of them witnessed such a wild sight. They looked south across the valley of the Coeur d'Alene River and saw in the mountains behind Wallace "a great white cloud pillar" as though from a long-delayed thunderstorm or a volcanic eruption. To the west, the sun set "in a flying black mass, looking like a great red ball of fire." Their ridgetop perch gave them a panoramic view available to no one else that dreadful day. "The weird scene greatly impressed" them all, and "one could not help having the feeling of fear and awe which the scene produced, as if a great tragedy was about to happen." The crew stared, thunderstruck, immobile, mesmerized. The very air, they thought, was "afire."[44]

Yet their blowup was hardly a flyspeck on the regional tapestry of burning. Had they been able to soar upward with the smoke over the St. Joe Mountains, and a bit beyond, they would have witnessed a vast tsunami of flame, set into motion by the tremors of a fast-paced cold front, sweeping across the Rockies like a broken-edged scythe. Their separate behaviors followed everywhere more or less the same scenario. The winds rose, the fires exploded, the winds shifted, the fires veered with them, the winds dropped, and the surge subsided. The longer the fetch of wind and fuel, the larger the fire. The biggest burns moved from the most westerly origins, rushing eastward along deep valleys until, with a roar, they broke over the crest of the Bitterroots.

•

THAT WAS HOW nature saw it. People saw it differently. The fires entered history to the extent that someone bothered to record them. Nowhere, however, is the documentation complete, or consistent, or even wholly comprehensible. Bureaucrats preserved more paper than settlers. Regional newspapers raged with daily misinformation, corrections forgotten in the next-day rush of new rumors and sensational details. Official records, sensitive to lawsuits, were more likely to forget successes than failures, more prone to detail damages and fatalities than near misses. Army officers filled out questionnaires.

No one saw it whole or had prior intimation that such a thing could happen and that he might be required to comprehend so profound a scene. Most observers knew the fires as smoke on the horizon and perhaps flame on the ridgelines or as the rumor of terror in the woods. Most of those on the lines knew, or, better, simply experienced, the fires as a welter of sense impressions: smoke, heat, roar, flame, sweat, dirt, trees, a world shrunk to a wild patter of monosyllables. But as the survivors and observers began to explain, or were compelled to explain, the fires to others, their renderings began to assume patterns beyond a cascade of sensings, scattered like leaves in the wind. They became stories.

The Big Blowup was a collage of smaller blowup fires, and likewise its chronicle is a massing of many stories. Yet almost every narrative conforms to a common formula. Each opens with a scene of the unsuspecting, lulled by the false calm of 19 August. There come the premonitions: the wind, the sudden darkness like a pharaoh's curse, a glow on the horizon, firebrands from the sky, a roar, a black cloud like a great bird of death. When the fire breaks upon them, a new set piece begins. Here are the fires of judgment; the crew reacts, each member according to his gifts. After the flames have passed, the crew rouses and assesses the damage and decides what the experience finally meant. Those who are willing ponder it. Mostly they see it only as danger or horror; a few are willing to chalk it up as simple adventure; most are grateful and puzzled that they have lived. Then comes the odyssey home, the messages missed and scrambled, the rumors of horrible deaths and losses, the welcome shock of contact, and the telling of the tale. Most of the accounts did not emerge spontaneously out of some inner hurt, some compulsion to tell, but from bureaucratic demands for records, which partly explains their common shape. Whatever their origins, the stories of the Great Fires repeat this pattern over and over, like a battle told through the eyes of individual combatants, each distinct yet all the same.

But history is more than story; the stories themselves must be shaped into a collective narrative. On this there is less consensus. Most often the outcome has been an arbitrary mosaic held together by the binding of the pages rather than the logic of a narrative driver. Yet a mapping of the fires suggests an organic order to those thronging accounts, less chronological than geographic. The fires gathered like an immense maelstrom, with the Big Blowup at their core: four gigantic burns blotting the Idaho Rockies like Rorschach ink blots. Around them stands a galaxy of lesser fires, as though caught in the gravitational field of the black hole burns. Along that periphery, the story develops at a pace still in the hands of its participants. But as the grand narrative spirals inward, the participants begin to lose control over their fires and over their tales. They react; they fill in the blanks of forms and questionnaires. The core stories have less leisure for foreshadowing and detail and explication. They dissolve plot into incident and incident into sensation. At the nuclear core of the Big Blowup, the narrative seemingly shatters into the literary equivalent of subatomic entities, moving randomly in a kind of storied indeterminacy.

That happened most profoundly on the Coeur d'Alene forest, which became ground zero of the Great Fires. The Coeur d'Alene felt the west winds first; it sucked in crews from its neighbors; it sent its worst fires beyond its borders into the Cabinet and the Lolo; it endured the greatest damages. Of the 116 claims filed in District One for injuries and death, the Coeur d'Alene accounted for 101. Of the seventy-eight firefighters who died, seventy-two fell in the St. Joe Mountains. In its flames, all the genres gathered: the crew escaped and the crew burned over, the settlers evacuated and the settlers killed, the towns threatened, burned, and saved. More tellingly, it broke down those stories into their smallest possible units, the phonemes and memes of narrative, until plot and place nearly vaporized in the flame and vanished in the pall. Remove the Coeur d'Alene fires, and the 1910 season becomes one remembered only by antiquarian chroniclers and raconteuring elders. Recall them, and you hold the torn fragments of an obscure sacred scroll of American experience. Understand them, and you touch the dark heart of a year of fires.

•

WHEN THE WINDS struck, Bill Greeley was where he wanted to be: on the line. The ever-festering Glacier fire control campaign needed stiffening. On the 19th Greeley had located a Great Northern track crew, worked all night on a fire on the Blackfeet forest, then headed for Kalispell. Greeley was hot-spotting; he was jumping from one crisis to another, knocking down flare-ups with sprays of encouragement, insight, money, zeal. At Kalispell he got word that "all hell had broken loose." Immediately he hurried to Missoula, where "everything was crashing at once"; more hot-spotting, this time administrative. He identified the blown lines and front office breakdowns, opened the supply offices in Spokane and Butte, readied headquarters to receive and respond, and "greatly worried about the strength of the fire fighters." As well he might. They were on their own, and they needed more than mass hirings to fill in gaps or jolts of coffee to ward off fatigue. The fires were upon them.[45]

•

THE FLAMING FLANKS of the maelstrom burned boldly but quietly. The Nezperce forest survived the Big Blowup with hardly a headline as Ranger G. I. Porter rallied a defense of Elk City, which narrowly escaped the rising tide of flame around it. The Kootenai forest suffered when the winds whipped up a large fire around Sylvanite and big burns spilled over from the Coeur d'Alene. The Kaniksu itself largely escaped, though the flames blasted through more settled country, incinerating mills, mines, and homesteads. Three settlers, two men and one woman, died in the conflagration.[46]

Years later Meyer Wolff recalled the firefight in the Priest River country. He had spent the summer with a reconnaissance crew of eight men and a cook. They were all of them "green," naive about the hard labor of such real fieldwork. But there was one job worse, and that was firefighting. Still, "with the enthusiasm of youth and general interest in forestry we earned the reputation of being the first ones on fire anywhere in our vicinity." They had found and fought fires all summer. Patrolling a line on the morning of the 20th, they watched a "huge black storm cloud" build up to the west. An hour later they recognized it for what it was, as ash, charcoal, and wind descended. They received orders to disband and join other crews. "It was with a feeling of youthful 'do or die' spirit and 'help in an emergency' that we separated, buoyed with the enthusiasm of youth to put in every ounce of effort of which we were capable." Wolff hustled on foot the fifteen miles to Priest River.[47]

What he found was a job, and "not at all a heroic flamboyant one." While fire scattered crews on the lines, it sucked in officials to orchestrate logistics. Wolff became "commissary man, time-keeper, fire fighter receiver, hirer and dispatcher, freight cars unloader, freight wagon loader, pay master and telephone central." Orders for crews, clothing, tools, food, transport poured in, until the flames burned down the phone lines. Meanwhile fires bore down on the villages. A shift in winds spared Newport; a backfire, organized partly under Wolff's "inexperienced direction," saved Priest River. They were "hectic days full of sweat, grease and hard work." He slept little, knew almost nothing about the big fires to the south, had no time for even the breathless newspapers.[48]

So too it had passed on the Pend Oreille forest. Another trail crew, another summer fighting fire, young forest guards suddenly thrust into command; several large fires come and gone. But ignorance of what was happening elsewhere here proved fatal. At DeFaut Gulch a trail crew had corralled and continued to patrol a small burn. Like most other fires, this one, once surrounded, smoldered. By the 19th it had subsided enough that rangers and foreman were dispersing, leaving a crew of ten under straw boss W. E. LaMonte to patrol it. They had a camp in a clearing about a mile from the fire and on the 20th had trudged there for lunch when LaMonte, sensing the freshening wind and another fire it brought from the south, "showed himself a thorough coward" (in the words of Forest Supervisor J. E. Barton) and fled. Soon he met Billy Brashear, a fire guard, who had seen the larger burn boiling over and had ridden for all he was worth to warn them. He reached LaMonte's party farther down the path, the men, worried and scampering, the fire nearly at his back.[49]

Their camp lay in a small clearing, an acre or two with a tiny spring in the middle. Brashear told the crew to throw down their tools and run to the camp. There he ordered them to gather at the spring, soak their blankets, and lie under them. They did, all but two men. The fire was then upon them. The official account says that the two men, J. Plant and J. Harris, panicked, leaped up, and bolted. Some crewmen tried to grab them, but the two wrestled loose and plunged on for a few steps until quickly felled by the flames and then burned to death only yards away from where the crew lay. Another version says they fled as the fire first approached, that they were found dead a few hundred yards down the road. Meanwhile the supervisor's office had recognized the danger and organized a relief party. They arrived that evening and found

Brashear's crew unconscious in the clearing. One account claims a few men suffered burns and temporary blinding from their efforts to constrain Plant and Harris. The rest were alive.[50]

•

ON THE CLEARWATER forest the flames found Ranger Ed Thenon's crew on Moose Creek. Thenon had been surprisingly casual about the early foreshadowings: the wind, the smoke, the sky that had become pitch black by late afternoon. At 10 P.M. he took to bed to think through the situation. He heard what he assumed were raindrops, jumped up and ran outside, and turned his face up without effect. Then came what he believed was a rain shower but proved only a dumping of pine needles. Later Louie Fitting shouted for him to come, that a "star" had fallen on the hillside across the creek and started a fire. This finally brought Thenon to his woodsman's senses. He looked west, the direction of the wind, and "saw the sky aglow with pink color spread across a width of several miles." He knew at once that the "star" was a firebrand, that an immense fire was on a collision course with his camp.[51]

Already its high red glow had begun to throw shadows around him as Thenon roused the men and turned to inspect the creek. It wasn't much: six to eight inches deep, eight feet wide, with a sandy strip six feet wide around a bend, and driftwood bunched at the tip of the strip. Now he inspected his crew, which was little better. He knew two by name, both rangers, Charlie Strite and Louie. As for the rest, some were crying and wailing, others "as cool and calm as if this was an everyday occurrence." When Thenon ordered the men to gather everything onto the sandy strip, the excitable proved helpless and wanted only to flee before the flames. Thenon climbed onto a log and delivered what may be the only stump speech ever recorded during a conflagration. He told them not to leave, to collect in the creek, to stay together. "If we all lie down in the creek during the crisis, no one will be hurt and we will pull through all right."[52]

The ordeal began. While the "cooler heads" moved their gear, Thenon contemplated the pile of drift slash. If it burned while the crown fire passed over them, they would fry. But he was reluctant to preburn it before the front arrived; it might linger, it might escape, and it was in any event too late. Already the pile had ignited and been doused with buckets of water. The crew pulled canvas over their camp grub and then wetted it down. Flames appeared faster in the drift pile than Thenon could swat them. Burning bark and embers began to shower down from the pall overhead. They soaked blankets in the creek and covered the horses and rolled in the creek to soak their clothes. The heat from the crowning flames dried everything as fast as they could wet them. The canvas over the grub pile caught fire. A commotion stirred by the creek as two men cracked. One, the cook, became so "violently insane" that it took three men to pin him to the creek. The other danced around and sang a lullaby. That spooked the excitables; they readied to dash off, though where to was impossible to say. There was nowhere they could go that the fire could not run them down. Thenon ordered everyone to lie in the creek and cover himself with a wet blanket. The coolheaded saved the day by doing just that and quelling the panicky. Curiously, the horses, their heads shrouded and blankets wet, remained calm. Meanwhile the two piles of combustibles nearby—the driftwood left by nature, the grubstake they had stacked on the sand—were ablaze. Thenon grabbed a bucket and began dashing water on the canvas until a downsurge of heat dropped him to his knees and he knew that his time had come. Instinctively, he thrust his head into the bucket. "This proved a blessing as I was able to draw a breath instantly and was relieved of the terrible strain. I got to my feet and with two or three steps I was in the creek where I lay down with the bucket still over my head. Having no blanket with me, I kept the bucket over my head for it had certainly saved my life."[53]

They waited; they endured. The crisis passed. Above the fire-reflecting waters of Moose Creek, the flames surged away, the heat lifted. Fire burned along the ground and within the drift, and as they pulled themselves from the creek, they drew near it to dry themselves. Snags blazed like enormous candles; the camp lit up like a ballroom. The grub pile was a heap of ash. Four men, Thenon among them, suffered a kind of fire-induced snow blindness so painful they could barely open their eyes and so stumbled around. Thenon had the roll called and discovered that two men were missing. From downstream, however, the lost answered the shouts raised for them. Doubting that anyone could survive in the camp, they had waded farther until they found an old cedar that had fallen across the creek and had its stump high enough for them to crawl under it. They thought they alone had survived. Around and into the camp snags began to crash down.

That remained the scene when dawn crept through the smoke. They scraped through the ashy crust of their grub heap and found a pot and pan, some half-baked beans and a slab of half-fried bacon, some coffee and sugar melded into a "sweet mess." The cook had recovered his composure. One man salvaged some table salt and splashed it into the eyes of the fire-blind; it helped. "We had," Thenon recalled, "some kind of breakfast."[54]

There was no longer a reason to stay. The fire was gone; it had won the field and taken motive with it. Now was the time to return home, and along the way Thenon collected fire stories as a prospector might collect rock samples from outcrops. First, Thenon and Strite tested the eight-mile route to the Three Forks Ranger Station, which had survived thanks to the clearing and the horse-trampled dirt that encircled it. Soon afterward Ranger Weholt arrived, shocked to find them there. They told their story; he told his. He had camped about three miles from them, at another fire, and had seen Thenon's burn sweep past and join his own. His camp, though, was within the burn and safe. He volunteered to retrieve Thenon's men, an offer Ed and Charlie gratefully accepted. When they reached the cabin, Ranger Ray Fitting (a cousin of Louie's) was there, with a fire story of his own. The big wind had found him alone scouting for camps near West Moose Creek, and a fire the wind was driving had cut him off from the station. Treading cross-country, he began searching for a refuge. He found a bluff with a shelf of rock projecting out over the creek, and as the fire rushed upon him, he crawled under the ledge and lay in three feet of water with his coat over his head. When dead fish began to float past, he assumed that they had boiled in the creek and had visions of meeting the same fate. Meanwhile Thenon's deserting packers had witnessed the spectacle of the conflagration from a high ridge and concluded that no one could have survived. They reported the disaster to Major Fenn, who fired off telegrams and phone calls and ordered crews to cut through the windfall and investigate. One of them met Thenon and told him of yet another escape. Forester Al Peterson had found himself cut off and had abandoned his camp and horses to dash to the Selway River, some six miles distant. He survived; his horses and outfit did not. The trek continued. Eventually they reached Darby, over the Bitterroots. Packers hauled the crew out. The "lullaby boy" went to an insane asylum.[55]

•

THE CABINET FOREST, like the Clearwater, burned a lot of acres yet flared into only a few stories. Even these, like the fires, seem derivative, an aftershock of the staggering firequakes that savaged the Coeur d'Alene. At least three fires soared over the Bitterroots and splashed broadly across the Clark Fork Valley. The great St. Joe fire, burning along the broken back of the St. Joe Mountains, was one. The other two spilled out of the North Fork of the Coeur d'Alene. A week earlier a warning fire had threatened Donlan's mill at Cedar Spur, until backfiring stalled it, or rather redirected it since the backfire then jumped the river and raced northward onto the Kootenai forest. But those were sparring rounds; the Big Blowup did the bulk of the burning. The great burns consumed mills, pigs, horses, homesteads, ranches, some thirteen million feet of sawn white pine, and at Swamp Creek, an appendage of the Tuscor fire, four firefighters.[56]

As elsewhere, the fires on the Cabinet had quelled prior to 20 August. Ranger H. S. Kaufman had a large force on the Tuscor and directly supervised a crew working near the mouth of Swamp Creek, where it enters the Clark Fork River. About ten to twelve miles up that creek Roy Engle oversaw a crew of twenty-five men. As winds quickened, Kaufman realized the hazard they posed upstream and dispatched a messenger. He arrived that evening with instructions for Engle to decamp immediately. The crew started out the next morning, trudging down the trail along the creek. They were four or five miles from the junction with the Clark Fork when they saw the fire.

This was a new fire, and so unexpected. It had run over the Bitterroot divide the previous night and was now racing toward them like streamers before a gale. They could not pass it; they could not stop it. They had no choice but to reverse their flight. Engle expected that when they came to their old burn, they could weather the new fire safely within. But the winds had whipped their old fire to life, and it too was spreading and blocked their passage. They were trapped. Their one exit, their one hope, was to reach a large rockslide farther up Swamp Creek. They hurried as best they could and reached the slide as the big fire spilled up the ravine like water through a flume. On the rocks they could run no more. Here they would make their stand.

The fire, pulsing through the conifer crowns, scoured out the gulch, belched embers in great fire showers, and spewed surges of heat and gas over the rockslide. The men sought protection among the stones. Some dug foxholes, and five elected to flee up the slope. The last in line, a man named Anderson, straggling, watched in horror and awe as the fire devoured the four men in front. He turned back, badly burned but alive, and stumbled into the rocks. All the crew were more or less blinded from smoke, all suffered some burns, but only the four who had shown their backs to the fire perished. The next morning the remnant of Engle's crew staggered through the burn to the river where they met Ranger Kaufman. The charred corpses of George Strong, George Fease, E. Williams, and A. G. Bourette remained on the slopes until parties were sent to fetch them.

It seemed a simple tale: a firefight gone bad when the flames blew up and a crew that refused to stay with its boss—a dark inversion of the Moose Creek fire. Yet the story had lapses, and where records exist, they quarrel one with the other. Williams and Bourette had only initials rather than names because that is how they had signed on, and if anyone on the crew knew their given names (if they were even their real names), he offered no record of that fact. They died as anonymously as they had chosen to live; their account died with them. The story of the survivor became complicated as official claims identified him as Joe Dixon, not Anderson, and testified that seven, not five, men scrambled up the slope and that those in the rocks had braved the flames to haul him back to safety as his cries rose over the roar. Regardless, Dixon was compensated $336.25 for medical expenses for treatment of deep burns on his left calf, right thigh, both shoulders, and right neck and for skin grafts to his badly scorched back and hips. Also defying Ranger Kaufman's official report, with its implication that the dead and injured had known the risks when they signed on and had suffered as the result of their own panic, was the plea of Mrs. Emily Haney, mother of George Strong, one of the identified dead. "I am a widow and depended on him for support," she wrote Secretary Wilson a year later. She feared she would soon lose her home because of sickness, her son's lost wages, and his funeral expenses. "He was a minor 17 years old," she explained, "ordered him out without my consent, never knew it until they sent him home in a box all burnt to a crisp."[57]

•

ON THE LOLO, what Koch later called "one long battle against fire from the latter part of June to the end of August" was reaching its climax. Over the past month ranger-led crews had beaten down half a dozen large fires over the Nine Mile Valley, many believed incendiary and sited in slashings of the Western Lumber Company. Not only did the Lolo have to defend its own territory, but westering winds threatened to splash firestorms over the high seawall of the Bitterroots. The Lolo staff thus carried its campaign into Idaho. One crew trekked over the Lolo Pass into the Lochsa country; two pushed into Fish Creek; another, to Trout Creek; another to Saltese; and others through the St. Regis country. Whatever could be found was thrown into the fight. A. H. Abbott only thought his round of fire rangering had ended when, on the morning of the 20th, he left his secured lines and headed to town. In the telegraphic prose of his laconic journal:

> AUG. 20—Left fire safe and paid men off. Went into St. Regis. F.F.
>
> AUG. 21—Went to St. Regis from Station with Beal. Bad reports of Fires west. Got bill grub and sent men out to watch tunnel 8 fire. Koch and Clifford and Beaver in town. Got 2 doz. acres in shape with Sayles. People go in St. Regis from fires West. Fires started in St. Regis. F.F.[58]

The Graves Creek fire showed how the logic of fire control had to follow the logic of fire. The only safe fire was one pursued and hit at its origin; the sooner it was contained, the safer and cheaper it would be; the longer it lingered, the more likely it would catch the right mix of wind and terrain to explode. Since anything burning to the west, even over the divide, was a threat to the Lolo, the Lolo sent crews after the fires.

When smoke was first spotted on 11 July, the fire was forty acres, attacked by a crew under Ranger H. P. Barringer from the Lolo, and uncontrollable. At 3:30 A.M. crews renewed their attack and held it until afternoon winds blew it away and Barringer rode after help, trying, unsuccessfully, to rouse enthusiasm from mining camps. The next evening Ranger Garrison arrived with six fire guards from the Clearwater. The combined force hit the fire, which again blew away. It was now eighty acres, and a second fire up the creek had reached ten acres. On 15 July Barringer returned from Iron Mountain with fourteen men and a packtrain. They cut trails, moved camp, fought fire. On 22 July a two-day outbreak of winds scattered the fires. The smaller one they contained; the larger burned more or less freely. Barringer returned to Iron Mountain for more supplies and men. The afternoon of 30 July brought high winds that powered the Graves Creek fire up the slopes about five miles and over the crest into Montana and down Trout Creek. Ranger Garrison again moved camp, this time over the divide, and with another eighty-five men had wrestled the fire under control by 4 August. On 20 August trenches more or less surrounded the burn. Had the "big wind" not come when it did, Supervisor Koch believed, the lines would have held.[59]

But the blast came. The winds "attained the velocity and force of a hurricane" and "uprooted or twisted off" living trees three to four feet in diameter; smoke, sand, and ash thickened the air into stygian darkness, such that no one could see to the end of his arm. The fire became an imploding cloud of flame that swept everything in its path. Barringer was on Iron Mountain, and "when he saw how conditions were," he mounted his horse and rode to his crews on Trout Creek. "With the cinders and ashes falling all around him, and so dark that he could not see his horse's head at three o'clock in the afternoon," Koch wrote glowingly, Barringer "rode up in the face of the fire to the summit, collected his scattered crews, quelled a mutiny of his packers, and saved every man, horse and all his camp equipment." It was, Koch concluded, an act of "the greatest personal courage."[60]

Yet the Blowup had struck before Barringer would begin his brave charge. The crew on Iron Mountain had had to save itself. William McPherson, then only a "kid," recalled how. The original fire was ten acres when they reached it by an old trappers' trail. They promptly began encircling it with a trench. The wind, however, "played the usual trick," and the fire blew over their lines. "If it had not been that my shoes were ripped down the back," McPherson claimed, "I could never have followed Johnson through the fire as sparks and coals were making me step fast and high." They reached their camp and began relocating everything, horses first, into the middle of a swampy patch of ground. Others soon collected, and "the move was on!" By the time they took to their heels, "the sky was all lit up," and that was fortunate, because they could not have traveled over rough ground without its glow. They made their way into O'Hara Creek at the foot of Iron Mountain, then pushed into bunchgrass. The horses badly needed fodder; so did the men. They paused to eat, with the flames "five miles below." But sparks arrived before the flames, the grass exploding like gasoline. The grass burned so quickly up the slope that the men scampered into the fresh burn and followed it "to the top of Iron Mountain!" By now "the eyes of men and horses were almost useless so we scraped away the cinders at a spot, covered the horses heads with saddle blankets, spread a tent over our heads and waited. After a few hectic hours, the follow-up fire passed up and we could get some better breathing." The next morning they saw Elk City "plainly," since "all else was burned."[61]

Just when the gallant Ranger Barringer arrived and what mutiny he quelled is not clear. Nor is the tally of those who died. Officially no one perished. McPherson remembered another register, which told of a Mr. Weiss, who had run into the Black Pine Mine and suffocated, and yet another man who died beneath a falling tree near O'Hara Creek, but neither was employed by the Forest Service so did not enter the roll call of those who had fallen in the line of duty. Koch as leader and McPherson as laborer experienced the fires very differently, told startlingly distinct stories, yet both had many fires over many years still to face. McPherson worked his last fire in 1961, seventeen years after Koch retired, before deciding he was "getting too old to fight fires" and wished only to retire "and shoe mules as a hobby."[62]

•

ELK CITY SURVIVED; other towns did not. The wooden rail and logging villages were almost disposable. They burned as regularly as trash piles, with or without drought and gales. Now they simply vanished in the maelstrom, nothing more to the flames that were rushing through the St. Regis Valley than convenient caches of combustibles. Unless one had ample time and room for backfiring, there was nothing to do but evacuate. Taft, Haugan, and Deborgia all burned to their roots. On the other side of the tunnel, Grand Forks had already burned in July, when a prostitute had robbed and poisoned a customer, then fired the building to hide the deed. The flames went through the entire compound. Immediately a tent city rose from the ashes, and prostitutes set up business in a treehouse. The Big Blowup scattered its residents to the winds and wiped Grand Forks off the land like tissue paper.[63]

On the afternoon of 20 August, Ranger Frank Haun mistook the black clouds to the west for a front of thunderstorms. When word came that they were firestorms, that the burn on Pine Creek had escaped, he arranged to ship forty men to the fire the next day, then returned to Saltese. At 11 P.M. a patrolman woke him to say the fire was at Borax. "I got up and telephoned Wallace, and the wire went down; then I got Mullan on the line and was informed that the fire was all around there at that time, and they were going to leave the telephone.

Then I tried to get Missoula, and got Hamilton instead, and all they knew was that there was a big fire; and about ten minutes afterward, that line went out. I went down town and sent messages to all the crews I knew of—Phillips' and Breen's crews, and told them either to stay where they were, if I considered it safe, or to move to some safe place which I designated; and they did."[64]

Shortly afterward Ranger J. E. Breen arrived and told Haun that he couldn't hold the camp at Borax. Haun told him to return and stay put, that the camp was in a big burn and hence safe. Returning, he met fifty soldiers and seventy others at the Borax bridge but convinced them to return and hold the camp, as they did. That done, Breen hurried to Taft. The fire had just arrived. He grabbed what men he could and "drove the fire around Taft," saving the lumber at the ranger station and perhaps a building. The remainder of the town vanished in flame.[65]

By now relief trains were shuttling along the Northern Pacific tracks. One arrived in Saltese from Wallace. Haun gathered up all the women and children and shipped them in boxcars to Missoula. He kept "all the men that would stay to fight fire." All day they waited; all day they carried lanterns through the inky smoke. Then a train arrived from Missoula with a hundred buckets and forty men. The newcomers didn't like what they saw and started to pull out. But the fire, which had burned out bridges as it approached, now leaped over Saltese and burned out the bridges ahead. The men had no choice but to stay and fight. When the fire struck the town about 9:30 P.M., they were ready: "water and water pails on every building, and ladders on every building" and seventy men strung out along a fireline. For an hour and a half they drove the fire "around the town by backfiring and whipping it out as it came in."[66]

They suffered one casualty, though in circumstances so macabre that only the greater wreckage accounts for its lost memory. The story begins with the realization that the onrushing fires doomed Taft and its stocks of liquor, so the residents had determined "to consume as much of it [liquor] as possible before the fire did." When evacuation came, drunks lay everywhere. The one casualty was burned "pretty bad" before he was heaved out to the street. Breen hauled him to Saltese, a doctor bandaged him, and they placed him in a boxcar with two others. There they left him, swathed in oil and cotton, unwilling to move him any more than necessary, ready to send him on the next train to Missoula. That night a friend, "having done his best to salvage the whiskey supplies in Saltese before they burned," decided to visit the man. When he lit a shaking match to see into the dark car, the flame caught the man's bandages. The dressings flashed; the man screamed, leaped up, and dashed down the tracks until tackled; and the once-burned victim burned again, this time to his death.[67]

Around 11 P.M., with the fireline encircling the town, the wind shifted and blew from the north, and Haun dismissed all but twenty-five men. A reporter from the *Daily Missoulian* asked for "some dope about the fire." After a few minutes Haun hustled to the north to check the line now downwind, and when he returned, he found the reporter "crawling into the N.P. water tank" and reckoned that was why the *Missoulian* had little to say about the Saltese fire. With the rails cut, they had to forage for feed. Since all the shopkeepers and butchers had evacuated, however, they had "no difficulty getting all the supplies there were in Saltese." Perhaps it was just as well the reporter was tanked.[68]

The next morning, hoping to see for himself, Koch rode a Northern Pacific freight to St. Regis, then to Deborgia. "The whole sky was yellow, then black. It was completely terrifying. New fires were breaking out all along the line. It became pitch black and the fires started breaking into Deborgia. The train had lights on. I got off at Deborgia and tried to set backfires, but it looked hopeless." There was nothing to do but fall back to St. Regis. By now the entire canyon was "completely afire." The train chugged through the middle when a flaming tree fell across the tracks. The freight ground to a halt. The heat, Koch wrote, was "terrible." He and some others jumped out of their freight cars and wrestled the tree off the tracks. The train, stuffed with survivors, continued to St. Regis.[69]

•

YET ONLY A few towns had ranger stations, with deputized rangers to serve as fire wardens. Many townsfolk, like most miners and homesteaders, had to fend for themselves. They tell a story common to the frontier, but out of sync with the grand narrative of the Great Fires. At Mullan what was to become the standard plot line was reversed: The town saved itself, while forest firefighters stumbled out of the hills.

The warning signs had appeared for days. By 3 P.M. on the 20th, the smoke so thickened that bats appeared, and the air became hot and oppressive and choked with falling brands. "Groups of men began congregating at street corners discussing the scene," recalled Mr. Swaine, "and a sort of reverential silence seemed to have settled upon the place." A few hours later townsfolk began soaking houses and offices, telephones spread rumors, and "alarm" replaced "awe." The scene worsened that night, as they learned Wallace had burned and the cruel flames were driving refugees through Mullan by rail as though they were frightened deer. Trains were evacuating women, children, and hospital patients, and many from Mullan joined them; telephone lines burned down; the sense of panic was palpable, as "all agreed that our worst fears were about to be realized." Still, the stalwart citizenry turned out, successfully backfired against the southern flames, and, as the wind calmed later, appeared to have saved the town.[70]

Early the next morning the weary townsfolk saw the appalling spectacle of a crew of firefighters, "almost charred," their hands held upward, "scarcely knowing how or where they were going," stagger down the street. Volunteers erected a temporary hospital in a vacant store building. Then the west wind resumed, and fire leaped over the river. A general evacuation of women and children commenced, moving across the burned area toward Wallace, where relief trains could carry them westward, through and beyond the burns. "The mountains so high and steep with the narrow gulches between, resembled curtains of fire suspended from the clouds." Those rimming ridges showered sparks down on the town below. All agreed that only a massive backfire to the west, north, and east could prevent the imminent immolation of Mullan. Under the unflinching direction of William Coumerilh, the volunteers formed a giant letter *S*, standing with torches but a few feet apart. At a common signal, all kindled the fuels before them, and building momentum, the separate fires joined and burst up the steep slopes until the valley resembled a "deep bowl . . . completely lined with seething flames." Midnight was as bright as day. Most felt as though they were immersed in "the infernal regions." A virtually unlimited supply of water from the river, though, allowed a bucket brigade to quench every spark that kindled houses and buildings. The Swaine family huddled in the brick schoolhouse, convinced that it would be the last structure to burn. When morning arrived—three days and two nights after the crisis had begun—the terror passed. No one had died. One and all, they scarcely believed their good fortune.[71]

The town survived because they defended it and had drawn a lucky hand. Their story survived because Elers Koch chose to preserve it. Somehow, even without rangers riding to the rescue, it seemed to belong to the larger chronicle. Probably it did. Almost uniquely, the Lolo had suffered large fires, fielded a major campaign, and retreated without havoc. Incredibly, during the Big Blowup, the old trenches in Nine Mile Valley held, and even more astonishingly, none of the crews scattered like buckshot over the Bitterroots lost a man, none on the Lolo proper. Elers Koch's labors had paid off. They loomed larger over time, a Legend of the Lolo, as Koch established himself as the historian of the Big Blowup.

•

NOT EVERYONE, HOWEVER, had passed through the flames as unscathed as Koch, and many hesitated to commit their experiences to paper. Roy Phillips, a ranger who fire-patrolled the tracks of the Northern Pacific on a speeder, found himself in charge of a large crew, one of several arrayed around a sullen burn, all caught during the Blowup. "I have always felt that many of us who were trapped were fortunate to escape," he wrote Koch in 1942, "and like all those who have been close to cashing in there is an inclination to talk as little as possible about it." That he had kept his head, that he had stemmed the "stampede of a pretty badly scared bunch of men," remained a source of satisfaction, not of pride. Young Phillips was a Lolo man, hired originally by Haun as a fire guard, now a ranger under Koch sent into the Coeur d'Alene in hot pursuit of the fires that one after another had blown over the divide and thundered like avalanches down through the Lolo.[72]

This fire had been Phillips's for more than a month. July lightning had ignited it near the Bullion Mine, and Phillips, pumping along on his velocipede, had spotted the smoke behind the ridgeline and reported it to the Coeur d'Alene's supervisor's office in Wallace. For ten days he continued to report it, without effect, since everyone was on fires. So he attacked it from the Lolo, after raising a crew of twenty-five in Missoula and assigning the "coolest Scotchman" he ever met, John Baird, the district lumberman, to head it. By now the fire had swollen too large to stuff back into the duff. The Coeur d'Alene had rallied sufficiently to send a crew under S. M. Taylor from the Idaho side. The Lolo removed Phillips from patrol and handed him a crew on the Montana side. Ranger Breen, before retiring to the St. Regis Valley, had overall charge from Taft, soon itself to be incinerated. The three gangs began to pinch off the fire around the vicinity of the Bullion Mine.[73]

The morning of 20 August differed little from those before. Baird had some trouble on the south flank. Taylor lacked only a mile or so of trenching on the west to encircle the burn completely. Phillips had downgraded his operations to patrol. A day before he had tramped around the perimeter and seen nothing out of order. Probably 150 men were on the line, and since the previous afternoon, a detachment of soldiers under Lieutenant Titus. By day's end he had removed his crew to camp. Everything seemed in "good shape," and he regarded night patrol, particularly on steep slopes, as futile. Only an extraordinary darkness, the difficulty of following their trail back, a lost man in the brush, and about 9:30 P.M. a "burning brand" a couple of feet long "that hurtled down out of the sky" a hundred yards away suggested anything unusual. "Dog tired," Phillips sent two men to investigate the errant flame before hastily eating and hitting his bedroll.[74]

The storm broke at midnight. The cook wakened Phillips. Below, they could hear the whistle of the relief train from Wallace, feeling its way east, sounding a warning for people to leave. Then flames poked above the western horizon, and the noise of the fire drowned out the locomotive's forlorn whistle. Phillips roused a few men he knew were dependable and hurried to their supply cache along the tracks. They gathered some provisions and were returning with four or five water barrels when they met the remainder of the crew, now decamped and demoralized and determined to flee the scene. But they were all of them too late. Those flaming brands, falling like a meteor shower, had cast fire widely beyond their lines and cut off their only escape. They turned to face the fire. It was "an awe-inspiring spectacle, the whole horizon to the west was aflame and the noise caused by the falling timber was terrific."[75]

They had to act. A foreman insisted, convincingly, that the railway tunnel at Borax was their best place of refuge. The crew was following him when Phillips stood against them. His endless patrols along the tracks had taught him that strong air currents passed through the tunnel. If those winds carried flame, or just heat, they would likely kill anyone within. All the crew, save the foreman and another man, agreed and turned back, and when they saw they walked alone, so did the dissidents. Before they reached the camp, they met Lieutenant Titus. The troops had no orders and no judgment about the fire, so they had decided to follow the firefighters. Phillips took Titus aside and explained his strategy: They would cut line around the camp, which was providentially sited on a small knoll, and backfire as the main burn closed in. The lieutenant was a veteran of the Boxer Rebellion, had won promotion for being the first man over the wall at Beijing, and was, Phillips happily conceded, "brave enough." The troops later confessed that they were badly scared but more intimidated by Lieutenant Titus than by the flames and so held rank.[76]

The spectacle of the conflagration was "awe-inspiring almost beyond belief and was sufficient to strike terror to the strongest heart. . . ." The water in the stream below them became "almost boiling hot," denying them that refuge. Winds flattened a nearby grove of large trees, lifting their trunks bodily from the ground. The roar was so great that it was difficult to talk to someone no farther than one's elbow. That they might stand against such forces seemed, even to Phillips, "hopeless." The usual crew drama ensued: Some men sagged into helplessness; some moaned that they were doomed; enough took up shovels and torches, and these were the ones who mattered. Hastily they trenched around the camp, wetted tents and supplies, and laid down their backfires. The new flames rushed wildly into the wind-sucking maw of the old. The backfire had spread only one or two hundred yards beyond the knoll when it met the main fire front, and "when they came together the heated air current filled with cinders swirled down upon us and for a short space of time that seemed an eternity, we gasped and choked for air and were blinded by smoke." Yet it was enough to break the fury of the flames. The wildfire sloshed around and over the adjacent hills.[77]

Then the stifling smoke and heat and roar, pressing down like an immense hand, lifted, and the air cleared. Everything not soaked was burning. A few men suffered from smoke and were fire-blind; one was so distraught at the thought of blindness that he tried to kill himself until thwarted. Mostly they were prostrate by smoke, too exhausted and weak for anything but to sit and gulp in air and sip water and wait for dawn to creep through the pall.

The next day they struggled to keep fire out of a railway bridge and tunnel. Small parties tried to contact the other crews, but the ground was thick with hot ash and impenetrable. Later they learned that Baird's crew had retreated into an old burn over the course of that terrible night, though Baird himself had assessed they were safe enough (if dazzled by the fireworks on the hills around), had disdained to leave camp "to roast in a heap of ashes," and had slept imperturbably through the night of terror. Somehow a timekeeper from Ranger G. W. Bell's crew on the Idaho side stumbled through the wreckage with the word that eight had died. Phillips headed to Saltese to relay the news but met Breen on a speeder along the way and passed it to him before reversing his travels back to camp.[78]

The Lolo had again slipped out of death's grip. The grand narrative spiraled, faster and faster, into its core on the Coeur d'Alene.

•

THE SMOKE WAS so thick that Percy Stewart, assisting Ed Pulaski, could hardly see ahead when he and forest guard Kenneth Robinson set out on 18 August to find a fire on Trout Creek. The smoke mattered little since they didn't know the country. All Stewart knew was "that the fire was in a certain direction and that if we came very near it, we could hear the burning trees fall." They located it on the 19th and then spotted a crew under guard Lee Hollingshead that was working a trench around it. The next morning they set off for Striped Peak, where Pulaski and Ranger Bell had combined crews of nearly 200 men, strung across the ridge that divided the drainage of the Big Creek that flowed into the Coeur d'Alene River to the north and the Big Creek that flowed into the St. Joe River to the south. The eastern crew was in turn split into two shifts of roughly 50 men each.

Pulaski himself was on his usual circuit of fire inspections. On the 18th he had trekked to Wallace to get a packer to bring in fresh supplies. On the way he found a breakover fire. He stopped and helped rally and organize the nearest crew (under guard D. H. Lewis) before continuing to Wallace. The next day he and the packer had got as far as Lewis's fire when the packer refused to proceed, claiming the ground was too hot. Pulaski whipped around and headed back to Wallace to hire another packer, and on the morning of the 20th he was heading back to Big Creek.[79]

Already winds were stirring the fires, spooking the crews, and each shift crew promptly decamped, broke into wandering bands, and headed off the ridge. One was working its way down the trail to Wallace, about nine miles out, while the other had stopped in the clearing of the McPhee homestead, much as Bell's crew had at Beauchamp's. Crews were scattered and listless when Stewart found them and told them all to halt until he tracked down Pulaski and received instructions. Then he set off briskly to Wallace, while Pulaski and packer Joe Reynolds guided their stock up the high ridge. The wind was "blowing something awful," Stewart recalled. The black mushroom cloud that shrank the sun into a red dot and, viewed from across the valley of the Coeur d'Alene River, had awed Will Morris's crew into stunned silence rose directly above them.[80]

•

ON THE OTHER side of the ridge, Ranger George W. Bell, a 35-year-old veteran of the mountains, had a crew of fifty men. The rising winds blew their fire beyond its trenches and as indrafts clashed with the gale, the air became violent with streamers of flame, gasping with a smoke thick in ash and dirt that shot up and slammed down and throbbing with a vast plucking motion that uprooted 150-foot white pines and flung them about like litter. This was a fire they could not outrun; it would flash up the west-facing slopes before them like a struck match. Nor, by the time they gathered, was there a place and time for backfiring.

But there was a possible site of refuge nearby, the tiny clearing and log cabin of the Joseph Beauchamp homestead. Beauchamp himself was there, had walked off paid duty as a firefighter to bury household goods before the fire arrived, and may have helped direct the errant men. Pulaski considered him "one of the best men on a fire that I ever met," but he had deserted the lines shortly before and no longer had official standing. Nor was there any foreman with the fleeing firefighters. They were a headless, fractured mob, racing for cover, any cover, the winds howling about a minute ahead of the throbbing flames, the flames on their heels. Most flung themselves into a small creek in the center of the cleared patch that passed for a garden, ten splashed about the clearing, and seven, Beauchamp among them, spying a small root cellar, crammed into it, squirming through one another's arms and legs like rats. When the wind struck, it leveled virtually all the trees around. One huge pine spun free and crashed into the clearing. It smashed two men, killing them instantly. A third had his foot crushed beneath it and, unable to free himself, writhed and screamed while the flames, wailing like banshees, bore down.[81]

•

WEST OF BIG CREEK, on the Trout Creek fire Stewart had finally tracked through the dry pea fog of smoke, forest guard Lee Hollingshead, a nimble 22 years old and a two-year veteran of fire duties, supervised a crew of sixty. Like others, this crew saw its trenches overwhelmed by the recharged flames, and like others, it found itself surrounded as firebrands fell like an artillery barrage. In all, forty-one crewmen, including Hollingshead, managed to squirm their way past the rekindled flames and find sanctuary in old burns. But nineteen did not. They were blinded with smoke, almost deaf from the din of flame and wind and crashing trees, and held in their heads only the obsession to find some shelter. Down the hill lay the small Dittman cabin, where they normally tied their pack string. To it they scrambled. With fire on all sides, they packed themselves behind its shielding logs. Soon afterward the roof caught fire.[82]

•

FORESTERS WERE NOT the only ones on Big Creek. The Milwaukee Lumber Company was laying down rails to support a logging operation—the trees Will Morris and others had cruised that winter—and fielded six camps with roughly 500 men. When the fire blew up, it startled them as much as the others.

The lumbermen had been fighting fires for days. Arthur Hogue described how an alarm at 2:30 A.M. had called out all hands for an hour of hot-spotting. The next day fires spilled over their five miles of trails, and the camp labored at shooflies until evening, when the bosses decided that it made more sense to relocate a wholly new fireline on the next ridge. They would rest on Saturday, 20 August, and dig new trenches on Sunday morning. By 4 P.M., however, the smoke thundering over the ridges told them they would have no further rest. An hour later they started burying their camp with the idea of retreating to Camp One. "Before we got them buried, men came running in saying that the fire had crossed the valley below and we were cut off from Camp One and a way out," Hogue wrote. "That it was coming up the valley our way almost as fast as a man could run.

> All thought of saving the camp was abandoned. Evanson and I jumped on some pack horses and galloped off down the creek to see if the report were true. About 300 yards from the camp we met the fire. It filled the whole valley and flames looked as though they arose 300 feet high. We wheeled our horses and raced back to camp where we met about 75 Italians, so frightened they were running every which way and crying out in their native tongue. We rode among them and they turned and went with us. Soon the road became so

> thick with men that we jumped from our horses, just as we crossed the creek, trusting that they would stay near the water and perhaps be saved. The bottom of the creek is very stony and many fell, rolling over and over in the water and being tramped on by the men behind. As soon as the Italians realized that they were caught they flocked to Evanson and me, as we had been their foremen and followed us now in a mob. About 200 yards above our camp we met Guy Rogers and the men from Camp Six, who told us that the fire had come in on them from above and was now coming down the valley almost on their heels.
>
> So there we were, 140 men caught in a valley not 50 yards wide with sides arising about 500 feet on an angle of 45 degrees, and covered with a thick growth of timber, and the bottoms covered with cedar trees that burn almost like tinder.

It was a sublime scene. Awe and terror mixed as they watched a gust of wind strike the flames on one ridge and send them in a great leap to another ridge, "in one continuous stream of fire for a distance of over a half mile." They were trapped like squirrels.[83]

The foremen decided to make their stand where a big, thirty-foot-high rock, clean of timber, rose from the creek. The waters would protect them from flame, the rock from falling trees. They kindled their backfires. But as fast as they lit them, the Italians put them out, yelling, "Firey, firey," and carrying water from the creek in their hats. The foreman fought them off, and at last—so dry were the woods—the backfires took. Slowly the mob retired to the creek, knee-deep in water, put wet blankets over their heads, stood with their backs against the rock, and waited.[84]

•

IT HAD TAKEN Joe Halm's crew days to slash a trail to their fire on Bean Creek, at the headwaters of the St. Joe River, some sixty-five miles from the nearest rail. Their supply line was a nightmare, so on the 19th Halm had released sixty-seven men. On the morning of the 20th Halm was returning from a supply cache when one of the eighteen men who had remained burst out of the bush and stood gasping for breath until the others arrived. The spokesman for the frightened gang, like rabbits flushed out of covert, blurted out, "She's coming! The whole country's afire. Grab your stuff, Ranger, and let's get outa here!"[85]

With the help of the foreman, the only one who still had a tool and who admitted laconically that their situation "Looks bad," Halm tried to calm the crew. Food might do that, so he asked the cook to set up his stove. Then they heard the roar, and three men determined that their only safety lay in flight. The flames were cresting to the west, like "a great wall of fire." Halm strapped on his gun. The sky was closing like a darkened room, and burning twigs cascaded like hailstones. The foreman observed quietly that the fire had just jumped a mile across a canyon. The 25-year-old Halm touched his holster and announced "with an outward confidence, which I by no means felt," that they were not moving. "Not a man leaves this camp. We'll stay by this creek and live to tell about it. I'll see you through. Every man hold out some grub, a blanket, and a tool. Chuck the rest in that tent, drop the poles, and bury it." He pointed to a sandbar where Bean Creek joined the St. Joe. The dazed men snapped to work.[86]

•

ON THE SLOPES of Stevens Peak, James Danielson, a 26-year-old house painter and student at Washington State, found himself scurrying over a place he had often visited but now under circumstances like none he had ever imagined. His crew had become suddenly surrounded by spot fires that, whipped like meringue by that blustery afternoon, quickly fluffed into a great ring of flame. Danielson led his men along the slopes to where an open park of bear grass spread into the timberline. To some of that worried crew the white-tufted bunches seemed like headstones blanketing a cemetery. Quickly the young fire guard had them burn off the park and then cover themselves with their wool blankets and wait. The blankets would shield them from heat, the wool from embers, and the hugged ground from the searing air above. About nine o'clock that evening the fire struck.[87]

•

FARTHER EAST, ALONG the Bitterroot summit, the Bullion Mine fire that had left John Baird nonplussed and forced Roy Phillips into a desperate backfire also threatened the crew under S. M. Taylor. It announced itself suddenly when a burning tree limb, "big as a man's forearm," fell out of the sky and bruised a sleeping crewman. The fire front was moving rapidly up the creek. A "conservative, intelligent fellow, thoroughly able to handle men," as Supervisor Weigle judged him, Taylor ordered his crew of sixty into the mine itself. One of the bunch,

Larry Ryson, had in fact helped build the tunnel. Another crewman carried blankets.

Taylor led and Ryson brought up the rear. In the main tunnel, however, the crew fractured, and eight found themselves separated. Probably in the darkness and noise they could neither see nor hear, nor perhaps did they much care. Here accounts differ. Some say everyone crowded into a side drift and hung blankets across it, while the separated eight milled outside in the main tunnel; others that the drift was an air shaft and the eight crawled into it while the main bulk of the crew crammed far back in the tunnel. The likeliest explanation is that of Roscoe Haines, who described a crosscut shaft between the tunnel portal and the air shaft at the rear. It was into this side drift that the main gang crowded and covered the opening with blankets. Regardless, the Bullion Mine soon had fire in its hole. Fresh air rushed out; smoke poured in.[88]

•

IF WALLACE DEFINED the northern flank of the maelstrom, the rail town of Avery defined the southern. Assistant Ranger Ralph N. Debitt, in charge of the district, had several large crews in the field and as of 6:00 A.M. on 17 August had Company G, Twenty-fifth Infantry, under the command of Second Lieutenant E. E. Lewis. On the morning of the 20th, the forestry crews were splayed in large gangs across the hills while the troops continued to labor on two fires east of Avery that threatened the rails. One soldier had his ribs fractured by a falling tree, and four others had narrow escapes. At Debitt's request Lewis ordered one noncommissioned officer and three troopers to march over the Clearwater divide "to bring in a murderer threatening [the] camp at that place." There was, the lieutenant noted ruefully, no civilian authority. Debitt turned to the Army, and Lewis hewed close to his orders that he act "according to the request of the forestry officials."[89]

By the morning of 21 August, civil disorder seemed as menacing as the natural chaos kindled by the fires. Lewis anticipated a "clash of authority between forestry officials and county officials" once the deputy sheriff returned; Debitt wanted the troops to close the only saloon and "disorderly house"; a flood of refugees from rail towns like Grand Forks, Falcon, and Kyle poured into Avery on freight cars, sliding in ahead of burned bridges and collapsed tunnels that threatened to close all escape to the east; and word reached Debitt from a man "badly burned and in dying condition" that immense fires had overrun crews on "Big Creek." Debitt departed to inspect the damage. At the request of Deputy Sheriff H. D. McMullan, Lieutenant Lewis sent another NCO and five privates to maintain order at Elk Prairie, and in their absence Debitt and McMullan asked Lewis to "assume absolute control of Avery and vicinity." By now the fires were utterly beyond containment. Lewis found himself not only the sole police authority but, with a lone hospital corpsman (without any supplies), its solitary medical institution as well. The four troops dispatched to the Clearwater were reported as "lost." Then the fires closed in from the west.[90]

What happened that extraordinary day holds among the best and murkiest of the recorded stories of the Great Fires. At its center stands Ranger Ralph Debitt. He was 35, had overseen the district for four years, and, in the judgment of Supervisor Weigle, "was thoroughly acquainted with all the conditions which might have led to the protection of the men." Sensing trouble, he claims he dispatched another deputy sheriff, Charles Sullivan, to a crew of seventy on Setzer Creek with instructions for them to flee to safety. Most did; twenty-eight refused, however, insisting there was no danger. That was the reported sum of actions taken and declined.[91]

On 28 August another account appeared in the *Seattle Sunday Times.* Thaddeus Roe, identified as a "forest ranger," vividly described a more militant version. Roe claims that he was on the scene, that he was directing a crew of eighty-two, that as the fires flared into vast pincers around them, he split the lot into two groups, one of twenty-eight men to advance on the fire before them and the rest to keep open "the only remaining avenue of escape" to their rear. By four o'clock that afternoon he realized the fire would simply overrun them and dispatched the eponymously named Ralph Waters, a water boy, to inform the vanguard to retreat. Waters never arrived. Roe and the remaining men began a race with the flames, now on both flanks and threatening to seal off their escape. They ran, and as they ran, the fires narrowed the opening left for their flight. When they broke out, the flanking fires were less than a quarter mile apart and soon closed the gap behind them with a surge. Within its great, compacting ring, squeezing the unburned middle, was the vanguard twenty-eight.[92]

In this stew of unreliable narrators, there is much to doubt about both versions. Debitt's is too sparse, and the assertion that a crew refused to leave because it felt unthreatened requires more proof than he offers. Pickup crews were notoriously skittish. They packed their gear, threw down tools, and hit trails on the slightest provocation. A gust of wind, a distant roar, floating ash (much less firebrands the size of femurs) all were enough to panic gangs of raw laborers. The ones who held their ground were those with strong bosses on the scene. Thaddeus's tale has a ring of truth, or at least of accurate detail conspicuously absent from the too-casual reports of Weigle and Debitt. Still, Roe's Run reads like a passage from Zane Grey and the Sunday supplements, where in fact the story first appeared. If Debitt says too little, omitting facts that should have been known, Roe says too much, sparkling with facts later shown to be in error, some minor, some simply unprovable. The *Times* claimed that Roe entered Avery a spry 32-year-old and today "looks like a man of fifty" with gray streaking his hair; that his arms and legs were "a mass of burns, the scars of which he will carry to his grave"; and that he planned to return to Avery the next day. Yet there is no "Thaddeus Roe" listed on Forest Service rosters, no one of that name filed a claim for medical expenses or disabilities, no one so named appears on the 1910 census for Idaho, Montana, or Washington; there is, apart from his riveting tale, not a shred of evidence that he ever existed. It is at least even money that he is a reporter's composite. But Debitt may have mislaid his fire facts as he did his fire moneys. A "short time" after the Big Blowup, his faulty disbursement (among other "irregularities") resulted in the official request for his resignation.[93]

However they got there, the Lost Crew at Setzer Creek faced the flames alone.

•

AT AVERY A nervous but steadfast Second Lieutenant E. E. Lewis twice a day, until the lines burned down, telegraphed his reports. On the morning of the 21st, the winds had seemed to unite all the fires to the west and a horde of flame—"20 miles of solid fire"—bore down on the tiny town. Ranger Debitt and Deputy Sheriff McMullan traveled on a special engine to inspect the scene. They soon telegraphed Lewis "to get all the women and children out and to notify all the rest of the people" to be ready to flee "at a minute's notice."[94]

The flight barely succeeded. The Milwaukee Railway had already evacuated by special train all the depot towns along its route. On the Montana side, relief trains had orders to pick up every stray soul—it was the forlorn whistle of a Northern Pacific train that Phillips's crew heard from the Bullion Mine fire—and then dash into the Taft Tunnel, which breached the Bitterroots. Probably the trains rescued a thousand people in all. The last fifty or so made it thanks to a volunteer crew with an engine and three freight cars that steamed downgrade from the tunnel and over trestles already aflame. The Avery evacuation proceeded in two special trains, one for women and children, another for men wishing to flee. Soldiers from Company G stood at the doors of each car, the windows were fastened down, the cars filled with water buckets, the seats loaded with refugees in under thirty minutes. "The engineers," Lewis explained, "had orders to make a dash through the fires and the soldiers were instructed, if absolutely cut off on all sides, to take the women and children into the river, keeping them together as well as possible, avoiding a stampede." The wild race with the flames succeeded, though barely, the train dashing to Missoula through countryside deeply burning and over bridges and ties already aflame and with heat peeling the paint off the wooden cars.[95]

What remained was Avery and those who, for whatever reasons, chose to face the flames where they stood. "The fires appeared to be coming in two waves, the smoke, roar and heat preceding the fire for miles," Lewis recalled, "and I am sure no person left ever expected to get out alive." They gave up "all hope" of saving anything. Those who remained gathered in the station to decide upon a course of collective action. Lewis took "no active part" because, as he explained, he "did not know the country and was not familiar with forest fires" and declared simply that "the troops would go with the greatest number of people." Debitt and McMullan decided to march up the St. Joe River and meet the fire head-on, although everyone was permitted to do whatever he believed would best save his life. The "procession" managed but half a mile when its futility became obvious and the throng returned to Avery. It now became, in an orderly sort of way, every man for himself. An old mining tunnel was stocked with provisions and wet blankets, and into it went a "few old men and lame men." As a rail division point Avery had ample trains, and one train, loaded with men, pulled out heading east. They knew that ahead the bridges were burned out and the tunnels collapsed but thought that if they could reach an old burn five miles east, they would survive. Meanwhile Debitt and others grabbed blankets and headed to the river at its fork. Deputy McMullan and Lieutenant Lewis, however, "agreed that the river would not do." They believed as many would drown as burn, and "subsequent events" proved them correct. That left flight west, through the ravenous flames. The two deputies, Company G, and the "remaining citizens" boarded a special train consisting of an engine, flatcar, and boxcar. They broke through the first fire wave but could not penetrate the second and found themselves "caught between the two fires." The scenes of "the fires, the dense, stifling smoke, the intense, blinding heat and the roaring and crackling of the flames were indescribable. The flames seemed to be over a mile and a half high." They traveled back and forth, attempting to break through at some providential pause; none occurred. One fire seemed to be on the north side of the river, a second fire on the south, with a distance of twenty miles of clear track between them. In fact, the track was rarely clear. Rockfalls, rolling logs, and uprooted trees constantly blocked it, and one "fireman was killed while picking rocks off the track." Then the front passed, and the night air turned cold, and the winds weakened.[96]

The defenders of Avery regrouped. Debitt and those who had splashed into the river returned, soon joined by stragglers from the hills. The first flames crested the outlying ridges half a mile away. An operator at the telegraph office sent a final dispatch that "Avery and all in it were doomed." Lewis believed that "nobody" would have considered that he was exaggerating. There was "no escape through both the fires"; there was only the chance of a "last stand at Avery." Everyone, "at different times," held out no hopes of being able to survive the approaching conflagration and "picked their last stands for an existence." Yet they made one final, defiant gesture. They would stand, they determined, behind a backfire. They hoped, as did everyone who set backfires that wild evening, that they could quickly conjure up enough fire that the vast draft of the approaching conflagration would inhale those flames toward it and by thus burning the forest candle at both ends break the furious charge of the fire front.[97]

Around midnight they began burning the town's outlying buildings.

•

ACROSS THE RIDGE, on the east side of Setzer Creek, Ranger William H. Rock, age 25, had a crew variously tallied as 70, 90, or 125 men. The Blowup cut off any retreat to Avery, about six miles distant. With conflagrations all around, the crew simmered with rumor and discontent, but before they bolted in panic, Rock—by sheer "personal magnetism and command"—held them together and led them to a hill previously burned over. There he had them cover their heads with blankets while the tidal wave of flame approached.

In all the commotion, however, two men had become separated from the crew and had managed to wriggle through the twisting flames and stagger into Avery. They were reliable men, known to Debitt, and they reported that they had personally witnessed the fiery end of Ranger Rock and his bold crew. They "described their death struggles so graphically and reasonably" that Debitt forwarded their report to Weigle, who passed along the word that 90 men had perished in one savage gulp.[98]

•

THERE WERE OTHERS besides fire crews, loggers, soldiers, and railmen in the mountains. Homesteaders and miners dappled the slopes and soon found themselves swept along the fire's riptides. Most had watched the skies warily, only too aware of the rhythmic ebb and flow of the flames. Most were not along the smoldering front when the winds arrived to fan them, so had some distance in which to act. They had mine shafts to retreat into, and they had trails to follow, although the fires often set them into motion along with the elk and bears, part of a great cavalcade of creatures in flight before the flames.

With her husband in Wallace, segregated by its ring of fire, Mrs. Speedy Swift and her baby found themselves alone along Placer Creek until they met a band of firefighters, a dozen in all. They made a stand at the Hords Ranch, swatting spot fires and digging line with wet gunnysacks over their heads. The outbuildings and woods burned. They saved the house and themselves. On the upper St. Regis River, Mr. and Mrs. George Cook were working their claim on the Silver Cable mine when the fire blew up and drove them over the divide and sent them on a harrowing thirty-mile trek down Thompson Creek. By hugging the creek, they avoided the worst heat and smoke, which rose as the fire raced by on both sides. They walked all night and the next day and reached Thompson Falls alive. The Pattison party almost survived intact. Mr. and Mrs. E. H. Pattison, along with five men, were at their mine on Sherlock Creek when the fire struck. All but one were able to find a break through the fire front and scramble into a burned patch where they weathered the blowup. They missed only Con Roberts, who had a wooden leg and had lagged behind. The next day they trudged thirty miles to Iron Mountain. A week later a search party discovered the charred, half-consumed body of Roberts.

Near Burke, Mrs. Henry Henderling found herself cut off from her husband, still laboring at the mines, when the word came that the town was sure to burn. She gathered some food and her two children, ages 2 and 3, and met another group, the Dube siblings—Lillian, age 20; Emma, 18; Philip, 23; and Arthur, 19. None knew the way over the mountains, but as they set out, they encountered a mountaineer who volunteered to guide them through. They spent that night in the open, the next day hiking and carrying the children, and the second night in a small cabin near the Arlington Prospector mine. The site burned shortly after they left. They arrived in Thompson at noon. Other refugees, not encumbered by children, were there to greet them. The Sparfeldt family—husband, wife, and young child—had a more terrifying exodus. Incredibly, they were on a camping trip outside Avery when the pincers fires that set off Roe's Run finally alarmed them. By the time they reached town, it was deserted. The relief trains had departed with the women and children; the able-bodied men clustered on the fireline. The Sparfeldts were offered refuge in a miner's cabin and accepted it. Then the flames reached them and sent them on a dash for the relative openness of the railroad right-of-way. Surface fires overtook them and burned away Mrs. Sparfeldt's skirt. She fainted on the embankment and was revived only after her husband hauled her to a creek and doused her with water.[99]

Yet the Big Blowup was not a fire that threatened settlers in the classic frontier tradition. Undoubtedly more died than the five officially recorded, but those numbers are small compared with conflagrations in the Lake States or even the 1902 fires in the Northwest. The reason is that the land was sparsely settled; it was public land, inhabited primarily by those with contracts for logging, mining, or railway construction; and the federal government in the form of the Forest Service had responsibility for fire protection. Almost uniquely among fire histories, those who perished were firefighters. They were the ones next to the flames, and they were there by choice, although it was very likely that few understood the choice they were making.

•

WALLACE HAD BEEN waiting for weeks. Twenty years before, it had burned, and the hills with it. Now, over and again, newspapers had forecast the imminent immolation of the town, only to have the winds sink or veer away and spare it, the largest entrepôt in the Coeur d'Alene. So apparent was the threat, and so lucky the residents, that insurance companies found themselves swamped on 14 August after awnings had caught fire from brands flung from flare-ups many miles away. They sold policies to everyone and, incredibly, continued to do so until noon on 20 August, when Wallace first felt the blast of the great winds. But the town, nudged against the mountains, deep in a valley, believed its luck would hold, that fires would hug the crest of the mountains, that flames and firebrands would leap across the ridges and spare the buildings below. As with the crews along the gulches, some townsfolk panicked, some prayed, some prepared.

As the afternoon wore on, the skies darkened, drizzles of ash and embers rained down, and scores of residents pondered what the Blowup meant for those—many of them friends or spouses—who stood in the mountains before it. Around 3:30 P.M. Company I, Twenty-fifth Infantry, deep in the hills, retreated from its overrun trails, at 5 P.M. broke field camp, just before the fires obliterated it, reestablished camp in the ballpark at Wallace, and there waited for duty as assigned. By 6:30 P.M. the winds had freshened, and by 7 P.M. they roared with gale force. By now it was unmistakable to all that the town would burn, somehow, somewhere. A great thunderhead of smoke towered above, leering over the crest of the high hills that framed Wallace to the west. Townsfolk heard a roar like "the sound of a storm at sea." The city prepared to fight and flee.[100]

The town became a flurry of bustle and confusion. What happened, for all the blurring of the details, is that flames crested on the western hills and spot fires ignited buildings on the east side of town, that relief trains pulled out for Missoula and Spokane, that some viewed the scene with horror and escaped while others scoffed at the danger and scorned those who fled. The classic accounts of citizen panic appeared in the *Seattle Daily Times,* which ran an extra edition and quoted Carl Getz, an evacuee, that the burning of Wallace was "horrible beyond words, and yet magnificent." Getz claimed he had been at the fire front and, when it collapsed, had joined the "mad rush," a riptide of townsfolk, to the trains. He had experienced "panics before" but what he witnessed at Wallace "was the worst I have ever seen. Men, women and children rushing through the streets helter-skelter . . . the buildings steaming . . . the flaring light of the fire . . .

▲ *Gifford Pinchot, served 1898–1910. Pinchot relished his close association with Theodore Roosevelt* (left) *and recalled fondly the time, when boxing, he knocked the president off "his very solid pins." When Taft denied that same freedom of access, Pinchot knocked the Taft administration senseless as well. He became an active commentator on the Great Fires.*

▲ *Henry Graves, 1910–1920.*

▲ *William Greeley, 1920–1928.*

*Not pictured: R. Y. Stuart, 1928–1933, the night-shift supervisor in the Missoula office during the 1910 campaign.*

◀ *Ferdinand Silcox, 1933-1939.*

▲ *Rangers or guards rode to prominent peaks like Mount Silcox, shown here, and surveyed for smoke. This worked fine when the skies were clear but proved ineffective in the vast smoke palls that characterized periods of stagnant air. A single guard could have responsibility, on average, for 450 to 670 square miles.*

▼ *Most fires started along railways, which were regularly patrolled by guards on velocipedes, or "speeders," like this one in North Carolina.*

HOW THE FIRES WERE FOUGHT

▲ *One could beat out the flames in light fuels—grasses, some sparse needle mats—with a blanket or burlap sack. In heavier landscapes, one had to scrape a fuel-free line around the flames and then set backfires.*

THE "INDIAN WAY"

▲ *October underburning in northern California, typical of the piddling fall fires that were the goal of light burners, probably photographed during Graves's inspection of Walker lands. Foresters found such practices even more threatening than conflagrations.*

## THE BIG BLOWUP

▲ *Ferocious winds caused intense burning and blowdown near Falcon, Idaho, close to the crest of the Bitterroots. Note the circular pattern of the blown trees, indicating powerful tornadic vortices.*

## THE BEAUCHAMP DEBACLE

▲ *The homestead of Joe Beauchamp before the fire.*

▲ *The Beauchamp homestead, from a somewhat different angle, after the burn. The large tree is likely the pine that crushed two men and trapped a third.*

▸ *The infamous root cellar* (bottom center) *into which seven men clawed their way and died.*

## THE BURNING OF WALLACE, IDAHO

▲ *The eastern third of the town burned after firebrands ignited a gasoline storage tank. The fire approached the town from the west, over the mountains in the background.*

## THE SAGA OF ED PULASKI

▲ *Ranger Ed Pulaski in September 1910.*

▲ *West Fork of Placer Creek, down which Pulaski led his crew to the Nicholson adit. Pulaski took this photograph.*

▲ *William Morris in front of the Nicholson adit.*

▲ *Closeup of the Nicholson adit, showing saddles, blankets, shirts, and hats amid the charred timbers.*

▼ *Emma Pulaski, visiting the entrance.*

▲ *A jaunty Joe Halm atop the blowdown.*

▸ *Elers Koch, an accomplished horseman, in the statuesque pose he preferred.*

▲ *Mealtime at a typical fire camp.*

◀ *Pack trains leaving Avery.*

◀ *En route to the front in the Bitterroot Mountains.*

▲ *Ranger Ralph Debitt* (in the white shirt and tie) *and fire crew, ready with a pack string.*

◀ *Ranger Debitt* (far left) *and troops of Company G, 25th Infantry.*

## "AND AFTER THE FIRE . . ."

▶ *Photographing the damage. R. H. McKay* (right), *a Service photographer from Missoula, and Joe Halm at the entry to the Nicholson adit.*

▶▶ *Opening trails through jackstraw blowdown.*

▲ *The towns of Baudette and Spooner, Minnesota, before the fire and after.*

SALVAGE

▲ *Locomotive hauling out the felled snags.*

*The Great Fires dictated forest operations for decades after 1910.* ▲ *Crews retooled from cutting firelines to felling timber to planting seedlings. Eventually the more accessible lands were restocked with millions of trees.*

▼ *The remote sites resembled fire camps and required arduous resupply programs.*

▲ *Intense burning along the railway through the St. Regis Valley.*

▼ *The same scene nineteen years later, thirteen years after replanting.*

▲ *Temporary grave, Big Creek.*

▼ *Firefighters' circle, Woodlawn Cemetery, St. Maries, Idaho.*

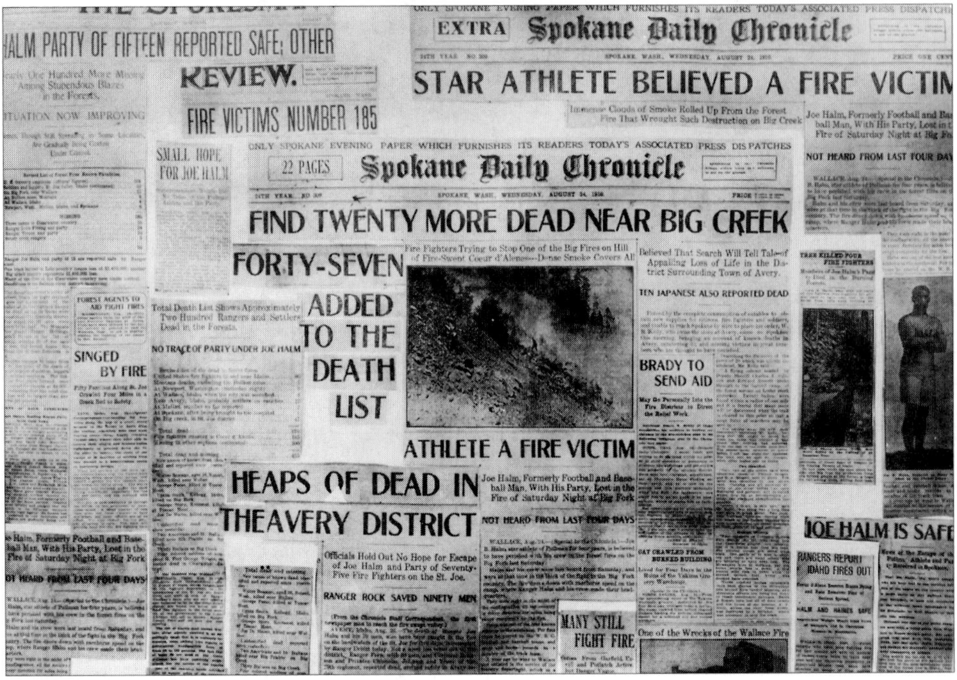

HALM PARTY OF FIFTEEN REPORTED SAFE; OTHER

REVIEW.

FIRE VICTIMS NUMBER 185

EXTRA Spokane Daily Chronicle

STAR ATHLETE BELIEVED A FIRE VICTIM

ONLY SPOKANE EVENING PAPER WHICH FURNISHES ITS READERS TODAY'S ASSOCIATED PRESS DISPATCHES

22 PAGES Spokane Daily Chronicle

FIND TWENTY MORE DEAD NEAR BIG CREEK

FORTY-SEVEN ADDED TO THE DEATH LIST

SMALL HOPE FOR JOE HALM

SINGED BY FIRE

NOT HEARD FROM LAST FOUR DAYS

TEN JAPANESE ALSO REPORTED DEAD

BRADY TO SEND AID

ATHLETE A FIRE VICTIM

HEAPS OF DEAD IN THE AVERY DISTRICT

RANGER ROCK SAVED NINETY MEN

MANY STILL FIGHT FIRE

JOE HALM IS SAFE

One of the Wrecks of the Wallace Fire

▲ *A sampling of front-page reporting from Spokane. Note the obsession with Joe Halm, the only ranger known to a wider public. The deeper story of the Great Fires would take years to sort out.*

THE CARTOGRAPHY OF CATASTROPHE

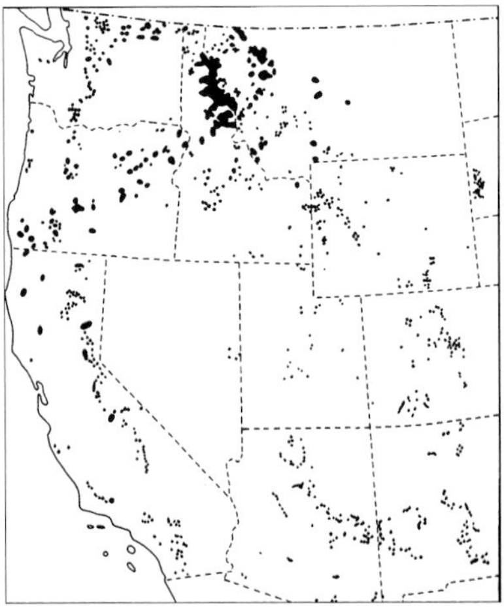

▲ *The fires, great and small, of 1910 as they registered on national forest lands in the West. State, private, and other federal lands are not included; a full reckoning of the year's burning could easily double or triple the total area. For other regions, notably the Lake States, 1910 was also a record-setting year.*

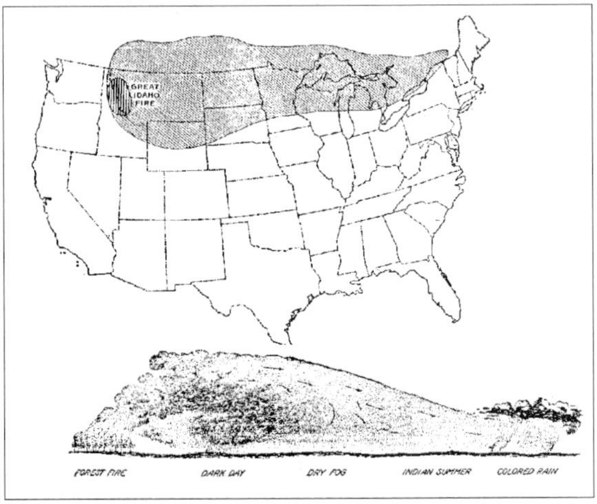


▲ *The track of the visible smoke from the Big Blowup, along with a record of the kinds of atmospheric effects the pall produced, from dark days to coppery suns. In fact, the thinning smoke extended over New England and dropped soot onto the ice of Greenland.*

the intense heat. . . ." Words, he continued, "cannot depict the horror of that night. The train whistles were screaming, the heavy boom of falling trees and buildings, the crackle of the fire, the buildings were swaying and steaming from the heat. . . ."[101]

Others told a less breathless story. When the fire crested, Mildred Hord Mellinger, then 13, was living with her parents in west Wallace. "We were not panicky," she recalled sixty years later, "and of course we didn't want to leave our home unless we had to as a last resort." She spoke of the Roach family, living in the line of fire, who were warned to leave but did so only after Mrs. Roach had seen that they had bathed, dressed in their finest, and scrubbed their teeth. While the Hords ate dinner, the wind swung cups on the dining room hooks. At last her father announced that trains were waiting to take the women and children away. Her grandmother and mother both refused to leave without their husbands, so Frank Hord put everyone into a horse-drawn wagon and hauled them to a rocky hummock known as the Tailing Pile. There they joined four other families and "watched the town burn." One couple sat quietly, the husband's arm around his wife, his wife clutching a satchel with all their possessions, while the flames destroyed their home. When the wind shifted, the fire blew back on itself and ended the burning of Wallace. The Hords returned for a second night on the pile, however, so hot was the town and so fearful was everyone about a flare-up. That night was far worse: more smoke, smarting eyes, difficult breathing, "dreadfully dark." Mildred was frightened, but of the locomotives that screeched and snorted nearby, not the fire. The Hords suffered a major loss when the fire burned into a load of uninsured coal that remained by the side of the tracks.[102]

By then 12-year-old Marie Alger, living in Osburn, was writing her grandparents with stories from refugees who were staying with her family. They said the fire was "simply terrible. The fire was so great the whole town was lighted up as at noonday; the roaring of it so loud it could be heard for five miles or more; and the wind so strong it broke and shattered the limbs of the trees. Many people were so frightened they left their homes with doors wide open and lights burning, carrying valuable dogs and cats with them. . . ." The Algers visited Wallace soon afterward and toured the burned district, the fraction along the town's eastern edge. "In some brick buildings the walls only were left standing, while nothing was left of the wood buildings. Of the furniture there was nothing left but the iron and steel parts, and those were sadly out of shape. All glassware was melted; apples were baked on the trees. We saw a roasted horse and cat. They were just as much roasted as if they had been in an oven."[103]

But mostly Wallace survived. It survived because of backfiring along the western and southern flanks, because citizens had wetted houses and lawns and fought fires on the roofs of buildings, because the fire chief led a strong fight, and because the front passed and the winds reversed and rushed from the north. The critical event occurred when the wooden building housing the *Press-Times* caught fire and the flames exploded gasoline stored there. Once the surrounding structures became involved, the fire blew out of control, driven east by the winds. Wallace survived because civil order never broke down, as either feared or rumored. John G. Boyd died when he rushed into his burning house to rescue his parrot. Possibly two others burned as well. There was likely less confusion in the town proper than in the outside world regarding the notorious Burning of Wallace, and certainly less controversy.[104]

Reportedly Mayor Walter Hanson had assumed control over the police department, deputized all able-bodied men not fighting fire, and armed them to prevent looting. Whether any occurred is hard to say, but the threat was perceived as real, and Mayor Hanson, as did the fire chief, turned to Company I, still sited on the ballpark. Certainly troopers assisted with firefighting. But ever-sensational newspapers claimed they might also be firing on citizens. Press dispatches from Spokane reported that the mayor had instructed the troops to shoot vandals, "whose depredations have become serious." The rumors sped to Washington, where the adjutant general shot back a telegram to the commanding general, Department of the Dakota, demanding that he "ascertain facts and take prompt measures to prevent this, or any similar violation of law by troops in your department. Provisions of article forty-eight Army Regulations must be enforced." There is no evidence that in fact it had been violated, any more than that Wallace had burned to ash with the loss of hundreds of lives.[105]

By the second day, however, Governor James Brady ordered out the Idaho militia from its American Lake maneuvers with the understanding that they would assist.[106]

•

PERHAPS THE MOST nerveracking moments, however, fell to those who watched and waited. Not everyone on the line was a hobo, stewbum, or floater. There were husbands, fathers, brothers, and sons on the lines, there because it was their job and their pride to beat back the flames before the fires could reach their families. They were men like Ed Pulaski, whose wife now peered into the pall.

Emma Pulaski was older than her husband by four to six years. She had grown up in Michigan and had "never heard of a forest ranger" but soon learned the joys and trials of that life. On the 19th, when Ed was gathering supplies, he visited her at their home and gave instructions for what to do when the fire arrived. "Wallace will surely burn," he told her, "so be prepared to save yourselves." While they talked, Weigle burst in and told of yet another fire that Pulaski would have to attend to.[107]

When he set off on the morning of the 20th, Emma and daughter Elsie went with him up Placer Creek until the road ended. "Mr. Pulaski said good bye I may never see you again he went up the mountain and we started home." Ed Pulaski and a packer began their trek up the West Fork to the summits where the smoky thunderheads were building. The drive home was harrowing. The flames were on the mountains, and the smoke caused their eyes to smart. They also crossed paths with a black bear that frightened the horse. Emma told Elsie that the creature was a large dog, but Elsie knew better and, after they reached home, told her mother so and added that Emma "looked scared." Emma replied, "It is all right now dear God took care of us." But the omens built all day. Ashes and moss and burning bark eighteen inches long fell into their yard, and Emma was sure they had not seen the worst of the fire and fretted that her husband and his men were "right in the middle of it." The wind blew a hurricane and rattled their house. The air swarmed with cinders and glowing needles. They watched the smoke roll over the hills and waited for the flames.[108]

At 8:30 P.M. Emma put Elsie to bed and lay beside her with a "sick headache" from the strain. A neighbor arrived and told her she would have to leave and could join the others who were gathering on the tailings dam with all the belongings they could lug, even furniture. She replied that they would not leave until they saw the flames. Half an hour later she did. They soared hundreds of feet upward and shot down "like great streaks of lightning." The flames "leaped from one mountain to another as though the whole world was afire." She knew that her husband was "some where in those burning mountains and all though he knew every foot of the ground and could have saved himself, I knew he would not desert his men and would save them or die with them. . . . I told Elsie to ask God to save daddy and his men, which she did in her childish way."[109]

They huddled all night on the tailings dam and watched "one of the most realistic fire works display we ever saw in our lives and one I never wish to see again. Though beautiful, most terribly cruel."[110]

•

THE LONG-SUFFERING and indefatigable William Weigle worried too. He knew he had crews under the firestorm—he had sent them there—so that afternoon he mounted his horse to probe up Placer Creek, the feisty stream whose narrow valley led from Wallace into the mountains. The trail to Pulaski's crews on Striped Peak veered up the West Fork. But there were others in the field as well, so Weigle pushed up the main trail south.[111]

There he found himself cut off by fire behind him. Perhaps that fire had kindled from the rain of firebrands, or perhaps it was one of the backfires strung along the edge of Wallace, a ring of fire that shut the town off from the mountains so that little could leave or enter. If it stymied the flaming front, it also blocked anyone fleeing those wild flames. For the moment Weigle was trapped. He rushed into and through a nearby mining mill, then burning, and darted into its tunnel. The building fell behind him, and the tunnel partly collapsed as a result. With his coat over his head, he crawled through the debris of the cave-in, then through the still-burning wreckage of the mill, and finally into a tiny creek. There he stayed until the fire had passed and the ash cooled sufficiently to walk. The hard-pressing flames had scorched his clothes and eyebrows.

Thus the supervisor of the forest hardest hit by the Big Blowup, a man with 1,800 firefighters and two companies of Army infantry under his control, the man who in practice was the fire chief of the Coeur d'Alene, found himself, during the height of the inferno, holed up and completely isolated from all contact. No one could query him, nor he others. It was nearly midnight when he left for Wallace. He arrived about 2 A.M. to find the town burning. An hour later a man staggered past the blazing buildings with the word that Ed Pulaski and his crew were dead.

•

THEY HAD MET, Stewart and Pulaski, beside the trail down the West Fork. The revived fire had scattered the crews along the ridge.

Those on the west side could squirm past the freshening flames or sprint to shelter at the Beauchamp homestead. Those on the east side could not. A cook set up a small spike camp, and most milled around it. But others were wandering, feebly looking for sanctuaries or stumbling down the trail to Wallace. They were a mob, their tools tossed to the side.

That was the scene when Ed Pulaski rode up. It was impossible to stay; they would die where they stood. Equally, it was doubtful that they could outrun the fire into Wallace. Yet a dash, leap, stumble, or crawl down the canyon of the West Fork seemed their best hope. "Boys, it's no use," Pulaski announced, "we've got to dig out of here, we got to try to make Wallace, that's our only chance." They would return the way he had just come, down the steep trail along the West Fork, through unburned forests, some still recovering from the 1889 fires, gambling that in a dash down the ravine they could outrun the flames cresting the ridge. Already its smoke blotted out the sun and made day into night, inspiring some crewmen to carry candles set in cans. Pulaski gave his horse to S. W. Stockton, a former Texas Ranger, now 44 years old and afflicted with rheumatism. They picked up stragglers as they plunged down the slopes, Pulaski eventually guiding a crew of forty-five men whose names he hardly knew, whose faces he could scarcely recognize, of whose very number he had only a vague idea.[112]

What happened next is murky, the narrative line twisted in smoke swirls. But then very little about the Big Blowup is clear. Facts vanished like pine needles in the firewhirls. Reports went missing; reports were never filed; reports varied; reports contradicted one another; accounts invented and passed along rumors; accounts written a year or even thirty years afterward are full of events forgotten, suppressed, embellished. Probably nowhere is that truer than with the Pulaski saga, a story that attracted more accounts over more years than any other, and so holds more ambiguities, lapses, and contrary details, and became encrusted with the barnacles of self-serving memory. By the time some members like F. R. Foltz and William Chance wrote versions, the story had become legend. Where the scattered men first gathered, how they collected together, where the fire came that cut them off from Placer Creek, how one man went missing, what happened at the tunnel entrance when the flames blasted, what mix of force, urging, fear, and sheer presence led them are not just unknown but probably unknowable. Nearly everyone misidentified even the name of the mine they fled into. What remains is the raw deeds. What remains is a handful of indestructible facts and the pith of a narrative.[113]

That narrative goes like this. The fire threatened to outflank them, breaking into streamers along both slopes leading into the creek. It was also spotting, kindling fires to all sides, dissolving the flaming front into an irrational thicket. They advanced but haltingly, as Pulaski would dash ahead to scout the way and then return to lead the terrified group to the next post. They fled, as one put it, like "scared rabbits." The only thing that held that flighty band together was the hard reality that they did not know the trail; that once off it, they knew they would die. They slogged ahead until they reached a short mine shaft, the JIC adit, and Pulaski ordered everyone inside. Already he was hoarse from shouting over the din of the fire and had to govern by gestures. The man who took pride in what he could make with his hands now used those hands to lead. The crew huddled in the tunnel while Pulaski, with a wet gunnysack over his head, moved off.

Here the story dissolves into shards. The core facts are these: Pulaski left; Pulaski returned and herded the men into a larger tunnel farther down the creek; Pulaski guarded the entrance of that mine adit when the firestorm struck. The pause created uncertainty. Perhaps he thought (as Stewart believed) the men were as well protected in the first mine shaft as anywhere he could get them before the flames overran them. Perhaps he was determined to reach his home before the fire did, even if it meant a risky dash through the flames. Perhaps he was making one more, longer probe ahead to scout out a better sanctuary and test the fury of the fire before leading his crew on. Perhaps no one, least of all Ed Pulaski, had any deep, much less rational, conception of what was happening and why. Their lives hung on a gasp, by instincts rendered in seconds. None of them had lived through such a scene before. Their world was imploding into a narrow ravine, a shallow creek, mining-scarred slopes, a black fog of soot and smoke, and a fire that screamed with a roar, as one man put it, of a thousand trains rushing over a thousand steel trestles. The fact is, Pulaski beckoned them onward, and they obeyed.[114]

The final dash was a horror. Only the fact that they were trailing the creek, tucked into the ravine, while the flames raced with the wind along the upper contours of the slopes, likely spared them from being instantly incinerated. By now the fire was around them, and the winds bellowing like thunder, and the embers thick as snowflakes. The tortured winds snapped off giant cedars and hurled them across the hills. Amid the darkness, the roar, the broken rhythms of spot fires, trees torching and tossing, the crew became almost senseless. They could neither hear nor speak nor see nor taste nor barely feel. They clung to one another and ran and stumbled along the trail, only because that took less thought than anything else they might do. Richard Wood lagged and died, possibly crushed by a flaming tree. Along the way a bear joined the cavalcade. Finally they halted, with the fires in front of and to all sides of them. The fire before them was likely the same that had hounded Weigle to shelter, not unlikely the backfire from Wallace or the old flaming edge now driven south by passage of the cold front. Whatever its origins, the shifting winds were driving the flames across their path. They were cut off. They could run no more. Instantly Pulaski led the remaining forty-four men and two horses into the Nicholson tunnel, a shaft 75 to 80 feet deep, barely the height of a man, with a trickle of water running through it. Even time had imploded. Within seconds the flames were upon them.[115]

Their black hole magnified the fire's horrors. Smoke rushed in; flames blazed outside the entrance and struck the timbers. The crew retreated as far back as possible, hugging the ground near the trickle of water, the men packed into the narrow passage like oats in a feedbag, while Pulaski tried to beat out the flames at the entrance with a horse blanket and a hatful of water and while others may have tried to hold blankets over the opening until the heat blistered their hands. Inside, with their fresh air shrinking and their fears swelling, the men showed the usual palette of praying, cursing, and encouraging. One man began to scream, "Oh, Lord!" Another shouted that they were doomed and were going to die. Several cried they could take no more. Then one man, and perhaps others, yelled that he at least was getting out and pushed to the entry.

There, in a murky silhouette against the flames, he met Big Ed Pulaski, pistol in hand, who said he would shoot the first man who tried to leave.

•

THE WINDS THAT had lifted men from their saddles on 20 August had blown from the southwest. As the front passed, they veered to the northwest. Places threatened by fire from the south now saw those flames driven away and along the north flank, back upon themselves.

The winds were brisk and cold, and gradually, over several days, they began to subside. The wreckage was immense. Regional newspapers trumpeted 400 dead and whole towns incinerated. No one knew the full scope of the disaster because those most affected were far from telephones and telegraphs and burrowed into tunnels and lying on burned-over hills isolated by miles and miles of trails now jackstrawed with immense trees. Word came from stragglers, who told what they saw, all of it horrible, much of it wrong. Days passed before relief parties made a final tally. The flames had scattered a thousand men like pine seeds. Loved ones waited for the news.

At 11:59 P.M. on 21 August, Will Morris had fought his way out of the hills long enough to reach a phone and have Supervisor Weigle send a telegram to his father in Chicago: "Safe and sound no danger."[116]

•

ON BEAN CREEK Joe Halm's crew spent a furious night in cold water and gravel. Firebrands and falling trees made it impossible to cower under their blankets, so they used buckets to splash creek water on the flames around themselves. They dodged falling trunks and showering sparks. Their clothing steamed and smoked. But gradually the flaming front passed, leaving a "hideous red glare" all around and a seeping chill that went to the bone. Weirdly, they passed the night wrapped in sopping blankets trying to find a place next to a still-burning log for warmth.[117]

For the first time in weeks, dawn broke free of smoke. The devastation extended in all directions. "Miles of trees—sturdy, forest giants—were laid prone. Only the smaller trees stood, stripped and broken." Halm gave inward thanks that he was alive, that they all were alive, and wondered what had become of the two packers. A cook had rustled a breakfast of sorts, rich with fried ham and coffee. Stiffly the men gathered around, as if in a huddle. The foreman asked Halm what his plans were, and the athlete whose motto was "Cheer up Joe Bunch your [*sic*] not dead yet" announced: "First, we'll dig out our tent, salvage the grub, and then look the fire over. We'll order more men and equipment and hit the fire again."[118]

•

AT THE BEAUCHAMP homestead, three men had died beneath a fallen pine, while seven, Beauchamp among them, had scrambled into a small cave, a root cellar dug to store provisions. They had fought to cram themselves into a space that promised some shelter from the heat, packed like putty. But when the flames arrived, the heat was too intense, and the men tried to exit, only to find that they were so tightly jammed that they could not escape, and though they fought and screamed and clawed and suffocated with fists clenched, they died like trapped rats. The cooked bodies pulled apart when rescuers later tried to extract them. Those who spread themselves out in the clearing and across the creek had their hair burned off and the exposed skin of their necks scorched, and they nearly choked on the foul air. But safe from direct contact with trees, flames, and one another, they lived.[119]

•

AT THE BULLION MINE the great throng crowded in the side shaft, huddling behind the blankets that separated them from the main tunnel. In stygian darkness, the roar of the fire front muffled, they waited. Outside that sanctuary, strewn through the stone and smoke of the main shaft, the separated eight still stumbled. Then they died where they fell.[120]

•

ALL NINETEEN MEN shoved their way into the Dittman cabin along the west fork of Big Creek. Then the roof caught fire, and dribbling sparks began to cave in. One by one the men scrambled out, each following right on the heels of the other. The first eighteen out the door fell dead in a heap from the scorching heat within paces of the cabin. The nineteenth, Peter Kinsley, stumbled while crossing the threshold and wrenched his ankle. He dropped to the ground, found something resembling fresh air, and crawled his way to a small creek. The heat blistered his hands and face, almost stripping off the skin, and burned away most of his clothing. For two days he worked his way down the creek for sixteen miles to the St. Joe River, where he was rescued. The scars around his eyes later required surgery.[121]

The main crew, hunkered down on an old burn, witnessed, to their shock and dismay, a reburn through the conifer crowns. Those with exposed skin had their hands and face scorched. But they lived. When fire guard Lee Hollingshead arrived at the ash heap that had once been the Dittman cabin, he found eighteen men, five horses, and two black bears dead outside. There was, he reported, "absolutely no identification on any body."[122]

•

ON BIG CREEK the logging crews cowered beneath the large rock. There were plenty of "white and drawn" faces, Arthur Hogue recalled. But plenty too who stood unflinching and some among them who even joked. Their backfire, however, broke the shock of the fire front. For two hours they stayed in the creek, perhaps half an hour under wet blankets.

About 9:30 P.M. the worst had passed, and the foremen slipped out, one by one, to scout the scene. They worried that if they all left as a bunch, the men would panic again. At Camp Four they found a full meal, cooked and sitting in big pots, waiting: boiled ham, cabbage, beans, and potatoes. They pressed on to Camp One, five miles away. They passed through hot areas, then met a rescue party waiting for the flames to cool. All the men got out safely. The next day Camp One burned. The fires cleaned the valley out. All six camps burned. The cruised and surveyed timber was charred and blown flat. But the danger had finally ended because as Hogue said simply, "All the country is all burned over."[123]

•

THE EARLY REPORTS on the cremation of Ranger Rock north of Avery proved premature. The crew had pulled through, galvanized by his stand, though all were variously terrorized by the experience. The torching trees and streamers of ignited gases bursting across the night sky had awed and frightened them all, but the spectacle had unhinged Oscar Weigert. Later, critics asserted that he should never have been hired, that he was too mentally unstable, that he was a risk on the line. In fact, he proved a risk only to himself. Convinced he was about to burn to death, he slunk off and shot himself twice in the chest. Out of Rock's crew of ninety, his was the only death.[124]

•

DANIELSON'S DARING BURNOUT only partly succeeded. Accounts vary on what happened. The bunchy bear grass perhaps required more ignition than the crew had given it or had time for. The burn proved patchy rather than clean, and the surrounding crown fire flung sheets of scorching, deadly air up the slopes and over their location. Whatever the blankets failed to cover of face and hand, the intense heat blistered. Many tried to save their faces by sacrificing their hands to block the flames. One man died when he bolted upright and inhaled the searing, perhaps fiery wind. Another, Claude Fanning, nearly perished when he stumbled on the track, "knocked insenseless by the extreme heat," and then burned when he fell and was nearly buried beneath falling debris until pulled free. The others suffered, wretchedly burned, yet lived.[125]

That was the official story. Will Morris heard another: that they had "backfired about forty acres on the Mullan road, when the big fire that swept over Wallace struck. . . . The fire went on either side of them all right, but a sudden shift of the wind blew the fire onto them. They ran in all directions, and one man ran towards the fire and fell unconscious. He never regained consciousness, and his remains were found the next morning." Possibly they were undone by the frontal passage; the same wind shift that spared Wallace, Mullan, and Saltese turned lethal on the slopes of Stevens Peak.[126]

Writing with hands too tender to hold a pencil for long, Danielson later told his story this way:

> Try if you can to place yourself at the head of twenty green men with your goal which you had expected no fire could touch, because of its rocky formation, completely covered with flames. Picture yourself holding up a courage which was superficial to yourself, but to the followers made you their leader. Now picture yourself rushing at 11 P.M. to a shallow rock cut continually warning the men that there was no need for alarm, when you knew that you might never see the break of the coming day. I say picture again twenty men at the only haven for miles around, gazing on a fire thirty miles wide, approaching at times with a speed of a train, and as it came near men half mad with fright wishing to leave the place in order to reach some fancied security, but the worst has not yet come. Imagine, if you can, the wind suddenly changing, the rock cut filled with sparks more dense than any skyrocket that could be shot off in your face, with a temperature that in an instant cooked every exposed part of one's body, with only a moment to realize your condition and then fall down unconscious, and then as if this were not enough misfortune, awake to find your clothes half burned off, men crazy with pain, some wanting to commit suicide, some wishing to leave through fire and smoke and darkness for Mullan, others throwing their arms around you begging for God's sake that you better their condition. This I say with the three hours' wait until daylight came and the long tramp to Mullan over burned debris is enough to

> weaken any man's mental as well as physical conditions. Many times I could hardly withhold the cries of pain which came from my whole system. Many times men nearly parted from the rest of the crew, but with my utmost power I was able to keep the crew together.[127]

Either version left the men badly burned. So scorched that he could walk only by holding his arms out to his sides, his neck and ears purple with blisters and his fingernails burned off, Danielson trudged into Mullan, five miles away.

•

DEEP IN ITS valley, Avery remained surrounded by a double arc of flame. The wildfires that burned south and north were still approaching relentlessly down the slopes, while the midnight backfires kindled as a last gesture against them struggled boldly out against them. But all remained oddly calm in the predawn amid the lulled winds. At 5:30 A.M. Lieutenant Lewis managed to maneuver his troop back to town and readied the place for the renewed assault that was sure to follow. Ranger Debitt had meanwhile taken a party to Kyle and remained cut off all day save for a still-working telegraph line. (His sole instruction: "If forty-nine still selling booze place guard to prevent it.") Lewis readied Avery. "Pools were dug and filled with water and barrels were filled and placed near buildings. All water carts were filled and men were placed all over the buildings to guard against sparks. Bucket brigades were organized." They gathered the empty rail cars together.[128]

The wind shift had dampened somewhat the threat from the south fire while strengthening that from the north. All day the winds picked up, and at 3 P.M. the three fires met in a wild, violent collision. Miraculously, at just this instant, the general winds "suddenly died out." Had they not, had the backfire not pushed outward the border of the fire front, Lewis was convinced that "nothing could have saved the town or people." The converging flames, in an orgy of self-immolation, quickly burned out all that could sustain them. An exhausted Lieutenant Lewis recorded a "universal rejoicing." Two hours later the telegraph lines were restored. An hour beyond that Captain George J. Holden arrived by train from the west to assume command. The next morning Major E. A. Dean of the medical corps and four hospital corpsmen arrived as well.[129]

The siege of Avery had lifted.

•

Two of his crew, his packers, were still missing, Halm realized. With the foreman, he set off to track them down. The supply camp where they had parted was a seared ruin. They plunged onward to the next camp, also a smoking wreck. Half a mile beyond they found the charred remains of a pack saddle, then a second, then the remnants of a horse, then more saddles and horses. By now they had chased the fire front far enough that the ash was still hot and residual flames were considerable, and as night settled, they elected to return for help. The wind rose, however, the fires renewed, and trees fell like wood chips. Halm probed ahead through the tangle of burning jackstraw while the foreman spotted for falling snags. Along a ledge a giant tree toppled and began to roll downslope toward them. They dashed headlong and nearly passed their camp in the rush.

The next day the whole crew pushed on, slashing open the trail, watching for the packers. They passed dead elk, deer, grouse, and fish floating in the sour, ashy waters. Drinking from the streams made them "deathly sick." Day after day they continued, with never a clue as to the packers. Not until they met a relief crew did they learn the story. The two men had fled before the flames, saving only a saddle mare, one holding her head, the other her tail. Incredibly, they outraced the flames to the summit of the Bitterroots, where the fire, starved of fuel, faltered. On they ran until they came to a small cabin and fell asleep. Two hours later the whinnying horse wakened them. The fire had caught up with them, and their run began anew. After two miles they came to an old placer and found safety amid the gravel. The fire swept past. By their reckoning they had traveled forty miles in six hours. They were among the very few that day who outran the flames.[130]

•

These men at least had a story to tell; the crew at Setzer Creek had none. Some twenty-eight men had remained behind; why, is not at all clear. Weigle's official report says they had dismissed the warning given them, though just when Debitt dispatched Deputy Sullivan is unclear. Lieutenant Lewis claims there was no civil police present until Deputy McMullan arrived on the morning of the 21st; he says nothing about Deputy Sullivan who likely arrived still later. The perhaps fictitious Roe maintains the Lost Crew had gone, under orders, to the fire front and never received the alert carried by young Waters, whose scorched body was later found short of the old fireline near a stream. Waters's death appears nowhere in the official records, though neither does the firefighter killed while removing rocks from the abortive train expedition.

When, two days after the Blowup, an Army search party discovered all twenty-eight of the Lost Crew, every single one was burned beyond recognition. They had apparently retreated up the ravine, seeking the high ground and collapsing their protective ring into a shrinking core, finally less than thirty feet wide, a last stand against the flames. This, the greatest single disaster of the Big Blowup, is the least understood, and it merited, in Supervisor Weigle's summary report, the briefest mention. Every other catastrophe had at least one survivor, one witness; most had several, often contradictory. The Lost Crew had none. The Forest Service dismissed it with odd, almost eager indifference.

The search party did not, however. It included a dozen members of Company G, four of whose comrades the fires had scattered and were still missing in action. Perhaps they were thinking of those four; perhaps they just had some sense of propriety. Regardless, the troopers dug a sixty-foot trench, wrapped the bodies in blankets, tagged each according to the number of its discovery, sewed them into heavy canvas, and laid them into the common grave. Then they fired a volley over the open pit, and as the dirt and ash were shoveled in, a bugler blew taps.[131]

•

THEY ALL HAD passed out. Yet one, and perhaps another, had suffered less, and when he came to some five hours after the crew had crammed into the tunnel, he managed to crawl out of the scorched timbers of the Nicholson adit, over the body of Ed Pulaski, and began a long, stumbling trek to Wallace. It was he who arrived at 3 A.M. and passed the word to Weigle that all, save himself, had perished. Quickly, with the flames dying down, Weigle organized a relief party. By the time they arrived, others in the tunnel—not dead, indeed—had roused themselves.

In the smoky darkness of the predawn, someone coughed out a cry to "Come outside, boys, the boss is dead." Out of a haze, Pulaski replied, "Like hell he is." He elbowed himself up and felt something like fresh air and sensed his return to consciousness. His lungs were a mess, his eyes almost useless. Those inside the adit were little better off. Charles Webb awoke in the muck, stench, smoke, and welter of bodies and tried to assist a nearby man more helpless than himself. He passed out again and woke up with "rocks falling on me this time was too weak to get up and I said to my self it's all over I am gone." The next time he woke a rock struck him in the head and knocked him into a pool of water "which had been dammed I believe by some unfortunate lying in the gutter." The rocks continued to fall, and Webb found himself unable to move. He roused himself enough to find, standing on his coat, one of the horses, "bleeding at the nose and his eyes bulging." Webb assumed the horse, though standing, was dead. "Finally after dunking myself in the cold water four or five times I got the strength to tear my self loose and crawl out, where I lay on the bank of the creek for several hours too weak to even get a drink of water."[132]

More men crawled out of the cave. They tried to stand but only wobbled and fell. They dragged themselves to the creek, ravenous with thirst, only to find the water alkaline with ash and too bitter and hot to drink. They called roll and realized some men were missing. The strongest of the lot went back into the tunnel and found five dead, perhaps from suffocation in the foul air, perhaps from falling unconscious in the deep muck and water ponded behind fallen bodies. Stockton claimed he had revived atop the bodies of two others, both drowned in the sump. The horses were alive but in such wretched condition that they were shot on the spot. The man who had lagged was nowhere to be seen. He was found days later, only after search crews had repeatedly passed by him on the trail and mistaken him for a charred stump.[133]

They began to stagger toward Wallace, coughing through the dense smoke, stumbling along the creek bed by the light of log torches. Along the way they met the relief party, who escorted them to the hospital. Emma Pulaski had wondered why neighbors had stayed with her through the morning and looked so distressed and had guessed that they had heard terrible news regarding her husband. About 9 A.M. word came to her that some of Pulaski's crew had survived but were badly hurt and that Pulaski himself had "his eyes burned out and probably would not live." An hour later she saw two men approaching, one holding up the other, and that the one stumbling was her husband. He was "staggering, his clothes coated with dry mud, his eyes bandaged he was blind and terribly burned, his hands and hair were burned and he was suffering from the fire gas." Weeks of hospitalization were to pass before he could see again and breathe freely and use his proud hands. But for now it was enough that he was alive.[134]

Ed Pulaski had come home.

•

ON 19 AUGUST, the day Ed Pulaski was gathering his supplies and preparing to leave home for the firelines, William James completed his own long journey from the Old World to the New. America's premier philosopher, one of the architects of pragmatism, had only days to live. Europe's cures, and Europe's ways, had failed to rally him. He had crossed the Atlantic for the last time. Terminally ill, he slumped into a chair beside the fire at the family cottage in Chocorua, New Hampshire, and sighed, "It's so good to get home."[135]

From the epiphanal day, 30 April 1870, when he decided to *believe* and to *act* even in the face of debilitating doubt, James had celebrated the deed over the idea, the fact over the theory, the world to be made over a world foreordained. The formal frame into which he placed this vision was a philosophy of pragmatism. Its test of truth—its measure of a life worth living—he summed up in his famous epigram "By their fruits ye shall know them, not by their roots." The world is a result of outcomes, not origins. "Truth," he insisted, "*happens* to an idea." We know things by what they do. We judge people by how they act, not by their pedigree but by what they make of themselves. It was a world of newness, of openness, of experimentation, not one predestined and not one that required complete knowledge before one could perform with moral vigor. Rather, the world was contingent and incomplete, our knowledge of it partial, our future what we chose to strive for, our reality centered in our own felt meanings. Jamesian pragmatism celebrated the daring and the risk takers and the doers. It was a marvelous philosophy for a self-made nation like America and an activist time like the Progressive Era.

In 1897, as Congress passed the Organic Act for the forest reserves, James lectured on "What Makes a Life Significant." A smoothed—what today might be called Disneyesque—world held no attraction for him. "What excites and interests the looker-on at life, what the romances and the statues celebrate and the grim civic monuments remind us of, is the everlasting battle of the powers of light with those of darkness; with heroism reduced to its bare chance, yet ever and anon snatching victory from the jaws of death." What we seem to require, he insisted, is "the sight of the struggle going on." Ever conscious that his own privileged class held no monopoly on life and meaning, he turned to ordinary folk, especially the ranks of manual workers. "Wishing for heroism and the spectacle of human nature on the rack, I had never noticed the great fields of heroism lying round about me, I had failed to see it present and alive."[136]

Yet it did not thrive equally among everyone. What made the difference? What created the "morally exceptional individual"? James's answer: a mix, "some chemical combination," catalyzed by struggle, among principles of common toil and idealism. Each by itself was inadequate. "Ideal aspirations are not enough, when uncombined with pluck and will. But neither are pluck and will, dogged endurance and insensibility to danger enough, when taken all alone." Inner meaning could come only when "inner joy, courage, and endurance" were infused with "an ideal." Thought without action was an indulgence; act without contemplation was mere physiology. But neither was this formula sufficient. After all, the ideals might be sordid, and the struggle merely a gritty mindlessness to plod on.[137]

Now as his own life drained away, James thought he saw peril as well as promise. What he saw was a growing militarism in Western civilization. The Great Powers were arming, not against feeble indigenes in distant colonies but against one another; conscription and reservists militarized whole societies; rival navies piled dreadnought upon dreadnought; social Darwinism had degenerated into a jingoism of martial struggle, of blood, steel, and soil. Earlier in 1910 Norman Angell had written in *The Great Illusion* that "military fantasy had become a mass sport in a sedentary, urban society." The trend alarmed James, and he wrote for the Association for International Conciliation a reply, "The Moral Equivalent of War," which *McClure's Magazine* published in its August 1910 issue.[138]

Hostile to militarism, James admitted reluctantly that war was "the romance of history" and that "the war-party is assuredly right in affirming and reaffirming that the martial virtues, although originally gained by the race through war, are absolute and permanent human goods." A life without the thrill of struggle or one stripped of desperate risk seemed contemptible even to a pragmatist committed to pacifism. Yet James insisted that there had to be an alternative, a *moral* equivalent to war, "analogous, one might say, to the mechanical equivalent of heat." What was needed was breed the "martial type of character" without war. What was needed was to "to inflame the civic temper as past history has inflamed the military temper."[139]

Then he plunged into his proposal. "If now—and this is my idea—there were, instead of military conscription a conscription of the whole youthful population to form for a certain number of years a part of the army enlisted against *Nature,*" one could have the martial virtues without the martial horrors. "The military ideals of hardihood and discipline would be wrought into the growing fibre of the people." Those who served "would have paid their blood-tax, done their own part in the immemorial human warfare against nature; they would tread the earth more proudly, the women would value them more highly, they would be better fathers and teachers of the following generation." His alarm was clairvoyant; the trenches of the Great War lay only four years in the future. Yet he saw no obvious surrogate.[140]

Had he looked west, however, he would have seen the shallow trenches of the Great Fires. It is unlikely that William James knew much, if anything, about the burns; he had reached his beloved hearth only the night before the Big Blowup, though as he slumped in his chair, the smoke pall was already yellowing the skies over Boston. It is even more improbable that anyone on the rumpled ridges of the Coeur d'Alene forest had read William James, if they could even read. But they all shared a common culture, the way bear and white pine and fireweed shared the St. Joe Mountains. They knew it as they knew Gifford Pinchot's call for a conservation crusade and as they knew Teddy Roosevelt's appeal for a "life of strenuous endeavor." They had that common culture on hand as they sought to explain what had happened, why men were cutting fuelbreaks over ridgelines so deep in the backcountry it took packtrains days to reach them, why they had died.

The military analogy was one they knew instinctively. Had not the National Academy of Sciences believed the work eminently suitable for military duty and wanted forestry taught at West Point? Had not the cavalry in the national parks shown the value of disciplined force—as a moral presence, no less—in combating fire? Had not the call-out of regular troops and militia demonstrated that at bottom, the firefight was a paramilitary campaign? Did not Elers Koch, in writing the fires' history, insist that "a forester in the Northwest dates the events of his life by fire years. The 1910, 1917, 1919, 1926, 1929, and 1931 fire seasons each have a character of their own, and in each year there are individual fire campaigns which the forester remembers as the soldier recalls the separate engagements of a war"? Did not Bill Greeley appeal for the regular assignment of troops on the forests during fire season? If war was the romance of history, was not firefighting the romance of forestry?[141]

Yes, yet no. The argument remained an analogy. The Army would fight wars; the Forest Service, fires. Fire protection would not militarize outright, but it would acquire, in Jamesian fashion, martial virtues that could justify what had happened. That task, unsought and unwanted, fell to the steadfast Edward C. Pulaski. His flight and stand before the flames attracted the most accounts, shone with the clearest meaning, and quickly shoved the other stories aside. Halm's exploits were a great adventure, not made tragic by death. The Lost Crew on Setzer Creek died unsung. Rock's brilliant defense was too uneventful and then compromised by lawsuits over Weigert's suicide. The crews at the Beauchamp homestead and the Dittman cabin were panicky fools and self-inflicted victims. The Bullion Mine fiasco occurred when a squad was cut out from safety. The Stevens Peak burnout had all the necessary story elements, but accounts varied too widely to bear the weight of the moral traffic it might have to carry. That left Pulaski, who led, shared, defied, suffered, and triumphed. He was almost unique in connecting with his crew and experiencing precisely the same dangers as they and suffering the same injuries. If the Year of the Fires telescoped into the Big Blowup, so the Big Blowup imploded with peculiar force into Pulaski's awkward saga—thrilling, daring, tragic, strenuous, heroic.

Yet this last adjective remained troublesome. Ed Pulaski never claimed—in fact, ignored and dismissed—any thought that he was a hero. Others made that assertion, and there is little evidence that Pulaski sought to boost that label or to play upon it. He declined to become a celebrity. He shunned publicity and only once, thirteen years later, wrote down his own account. Almost alone he remembered the fallen firefighters and tended their graves. He remained rooted on the Wallace district for another twenty years until he retired. Uniquely among those young rangers, he had a family, to whom he was devoted. He had done only what he had to do and regretted that the horror had happened at all. He exulted only that his sight returned.

He was not a classic hero, one who knew right and acted on it, who understood and played out his destiny. He had been wrong, and confused, and surprised. More than once he had made questionable choices: leading the men through an unburned patch of forest, gambling that they could dash down the West Fork trail faster than the fire could race through the enveloping forest; putting the men into a shallow shaft and leaving, if only to look for somewhere safer for them; bringing horses into the Nicholson tunnel. Yet he had made more good choices than bad ones, and ultimately the crisis had demanded what all fires demand: that he act. The Blowup required only that he do or die, and likely die if he acted poorly. For all the accounts that spilled out afterward, from half a dozen survivors, not one doubted that Ed Pulaski, alone, more or less by sheer force of personality, had pulled them through. He was not a promised hero who met his destiny and triumphed. He was a man who found himself, reluctantly, in extraordinary circumstances that he had never wished for and had risen to meet them and for one stupendous instant reached beyond himself.

For that reason he was perhaps a Jamesian hero. His was an Age of the Act: It preferred gerunds for nouns; it sought strenuous engagement; it believed the future was there to be made. Progressivism gave that impulse political expression; Pragmatism, philosophical expression—the one a call for reform, the other an appeal that sought to free people to believe and to do. Perhaps that explains the era's eagerness to interpret the Big Blowup, in general, with approval. That was not a given. One could have interpreted the dollars and deaths as Koch did: as a complete failure of field operations. Or one could have seen them as Ballinger did: as a failure of conception, a commitment to flawed ideas.

The informed public, however, saw the Big Blowup as a bold campaign. At the 24 August meeting of the Service Committee, the Forest Service's general Washington office briefing, Will Barnes reported:

> [T]he clippings coming in regarding the fire situation were extremely satisfactory from the Forest Service's point of view. In a large majority of cases the influential papers of the country were advocating the extension of the powers of the Forest Service and of furnishing funds for the employment of more rangers so as to give a better fire protection to the Forests. It was felt that this was very encouraging and showed that in all probability the general public sentiment would favor increasing the number of men rather than feel discouraged over the fire conditions and advocate doing away with any efforts at fire prevention or protection.

Its fire crews had pulled the Forest Service along with them and had engaged American culture in ways that abstract talk of monopolies and New Nationalisms and arcane land laws could never do.[142]

The day after Ed Pulaski staggered from the Wallace hospital to his home, William James slumped into a long slide with death, and on 26 August, the day after Company G blew taps over an open grave on Storm Creek, while smoke from the Big Blowup still turned the Boston sky copper, the philosopher who had championed action in the face of uncertainty passed away from the worlds of both deed and doubt. He died knowing his last great idea had gotten into print, but not knowing that truth was already happening to it amid the smoking wreckage of the Northern Rockies.

•

THE BIG BLOWUP lasted two days, 20–21 August. Once the winds faltered, the firestorms rapidly decayed, like aging thunderheads. The fires were still present, more widely flung than before, like great black tears across the mountains. They still smoldered and flared in stumps and logs; they still torched snags; flames still prowled their fronts, alert to any gust of wind or fresh fuels. Trees continued to tumble down. Streams ran sour with soot. Ash lay so deep in places that it took days to cool enough to walk through. The great pall hung, like a terror suspended, over the land. Although the air chilled and the winds subsided, the fires still menaced. The lost firelines had to be rebuilt. But the fury had passed.

Grazing Inspector A. H. Abbott only thought his long tour had ended on the morning of the 20th. The Big Blowup sent him back into the field, as it did hundreds of others. The gritty business of trenching, backfiring, patrolling went on.

> AUG. 21—Went to St. Regis from Station with Beal. Bad reports of Fires west. Got bill grub and sent men out to watch tunnel 8 fire. Koch and Clifford and Beaver in town. Got 2 doz. acres in shape with Sayles. People got in St. Regis from fires West. Fires started in St. Regis. F.F.
>
> AUG. 22—Went out with Clifford and Beaver on fire line west of town. Blackfoot men and Japs. F.F.
>
> AUG. 23—Built fire line with same gang along Mullan gulch ridge. F.F.
>
> AUG. 24—Sent Japs out after tools. Took gang out to water tank. F.F.
>
> AUG. 25—Fought fire all day. Built trail. Fire not bad. F.F.[143]

That day J. E. Barton, supervisor of the Pend Oreille forest, sent out a letter to all forest officers instructing them to be "exceedingly careful" with the men under their charge, that "they are not sent into fire traps or situations in which there is great danger," that they have some "avenue of escape." The recent loss of life, Barton suggested, emphasizes the necessity of such precautions.[144]

If the letters had any effect on Abbott (or even reached him), his diary shows no change.

AUG. 26—Ordered more men. Fought fire. 6 men in camp at night including Davidson and Burton. F.F.

AUG. 27—Fought fire. F.F.

AUG. 28—Ordered more men and grub. Fought fire. F.F.

AUG. 29—Crew met other men. Fire corralled.

AUG. 30—Fire across line but not bad. Under control. 8 men gov't. account of hard lint. F.F.

AUG. 31—Ordered more men and supplies. Fought fire. Good rain. F.F.

SEPT 1—Fire practically out. Cleaned up camp, checked up grub etc. tools. Went to St. Regis. Called up Supervisor and ordered to Missoula. Turned over statements of property, grub, and time to Beal. F.F.

SEPT 2—Went to Missoula. Helped check up accounts in office. F.F.[145]

•

TWO DAYS AFTER the Blowup, still on the fireline, Will Morris wrote a letter home. That first night had been a horror. The wind blew, men dropped off to sleep in rough shacks of lodgepole, and Will fretted. The scene seemed to him far too serious "to think of sleep." At 9 P.M. he decided they had to move. He roused the men, had them bury their tools, and while each man carried his blankets and belongings, they trudged down the ridge. It was "rather dangerous," he admitted. They passed through a gap in the flames, but trees still burned and fell, and the darkness made footing treacherous. After a few miles they came to a clearing and slept. Will recalled the night as "quiet and peaceful" and had "some fine dreams of going on a trip somewhere on a steamboat in a pretty lake." Later one of the night patrolmen wakened Will and informed him that their own camp was no more. He trudged back up the hill and found it was true. "The lodgepole shacks, provisions and all tools that had been left were completely gone, and the ridge was swept bare."[146]

Their situation was more forlorn than desperate, but something had to be done. They had no food, few tools, no water, little stamina, and almost no resolve. Will sent a party to a nearby logging camp for provisions, then hurried to the Graham Creek Ranger Station to phone Weigle for help. Weigle told him he would have to do with what he had. He picked up a few loaves of bread and headed to their spike camp. "It was a dark day and the sun was hidden, as it was for many days following."[147]

The men were leaving. They had seen enough, and neither pleas nor threats could halt them. A few stayed; among them fortunately was the cook. The foreman of the logging camp cut line around the lower part of the fire, while Morris and his "faithful few" completed a trench along the top. He told his mother not to worry, for "I am in a safe place and all of Graham Creek is already burnt out so it is perfectly safe." When they finished, they had a line four or five miles long. They patrolled until the winds abated and the air turned chilly with the hint of autumn. They knew the end was at hand. In time Will came to look back on those final days "with somewhat of a feeling of pleasure."[148]

•

IT WAS THE kind of organizational crisis in which Bill Greeley thrived. Almost alone, he seemed to understand what had happened and what had to be done. He fired off telegrams, phone calls, letters; found more men, more tools, more money; renewed the firefight. Yet he never wavered in his core values, that what mattered first were the casualties, the men who had died, those who were injured, those perhaps still unfound amid the ruins. He made no distinction between those who wore Forest Service green and those whom the Forest Service had hired willy-nilly off the streets. They all were comrades-in-arms; they merited equal care. The bureaucrats would disagree, but Greeley insisted as a matter of decency that casualties receive proper treatment, or proper burial, and that the Service pay the bills. All this, he confessed, was "difficult," "necessary," and urgent. The bodies of the unidentified should go into "suitable plots," fenced for protection, at the nearest ranger stations. Greeley promised to discuss later "the preparation of suitable tablets. . . ."[149]

To do anything, however, required men. Morris's experience was typical: Most refused to carry on and walked off the line. Most, as Roscoe Haines blandly put it, deemed the work too hazardous even for 25 cents an hour and expert grub. "Recent experiences with Forest fires made it extremely difficult to secure men for fighting the same." Those crews still intact were outfitted for relief operations. Somehow, new crews were scraped together. "About two hundred fire fighters including tramps and undesirables shipped St. Joe this morning," one Army officer fumed. "About same number came in since." Whatever their numbers, they still needed rangers to lead them, and most of the best were either exhausted or injured. Throughout the summer Greeley had shifted men across forest boundaries as the need arose. Now he reached across districts and called up fifty rangers from Utah and Arizona to assist. From the Arizona Strip, Sharlot Hall glowingly reported:

> He was out on the Kaibab when the word came, but he rode in to Fredonia as fast as his horse could take him, got food, outfit and fresh horses, said goodbye to wife and children and parents, and was on the road again, riding through the night without sleep or rest, still pushing on by day and night the long distance to the railroad, then still on to the post of duty far in advance of what had been thought the quickest time he could make—and his service there befitted the [pioneer] blood of which he came. . . .

By the time they arrived, however, the fires were sinking into sullen coals. Will Morris met some of the relief, "a bunch of boys from the Uintah Forest in Utah" sent to help, who didn't see "enough fire to keep warm by. They have had a regular pleasure excursion."[150]

Mostly, though, the civilians turned to the military. Companies G and I, already on the Coeur d'Alene, became the backbone of a search, rescue, and burial mission. For days crews in the burned area tried to cut their way out, while parties on the outside tried to cut their way in, a kind of *danse macabre* through what had become a no-man's-land in a ghastly war with nature. On the evening of the 22nd Captain George Holden arrived in Avery from Fort George Wright to assume overall command of the Twenty-fifth Infantry. He shot off an immediate telegram to the adjutant general:

> Report arrival six-thirty tonight on relief train from Malden. Bridges destroyed East and no traffic or communication beyond this point Eastward. Fires burning themselves out for miles surrounding but danger considered over here. Avery saved but congested. Troops, fire fighters and inhabitants gathered here nearly exhausted. Special trains leaving tonight and tomorrow will carry out those not needed for relief work. Ample provisions for present. No surgeon or medical supplies here. Endeavoring to get some from St. Joe or Tekoa. Hospital at St. Joe reported congested. Will commence sending injured to Tekoa and Spokane tomorrow. Impossible to intelligently estimate dead, injured, and missing at present due to great dispersion of about four hundred still in mountains. Four enlisted company G still missing. Lines of communication uncertain and frequently broken. Searching parties will be sent out for dead and missing as soon as conditions warrant.
>
> Holden, Captain
> Avery, Idaho, August 23, 1910[151]

The next day the long-missing troopers were discovered thirty-five miles outside Avery. Holden dispatched "couriers" to guide them to town. He expected them, if "not cut off by fire," to arrive within another day.[152]

•

FOR DAYS AFTERWARD the Coeur d'Alene troops did some desultory patrol and trenching, but mostly they fed firefighters and scoured the burned lands for bodies. They gave the dead military funerals and buried them where they lay, since the Forest Service "found it impracticable to identify or remove bodies." On the 23rd they buried forty-two; on the next day, twenty-four; and on the day following, eighteen. They discovered one more body on the 27th and another on the 30th. (That adds up to eighty-eight dead, excluding those around Wallace; the Forest Service acknowledged seventy-two on the Coeur d'Alene, another of officialdom's innumerable discrepancies.) Meanwhile Forest Service crews inspected every mine shaft and minor habitation. Pulaski, in particular, was convinced that they would discover more dead, and from time to time over the coming weeks they did. A body by the tracks. A body, mostly consumed, by the creeks. The official tally of dead is incomplete. The Forest Service counted only those civilians who had worked alongside them, but there were others not on the payroll or widely known, at least totaling seven. Almost certainly the numbers of dead were larger.[153]

The "most harrowing experience" for Roy Phillips came later, when the bodies dumped into common graves had to be exhumed, lashed to horses, and hauled to towns for reshipment to families or reburial in local cemeteries. For that Weigle waited until the railway was repaired. Phillips led a group of fifty to retrieve the local Wallace men who died at the Bullion Mine. But only his packer would help. He "recalled clearly" too the "reluctance of the negro soldiers to handle the dead bodies, and the captain was compelled to exercise considerable persuasion to get them to touch them." Still, the grisly work went on.[154]

Their response differed in other ways as well. Frank Haun had "quite a job" convincing Phillips, his bags packed, to stay. The young guard had tramped days through a landscape that hadn't so much as a green twig and was sure that "a forester's job must be all washed up." On the 25th, Captain Holden reported from Avery: "Conditions normal except damage done by fires."[155]

•

THE ARMY HAD its limits, however. It was not that large, and it was never quite clear who was to pay for its services or for its frayed uniforms. On the 22nd, after a conference between General Wood and Associate Forester A. F. Potter, another five companies, the last in the region, were rushed into the fray. That brought a total of thirty-three companies the War Department had fielded along with extra packtrains and medical corpsmen. It was all "most serious," President Taft telegraphed the governors of Idaho, Montana, and Washington. Yet there was not much more the federal government could do. Thus Taft sought "exact information" and pointedly asked the governors how they intended to assist, specifically whether they planned to call out state troops for "police work" in the threatened towns.[156]

Later that day Governor James H. Brady of Idaho replied, thanking Taft for his aid and reporting that matters seemed to be "under comparative control" unless the wind changed. The next day he ordered the Second Infantry Regiment of Idaho's National Guard, then encamped for training at American Lake, to Coeur d'Alene. Brigadier General Marion Maus requested approval for them to receive ten days' rations and dispatched Lieutenant Henry M. Fales to accompany them and to report as well on the troops already on the scene. They settled into the old post grounds of Fort Sherman and awaited orders. None came.[157]

What followed was an object lesson in political buckpassing, a bureaucratic opéra bouffe. The civilians informed Lieutenant Fales that no troops were necessary, that the bad fires were farther east, that the worst, in their opinion, had passed. The president of the Coeur d'Alene Lumber Company had already sent a telegram to Governor Brady stating that the troops weren't needed. Brady replied that he saw no reason to countermand his order. The troops' maneuvers were scheduled to end in a few days; they could bivouac at Coeur d'Alene rather than return to American Lake before heading home.

The Second Infantry finally roused itself to action on the 27th. One battalion went to St. Maries; two companies headed to Harrison; and one, C Company, traveled by "electric car" to Post Falls. None of them saw so much as a match burning. Within forty-eight hours they had returned, their principal casualty one private who contracted smallpox. Meanwhile the ever-vigilant Greeley had wired General Maus to recommend urgently that the Avery troops move to Wallace, where they could help protect towns along the Coeur d'Alene River. The Army wondered aloud why the Idaho guard wasn't used, instead of boating and touring around the countryside. Nor was the guard happy. Political dissension had been chronic; the guardsmen saw little reason why the state should bail out the federal government; they wanted to go home. On the 29th, they did, conveniently timed so they could vote in the election. The next day Greeley replied to pointed queries from Maus that he knew nothing about the Idaho militia, but that, regardless, the danger had passed and concurred that the regular troops could return to their barracks.

The episode did not amuse Lieutenant Fales. Apart from political posturing, there had been no reason to activate the guard. Coeur d'Alene itself lay outside the maelstrom. The news reports were a jumble of exaggeration and misinformation. Lumbermen asserted that their losses were less than reported, provided they could harvest the scorched timber within two years. Civilian authorities assured Fales that the fire's casualties were not helpless homesteaders but "paid men of all nationalities, brought in from different points to fight fires, and who were not accustomed to the work and would not in many cases follow the advice and directions of their leaders." On 29 August, when they decamped, the skies were clear.[158]

•

THE WAR DEPARTMENT was a tempting target. Obedient, cheap, patriotic, with good press; the political capital invested was small; its payoff, large. It promised the illusion of vigorous action at trivial cost. But the impulse reached its most bizarre expression with a scheme to have the department blast rain out of the dry skies.

Perhaps the muted thunder of the Big Blowup was its inspiration, perhaps an instinct to return fire. Whatever the logic, on 25 August George M. Cornwall, editor of the *Lumberman,* telegraphed the secretary of war that he believed a "discharge of heavy artillery might produce rain" and that he "respectfully" urged "that orders be transmitted to Commanders in Oregon and Washington for discharge of artillery at eight A.M., Pacific time tomorrow." The Army would fire its coastal batteries, the Navy its ship guns. A duplicate telegram went the next day to the White House. The plea was joined by others from the Washington Forest Fire Association and the Seattle Chamber of Commerce. Senator S. H. Piles and Representative W. E. Humphrey of Washington and Senator Jonathan Bourne of Oregon joined the chorus. Associate Forester A. F. Potter added the Forest Service "as an interested party" and urged "compliance" because it would "satisfy public sentiment regardless [of] probable success." Then, with proper bureaucratic caution, he added that it should be done "if possible without heavy expenditure." All that exploded on the morning of the 26th, however, was a barrage of confused telegrams.[159]

By the 27th the War Department had estimated the cost of a single, collective discharge at $10,000 and that "of any reasonable number of discharges" would cost not less than $100,000. Granted the expense, the limited number of shells available, and the "practical certainty" that none of it would do the slightest good, Chief of Staff Wood recommended against the demonstration. A quick reply from Willis Moore of the Weather Bureau confirmed that decision. Moore reported on an earlier congressional experiment at rainmaking by political fiat that yielded nothing. The popular association of battles with rainstorms he dismissed as simple statistics. Commanders move armies during fair weather; rain falls in temperate lands an average of one day in three, such that the "regular operations of nature should bring rain during, or at the close of, a battle begun during clear weather." Worse, the mere attempt would damage the bureau's efforts to combat "the mercenary efforts of charlatans" to create rain and would open "a fruitful field for their fraudulent work." All this Wood passed along to Taft with the firm recommendation that the president cancel the experiment.[160]

On 29 August, with the Big Blowup safely over, Taft finally did.

•

IN ITS SWIRL the front that had whipped the Northern Rocky fires into the froth of the Big Blowup topped them on 24 August with a dusting of drizzle and snow. The crisis persisted, but only in potential; a second such front could well inspire another, larger and more comprehensive blowup. There was no reason to expect it. But then no one had forecast the first either.

Greeley summarized the situation in a telegram to Graves:

Missoula, Mont., August 24, 1910

Forester,
Washington, D.C.

Light rain and snow extending Absaroka to Lolo Forest. Greatly improved fire conditions. Practically all fires east of divide under control. Pend Oreille fires practically under control. Flathead and Blackfeet fires partially checked and work well organized. Kootenai fires still serious. All settlers brought in from dangerous localities. Troy and Libby safe for present. Kaniksu fires serious but Newport and Priest River safe. No definite information Cabinet. Conditions Coeur d'Alene extremely critical. Two companies state militia in readiness for duty there. On Lolo, Coeur d'Alene and Clearwater Forests present work mainly relief of missing fire crews and settlers. Fires still critical. Fighting being organized as rapidly as possible. No known deaths of regular Forest officers. Eight accounted for. Deaths temporary employees aggregate at least twenty-five. Arrangements made care and medical help all injured.

Greeley,
District Forester[161]

The larger firefight shifted to Oregon and California, where large fires flared up along the Coast Range and Sierra Nevada. The political contest rode the rails with peregrinating politicians, spread in a pall of newsprint, and left mining caves for the halls of Congress.

•

THE ARMY DID as it was ordered: The last of its uncommitted companies it threw into the fray. A hospital corps from Fort George

Wright hurried to Avery. Fort Missoula sent two companies to the Flathead Reservation, two troops of the First Cavalry rode to fires on the Yakima Indian Reservation, and four companies of the First Infantry left Vancouver Barracks for southern Oregon, where they joined Companies E and M, already on the lines. Five companies of the Oregon National Guard mobilized to protect the watershed of Portland. From the Presidio two companies of the 60th and 147th Coast Artillery rushed to fires on the Tahoe National Forest. By this time the western Army was on general alert for smokes. While on maneuvers near the Black Hills of South Dakota, the Fourth Cavalry "encountered heavy forest fire" and engaged. By 30 August it was breaking off to secure rations from Deadwood.[162]

The First Infantry detrained at Medford, where it met Ranger C. J. Buck, who parceled the men among three fires. Company A went to Ashland, two companies traveled to Prospect (the scene of the most alarming reports), and two to Butte Falls, where troops were already on the line. The burns were indeed large and serious, but they were "exclusively ground fires," except in Dudley and Prospect, where surface flames were apt to torch canopies in the afternoon and make short runs through the crowns ("to the uninitiated it was most terrifying," Major C. H. Martin wrote). One such rush threatened the camp at Upton until halted fifty yards away. In general, this was classic firefighting, tough, fatiguing, miserable, exhilarating, systematic. There was nothing of the ineffable, no eruption beyond the ken of experienced men, no Big Blowup. By 5 September everything—even the stubborn Imnaha Creek fire—was under control. By the 9th the 378 enlisted men, 17 officers, 10 horses, 69 pack animals, 8 escort wagons, and 2 ambulances dispatched to southern Oregon were being released.[163]

The California fires demanded even less. The rangers themselves acknowledged that no real crisis existed, that they were calling upon the troops because they had been made available. They attacked five fires, one outside the Tahoe forest proper but threatening its borders. The hardest fought was at Forest Hill near Auburn, but there reports circulated about a fire threatening Nevada City, fifty miles away. The tired troops left the one for the other, closing the distance in twelve hours, and suppressed the fire front before rising winds hit. Supervisor Richard Bigelow wrote glowingly that "this move and the rapidity with which the fire was extinguished was [*sic*] one of the prettiest pieces of work I ever saw in fire fighting." He congratulated the troops on their "bully work." When they departed on 8 September, they were, unsurprisingly, "a ragged looking bunch."[164]

That was true. Over and again the chief complaint by the troops in the field was clothing. Fire duty ruined their uniforms and shredded their boots, and their standard uniform allowance could never cover the losses. The War Department appealed to Agriculture (which after all had a deficit fire fund) to make good those costs, along with the expenses of transport and some rations. In effect, the military refused to act as a cheap commissary for the Forest Service. The fiscal sparring continued for months.

The strangest voucher never got that far. Major A. W. Chase of the Coast Artillery Corps submitted two bills from the firefight at Forest Hill. One was $1.85 for drugs; the other for two gallons of whiskey at $4 per gallon. The adjutant general, department of California, recommended payment and cited the laudatory letter from Supervisor Bigelow. The surgeon general, however, disagreed. The medicines should have come in the authorized medical chests. The whiskey, he concluded, was administered "as a diffusible stimulant, not to sick and wounded, but generally to the men on the fire lines. . . ." The judge advocate general nonetheless concluded that "it is equally lawful to incur necessary and proper contingent expenses in connection with the same employment (fighting fires)," that "the issue of whiskey to the men ⋆ ⋆ was necessary ⋆ ⋆ . . . ," and that reimbursement was in order. General Wood passed along the memo to the acting secretary of war.[165]

They left on good terms, and each side, the War Department and the Forest Service, passed its judgment on the exercise. Both sides agreed that the National Guard had proved more or less worthless. The Idaho guard had done nothing; the Oregon, only little better. They had extinguished ("it is believed, with credit") the fires outside Ashland, but once regular troops arrived, at least some guardsmen seem to have "abandoned the work." Major Martin's summary held generally: "I do not consider that the national guard troops, as a rule, are fitted for this class of work, as undoubtedly it requires the highest order of systematic direction and discipline, which can only be had under an officer with absolute control over his men, and such conditions prevail only with regular troops."[166]

Was it worth doing? Most officers thought so. Those who found fires believed their labor valuable. They admired the rangers who directed them as knowledgeable and hardworking (though they scorned most of the laborers they met in the trenches). Some thought the exercise better than drills and normal maneuvers, and hard marches through pumice and long hours on firelines still beat the numbing routines of barracks life. The medical corps in particular had very real casualties to deal with. Brigadier General Tasker Bliss cited the tough duty to refute "any impression that may prevail to the effect that our troops are not in condition to meet unusual conditions of hardship and deprivation." Several officers enthused over the idea of fighting fires on the forest reserves regularly, just as the cavalry was doing in the parks. But that scheme aroused more interest in the lower ranks than the higher. Congress, the Western Pine Manufacturers Association, and Bill Greeley might like the idea, saw it as efficient and cheap; the War Department did not. Chief of Staff Wood announced flatly to Taft that the "suggested use of troops from May until October each year . . . is wholly impracticable."[167]

As it was. What field officers affirmed, almost to a man, was that the civilians needed to create for themselves a suitable force, establish regular patrol, and lay down a system of barriers, trails, observation posts, and phone wires—a network of fortifications, if you will. While this bore resemblances to military operations, it was not war, and the War Department should decamp as soon as the crisis passed. If the Forest Service wanted a militarylike force, it should create one for itself, and in a way, it did.

The fact is, the Army meant more to the Forest Service than the Forest Service to the Army. The big call-out was, in American military history, a footnote at best. For the Forest Service it was a defining moment, and it fed the military analogy that was progressively dominating discourse about what fire control meant. The reports assembled for the adjutant general are far more accurate and comprehensive than those scribbled haphazardly from the burned-out forests and posted to the chief forester and, through him, to Congress. The lengthy submissions by Lieutenant Lewis and Captain Holden, for example, are almost the only reliable accounts of what happened around Avery. The Army proved to be a better bureaucracy as well as a better force in the field. Yet its reports barely entered into the master narrative penned by the Forest Service. The early historians of the Big Blowup like Fred Morrell and later Elers Koch had hardly a word for the troops. The story, as they saw it, belonged to the rangers. The martial virtues they transferred to the fire front. For the Army the fires were just another detail, a welcome break from the barracks (or a waste of time chasing phantoms around the woods), a curious adventure, and perhaps, as with Company G at Avery and Company K outside Glacier, a brush with death. For the Forest Service, however, the Great Fires birthed a creation story.

•

THE BLOWUP HAD happened so suddenly and so hugely that the fires waned before the politicians could fully wax. They quickly reacted, however, though spasmodically. The hasty call-up and dismissal of the Idaho guard were one such spasm. So was the proposed Big Blast. The arrival of Senator W. B. Heyburn of Idaho in Wallace by special train on 23 August was another (that was where the 1910 census finally caught up with him). On the 23rd the *New York Times* ran a lengthy feature on the fires, and on the following Sunday, a heavily illustrated spread. At the time losses were still estimated at perhaps 200 dead; Fort Assiniboine, 200 miles from the nearest fire, reported an ash fall that covered the ground for half an inch; two days later Bostonians saw the sun as a copper disk through a yellow haze. Charges and countercharges—who "lost" the Coeur d'Alene—splashed across newspapers for days. Editorials followed. Departmental secretaries and bureau chiefs demanded reports. Congress prepared special hearings.[168]

The fight over the meaning of the Great Fires had begun. In truth the wrangling was no abrupt intrusion by politics into a field that politics had previously spared: the politics had always been there. The political establishment had never unshackled—had no intention of unshackling—fire protection to pursue a destiny as a self-contained negotiation between nature and engineers. Neither did the Forest Service intend to decouple its firefight from politics. This was not the case of an agency that had simply done its duty only to find itself blindsided by blundering and posturing politicians. From its origins under Pinchot, the Service had had a political mission; its power derived, according to the precepts of its charismatic chief, from its ability to sway public opinion, and it had exploited fire imagery shamelessly for publicity and had openly declared fire protection its primary charge. As Ucker understood, the Forest Service had itself invited fire control as a public demonstration of its capacity to govern the public domain. Since January, because of the Ballinger-Pinchot quarrel, a political battle of its own choosing, the Service had been in chronic crisis. Inevitably, the

Big Blowup would act as a catalyst for further political debates. But just what reaction the fires would catalyze was unclear.

There were principles at stake. The *New York Times* on 23 August expressed the received wisdom of the elite when it observed that the "conflagration" in the West was "much like the fires of yesteryear, and like more fires that will sweep the forests this year from Maine to California," and congratulated New York and Massachusetts for their inestimable efforts that had so reduced losses from 1908. On the 25th Secretary of the Interior Ballinger, speaking in San Francisco, weighed in with a judgment that the Forest Service might be wrong in its approach, that light burning was likely superior to aggressive fire control. The next day Gifford Pinchot responded. The real struggle, he had always believed, would be won in the trenches of public opinion, not on those cut across the Bitterroots, and he knew that abstract principles were less convincing than the actions of brave men. Adjacent to his quotes in the *Times* ran the tally of the dead, then set at 160.[169]

He was proud of the "splendid work" the Forest Service was doing. They all had labored and many had died in the service of the nation. "To my mind," his formal statement reads, "their conduct is beyond all praise." So too it must lie beyond all criticism. There could be no discussion over the ultimate policy that brought them to the fire fronts, no alternative explanation save that these men had seen their duty and done it and had paid, many of them, the ultimate price. Pinchot then lashed into their dark doubles: the politicians, particularly western, who opposed the expansion of the Forest Service and who challenged, as Ballinger had, the special vision of conservation the Forest Service embodied. "The men in Congress like Heyburn, Carter, and Mondell, who have made light of the efforts of the Forest Service to prepare itself to prevent such a calamity as this have, in effect, been fighting on the side of the fires against the general welfare." Forest fires, Pinchot continued, were "preventable"; losses like those suffered in the Rockies were "wholly unnecessary." A "fire in the forest is the same kind of a thing as a fire in the city" and should be controlled according to the same principles: rapid detection, rapid response, dedicated crews, building and slash disposal codes.[170]

Senator Heyburn dismissed Pinchot's statement as "not worthy of serious consideration." The problem, he insisted, lay with Pinchot's "theory of forest protection," which was now "discredited by the administration and by experience." Congress had appropriated ample money for "necessary purposes"; the Forest Service had lavished it instead on its propaganda machine. While the senator deplored "the loss of life" and commended "individual efforts," he denounced Pinchot's explanation for the failure as "silly." The efforts of his Forest Service had been "spectacular but ineffective." Senator Thomas Carter of Montana went further, retorting that vast sums had been spent by the agency for Pinchot's "absurd campaign for the presidency of the United States." He then advocated the traditional approach to fire protection: settlement. The Forest Service had ruthlessly and tyrannically driven off the "settlers, prospectors and miners" who had constituted "a splendid fire fighting force within the forests." Removing them had left the woods "easy prey to flames."[171]

The *Times* responded with a Sunday supplement feature on the fires, richly illustrated with photos. Its sources were Pinchot and Graves. Both discounted the prospect of truly fighting the Great Fires by considering them a force of nature, like the San Francisco earthquake or the Galveston flood. The only solution resided just where Graves, Greeley, Silcox, and Will Morris put it: the full-scale development of the forests with roads, trails, telephone lines, lookout towers, and a resident staff sufficient to patrol and attack fires while they were small. Fire protection was a simple matter of "force enough, fast enough." What the *Times* and the once and future chief foresters failed to explain, if they saw the irony, was that this was precisely what the Service's critics sought. Both sides argued for full-bore development, one by traditional means, the other by government bureau. The issue was not whether the lands would be settled but how and by whom. As with waterways, the question was whether public or private capital would erect dams and cut canals or, in this instance, build trails and staff patrols. The *Times* concluded that the question of increasing the firefighting force was "apt to receive attention at the hands of Congress in the near future."[172]

So it would. The Great Fires had profoundly unsettled the Forest Service in the field. No one on the Cabinet or the Coeur d'Alene spoke of victory; they muttered only about survival. The fires had also, to anyone with an open mind, called into question the strategy of fire protection promoted by the Forest Service. Aggressive fire control would invoke huge costs, and if light burners were correct, it would prove self-defeating in the end. Money had not inhibited the firefight; easy access to money had, if anything, contributed to the fatalities because without the deficit option the undaunted rangers could never have herded hundreds of errant laborers into the backcountry.

But the Washington office saw it differently. It dealt with policies, personalities, and popular symbols. For those ends the Great Fires gave the foresters exactly what they needed and what their critics lacked: a magnificent story, folk heroes, a drama so elemental it became its own morality play. The emerging story of dedicated fighters battling in the national interest made vivid conservation's message about waste and its self-image as a crusade. Light burning had no Ranger Rock to communicate its message wordlessly. Critics of the Service's settlement program—not only those who preferred traditional homesteading but those who wanted the wilds untrammeled—had no Nicholson adit, pummeled by a firestorm, to be photographed. None of them could institutionalize the Great Fires as the Forest Service did so thoroughly that it became close to a founding myth.

Over the course of the twentieth century, the Great Fires' most monumental impact was ecological because they defined how Americans would relate to fire, that most ancient and profound medium by which humanity has shaped the world around it. But the means of imposing that ecological outcome would be politics. Politics did not attach itself leechlike to the fires; it was there before and during as well as after. What the fires did was to rattle politics out of its comfortable niches and set it roaming like bears and bewildered mule deer across a once-familiar landscape, now rudely altered.

# SEPTEMBER

AND THEN IT ENDED.

For four days the wind blew. On 24 August snow and rain briefly bathed the still-raw lands and quelled flames lodged in snags and downed logs. The next day Associate Forester Potter informed the War Department that the crisis had passed in the Rockies, that the action had shifted southward to Oregon and California, where frontal winds had brushed over lands beyond the reach of the rains. In the Rockies the air grew cooler, the winds softened, and the fires sank deeper into embers and blew away with the gray ash. On the morning of the 28th Will Morris noted ice in the water pail and concluded that the fires would soon be out. Then, on 4 September, Will and his crew awoke to raindrops.[1]

"First only a few fell, and then, increasing, it soon began to come down quite heavily. We lay there and enjoyed it. We were glad to get wet, for we knew our long fight was over." Everywhere people rejoiced. Meyer Wolff recalled how "practically every man, woman and child . . . walked around the streets of Priest River bare headed, getting soaked by the showers that began to fall." The great strain of work and worry eased, the tension broke. "Never do I remember having before and never do I expect again," he wrote, "to have a similar feeling of high exultation over the fresh smell of rain filled atmosphere."[2]

But if the rains extinguished the fires, they did not end the firefight. As overwhelming as the buildup had been, Wolff now found himself with an equally frenetic builddown, a mass demobilization of men and supplies. An immense "reverse eddy of fire fighters," as he called it, began to flow out. He had had some experience paying off a few "stragglers" and "truly incompetents"; he had no preparation for the "horde" that now descended upon him, each arguing over time slips, a few submitting vouchers, all demanding immediate payment. Wolff set up a table near his cot by the telephone booth at the drugstore and plowed through the shuffling line of workers and wheedlers, while the druggist gossiped, mixed pills, and dispensed "booze of shady legitimacy." His fund quickly emptied. After conferring with Greeley, the bank honored his "very considerable" overdraft. What happened in Priest River was repeated in scores of towns, with overdrafts that staggered those who finally summed them. The long mop-up of paperwork and money continued for months. The inquiry into what had happened and who owed what to whom crawled through bureaucratic corridors for years.[3]

•

AFTER A SUMMER spent looking forward with dread, in autumn people looked back with nostalgia. Meyer Wolff recalled as indelible the delicious smell of fresh rain. Mrs. Swaine of Mullan remembered it as "a terrible ordeal, but I wouldn't have missed it for anything." Frances Eaton was "glad to leave this land of snowslides and forest" and confessed that "if ever I come back, it will be when I want to die more than I do now." Bill Greeley never forgot, for "the summer of 1910 brought home the hard realities of the job." Ideals and inspirational rhetoric plummeted to earth with "the cost in hardship and sweat, in danger and human lives. And I had to face the bitter lessons of defeat. For the first time I understood in cold terms the size of the job cut out for us." Elers Koch remembered, and worried that the collective memory might fade if it were not properly recorded, as he determined to do, not for publication but "primarily as a record for the Forest Service, so that the story will not be lost." Ed Pulaski remembered, and asked Percy Stewart if he still had "bad dreams of forest fires." Will Morris remembered other fiery dreams and how, during the long ordeal, even in their sleep, they would "be fighting fire all night." But he also recalled fondly those last days with the "faithful few" who had stayed with him on the line and how, around the evening campfire, he had a chance "to size [them] up." He recalled a young Englishman, a singer and poet, a veteran of the Boer War. He recalled two Montenegrins, the best and most faithful workers he ever had. He recalled two southern boys, "a different type" from the others, good workers, out for adventure in the West, which he believed they got. He recalled young Burke, a foreman, later a guard and then a ranger, the "wag of the camp," who said of their first cook that "he was so greasy that every morning he had to roll in the ashes of the fire to keep from sliding down the hill." He also recalled the rain and how they had let it pour off their faces and wash away the grime and the weariness and the fear and how they had bidden "affectionate farewells," knowing that they would never see one another again.[4]

The land remembered too. How much land burned from how many fires is impossible to say. On the national forests of the Northern Rockies, some 2,595,635 acres burned, according to the official record. That doesn't include national parks, Indian reservations, private lands, or public domain outside the forest reserves. Nor does it include everything on the forests. Roscoe Haines was "quite positive" that the formal figures slighted the fire load on the Coeur d'Alene. Fire patrolmen had become foremen of fireline crews instead, and their replacements rarely bothered to report every fire; they had all they could do to control the ones they saw almost daily from July on. After 14 August, Haines believed, the record simply ends. "We fought the fires the best we could wherever and when ever we found them" and had little zest for completing paperwork. The acres burned are estimates. Burned acreage outside the forests was so crudely tallied that the sum was not worth transcribing. Officials argued loosely by analogy, that the Big Blowup had incinerated an area of national forest the size of New Jersey. The burned area outside the reserves could easily have doubled or tripled those numbers. Official statistics in the mid-1920s—including estimates of burned area in "unprotected" lands—ranged from forty million to fifty million acres nationwide. The 1910 figure must have reached at least such sums.[5]

The sheer areal dimensions of the burns mattered less, however, than their intensity. The core conflagrations had leveled and fried vast swaths of mature forest. A back-of-the-envelope calculation by Greeley estimated that a billion dollars' worth of merchantable timber burned. No one had any means by which to reckon the damages to soils, water, and wildlife except by the cost of replanting and protecting. The St. Regis River became unstable, the steeper slopes shed soil down to bare granite. Nor could they calculate the biotic significance of a massive, internal shift within the geography of Rocky Mountain conifers, the replacement of white pine by lodgepole, for example. The burns fostered a bark beetle infestation that, by 1914, had spread into green timber with further, serious losses to white pine and that readied more tinder for more fire.[6]

Perhaps more spectacularly, the effects of the Big Blowup did not completely cease in September 1910; fiery aftershocks continued for decades. Large fires tend to create conditions for more fires, a "vicious circle," as Koch called it. Not all trees, for example, fell during the fire front. The burns created more snags than they consumed, and these continued to fall and burn for many years, particularly when underlain with a carpet of conifer reproduction. Some of the 1910 fires fed on sites burned in 1889; the large outbreaks of 1914, 1919, and 1929 fed on the lavish scraps of 1910. Koch believed that 30 to 40 percent of the Big Blowup reburned, despite salvage logging and intensive protection. He thought it likely that the burned area subsequent to 1910 was "twice as great" as would have occurred had the Great Fires not happened. Those reburns yielded different landscapes from once-burned sites.[7]

Outside the incinerated forests of the conflagration corridors, many observers, though not foresters, found benefits. Ranchers could imagine the thronging greenup of the following spring; hunters and trappers saw a sprouting carpet of young growth to feed prime game. Those who approved the "Indian way" of forest protection saw thousands of acres flushed free of combustible clutter. The greatest ecological impact, though, did not reside in the direct immediacy of wash and bloom. The greatest burden of the burns came indirectly through their impact on the fire regimes that followed, on how people attempted to apply and withhold fire not only on the Flathead and the Lolo but in Florida and Colorado, throughout the whole United States.

Because institutions, too, remembered. In some critical respects the federal government would never forget; the Forest Service never could. The Big Blowup altered the bureaucratic and political landscape as fully as it did the dynamics of Northern Rockies larch and white pine. In the weeks that followed, crews searched, exhumed, photographed, tallied. In the coming years, they salvage-logged and replanted. For decades the Big Blowup served for the politics of fire protection as the Munich accord did for the Cold War. By its sheer fact it repudiated alternative strategies of fire management. It became the immutable standard against which to measure success in fire control. It warned of the insidious consequences of appeasement. It must never be allowed to happen again.

For now, though, it was enough that the rain and snow had snuffed out the implacable flames. Will Morris wrote his mother not to worry. The days were wet, the nights cold, and "there is very little left to burn."[8]

•

THE DAY AFTER the joyful rains settled over the Rockies, the National Conservation Congress convened in St. Paul. For weeks the major figures of the conservation movement, both the politicians and the provocateurs, had circulated about the West and Midwest, barnstorming their political and personal agendas. Ten western governors had assembled in Salt Lake City on 18 August to prepare a common front. Now they all converged on St. Paul. Graves had expected to proceed directly from Washington, but the Big Blowup drew him to District One for a personal inspection instead. Full of maps and estimates of losses and deaths, he traveled to the four-day congress from Missoula.[9]

The National Conservation Congress had emerged out of conservation's *annus mirabilis,* part of the political pyrotechnics of 1908. The first congress had followed in September 1909 with the intention of creating a national forum for federal, state, and private interests. It fell prey, however, to Pinchot's ambitions. Almost Lenin-like he arranged a large delegation that took over the machinery, and for the next four years his agenda became the congress's. During the 1910 session the mention of his name, well after his speech, was sufficient to arouse such wild applause that he returned to the platform and declared, "There are but few moments in a man's life like this. It is magnificent to hear the principles of conservation of natural resources acclaimed as you have done. I have fought many years for conservation, and conservation has won. I thank you."[10]

Not everyone agreed. There was method here, as well as a touch of madness. Pinchot had tried to seize the American Forestry Association and failed. He had created the National Conservation Association and assumed its presidency in January 1910. Now he tried, unsuccessfully, to absorb the National Conservation Congress within it. The effect, as Samuel Hays has observed, was to narrow rather than broaden the constituency and finally to disrupt the organization completely. But that became true for conservation overall: Pinchot's quarrel with Ballinger split the movement and eventually the Republican party. He had become a professional insurgent. He made clear what victory meant when he wrote that "conservation has captured the Nation. . . . It has taken firm hold on our national moral sense, and when an issue does that it has won." In such matters, he insisted, "there is no third course."[11]

For the present the Conservation Congress was Pinchot's personal triumph. Taft delivered a long, somnolent, judicious speech about conservation that aroused no one. Roosevelt spoke to ovations from a text first drafted by Pinchot that he had delivered some days earlier in Kansas about a "New Nationalism." A strong federal role suited Pinchot perfectly. His obsession with the public domain was in fact part of his divisive role, since most citizens were at least as concerned with state, local, and even private matters. Pinchot preferred to relive his very public brawl with Taft and Ballinger over abstract principles and murky land law. With impeccable timing a resolution that condemned Ballinger and urged his dismissal appeared from the congressional committee that had kept the Ballinger-Pinchot controversy festering. Of the twelve members of that committee, only five (four Democrats, one Republican) had voted for the resolution, leaving ambiguous whether a quorum had existed and what the full committee might do. (It eventually exonerated Ballinger.) But in the court of public opinion the damage was considerable. Ballinger stood convicted, while Pinchot's public persona soared. Pinchot found the acclaim intoxicating. His liege, Roosevelt, had not yet dismissed Taft as hopeless, and he urged Pinchot to seek political compromises that would prevent unbridgeable rifts in the Republican party. That was hardly GP's style; he preferred confrontation to compromise. He sought alliances only if they offered him a free hand. So before he despaired of Taft, Roosevelt despaired of Pinchot. He wrote his son, "The wild-eyed ultraradicals do not support us because they think we have not gone far enough. I am really sorry to say that good Gifford Pinchot has practically taken his place among the latter."[12]

Still, the Forest Service remained Pinchot's primary legacy. Graves addressed the Conservation Congress at length regarding "The Forest and the Nation." The conservation movement, as he saw it, had succeeded in its public message. What remained was the "practical application" of its principles. For forestry, those principles were three:

Shield the woods from fire, reduce waste, and ensure a future timber supply. That in fact was their order of importance. The "first task" for the national forests, Graves lectured, was comprehensive fire protection. "The past summer had demonstrated just what could happen" should foresters—should the nation—shirk from that duty. Only days before he had seen the outcome for himself.[13]

While no celebrant in the Pinchot mold, neither was Harry Graves a defeatist. "I meet some men who say that forests can not be protected from fire and that sooner or later every extensive forest will be burned. The experience in the Northwest this year only strengthens my conviction that forests can be protected from fire even under the most adverse climatic conditions." The answer lay in right ideas, system, and steady application. When the national forests were properly developed, the fires would cease. When the means became sufficient, the ends would follow.[14]

Three months later, having digested the reports from the Big Blowup, Graves informed the American Forestry Association that the past year had been one of "great advance" in practical forestry. "I say this," he conceded, "in spite of the great losses during the last season by forest fires." This was, he continued, "the first year that there was a systematic effort to control forest fires on a large scale during a season of great drought." He disputed, as Pinchot had, those who claimed that forests would burn eventually regardless of efforts at fire prevention. The basis for that popular superstition was that large fires had broken out in the past, but the reason for those outbursts, Graves argued, was that systematic fire protection had never been truly tried. This year it had. This year, despite extreme conditions, the Forest Service had extinguished thousands of fires. Only 15 percent of that total had escaped to power the Big Blowup, and those too could have been caught early had an adequate infrastructure existed and had the payroll included a sufficient number of fire patrolmen. Let the carpers and whiners and standpatters insist that nothing could be done, that the Big Blowup had reduced forestry, whether "practical" or merely principled, to lethal mockery. The Forest Service knew better. "The occurrences during the past season furnish a clear demonstration, not that the government can not protect its forests, but that with means provided for their proper organization and patrol the forests can be rendered safe." From Pueblo, Colorado, Theodore Roosevelt lavished his bully praise on the "heroes," that despite "very inadequate appropriations," the Forest Service had by "absolute honesty and efficiency" so conducted itself "as to make an American proud of having such a body of public servants."[15]

No one in the field during the Big Blowup considered the outcome anything but horrific. To politicians, particularly those campaigning from trains or lodged in Washington offices, the fires were a test of the conservation crusade, a bold sortie against entrenched political positions. Especially they were a test of Pinchot's brand of conservation in which agencies like the Forest Service would become model institutions to govern the nation's natural resources. Such bureaus stood for the common good and against the "special interests," which, Pinchot insisted, "must be put out of politics. I believe the young men will do it." He had no sense, as others did, that the National Conservation Association, the American Forestry Association, and the Forest Service constituted themselves special interests as fully as the Great Northern Railway or Guggenheim coal. In the Northern Rockies the young men had removed the special interests, and in Washington and across the pages of the *New York Times* the old men had put them back in.[16]

•

WHEN GRAVES REPORTED to the Service Committee on 14 September, the Big Blowup was much on everyone's mind. Its "great lesson," he told his staff, was the need for trails, telephones, and close patrol. The untreated fires had overwhelmed the controlled ones; the unprotected backcountry had spewed out the fires that savaged the frontcountry. A handful of uncontained burns had wrecked the good work of the many fires caught and controlled. The Lolo, for example, had shown what careful fire planning could do yet had been overrun by fires pouring in from beyond its borders. Extend a proper system to every acre, and the Great Fires would blow away with the smoke of history.[17]

Most high officials, except for the despised Ballinger, agreed. President Taft expressed "great interest" in the catastrophe, particularly in the cooperative work with the Army. Secretary Wilson had authorized a deficit in the fire fund of $650,000, with more to come. Lumbermen had approached the chief forester at the St. Paul conference and sought to help campaign for additional moneys for protection. But success demanded that the general public also agree. In this regard, the good news was that the press was clamoring for photographs. The demand ran so high that the Service considered contracting with private individuals to get an ample supply.[18]

Thus it happened that Will Morris and Joe Halm turned back to the Big Burn with R. H. McKay, a Forest Service photographer from Missoula, in tow. For several days they trudged through the wreckage with a glass plate camera, whose care required a separate packhorse. They all took photos. McKay's were destined for district office headquarters and consumption farther up the bureaucratic food chain. But Halm and Morris shot batches, some for themselves, and Will promised his mother he would send her a few. After he left the hospital, Ed Pulaski added to the collection, including one stunning view up the gutted ravine that was once Placer Creek's West Fork. When they finished, they had assembled perhaps the most stunning visual testimony of the effects of a large fire until the media frenzy over the 1988 burns at Yellowstone.[19]

On the ground, through an unblinking glass lens, the scene looked far grimmer than it did at Forest Service headquarters a few blocks off the Mall or in the St. Paul convention hall. Grandiose plans for a public works–style infrastructure seemed vapid when crews were still struggling to hack their way through trails so densely jackstrawed with blowdown that they could hardly advance a mile a day. Public speeches that proclaimed the past summer a victory for the forces of conservation rang hollow (or worse) when compared with panoramas with hardly a green needle in sight, with ravines clotted with white pine flattened into whirls, with streams still running thick with ash. Assumptions that greater means—more money, more men—would lick the fire problem came up against another costing, in the photos of canvas body bags exhumed from their hasty slit trenches for reburial or shipment to next of kin. That small corps in the backcountry photographed railroad rights-of-way gutted on all sides. They photographed the Nicholson adit. They photographed themselves: McKay sardonic, Halm jaunty, Morris short, a bit stiff, eager.

The photos were themselves ambiguous. They showed, on one hand, an almost total failure to control wildfire and, on the other, an astonishing, even reckless attempt at trying. They are ambiguous in the way that photos of the western front were to be ambiguous a few years later. Captions alone were insufficient: The photos had meaning not in themselves alone but as the decorated borders and leafy vignettes of an illustrated manuscript, a narrative. One could understand the photos only after having read the story. The image derived its meaning from the word. A generation that could, in a few years, imagine Verdun as a victory had no trouble projecting into those appalling landscapes a vision of heroism, of a war zone in the firefight to end all firefights.

When, over the coming decades, the Forest Service needed photos to illustrate its argument that fire damaged forests, that anything less than absolute fire control was dangerous, it retold the story of the Big Blowup and reprinted images collected in its aftermath, an album that the emerging narrative was already editing into a bureaucratically usable past.

•

AT THE ST. PAUL congress, Graves claimed that he had found lumbermen "very cooperative," anxious to assist in fire protection and keen to help ramp up federal appropriations to that end. From the Coeur d'Alene, Will Morris could tell him why. The fires had gutted many sites, like Big Creek, that were being logged and many others that were out for bid. Prime timber that Will had cruised over the winter now lay charred and broken. "I suppose," he wrote home, "there will be a good deal doing selling the burnt timber. . . ." There was. The Forest Service saw the millions of acres left by the Great Fires as a lurid example of the unnecessary wastage caused by fire yet, equally, as an unparalleled opportunity to turn that loss to profit by salvage logging.[20]

How much charred timber was there? The Forest Service settled on a figure of six billion board feet, about twice the entire national output and that in a year of record production. The Big Blowup had consumed 1 to 2 percent of the total timber of the national forests. Foresters believed that they had about two years in which to harvest the western white pine, which would deteriorate rapidly, and perhaps four to five years for larch, Douglas-fir, and white fir. Accessibility was a serious liability; so was a market already sated with wood. So too were sales from private lands burned outside the forests, which would depress demand, and so were sales of green timber on the reserves, which might compete with the salvage sales and were accordingly suspended. Greeley assumed that a vigorous operation would mill half a billion board feet. "Hardly had the smoke cleared," he admitted, than he had reconnaissance parties running estimates. The salvage—a true fire sale—he regarded as "the most urgent administrative question of the District."[21]

There was, perhaps not surprisingly, little debate over the program. Secretary Wilson was not keen to sell off national forest timber, unless demand was strong (it was not), since one purpose of the reserves was to hold that wood for the future. But the fires had burned away normal fiscal and political caution. With fire-killed timber, the Service noted, "it is a case of now or never." There were unusual opportunities for lumbermen to buy stumpage "at bargain prices." Weigle wrote A. W. Cooper of the Western Pine Manufacturers Association to learn "of any lumber companies wishing to get hold of some cheap timber." The Service waived some other requirements as well. It allowed, even encouraged companies to cull the white pine first, hoping that they might return for a later sweep of the lesser species. The usual small slash and brush were gone, already burned, so regulations governing their disposal vanished. Instead protection took the form of cutting strips around the sale areas or sites of greatest hazard and burning the debris where it lay, without the bother of piling. Not least, a legal ruling by the attorney general allowed for cutting in the checkerboard lands along railroad grant lands, script lands, and homesteads where patent was not yet perfected. Timber companies would post a bond to indemnify the government for the stumpage of such lands should they revert to the public domain.[22]

Even so, salvage succeeded in hauling off only a fraction of the total kill. Koch estimated the logged cut between 1911 and 1914 at three hundred million board feet, or less than 10 percent of the total. Many rangers could not overcome their reluctance to let loggers cull the best sites; too many still did not appreciate the need for haste and for a suspension of normal protocol. As a result, Koch insisted, some operators actually lost money. The lesson in salvage was the same as in suppression: Fires were emergencies that demanded action and money; an overreaction, an overspending. There was no time to dally over principles and nuance. The Big Blowup broke down normal senses of caution and consensus. As with funds, which went off budget, so with rules.[23]

In this way, at least some of the fire's immense waste would be eliminated. There was no thought that over such expanses, nature could restore itself to productivity. Nature, if left alone, foresters insisted, would require years to stabilize the soils and then would clothe the hills with "inferior" species. Their solution was to rehabilitate deliberately. The firefight would continue into the postburn period.

Gangs of men who had, during the crisis, scraped trenches and thinned reproduction to halt flames now dug hillsides to slow erosion and planted new stocks of commercially valuable trees. That required seedlings. Immediately after the burns the Forest Service shipped in a ton and a half of walnut seed, red oak acorns, and hickory nuts, "an experiment" that began the following spring and whose final outcome, Will Morris thought, would be "interesting." Closer to home, the Savenac Nursery, which Koch had established in 1909 near the junction of the Northern Pacific and Milwaukee railways, had burned away during the Great Fires. It was quickly rebuilt, and seedlings were parceled out to crews on the gutted slopes. They went first to Wallace, then to Prichard, both by rail, then by wagon six miles up the Coeur d'Alene River to Lost Creek, where they were packed on horses five miles over a temporary trail to a camp. Over the next thirty years millions of seedlings went into the mountains. The Big Blowup, in brief, dictated the practical field program of the Northern Rockies for decades to come: fire control, salvage logging, replanting.[24]

There were national lessons as well in what Greeley considered "practical conservation": that it was better to intervene than to leave to natural processes; that it was better that dead timber should be "utilized than that it should go to waste in the woods"; that it was necessary, in order to reduce the waste of the fires, to open up the country as rapidly as possible. Better access could keep smokes small, prevent big fires from becoming conflagrations, and allow the efficient harvest and rehabilitation of lands "destroyed" by flame. In this matter, as in so many others, the Great Fires had forced decisions; flame required action, not reflection. That was inevitable. The tragedy was that after the flame had passed, there was no still, small voice to listen to. The din of sheer doing continued to drown out thinking. The rehabilitation of their impact on policy was to last longer than those busily logging and planting could ever imagine.[25]

•

THE GOVERNMENT TREATED its burned trees better than its burned workers. Incredibly, the Forest Service did not come under the provisions of federal compensation acts. Employees on the Panama Canal, those with the U.S. Life-Saving Service, even workers with the Reclamation Service had provisions for relief or pensions in the event of injury. The firefighting Forest Service did not. While revisiting

Stevens Peak with James Danielson, still swathed in gauze and with his fingernails burned away, Will Morris pondered the unfairness. It was a "pitiful sight" to see Danielson's crew, heads and hands bandaged, arms crossed and bound, their burned fingers exposed. "I think the Government ought to give them a pension," Will concluded. "But they have even refused to pay their hospital fees, so we are going to each subscribe something ourselves."[26]

Of all the aftermath of the Great Fires, the treatment of the human casualties was the most confused, and perhaps most shameful. Bill Greeley had never doubted the Forest Service's duty: Everyone who served it, be he ranger or field cook, deserved medical care, compensation for work lost, and, if need be, burial. The injured—101 from the Coeur d'Alene alone—had gone directly to hospitals. But hardly had the rains squelched the flames than the solicitor for the Department of Agriculture ruled that all such expenditures could not be paid from official funds. Greeley was outraged, and in a circular letter to all the forest supervisors on 6 September, he insisted that the work would be done even if it be paid "entirely from personal funds." The American Red Cross donated $1,000. The town of Wallace organized a Fire Relief Committee, which accepted donations. Greeley suggested that the remainder of the expenses be met by subscriptions from members of the Forest Service "of not over one dollar each." The Washington office contributed $180. In the end the appeal raised $2,190.86.[27]

Fortunately Idaho senator Heyburn—maligned by Pinchot for his tightfistedness toward the Service—sought compensation for the casualties through legislation. These were, after all, men from his state. Secretary Wilson too believed that they warranted relief and prepared to recommend to Congress that it pass a special appropriations bill to cover the losses. Accordingly, he requested detailed information about those killed and injured and the extent of their probable claims. On 4 January he submitted a request for supplemental funding to the Treasury in the amount of $15,000 to provide for "burial expenses and the relief of dependent relatives." The exact amount he could not declare because most had not yet been fully identified. He recommended urgent passage "as a slight and altogether just and reasonable recognition of the heroism of the men who lost their lives while serving the Government as fire fighters." The treasury secretary, Franklin MacVeagh, agreed and forwarded the request to Congress, which enacted the request into law and provided that it would extend through the 1912 fiscal year. The bill also authorized reimbursement for those who had lost horses or equipment through government service during the fires. By the time it expired, Congress had amended the act of 1908 that defined hazardous duty in government employment to include the Forest Service.[28]

Meanwhile word came from the field that the Army troops stood in need of new uniforms. A canvass of damaged clothing suggested a loss of $40 per man; this was a significant sum for a poorly paid private. Graves considered that reimbursement from Forest Service funds was "out of the question," even though the losses occurred in duty to the Service, but asked Wilson if something might be done. Unhesitatingly Wilson agreed that the "soldiers should be reimbursed." The question was by whom. If by congressional act, then Greeley also urged that the bill reimburse those "Forest Rangers whose stations were destroyed by fire and who lost, in at least half a dozen cases, everything that they possessed, clothing, bedding, furniture and household goods of every description." He noted pointedly that they had resided in those structures by assignment, not "personal desire or initiative." What they lost, they lost in the line of duty. In this way, a new round of buck-passing commenced. The bills before Congress mounted.[29]

Thus began a tedious, often futile accounting of those injured and killed, an exercise that exposed the ramshackle process by which the men had been hired and shipped to the firelines. In comparison, the salvage of scorched white pine seemed simple and masterly. No compensations were paid until Congress passed the General Deficiency Bill of March 4, 1911, and none was to be paid after March 31, 1912. The inquiry began.

Those who survived and remained in local residence were relatively easy. They had to submit their claims on proper forms, suitably notarized. Rangers then submitted letters testifying to the facts presented, and doctors to the extent of injuries. For those who had departed, the task was similar but tougher. The real challenge came with those who had died. In most instances the deceased left no identifying papers. Rumors, reported friendships, fragments of letters, telegrams thrust into pockets all provided clues. Newspapers across the nation printed the list of casualties, as the dead had recorded their names. Queries rushed in; counterqueries poured out. From Upland, Pennsylvania, came a letter from James Denton, who had read in the Baltimore paper the register of names, among them the names Joe Denden and

Jim Denden, who "i Think our sons the last we Heard from them was the sixteen of August they were Then at Spokane Wash." C. S. Chapman was pleased to report only one injury in his district, the death of Louis Sego, a "transient" killed by a falling tree, about whom nothing was known except that he came from California. For the Coeur d'Alene, now in the hands of Acting Supervisor Roscoe Haines, the clerical exercise was enough to virtually paralyze office operations.[30]

But let Haines, who thought he had signed on as a forester, describe his efforts on behalf of one member he thought belonged with the Lost Crew of Setzer Creek.

> The man known to us as J. Rusick was among those to lose their lives in this fire on Setzer Creek. Among the effects found on the person of J. Rusick was an old note-book from which we were able to obtain only a small amount of information. We were able, however, to determine that he evidently was friendly to M. J. Merrick of Spokane, Washington. During the summer of 1911 at various times I called upon M. J. Merrick and George Scojat of Spokane, Washington, relative to Mr. Rusick and obtained the names of father and mother of Joe Ruzic. I took the matter up with the Imperial and Royal Austro-Hungarian Consul and secured his assistance in locating the relatives in Hungary. These relatives then appeared before the U.S. Consul at Fiume, Hungary, and executed an instrument, which, altho I am unable to read it, I would judge is a certificate of relationship. Altho there appears to be no means at this time for us to determine beyond every possible doubt that the man known to us as J. Rusick is Joe Ruzic, there is little question in my mind from my conversation with Mr. Merrick and Mr. Scojat and various correspondence from the Imperial & Royal Austro-Hungarian Consul of Denver, Colorado, and the papers furnished thru the U.S. Vice Consul at Fiume, Hungary, but that the man who lost his life and who was known to us as J. Rusick was Joe Ruzic, the son of the parties who are now making this claim.

There followed other conversations that confirmed, if circumstantially, that Ruzic had died at Setzer Creek. But did Stipan and Ulijana Ruzic have a valid claim?

> They state that they were entirely dependent upon the earnings of Joe Ruzic for their support, but they do not state the amount necessary for their support. It is observed that the father is sixty-two years of age and that the mother is sixty-one years of age, and also that the

> father is now employed in a stone-quarry at Fiume, Hungary, in order to earn a living. It is evident, therefore, that the father is able, or at least is earning a living for himself and wife. With the assistance of the American Consul at Fiume, Hungary, I attempted to determine the nature of the dependency of the father and mother of Joe Ruzic upon the earnings of their son for their support. I also endeavored to determine whether or not they had any other means of support, as well as the amount necessary for their support.

In any event, there was no longer time to exchange more letters across the Atlantic before the claims period expired. Carlo Rusic, a brother living in Chisholm, Minnesota, sent a letter asserting that Joe had sent to his parents $15 to $20 each month and that they depended on this stipend. Haines also obtained a photograph of Joe Ruzic from the consul at Denver. Carlo confirmed that the photo was of his brother and sent another, more recent picture. These were shipped around to rangers, foremen, and others of the crew who could be found. No one could state "whether or not the man shown in the picture was among those who lost their lives on Setzer Creek, or among those who fought fire on Setzer Creek." Still, Haines felt there was "little question" of the man's identity and the parents' dependency and recommended approval even without another round of forms.[31]

And so it went.

The crews were full of floaters and foreigners, not all of whom gave their real names, few of whom left any form of forwarding address, many of whom were burned so badly that bodies could not be matched with signatures. They had come from Canada, Serbia, Finland, Norway, Germany, Hungary, Nova Scotia, Austria, Italy, Persia, England, and heaven knows where else. Some had enrolled through employment agencies like Lyons or Inland Empire in Spokane. Most had just signed on with only a name, and had they lived, they would have carried away their wages in cash. No other record was needed or desired. Many passed under assumed names, and the haste of hiring had argued against statements about next of kin or permanent addresses, if any existed. Since they died, however, the ramshackle accounting system of folding tables in drugstores and tents near train depots proved inadequate. The government still owed them salary; it also could provide for the costs of interment; but it could do nothing unless it could locate relatives. For twelve long months the inquiry continued, an interminable, thankless stream of letters sent, returned, resent, answered, redirected, returned again; of files opened and closed, full of empty correspondence; of charges, confusions, grief, occasional frauds, and sluggish payments.

Of the seventy-eight government firefighters killed during the Big Blowup, only twenty-nine could be sufficiently identified to send their remains and their wages due to their next of kin. Most had no addresses or known friends or means of positive identification. Henry Jackson was identified by the heel plate worn on his shoe; Frank Sanders, by a partly burned Poor Tax receipt. A Mrs. Casey from Helena thought that the man who signed his name as "Wm. Casey" was her husband but had "no positive way of identifying him." (Her actual husband returned home two years later.) Mailed a photograph of Richard Hill, Mrs. J. C. Hill of Seattle was "still not quite positive as to the identification" of the man in the photo, the man buried at Setzer Creek, and her son. Louis Schwarz saw his son's name among the list of missing published in the newspaper and established identity "through the German Consul at Seattle." Louis Holmes had in his pocket a photograph of his mother, Mrs. Lewis, with her address in Birmingham, England, inscribed, and she claimed his salary due. One of those reported as "name unknown" in the Spokane paper became "E. Smith" when his mother sent a picture that others on the crew identified. He had been given a time slip at noon on 20 August and along with two others had started for Wallace. They never arrived, and both the "time keeper [and] records burned." August Berger, "address unknown," had worked 6 hours on 2 August and then 12 hours a day through 20 August, a total of 222 hours for wages of $55.50. "Died in tunnel with Pulaski's crew. Had white hair." Walter Beamair had worked only 12 hours on 19 August and another 12 on 20 August. His father claimed both his body and his $6 in due wages. Most entered the final roster as did "C. Bing": "Address unknown. Buried on Setzer Creek. No clue to this man's identity." Eight of the dead had no names at all.[32]

One by one, the rangering staff passed through the claims and queries even as they became more macabre, poignant, ironic, eerie, as the social reality of American labor and the indifference of the American landscape collided with legal language and political posturing.

The claim of Salvar D. Adams, whose son died at the Bullion Mine, appeared to be "very deserving." Still, Haines had to qualify that judgment by observing that "the affidavits and the claim have not been executed before a notary public, but before the Chairman of Legal

Board of what I take to be the Evangelical Church, who, I take it, may be authorized to administer oaths in Persia." Eventually he located a cousin living in New Britain, Connecticut, who could verify that the mother did in truth depend on the small sums sent home and thus merited compensation.[33]

Peter Schmidt filed for relief because of extended incapacitation. Yet after leaving the Wallace Hospital, he was "evidently feeling very gay, for he got on a big drunk and went over to the Providence Hospital where he stayed for several days. It also appears that after he was in the Providence Hospital for three days, that he went to Missoula and secured, or attempted to secure, treatment at the Sisters Hospital and told them that the Forest Service would pay the bills." C. W. Griffin decided Schmidt was not acting "in good faith" and recommended against payment.[34]

William Adsit, who had given his name as William Anderson, claimed damages from work on the Moose Creek fire. He was known to the crews as "Happy," William Adams (another firefighter) wrote, and "he appeared to be a man of feeble mind possibly a drug fiend, he never done any work outside of walking to and from the fire, every time he got out of sight of the camp he got lost and some of us had to hunt him up and bring him back." Five firefighters on the Moose Creek fire on Clearwater testified that he had done no work, had suffered no harm, had undoubtedly eaten better than had he been left in town. But he had an attorney in Seattle, and one (or both) were pressing claims for physical damages and emotional harm. Application denied.[35]

The widows and relatives of three homesteaders—Roderick Ames, Joseph Beauchamp, and Joe Robicheau—filed for compensation as surviving dependents. On 11 August, Pulaski had hired Ames to blaze a pack trail, but he had deserted after two days. He and the others reappeared during the Big Blowup to try to protect their properties. They were volunteers, not employees. All died at the Beauchamp homestead. Recommendation: no payment since not Forest Service employees.[36]

William Anderson, sawmill worker, was injured fighting the Swamp Creek fire on the Cabinet forest. "Entire breast surface burned, over abdomen in two or three places, burning through to intestines; two-thirds of back's surface burned; on right hip and both forearms for about 4 inches in length almost around; slight burns on privates." He received $115 for medical bills, $145 for time lost, and an additional $80 because of another month of lost labor.[37]

Justus Beaman of Sunset, Washington, requested reimbursement for the interment of his son Walter, killed at Stevens Peak. The government offered $20 to cover expenses for which he had receipts. Of the $53.50 for undertaker's bill, the Forest Service subscription fund paid $30 and the Wallace Fire Relief Committee $23.50. Beaman advanced an additional claim of $12.25 for transportation to and from Wallace that officials considered "undoubtedly valid" but denied since Beaman could produce no receipts and had "not properly presented" his bill.[38]

Josef Omerza of "Duruvar, Kingdom of Croatia and Slavonia," claimed relief as a dependent of his son, Carl Omerza. He stated that three years earlier he had loaned his son 400 crowns to send him to America, where he would earn enough money to repay his father and also support him in his old age. No one had heard from him again until a relative spied his name on published death lists. Recommendation: no payment.[39]

Vika Polic of Hreljin, Croatia, claimed payment as a dependent relative of her husband, Frank (or Ivan) Polic. Initially, the claim was denied because Vika could not identify her husband with anyone who died. Later a saloonkeeper passed along word that other "Austrians" had told him that the man had in fact died at Setzer Creek. Further investigation suggested he was the "Polk" on the time cards and was among those whose bodies had been found but not identified. Although the evidence was "circumstantial," the Forest Service recommended payment of $200.[40]

Young William Polleys of Missoula had died when a falling tree threatened the crew under his command. He had scattered the crew and taken the blow himself. But since he had volunteered his service, his relatives could make no claims for compensation. Instead Greeley and Silcox recommended that President Taft send his family a letter of condolence and drafted one for consideration.[41]

The claim of J. W. Siphers on behalf of Nina Siphers for relief as a dependent relative of Harley Siphers (signed "H. Sipheas"), killed at Setzer Creek, included "perjury . . . so flagrant" that the solicitor recommended further investigation with possible criminal prosecution for fraud.[42]

Jason Lalor wrote his Montana congressman to protest being stiffed by the Forest Service for time worked. "Now the facts of this case are Mrs. Everlith the ranger's wife (who is also appointed deputy), came to Stanford and made an appeal in the name of the Government for help to fight the forest fires which at that time threatened the whole reserve in the Little Belt Region directly west of Stanford. A large number responded and went up." Along the way a rancher named Taylor diverted thirty men to work a fire that Lalor believed was on the reserve and that threatened Taylor's ranch. The Forest Service then claimed that Lalor had worked for Taylor, not it, and he would have to sue Taylor for payment. Lalor noted that such behavior did not encourage men to turn out for fire duty in the future.[43]

Investigators lavished little sympathy on M. J. Carnahan of Mullan, injured on the Stevens Peak burnover. Carnahan had spent forty-two days in the hospital and would require some time more, perhaps up to three months, to restore his burned hands. Now he claimed incapacitation to the amount of $945. Haines attributed this excessive sum to two causes: One, the saloonkeepers of Mullan had taken pity on him and let him drink himself silly (and work off the debt as a swamper at the Elite Saloon), and two, he had hired two attorneys who had included a generous fee for themselves into the claim. The Forest Service recommended a counteroffer of $255.[44]

Doctors proved as greedy as lawyers. Two in particular, T. R. Mason and Albert Knudtson, charged bills so "exorbitant" that in Weigle's opinion, "without question whatever [they] should not be paid." Dr. Mason, when called upon to join the rescue party for Bell's crew, then demonstrated why he had "little standing" in the community. Bell claimed he engaged the "two of the Best Guides" he could, but the dark and gutted landscape bewildered them. Mason explained, "I found it necessary to walk thro' fire, fallen timber etc. climbing over and under burned logs, at night with no light except an ordinary 'Palouser' which gave very poor light, and having lost my Notch-Stick cannot tell you how many times I fell head-over-heels in the dark, tearing and completely ruining my clothing. It was the hardest trip a man ever took and had I known what I was getting into, money could not have hired me to go." He had had no blanket and had slept in "dust and ashes six inches deep." Dinner consisted of a can of pork and beans. Moreover, he had ruined a $50 suit. The Forest Service should pay for his inconvenience. It paid instead for his labor in dressing burns and splinting two broken legs.[45]

Miss Maude Early received $150 for the two horses that died at the Nicholson adit and for two saddles and bridles burned up. The fire also consumed a saddle of Roscoe Haines's. L. H. Cahoon lost a bay mare (value: $22) when it "fell off grade and was injured and had to be shot to prevent being burned as fire was almost upon her."[46]

The Forest Service recommended against Charles Bratton's claim of rheumatism brought about by exposure during fire duty. The claim was filed several months after the season; a chiropractor, who had prescribed treatment, refused to sign an affidavit for fear of being prosecuted for practicing medicine without a license; and as R. P. McLaughlin, forest supervisor, noted, "Men employed in Forestry work and in fact all kinds of work of this nature usually make such choice of work because they like it, or are driven to it because of necessity. It is always optional with them and most of them understand the hardships to be incident to the work, and this, in fact is one of the alluring fascinations connected with any kind of mountain work. Oftentimes too these so called hardships are really self imposed, especially by those who are most fascinated with it, and least experienced." In brief, Bratton had known the score and would have to live with his choice.[47]

Some of the most pathetic appeals were among the least effective because the law dealt with fine print, not with the cries of the human spirit. Mary Ella Nicolson explained how her son Val was only 17 and "had no written consent from either his father or myself as we thought it too dangerous work for a boy, but they needed men, and offered to pay good wages, and this lured him away at first, and then he felt he [was] needed, and the last time he came home he said mother I came up to see if you were in any danger here or needed any help, and when he went away he took me in his arms and kissed me and said mother you and father don't need to worry one bit about me our camp is perfectly safe it has been burned over once and can't burn again." But it did, and Val Nicolson died in the retreat to the Bullion Mine. His father was among the party that disinterred the Bullion Mine dead and brought them to Wallace for reburial. He himself died two weeks later, reportedly from grief. That left mother and daughter destitute. Since, at the time of his death, Val's mother had not depended on him, the law permitted no compensation. At least, Mrs. Nicolson replied, the government could "put a suitable stone to mark my son's grave." She received money for the cost of interment.[48]

Others had claims but little sympathy. Thomas A. Noonan was "just getting over a drunk" when Danielson hired him. "The next day he had to lay off owing to his spree of a few days previous. The fire burned the side of one thumb and singed his mustache. When we started down the hill to Mullan he feigned helplessness and was carried for miles by several of the boys who could hardly walk themselves. He stayed in the hospital one night and left and was seen in Mullan drunk two days later." His claim for compensation for wages lost was accepted but downgraded.[49]

Undoubtedly the most protracted claim came from Mrs. Antoine Weigert, mother of Oscar Weigert. Weigert was the only one of Rock's crew to die, and did so by his own hand, in a panic. The mother, however, insisted that Rock had imposed some kind of martial law and had shot Oscar as a means to enforce his will. It was a sensational claim, perfect for newspapers and lawyers. A thick file of affidavits, however, amply proved otherwise. The impending Big Blowup had unhinged Oscar; others in the crew had taunted and teased him, playing on his fears until he announced that he had a gun and would use it rather than let the flames get him. The "more considerate ones saw that he was in earnest and asked the others to desist, which was done." Yet the fear swelled, and so horrified was Weigert when the smoke and firefront arrived that he escaped from the sanctuary into which Rock had moved the crew and shot himself. John D. Jones, acting assistant district forester, deferred to the solicitor the question of what was owed to an injured employee and what not because the injury had been self-inflicted. Mrs. Weigert verged, in his opinion, on "nervous collapse and mental derangement." The charge was wholly unfounded, as was her claim to be dependent. Reimbursements on the order of $320 for burial expenses, however, were in order.[50]

Catherine Hansen's husband had died eighteen years before and left her with two sons, a daughter, and heavily mortgaged property. Until her health gave out, she took in boarders and relied on her sons. Then her older son died. That left son Harry to provide for her care, and he did, about $15 a month for eight years. He went west to make more money and find a new home and decided to bring his mother out to live with him in Oregon. He "loved the west," Mrs. Hansen explained, "and wrote he could never be content back east again." He told a friend in Kellogg, D. W. Price, that "he was going to fight fire I tried to talk him out of going I told him [he] would get a position at $3.00 per day and stay in Kellogg but he said he could make more money fighting fire and needed the money to get his mother out west." He died instead in the Nicholson tunnel. She was reimbursed $342.40 for the cost of shipping the body to Racine, Wisconsin, and reburying. Investigators recommended another $500 as a dependent relative.[51]

When the deficiency bill expired in March 1912, three claims still clamored for supplemental relief. D. R. Sullivan, a temporary, had permanently crippled hands, too sensitive to stand "any severe exposure." His left hand had no feeling and was useless. Moreover, "his sufferings in the forest fires have seriously affected his mind." James Danielson also sustained injuries to his hands and eyes that would leave him partially but permanently disabled. He had used his annual and sick leave to cover his time in the hospital, but he could not return to house painting, so he had reenrolled at Washington State College. The solicitor, George McCabe, considered it was impossible for him to do anything else, and "no man should suffer for doing the best that he can under the circumstances." In fact, he struggled through his studies, "seriously handicapped by his burned hands and inability to sleep well," and had to borrow $170 from his sister to survive the year. The recommended relief was for the amount of $550, half the annual salary of an assistant forest ranger. Then there was the "particularly distressing" case of Anton Canyor, another temporary, whose injuries would never allow him again to do manual labor. Secretary Wilson suggested that these expenses be absorbed into the emergency fire fund. The legislation passed.[52]

Still, the claims continued to trickle in, their sum exceeding the $15,000 originally allotted. From Phoenix came one from Samuel Stockton, who had traveled with Pulaski's crew on a horse and had survived the Nicholson adit ordeal. From Goff, Idaho, came a claim from Frank Freeman, who had voluntarily attacked a fire on national forest lands, crossing the Salmon River to do it. Since the original act allowed only for bona fide employees, Freeman required a supplemental appropriation. So did Dr. T. R. Mason, still grousing over his soiled suit. Secretary Wilson thought he deserved compensation. Senator Heyburn sponsored an amendment to that effect.[53]

•

PERHAPS THE MOST startling—surely the most exasperating—story was that of Edward Pulaski. Like many others, he had languished for several weeks in the hospital. Like theirs, his injuries had loosened their grip only slowly. His lungs never fully recovered. But he dreaded especially the tedious healing of his eyes. In November 1911 Haines explained to the district forester that there was "no question but that sooner or later Mr. Pulaski will necessarily have to submit to an operation on his eyes" and that it "would seem no more than right that Mr. Pulaski should receive a sufficient amount from the Government to pay the cost of this operation."[54]

But "right" didn't enter into the matter. Pulaski had no out-of-pocket expenses to report, had used sick and annual leave to cover his days in the hospital, and was still waiting for his eyes to recuperate as fully as they could on their own before undertaking surgery. The solution was to include Pulaski's claim with those others that fell outside the original appropriation. Incredibly, that claim never made it properly in and out of bureaucratic pigeonholes. Acting Assistant Forester F. W. Reed wrote the district forester on 26 February 1912 to lay out the confusion. The 8 February reply by the supervisor to the Heyburn resolution did not include Pulaski's case because, it was believed, his claim had appeared in the report of 3 February. In fact, that report had overlooked Pulaski, as did its sequel. Since Pulaski was "still on the rolls as a Forest Ranger," Reed did not understand "the delay in getting his claim in." The fact remains, it wasn't submitted. Acting District Forester R. H. Rutledge lamely excused the omission by explaining that "in the opinion of this office," Pulaski's claims did not fall within the scope of the Deficiency Act and so had not been forwarded. That brought the unforeseen consequence that he would not be considered for the supplemental bill.[55]

Everyone felt strongly that Pulaski's injuries entitled him to compensation. No one, however, could imagine quite how to do it. Rutledge thought that if Congress extended hazardous duty statutes to the Forest Service, Pulaski might submit a claim under those provisions. Acting Assistant District Forester J. D. Jones thought Pulaski had two options. He could try for special legislation in Congress, although this was unlikely since the deadline had passed for the Heyburn resolution (which, for example, had helped Danielson). Or someone could submit his name to the Carnegie Hero Fund Commission for consideration.

Jones noted that a ranger on the Kootenai had saved a woman on a ferryboat and received a medal and $1,000. Nor, it was decided, as the paperwork crawled through the corridors, could Pulaski be reimbursed for expenses he had incurred in obtaining affidavits on behalf of injured crewmen who were submitting claims of their own. He had footed the bills for the indigent in the expectation that if he did Forest Service work, the Service would repay him. It didn't.[56]

The Carnegie Commission decided it could not either. The purpose of the fund was to reward those who acted above job and beyond instinct to save the life of another. While Pulaski's actions had undoubtedly spared lives, the commission reasoned that he had performed within the scope of his duty as a forest ranger and that he had been in cold fact part of a mob fleeing for its collective life. He had struggled to save himself as well as others and thus fell outside the scope of the fund. In 1916 Meyer Wolff, then supervisor of the Coeur d'Alene, handed the file to Richard Eggleston to "try to work up a strong case for the Carnegie Medal" regardless. Eggleston, however, who was transferring to the Missoula office, found himself "swamped with work," pushed the matter aside, and then forgot about it altogether. He finally returned the files, with apologies, in 1949.[57]

There remained a weirder sidebar to this particular narrative. Even as field officers mailed out scores of letters to search for next of kin, bureaucracy and politics clunked along according to rhythms all their own. Taft's ballyhooed reform of government to make it more efficient and businesslike led the Department of Agriculture's Committee on Economy and Efficiency, chaired by George McCabe, the solicitor, to inform Chief Forester Graves on 8 February 1911, the same day Pulaski's claim failed to appear in the supervisor's report, that "The President desires a complete and specific description of the method and procedure followed in the various Departments in the handling and filing of correspondence." The directive produced detailed questionnaires regarding how, stage by stage, letters were received and sent, what forms the Forest Service used to record expenditures, how many paper clips clerks used in filing. There was a discussion over the exorbitant cost of library paste. There were letters exchanged over the disposal of waste papers. Moreover, in a crowning gesture, the committee secretary, C. C. Carroll, informed the Forest Service: "It appears that this Committee's report to the White House transmitting your reply to this communication has miscarried, and I have to request that you furnish this Committee with a copy, *in duplicate*, of your reply. This matter is urgent. . . ."[58]

The fact remained, if anyone needed further proof, wildfire was not a bureaucratic entity. It never would be.

•

AMONG HER EXPENSES, Mrs. Antoine Weigert had included $100 for a "monument." Mrs. Mary Ella Nicolson had also requested a "suitable stone." Acting Assistant District Forester Jones believed, however, that "in view of the shortness of the fund and the large demand upon it," such claims could not be included as "legitimate expenses." The question of what to do with the dead, as distinct from the money owed them, rankled for years. There were abundant claimants for the former, few other than parents for the latter. As the Great Fires proved over and again, the government would have to do what in the past ordinary citizens had done. The Forest Service had demanded to "settle" the reserves on its own. That meant it would have to fight its own fires, and it would have to take care of those who died doing so.[59]

The immediate problem was simple burial. For days after the Big Blowup, the troops of Company G at Avery had searched the charred slopes for bodies and then given military burials to those they found. The fallen firefighters nearer Wallace, Will Morris explained, received a "Christian burial" from the Reverend Carter, a Congregational minister from Nova Scotia. Greeley explained forcefully to Weigle that those "temporary laborers" who had died and could be claimed by relatives should have their remains "prepared for shipment and shipped as soon as possible at our expense." The rest "should be collected when practicable at the nearest Ranger Station and interred in wooden boxes in suitable plots which can be fenced off to protect the graves. I will take up with you later the preparation of suitable tablets at these plots." Greeley wanted the business of proper burial "prosecuted as soon as practicable after the immediate fire emergency is past."[60]

The original thought was to disinter the bodies after fire season and rebury them properly. Those who had died at the Nicholson adit, not far from Wallace, and those who had perished in the Bullion Mine, most of them local men, were exhumed and reinterred in Wallace cemeteries. They were reburied in the order and number they arrived: Five went into one grave; six into another; the two Nicolsons, father and son, into a third. Weigle had to wait about ten days for the railroad to rebuild its line before dispatching the disinterring crew to the Bullion Mine. The Northern Pacific supplied a special car to carry the bodies over the mountains to Dorsey. There, blocked by an unrepaired trestle, the bodies were transferred to another special train, this one bound for Wallace. By 3 September, the day before the season-ending rains, thirteen dead firefighters came to rest in Wallace. Seven other bodies were claimed by fathers, mothers, sisters, and brothers and brought home to Gem, Idaho; Sunset, Washington; Missoula and Butte, Montana; and Racine, Wisconsin.[61]

But many of the slit graves resided in remote sites; most of the dead had no kin that anyone could identify, much less relations willing to oversee transport and reinterment; they stayed where they lay. Small rock cairns over mass graves marked their unrestful resting places. On 31 May 1912, Roscoe Haines wrote to the district forester regarding the claim of Klara Johansen, wife of Gust Johansen, one of those who had fallen in a heap outside the Dittman cabin. He mentioned that "it is planned to remove the bodies yet this spring." They weren't.[62]

There was money to reimburse relatives; there was none for those without relations, who were in effect wards of the Forest Service. At the Wallace plots, wooden slabs substituted for headstones. There was no provision for maintenance. For years Ed Pulaski took it upon himself to make repairs, clear out weeds, and plant flags annually.[63]

•

IN ITS 24 September issue, *Collier's* published a feature on "Idaho's Thirty Days' War," which introduced the Big Blowup to a national readership. Newspapers had of course run accounts from major wire services as the drama unfolded, and the *New York Times* had printed a special feature on 28 August, based largely on interviews with Graves and Pinchot and comparing what the federal government was doing with what the enlightened state of New York was doing in the Adirondacks. The *Collier's* piece was a bid to define the fires' meaning for a larger audience.[64]

Neither theme nor magazine was coincidental. Under editor Norman Hapgood, *Collier's* had championed Pinchot in his quarrel with the Taft administration. Probably its influence was never greater than when, in August 1909, it had editorialized that "Ballinger Should Go." Taft invited Ballinger to fire Louis Glavis, the prickly Interior agent whose relentless proddings had prompted the scandal, which he did on

16 September. In November *Collier's* published Glavis's stinging exposé on Pinchot's rival, "The Whitewashing of Ballinger." It was exactly the kind of trial-by-media in which Pinchot excelled and that reduced Ballinger to sputtering. The beleaguered secretary muttered publicly about suing *Collier's* for libel. Hapgood retained Louis Brandeis to represent both the magazine and Glavis. On 21 September 1910, Ballinger laid bare before the Denver Chamber of Commerce the nature of the campaign against him. "I have been the victim of a wicked, unconscionable cabal of bureaucrats, politicians and muckrakers," he fumed. The *"fatal charge"* against him was solely that he disagreed with those who had a different vision of how to administer the public domain and that "not being in accord with the doctrines of the Chief Apostles of bureaucratic conservation, I should be ruthlessly removed from office." He believed in conservation; he did not believe in converting the public domain "into a great national preserve and to destroy the opportunities of the West for the useful and just development of its resources." His critics' quixotic quest was not merely unfair, it was unworkable.[65]

Now, one year after its sensational declaration, the Big Blowup offered a test of Pinchot's and Ballinger's competing theories of government-sponsored conservation. The firefight in the Rockies became politics by other means. If, as a result of its brash campaign, the Forest Service rose in public esteem, so would the deposed Pinchot, Roosevelt's New Nationalism, and federal-based conservation, while by implication the despised Ballinger would plummet in stature and drag state-sponsored conservation along with him. Roosevelt had informed the Second National Conservation Congress that the recent fires had proved that "forest protection is a national duty"; even with the aid of the Army, the Forest Service had been overwhelmed; nothing less than a federal system could succeed. The normally Pinchot-friendly *New York Times* laid out the choices: "Mr. Pinchot is largely responsible for the creation of the national forests" and has argued that "we can get conservation best" by buying up private lands "equivalent in area to many States and entrusting their welfare to a bureaucratic central government." But why, the newspaper asked, did he not during his "long years" of stewardship "make their 'efficient' federal machine work to provide a system of fire protection?" The state of New York amply demonstrated an alternative.[66]

Yet public opinion read a different narrative, and eventually so did the *Times.* Wrapped in the firefight-as-battlefield metaphor—which over the coming decades would be almost mandatory, a kind of autonomic reflex—the Big Blowup became a patriotic story of gallant, outgunned rangers standing against demonic flames and the shameful waste of natural resources. Yes, the fires had escaped. But they had exploded because Uncle Sam's rangers had not been granted the weapons they needed, because a cabal of Western politicians and standpatters had refused to accept the logic of Progressive conservation and had denied the funds that would have made trails and patrols possible. Pinchot had been right, Ballinger wrong. When the land was properly laced with roads, trails, telephone lines, and lookout towers, and staffed with a tough corps of forest guards, the fires would cease. To suggest otherwise was to agree with Secretary Ballinger and senators like Heyburn that fire suppression might not be the ideal method of forest protection, that forestry was not necessarily the best profession to oversee the public lands, that more money would not solve the problem, that some core premises of federal conservation were flawed.

# OCTOBER

THE FIRES ON the Coeur d'Alene were over, and Will Morris was glad. "I haven't been to church now since June," he wrote his mother. This Sunday, in mid-October, he would at last attend in his congregation's "very pretty little pressed brick church." He was looking forward to visiting the family at Christmas; they would hardly recognize him, he had so filled out and eaten so much. He longed to be somewhere where he could walk on level ground. Mostly it was a relief to find the fires had gone elsewhere. "I was reading today about the bad fires in the Rainy River region of Minnesota."[1]

They were worse than bad: They were dreadful. The endless drought across the northern borderlands had rendered the fall fire season into a horror. The usual fires broke out in the usual ways as settlers burned brush, locomotives cast sparks, drying mires held smoldering combustion through the rainless summer; slash from logging and land clearing blanketed the land around the railways and towns; a cold front drove southwesterly winds over the scene, and the flames exploded. There was nothing—absolutely nothing—extraordinary about either the fires' causes or their consequences. The fires were extreme because their informing conditions in 1910 were extreme. Deal enough hands of stud poker, and eventually you will draw a full house. On the evening of 7 October the last card turned over, and a regional conflagration resulted, exactly one day ahead and thirty-nine years after the great fires that gutted Chicago and Peshtigo on 8 October 1871 under virtually identical circumstances.[2]

The worst of the whirlwind struck the communities of Baudette and Spooner, Minnesota, rival rail towns across the Rainy River, around 8:30 in the evening. Four fires—three from locomotives, one from brush burning—roared out of swamps, stoked by slash, and pummeled the towns. It happened so suddenly that no alarm had been raised. No one had been fighting the fires. The flame seemed to fall from the sky with the fury of an earthquake. When many first heard the roar, they thought a thunderstorm had at last broken the drought. But embers fell instead of raindrops. Some never escaped their dwellings; others struggled into the streets or into fields or waded into streams where they stood for hours, a few shoulder deep in the water, holding their babies above their heads. The towns burned in less than two hours. The railway bridge that linked them melted away. Whole families died in their houses. The earliest reports estimated 1,000 dead, 200 bodies recovered, and more than 5,000 homeless, many wandering the smoking woods shell-shocked.[3]

Immediately, telegraphs sounded warnings to other villages along the Canadian Northern Railway and requested aid. Fifty militia from Bemidji arrived and set to work in the ruins of Baudette. Fire wardens rallied settlers and commandeered citizens to cut line, backfire, and douse kindled roofs. G. G. Chapin, a student at the University of Minnesota, who had worked as a ranger during the summer, wired the Minnesota Forestry Commissioner: "Give me fifteen men and I can prevent town's destruction in case fire." He got them, and did. More towns burned, wholly or in part, on both sides of the border: Pitt, Swift, Zipple, Gravel Pit Spur, Engle, Rainy River, Pinewood, Stratton, Warroad, Sprague, Cedar Spur, Roosevelt, Williams. The Canadian Northern dispatched trains to evacuate residents, fifty boxcars in all, hauling out townsfolk "like cattle." Relief trains from Duluth and St. Paul soon steamed in with more militia, tents, blankets and clothing, medical supplies and physicians, and Governor A. O. Eberhart. Relief committees appeared. Custom barriers across the Canadian border were suspended to allow aid to cross freely from the north. The Minnesota militia began the grim work of sorting through the ruins and burying the dead. Eight bodies were found along the tracks. Other corpses arrived in wagons. The Roulins, nine in all, were discovered in the clearing in which they had gathered until a firewhirl incinerated them on the spot, mother and father still sitting upright, arms outstretched to their children.[4]

When the flames finally quelled, the wreckage was less than feared.

Some twenty-nine persons had died. The destroyed towns were already rising from the ashes. "Every encouragement will be given settlers to remain," the *New York Times* reported. Local lumber companies planned to buy the burned timber and resell it at cost to help rebuild the towns. Relief committees were shipping nails and hammers ("especially welcome") as well as blankets. Neighboring towns were providing 1,500 meals a day. Some even saw benefits. "Thousands of acres of land has been cleared and can be made ready for farming with but little clearing." Schoolteacher Mary Donaghue concluded, "The land can't burn and I'm here to stay." Perhaps too, officials wondered, this might be the fire that finally broke the region's melancholy chronicle of wanton conflagrations.[5]

In a way, it was. Wildfires continued to plague the Lake States for another twenty-five years, but the 1910 conflagrations were the last million-acre eruption. The response by both settlers and officials shows why: Institutions were in place to cope with them, even if not running at full throttle. Tallying the year's burns, Forestry Commissioner C. C. Andrews reckoned that more than one million acres had burned in Minnesota alone and that wardens had relied on 15,260 firefighters, to whom the state owed $94,507.31. (Since many people had worked more than one fire, Andrews downgraded the actual number of firefighters.) "The unpaid service of these 8,944 Minnesota people in fighting fires was legally commanded by the fire wardens. In most cases they left their own, to them important, work, to render this public service. They sometimes went many miles from their homes. They saved settlements, human life and property from destruction. This work was sometimes at the peril of their lives." Six months later they were still waiting to be paid.[6]

Andrews insisted that Minnesota and its citizens deserved better. "The dignity and humanity of the State demand that every reasonable means of protection be provided." His solution was to rationalize the process of settlement: to restrict burning to certain periods, to continue summer fire patrols into the autumn, to insist that logging companies trim and burn slash, to demand that firebreaks surround burned plots, to require locomotives to burn diesel rather than coal and to outfit their smokestacks with spark arresters, to extend patrols into townships that held little valuable timber but could harbor long-smoldering fire in muskeg. Not least, he urged tougher enforcement. "The forestry commissioner's office must be strongly reinforced," he insisted, "and not with cheap men."[7]

If it all sounded familiar, that was because much of what Andrews prescribed was the common wisdom of foresters. Graves said much the same thing in his treatise *Protection of Forests from Fire.* Yet the Minnesota model looked to New York, not Montana. It urged means to expedite, not to eliminate, settlement. The state did not propose to do itself what it did not allow its citizens to do. Fire protection relied upon, and served, rural communities. Eventually wildfires would pass away along with other violent expressions of the frontier. With its mix of rural fires and the Adirondacks Preserve, New York offered a suitable model; the forest reserves of the Northern Rockies did not. There the government would have to assume the roles that citizens and settlers performed in Minnesota. It would have to develop the countryside; would have to staff firelines with whatever bodies it could get, almost none of them residents; would have to furnish relief; would have to rebuild; would have to assume responsibility for the unidentified dead. In particular, Forestry Commissioner Andrews could imagine only regulating fire, which rural Minnesota required, not abolishing it. Chief Forester Graves could, in principle, imagine fire's abolition on lands that would never be settled under the regimen of a rural economy.

Yet there was a deeper contrast, one that accents how strange the Great Fires were. The Baudette Burn raged within a specific social context. It savaged a working community along a frontier that had crunched through the North Woods for more than half a century. The fires occurred within a tradition, however macabre, of catastrophic burns. That society knew how to respond. The state sent in militia; the railroads dispatched emergency trains; the Red Cross erected medical tents; the citizens organized relief committees. The town promptly rebuilt. Its residents stayed and raised children. The dead had families, friends, and relatives to bury them, mourn for them, memorialize them. Someone, usually a schoolteacher, wrote up and published the fire's story. In brief, a narrative existed to explain what had happened, and institutions to cope with consequences. Baudette plugged itself into that chronicle. The frontier absorbed this tragedy as it had others.

None of this, however, applied to the Great Fires farther west. If the Baudette Burn was the last million-acre burn from a century of great settlement fires, the Big Blowup was the first in a century of fought fire in wildlands. No one knew how to behave; no one had invented the proper procedures; no one had the least idea what such a campaign might cost; no one had yet written the controlling interpretation. Not local citizens but throngs of errant laborers fought the flames. Not relatives and neighbors but anonymous bureaucrats had to collect the separate tales, bury the unknown dead, devise the land's reconstruction, ponder how, if at all, the trauma might be remembered. Almost to a man, the rangers and fire guards left for new posts elsewhere within a few years. In brief, the Big Blowup burned outside any true social order. No obvious narrative claimed it.

Thus the Baudette Burn was less an eastern echo of the Big Blowup than it was a symbolic passing of the torch. The frontier of eruptive fires was closing; a new era of wildland fires was opening. The inability (or unwillingness) of officials and the public to discriminate among such different fires complicated enormously the debate over fire policy. The fires that savaged towns seemed no different from those that blasted through forests, and as Pinchot insisted, the response should be the same. But they were, at base, different fires. The contrast between how Baudette coped with its fire tragedy and how the Forest Service did it shows this brilliantly. The Great Fires had a disproportionate impact because in 1910 the Forest Service was a raw and inchoate institution. It was not inevitable that it would respond to the Great Fires as it did or that the agency should preserve the fires' history. But the timing was right for something big to have a big impact. That the Big Blowup provided.

•

THE PAIRING OF the Baudette Burn and the Big Blowup holds some larger lessons. One was that neither the states nor the federal government could alone control fire. Another was that both exploited the fire menace as a means to install institutions for general forestry. The contrast between the two fires makes a convenient point of departure: Minnesota stands in useful counterpoint to District One, much as Forestry Commissioner Andrews serves as a foil to Chief Forester Gifford Pinchot. The one reminds us that forest fire protection did not originate with the U.S. Forest Service; the other that Gifford Pinchot did not implant forestry in America.

There were in truth other "prophets" of forestry, other visions of forest management, other institutions and schemes to halt and perhaps reverse the devastation of America's woods. In 1864 George Perkins Marsh had addressed the link between deforestation and destabilized lands; Charles Sargent had inventoried America's forests for the 1880 census, sketched the panorama of its fires, and chaired the National Academy of Sciences committee to review the forest reserves. Christopher Columbus Andrews belonged with them. Like Marsh, he had grown up in New England, and like Marsh, he parlayed extensive experience in Europe into a vigorous critique of the extravagant havoc that his fellow Americans wrought on their lands and woods. Unlike them, and Pinchot, he focused on the state as the vehicle of public control.

Born in 1829, he had studied law, gone west to Minnesota, and, when the Civil War broke out, quickly volunteered and then recruited a company of Minnesota infantry. By the time the war ended, he had risen to the rank of major general of volunteers by brevet and distinguished himself not only in the field but in politics. In Arkansas he oversaw a constitutional convention to reorganize Arkansas as a free state. When the war ended, he had command of districts in Alabama and Texas. After the war he returned to Minnesota and added the politics of public service to his law practice and plunged into library boards, soldiers' homes, war memorials, chambers of commerce.[8]

The breakthrough came in 1869, when he began eight and a half years as minister to Sweden and Norway. Both were experiencing a surge of industrial logging, in purpose and practice almost identical to that in Minnesota. Tirelessly Andrews studied the scene, particularly noting the general European commitment to forestry as an institution of state administration and Sweden's increasingly tough measures to contain the wastage. After a stint as consul general to Brazil, Andrews returned home to commence a long campaign to bring to Minnesota something of what he had seen of Swedish forestry.[9]

Meanwhile the model he hoped to achieve was, if laggingly, being developed in New York. Andrews regretted that New York had waited too long, that much of its vast forests were already "desolated." But he attributed to Grover Cleveland as governor, and later as president, the origins of forest policy in the United States. Interestingly, C. S. Sargent chaired New York's forestry commission of 1883 upon which Cleveland acted, as he did the 1896 NAS committee on the national reserves, the first of which had been created during Cleveland's administration. That this history has more or less faded from memory is testimony to the power of Gifford Pinchot's propaganda that he was the father of forestry, that forestry and conservation began with the federal government.[10]

General Andrews recognized that fire protection lay at the core of forestry. In August 1894 he read a paper titled "The Prevention of Forest Fires" only nine days before a fire killed more than 400 people outside Hinckley. That prompted Minnesota to enact in 1895 its first forestry law, which Andrews drew up and modeled on New York's. The core provision was an office of chief fire warden, which Andrews, not surprisingly, initially occupied. Over the next sixteen years, he tried overtly and surreptitiously to leverage the fire statute into a general institution of state forestry. The state remained both skeptical and frugal; willing to aid around settlements, reluctant to push into the unsettled backcountry. By 1905 the chief fire warden had 2,000 local wardens under him. Andrews watched the 1908 Chisholm fires terrify the northern counties, and he remained chief warden when the 1910 disaster overwhelmed Beltrami County. Until then, he noted approvingly, Minnesota had been doing a better job than its prairie and Lake States neighbors. Had he enough money to keep a ranger staff through the fall season, he was convinced the Baudette Burn could have been suppressed before it escaped from the swamps and rail rights-of-way that nurtured it. Even so, his warden staff had fielded 15,260 firefighters across 1,051,333 burned acres.[11]

He despaired, however, that Minnesota would ever staff the ranger force sufficiently or that it would ever allow the office of fire warden to expand into a department of forestry. Accordingly, he simultaneously campaigned to have some of Minnesota's expansive unclaimed forests (lands unsuitable for agriculture) set aside from the public domain as federal forest reserves and to have one patch endowed as an experimental forest. Both eventually happened. Also, by the time he retired, after the 1910 season, the legislature had established a Forestry Commission, of which he became secretary. It was not all he wanted, or all he thought the citizenry deserved, but it left Minnesota with a mixed economy of forest lands, intermediate between those eastern states with almost no public forests and those western states with only public reserves. When he retired, General Christopher Columbus Andrews was 82 years old.

In the twentieth century federal forestry became so powerful that it has by and large trumped the story of state forestry. But despite the mirage that forestry might be nationalized, or at least that federal regulations could extend over all forest practices, the reality remained that most fires did not occur on federal lands, that fire control belonged with local communities, that federal forestry would become powerful through alliances with the states. Pinchot had argued otherwise. In the *Use Book* he lectured that only "the Government," meaning the federal government, could afford the outlays necessary for fire protection; and for the public domain, this meant the forest reserves. Neither the states nor the federal government could individually acquire the critical mass needed to overcome the public's skepticism or indifference. What the 1910 fires showed, if anyone needed so obvious a demonstration, was that fire protection was the means of joining those separate visions. The states could not accept Baudette Burns any more than the federal government could tolerate Big Blowups.[12]

By 1910, in fact, eighteen states had organized fire protection systems. Few had adequate funding, but then neither did the U.S. Forest Service. What they collectively lacked was a kind of institutional linkage, a political valence that could bond them together. For that they needed a catalyst or a jolt of heat to speed up the tedious reactions. In political chemistry, as in molecular, that is precisely what flame could furnish. That is also precisely what the Year of the Fires did supply.

•

FOR MOST OF October, Harry Graves toured the West, inspecting the major challenges to the forest reserves. On the 4th he was in Boise; on the 6th, Spokane. He joined Greeley and Silcox for a three-day pack trip, before heading to Portland and Sacramento. There were the usual squabbles over land classification—what portions of the reserves might be opened as forest homesteads, what sites might serve as damsites and reservoirs—and of course there were the enormous fires and the crises posed by their salvage. Graves informed the Mountaineers Club in Oregon that fire was the "first problem" of the Forest Service and that "we believe in fire prevention." But he saved the longest entries in his field diary for an excursion to Grass Valley, California, and a scrutiny of light burning on the lands of T. B. Walker.[13]

He had known of Walker before, knew him to be more progressive than most lumbermen, may in fact have later approached him to underwrite a chair on fire protection at Yale (for $100,000). Walker owned vast acres of pine, largely sugar and ponderosa, in northern California. Most of the land was flat, the forest open, the soil hard. To protect those big trees, Walker adopted a strategy of light burning. He did so methodically, in many ways adapting the techniques long practiced in the turpentine groves of the South. Raking the needles around every tree proved impracticable, however, so crews concentrated on protecting those trees that had basal wounds, filling the cavities with a mound of dirt. Thus fires could not reenter and falling debris could roll off. Sometimes they filled the "cat-face" with a large stone. This preparatory work occupied a crew of thirty men through spring and summer. Graves estimated the cost at 6 to 10 cents per tree, or 37 cents an acre. More frustrating was brush control; the scrub kept resprouting, far faster than labor-intensive weeding could remove it. The solution to both brush and the threat of wildfire was the same: to burn.[14]

The burning commenced, with dripping pitch torches, after the first fall rains. The fires were light, patchy, slow, easily contained. Probably not more than 50 percent of the area actually burned—largely, Graves thought, because "Squaw weed" inhibited the flames but also because the frequent firing meant that few combustibles built up on the ground. The fire destroyed a "good many seedlings" but "practically no saplings except an occasional patch and this chiefly white fir." The cost was about 15 cents per acre. All in all, Graves found "very surprising" the "lack of damages."[15]

That did not mean he liked the practice. He had seen it all before, in India, where it was known as early burning and was common in teak. There the laborers surrounded a coupe with a fireline and then fired off the fallen leaves and grass within. "They seem to have it under perfect control and beat it out with ease at will." But whatever its local name or wherever it appeared, he deemed it intrinsically hostile to good forestry. As long as burning was abundant, fire control was impossible. Yet, once well rooted, fire control no longer required prosthetic burning for assistance. In fact, sound fire suppression demanded aggressive fire prevention; the fewer the fires, the fewer the escapes that could occur.[16]

Besides, broadcast burning confused the public. It required discriminations between good fires and bad fires, which complicated propaganda messages. Most of the rural public liked to burn and wanted access to the torch. Many thought that outside the conflagration corridors of the Big Blowup, the fires of 1910 had done more good than harm. But if foresters executed the same fires as the public, then what was the purpose of the forest reserves? To sanction public ownership, rangers needed to act for a greater good and to adapt practices derived from scientific (or at least academic) precepts.

Accordingly, foresters labeled folk burning as "incendiarism" or "woods arson." Those who set fires were saboteurs, and their insidious acts were likely one of the reasons why the fires had persisted as they did. Elers Koch admitted that in the early days, including 1910, incendiary fires were "quite common" and "most infuriating," the outcome of "general cussedness." Secretary Wilson even offered a reward for the conviction of incendiarists. Will Morris thought that forest homesteaders, unhappy with Forest Service inspections, were a source of "many of our recent fires." In southern Oregon similar groups—cattlemen, those dispossessed by the Crater Lake reserve, forest homesteaders angry over inspections—kept the pot boiling; for every fire put out, another would spring up. That ended only after a rumor circulated that the soldiers called to the firelines would shoot fire starters on sight. Of course, as Major C. H. Martin intoned innocently, "no such order was ever thought of, yet it was never denied."[17]

The more troublesome charge raised during the past summer, however, was that firefighters were themselves setting fires. In the aftermath of the Big Blowup, the *New York Times* editorialized that such an accusation seemed "incredible." "That many, or even any, of the forest fires now devastating the West are of incendiary origin is a charge that comes from several sources in frequent repetition, but it is made hard to believe by the inadequacy of the motives which are offered in explanation of the atrocious crime." Some thought that incendiarism had as its purpose to embarrass the Forest Service; others, that the firefighters did it to "secure employment." The *Times* dismissed both explanations. Its firefight only ennobled the rangers, and there were easier and safer jobs open to workers "as strong and courageous as the fire-fighters must be."[18]

Those on the scene, however, did not find it so incredible; they knew the caliber of men they were hiring. They knew the simple economics: that if you pay someone to fight fires, those someones have an interest in seeing that fires continue. Koch openly confessed that "sometimes" their temporary firefighters set fires to get work (and good grub). The most acidic reports, though, were those filed by the Army. Many officers found evidence of incendiarism; those patrolling along railways considered job hunters as common as locomotives in starting fires. Lieutenant W. S. Mapes expressed the opinion of most when he doubted that "the employment of labor at such high wages and furnishing them such extraordinary food is good policy as the temptation to create the necessity for fire fighters is too great for a certain class of citizens." Captain Charles Bates urged regular patrol to the "present system of concentrating unknown gangs of hoboes who as Major Morgan well said 'probably set more fires than they put out.'" A dedicated corps would "feel an interest in doing their patrolling work, just as the hobo gangs now take an interest in prolonging the life of the fires."[19]

More embarrassing was eventual court-martial of two soldiers from the Fourteenth Infantry for arson. They had been overseeing evacuations, but after whisking residents off with nothing save the clothes on their backs, often nightgowns, they had looted the houses, doused them with kerosene, and set them ablaze. The scheme unraveled when a resident subsequently saw some of his clothes being worn by a soldier outside Borax. The soldier gave an unconvincing explanation for how he came by them, so C. H. Hopkins filed a formal complaint with the officers of Company H. A search revealed other articles stolen from the residence and elicited a confession about an accomplice.[20]

Yet there was more than embarrassment at stake. Conviction was difficult. As Bates observed, "If apprehended under suspicious circumstances setting fires, their defense would be that they were simply 'back fighting the fire.'" As long as fire control demanded controlled fire, it was hard to prove one fire damaging and another not, hard to distinguish one fire set maliciously and another set, perhaps desperately, to control a wildfire. So too it was difficult to discriminate between light burning as a fire-preventative measure and an identical free-burning fire that required suppression, or indeed any fire kindled by settlers or tourists with the intention (or not) of cleaning up surface needles and brush. Anyone littering the woods with fire could claim that he was only doing his duty to ensure that forest fuels remained scant. So long as fire furnished the best defense against fire, the case against "incendiarism" was problematic, simply a political definition granting the power to hold the torch to some while denying it to others. One could argue that the Forest Service was in fact setting more fires than it was suppressing.[21]

Just as the Forest Service found it had to "develop" the land to save it, so it discovered that it might have to adapt an alternative tool kit of fire practices that met its needs to replace those that did not. Light burning for forestry might be a surrogate for rural burning in much the way that hiring gangs of floaters to fight fire was a surrogate for calling out settlers. In 1910 anyone who lived on the land still required fire to make it habitable. The Forest Service, however, had an advantage: It did not truly live off the land. It did not need fire to clear fields or to renew pasture or to jolt garden plots. It needed fire only to protect the lands from wildfire. But it believed that it could ultimately contain the dangers with better fire suppression. In time, slash burning would disappear, and even backfiring would be unnecessary. In time, good forestry and intensive silviculture could abolish fire altogether and, along the way, scrap the confusing distinctions between fires set by one group or another for one purpose or another. A necessary evil would become an unnecessary one.

Moreover, the Forest Service clearly understood that just as many fires had been set to embarrass it, so many light burners wished to discredit forestry or the Service. It didn't hurt that the Service was literate (politically as well as in letters) and many light burners were not. No doubt the Washington staff would have delighted in the 6 November letter of E. T. Abbott of the Klamath Lake Railroad Company to Secretary Ballinger in which he jeered at Forest Service policies: "I have taken the Pains to get the Opinions of Intelligent Residents who have resided in here 20 to 30 years and to a Man they pronounce the Govt Methods as outlined by Mr Du Bois as Rank Fakes, impracticable and impossible." Ballinger thanked Abbott for his letter and agreed that "the conservation of resources, including the prevention of destruction of forests by fire, should be handled in a practical, common sense way rather than by the attempted application of impracticable theories." He had, he continued, no objection if Abbott wished to quote from his reply. Abbott didn't, but he did fire off a letter (better edited) to *Engineering News,* which had published a forester's arguments for systematic fire control. In it he sounded the popular opinion that "the general policy of putting the fires out indiscriminately is all wrong."[22]

Foresters alternately smiled and sneered. They knew that their theory was right and that they lacked only the means to apply it fully. But their real reply was the Big Blowup, which vaporized nuanced definitions of fire and wiped out alternative explanations of how the public lands should relate to fire. Firefighting, not fire lighting, was the core act of proper forest protection. It was incredible, as the *Times* thundered, to suggest that the forest reserves needed more fire, and it was no less incredible that forest rangers might choose to set fires in the hope that they could eliminate fire. As Gifford Pinchot had declaimed, there was no distinction between fighting fire in the woods and fighting fire in a city. No one would suggest regularly burning through the living rooms of houses to control possible city conflagrations. The cranks and crooks who suggested otherwise were, if the truth be told, simply incendiarists.

# NOVEMBER

THE GREAT FIRES were dead. After the Baudette Burn some troublesome fires broke out in Colorado's Big Chief Mountain and across the Black Hills, and then a large fire (by eastern standards) threatened the watershed of Newark, New Jersey. The South simmered, as always. But the crews were home, battered tools were back on racks in fire caches, and the paperwork began to pile up. November was a time of stocktaking. What had happened? Why? Who was to blame?

*American Forestry* published a special fire issue for November. All the participants in the Great Fires contributed, although the Forest Service naturally commanded the lion's share of the issue. Graves addressed the significance of fire control: that "no single forest problem is so important as fire protection, for the risk from fire to-day stands as a great obstacle in the way of the practice of forestry" and that the burden of protection must be "borne by the public." The magazine then printed another installment from his fire treatise. Silcox described how the fires were fought. C. S. Chapman outlined the perils faced by District Six. But there were plenty of others ready to comment on the Great Fires. Professor Chapman breathlessly described his own firefight on the Flathead. E. T. Allen explained what cooperative protection (and private landowners) had accomplished under the aegis of the Western Forestry and Conservation Association. Joel Shoemaker of the Washington Conservation Commission discussed the fear that 1910 might prove as lethal as the Black Friday fires of 1902 and the steps the state had taken to prevent it. C. J. Buck recounted the role of telephones in the Oregon fires, not only in directing Forest Service and Army crews but in saving settlers. That no lives were lost was not to say that no danger had existed; strong backs, cool heads, and modern technology had prevented disaster. Gripping photos of fire crews, packtrains, Army encampments, and smokechasers perched on rocky summits sprang off the pages.[1]

Perhaps consensus was foreordained; perhaps not. In any event, there was no dissent to the argument that forestry knew how to prevent another blowup, that its methods were right and it lacked only the means to impose them on the ground. Speaking for the private associations, Allen agreed. Control had failed owing to the insufficient application of known techniques, to the violation of fire laws, and to an unstable compound of lands that sprinkled unprotected patches among protected places. Where laws were enforced, the fire trails patrolled, and fire sanctuaries eliminated, fires did not break out or were quickly corralled. The solution was to extend heavy-gauge fire suppression everywhere. Ultimately, to be truly effective, fire control would have to be compulsory.[2]

Yet there were critics, not members of the forestry fraternity, who had dared propose an alternative. To true foresters, those critics' methods were flawed, and their motives suspect. Thus *American Forestry* answered Hoxie's *Sunset* article on light burning by reprinting the reply California Deputy State Forester William C. Hodge had written for the *Timberman* in September. Patronizingly, Hodge explained how Hoxie's "misunderstanding" of government policy was "almost perfect." Anyone with a smidgen of sense understood that forests needed less fire, not more, that protecting reproduction was more vital than shielding old growth. But the editors knew the real issue was not technical. It was political.[3]

As Pinchot explained in his address to the St. Paul Conservation Congress, "When any great movement has established itself so firmly in the public mind that a direct attack on it will not pay, the regular method is to approve it in general terms and then condemn its methods and its men." This was, the Forest Service hinted, precisely what was happening in the California pineries. Critics disingenuously protested that they supported forestry, conservation, and the forest reserves and sought different techniques only in the practice. Their real intention was otherwise. They represented "two classes": one, the "great combinations of capital" that wanted no truck with conservation or government bureaus, and two, "private and corporate owners of timberlands." It was the latter that had "recently worked up an organized attack upon the whole principle of protection against forest fires as practiced by the national and state governments." T. B. Walker, for example, held half as much timberland in California as did the Forest Service.[4]

In brief, the light burning controversy was not a credible quarrel over proper techniques of fire protection; everyone understood the unalterable importance of fire prevention and the proper techniques to control fires. The critique was, rather, a veiled political conspiracy to discredit the core precepts of forestry. If unchecked, it would corrode away the pillars of conservation the way light fires gnawed into the butts of trees until even the grandest specimen must eventually topple. In its 19 November issue *Outlook* agreed and saw in the attacks the work of political sappers. "They might as well blame the Weather Bureau for its failure, first to prevent a drought, and second, to permit the development of a hurricane." The Forest Service's "failure" was a failure of Congress to grant it sufficient funds. The Big Blowup was a force of nature, irresistible and ineffable. Yet both sides argued that they could forestall a repetition. The Forest Service, especially, had insisted that with more money, it could prevent such eruptions in the same way that proper engineering could prevent even the Mississippi River from overflowing its banks.[5]

The politics remained, for the public, a subtext or at best an interlinear gloss or simply an annoyance. They read the harrowing accounts of rangers in desperate struggle for their lives, men whose only reason for being in the path of the devouring flames was to serve the commonweal. Personal accounts, larded with "human interest" anecdotes, carried more weight than field trials on sapling survival; personalities crowded out arcane politics. The literate public sided with those lying in the ash and cowering in tunnels and boldly backfiring against fire fronts as huge as thunderheads. The survivors too shed overt politics for a personal narrative. Ranger Buck spoke for most when he recalled for the *Oregon Sunday Journal* how his beleaguered office had come to resemble a "headquarters in war time." It was such a time "as a man never forgets."[6]

What the public and the Forest Service would never forget were the stories of stirring heroes, brave causes, and, if they thought of politics, congressional carping. Rarely did anyone raise the question of why those crews were there at all or if they had failed and died because their task was premature, perhaps misguided. For *American Forestry*'s fire special, Gus Silcox did, however. "The question will be raised as to whether it is possible to protect these areas from fires and whether or not it is worth while." He answered both with an unequivocal yes and systematically laid out the means necessary to accomplish that task. At the end of his essay the editors reprinted a poem that had appeared earlier in the *Denver Republican*. In doing so, they captured precisely the interpretive outcome of this skewed discourse as critical policy and partisan politics succumbed to sentimental poetry.[7]

**The Fire Fighters**

*"Where's Smith and Hennessy, Edwards, Stowe—*
*Where's Casey and Link and Small?"*
*The ranger listened, and murmured low:*
*"They're missing, Chief, that's all.*

*"Where the smoke rolls high, I saw them ride—*
*They waved good-bye to me;*
*Good God! they might as well have tried*
*To put back the rolling sea.*

*"I rode for aid till my horse fell dead,*
*Then waded the mountain stream:*
*The pools I swam were red, blood red,*
*And covered with choking steam.*

*"There was never a comrade to shout 'Hello,'*
*Though I flung back many a call:*
*The brave boys knew what it meant to go—*
*They're missing, Chief—that's all."*

—Arthur Chapman

•

AFTER ASH CAME ink, and on 10 November annual fire reports for Forest Service District One fell due. Those forests with fatalities had earlier submitted preliminary reports; these documents were to percolate through the bureaucracy, repeatedly revised, until the end of the claims period in March 1912. Those forests that had overspent their budget—virtually every forest in District One—had had to cobble together financial summaries in time for the House Committee on Deficiency Appropriations, which met in early December. Supervisors on a few of the hardest-hit forests had succeeded in submitting their annual reports on time. A few still lagged.[8]

Not for another decade, not until the Mather Field Conference of 1921, would truly standard forms appear. Until then the annual summaries served as a statistical record, very imperfect, of what the Forest Service had accomplished and what it needed to achieve its mission. The reports listed the number of fires by size classes, their causes, firefighting expenditures (both regular and emergency), damages, and fairly detailed discussions of how fires related to "permanent improvements." One intention of this exercise was of course to learn, but the stronger motive was to teach. The Service accepted as an axiom that rapid development of the lands under its stewardship would reduce the area burned. The reports showed this, were intended and skewed to show this, and they did.

Before the next fire season the Service commenced the first of what proved to be a series of nationwide fire-planning programs. Within two years it expected every forest to possess a working plan that specified what improvements it needed to control fire. The gaps between what was on the ground and what was needed would justify the coming fire budget presented to Congress. More money spent on these "permanent improvements," it would argue, meant less money spent from emergency accounts. Fund the annual fire budget sufficiently, and there need never be another deficit binge like the million-dollar Big Blowoff.[9]

The Forest Service found, however, that there was greater diversity in the field than it had anticipated. Model plans bubbled up from Florida and Arkansas, Montana and California. The most significant surfaced in California, where foresters had to battle not only wildfire but light burning. A young forester, Coert duBois, created that model out of what, from a national perspective, was a sideshow around Lake Tahoe. But the Stony Creek fire affected duBois deeply, and through him, the Forest Service, and through the Service, virtually every landscape of the public domain. The episode demonstrates vividly that a fire does not become important because it is big but because it has big outcomes, and the way it acquires big outcomes is through its cultural context, especially its institutional impacts, and those through its effect on particular people. The Stony Creek fire had, arguably, immense influence on American fire ecology because it created a scheme to harness the outrage triggered by the Great Fires and send that zeal for reform back into the field.

Coert duBois was, as he put it, "a young, impressionable and enthusiastic idealist at the time this crusade got under way and metaphorically crying, 'Gifford Pinchot le vult!'" went into the Forest Service "head down and tail up." His family had suffered financial reverses, too much to afford sending him to Yale, as he expected, or to train him as a naturalist, as he wished, and his father had insufficient political connections to secure an appointment to West Point, his other choice. Yet the Forest Service promised them all, after a fashion, and his father contacted Pinchot. Young Coert soon ended up in California. Traveling extensively throughout the northern forests, he realized that fire protection was "the *sine qua non* of forestry in California."[10]

Then came 1910. DuBois had to cut short his honeymoon to fight fire around Tahoe for two weeks. The Stony Creek fire started him "thinking seriously" about fire. The prevailing attitude was that fires were acts of God, "unfortunate but unpreventable." One ranger told him, "When a fire starts, we go and try to put it out." That wasn't good enough. Without fire protection, the reserves were hollow shells. But protection, to be effective, had to be methodical. DuBois's solution was to apply Taylorism, the efficiency engineering so beloved of the Progressive mind, to the problem of fire control. He broke down fire suppression into its elemental parts, then reassembled them into a rational whole. The first result was a model fire plan for the Stanislaus National Forest, which duBois likened to "a war plan" for "Operation Hell." In 1914 he published the process itself as *Systematic Fire Protection in the California Forests.* DuBois considered that the effort took "the hardest mental work I ever did and was the most important contribution to the public that I ever made."[11]

*Systematic Fire Protection* defined what went into fire planning and what came out. The duBois model demanded more data—better data of a particular sort—so fire reports adjusted their categories to provide it. Yet duBois emphasized that his program said nothing about goals. It was assumed, of course, that fire protection was its purpose, but fire control could take many forms and advance many ambitions. What duBois devised was a means to meet whatever ends the organization thought suitable. It explained how best to lay out the trails, lookouts, guard stations, and other "permanent improvements" to hold fires to whatever standard the Forest Service thought suitable. (DuBois proposed for California that while "arbitrary," the goal should be to hold timber fires to under ten acres, and brush and grass fires to under a hundred.) In good American fashion, however, the process became itself the purpose. As due process informed the legal system, as Pragmatism informed American philosophy, so the process of doing shoved aside the calculated determination of national objectives. The duBois model nominally solved the question of means and ends by making the means into the ends; efficiency (a good Progressive word) became itself the administrative goal. While written for California, the duBois model propagated until year by year it became the national standard.[12]

As administrators tallied the year's fires, they might well ponder what made a fire significant. Some big fires had proved inconsequential; some little fires had loomed large in their effects. What mattered was how the fire interacted with its surroundings. No one save Coert duBois thought twice about the Stony Creek fire. Yet because he thought long and hard about it, an obscure burn around Lake Tahoe had ecological reach more pervasive than even the far-drifting smoke of the Big Blowup.

# DECEMBER

THE YEAR ENDED as it began, as a prolonged study in the political ecology of fire. From January to December politics and flame had orchestrated a curious fugue. Politics could not leave fire alone, and fire could not help challenging politics. So it happened that the first major conference devoted exclusively to wildland fire opened on 6 December 1910 in St. Paul, three months after the Second National Conservation Congress had convened in the same city.

The scheme had originated the previous spring when Governor Eberhart, still rattled by the 1908 fires, had urged the Minnesota State Forestry Board to appoint a committee to recommend additional legislation to prevent another such outbreak. The model, as in so much of Minnesota forestry, was New York. After its own 1908 fire debacle, New York Forest Commissioner James Whipple had invited all interested parties to meet; they did, 150 in all. A smaller committee of 15 then proposed new forest fire legislation, which the Albany legislature enacted. Probably with the prodding of General Andrews, Minnesota wanted no less. It quickly invited Michigan, Wisconsin, prominent lumbermen, the railroads, forestry professors, insurance companies, the Department of the Interior, and the Forest Service to join. Between conception and convocation, both the Big Blowup and the Baudette Burn worked their catalytic magic.[1]

The usual speakers delivered the usual advice. Control folk fire practices and railway ignitions. Dampen slash. Establish a chain of fire authority and fund it. Send out regular patrols, not only to find fires but to advertise a fire prevention message. In undeveloped lands—the vast forest reserves of the West, the new national forests of Minnesota, the "forever wild" parks of New York—create a network of roads, trails, and firebreaks sufficient to swat fires out as quickly as they start. All these, the delegates believed, were political matters. Forest protection was a public good and deserved public moneys. If legislation could not by itself solve the problem, no imaginable solution could nonetheless occur without political buttressing. The firefight could not succeed in the field alone: It had to be won in legislatures and in public opinion. So it was that Chief Forester Graves, with "deepest regret," dispatched an assistant to read his paper while he remained in Washington to fend off assaults on the Forest Service budget.[2]

There was only one dissenter. William O'Neill, representing the Chippewa Indians, joked that the year before, when he was "young and innocent," he had become a member of the legislature, "an enthusiast, a reformer you might say, who believed in passing laws to have things right, and stringent laws at that, to make the world good, as it ought to be." Yet he could not now recall any law that he helped pass "but what the world could have got along just as well as if it never had been passed at all." The only solution to the fire problem, he concluded, was to rally public sentiment and show people what good behavior meant. Do that, and the fires would fade away.[3]

This was not the Progressive way. The audience laughed and applauded O'Neill, then passed a laundry list of resolutions to inspire the political system to apply its force, legal and fiscal, to the suppression of free-burning fire. Yet, in the end, O'Neill's vision lay closer to reality. The truth was, America never solved the stubborn problem of rural fire by deliberate action or political resolve. Those rural flames simply and slowly faded away without regard to policy or committees. The great burns in the East vanished with the migration of industrial logging to other regions, with the end of frontier land clearing for farms, with the demographic tectonics that made America urban, with the sea change of the American economy from agriculture to industry. The savage fires that had haunted the Lake States from the time the railroads first punched into the North Woods ceased. A rural population moved to cities; farming looked to fossil biomass for its fertilizers, pesticides, and herbicides; much of the land was abandoned to stumps, sand, and weeds. When the forest returned, it did so under a different regimen from agriculture. Politics had lubricated that transformation, but no fire code could abolish slash, wrench farms out of woods without burning, or renew fallow without flame. Those flames were merely whitecaps on a landscape whipped by larger, far distant social and economic storms. In the Lake States the cycle of conflagrations lasted roughly sixty-five years.

Yet matters were different in the forest reserves. By prohibiting rural settlement, the reserves had banished rural fire. That did not mean, as it did in New York or the Lake States, that fire had largely gone. Graves considered fire's "enormous destruction"—so great that one could frequently stand on peaks and not see half the area covered with trees—one of the "most striking features" of the western scene. Contrary to popular myths, the national forests did not harbor old woods; vast areas were snag fields or young woods, both the outcome of fire. This pattern predated white settlement. Graves in fact did "not believe that the fires have been any greater, or as great as in many years in the past." The 1910 fires appeared exceptional because they attracted exceptional publicity, and that because "for the first time in history there has been an attempt to check the fires in a season of exceptional drought."[4]

The character of the Big Blowup thus differed from that melancholy register of frontier fires of which the Baudette Burn was the latest, brutal entry. Its politics would differ no less. The Great Fires happened early in the historical cycle of big wildland fires; they had young, malleable institutions on which to impress themselves; they occurred within an era that had declared conservation important and had, as part of a New Nationalism, looked to the federal government for leadership; they challenged that political order at a time when the country was not otherwise in crisis. National politics were agitated enough for the fires to catalyze reform, yet the nation was not so overwhelmed with depression, war, or other calamities that the fires did little more than add smoke to a national holocaust. The timing of the Big Blowup was impeccable. Much as drought had allowed small fires to smolder and wind had fanned sparks into flame, so the national scene allowed fires burning in the mountainous backcountry to become significant at nearly all levels of the political hierarchy. The Big Blowup would align symmetrically with the political firestorm that Pinchot's dismissal had kindled and that would end over the next two years in Taft's collapse, Ballinger's resignation, and Roosevelt's second coming.

Even the states not scorched by the flames still sensed their heat. Forest advocates pointed to the Great Fires as object lessons in the failure to provide adequate protection. New York, for example, basked in self-congratulations for permanently banning such burns. The governors of the states most savaged, Idaho and Montana, had struggled for years to reform fire legislation to a more progressive standing. But the states that responded and achieved results were those along the periphery, Washington and Oregon. In 1911 Washington adopted fire reforms as part of a general overhaul of forest policy, while Oregon enacted the first statute requiring compulsory fire patrols. Both Governor Edwin Norris of Montana and Governor James Brady of Idaho had sought improvements, but the state legislatures refused. The fires had been a peculiarly federal problem; let the feds pay for them. The primary local impact was to stimulate interest by private landholders, all of whom relied on cooperation for their punch. The "Idaho idea" was already famous as an alternative to state-directed programs such as New York's.

In this way the region overall responded. Railways that crossed several states, timber protective associations that confederated timber owners within and between states, the Western Forestry and Conservation Association (which added California after the 1910 fires) all spread influence and helped soften the hesitation of the states. More important, they all cooperated with the U.S. Forest Service. That was the critical fact. The Forest Service provided an institutional medium for scaling up fire protection even across state borders, and it promised some degree of standardization. Each new private contribution did not have to sign agreements with every other group; it had only to relate to a single master organization, the Forest Service. Whatever the Great Fires' impact on the Forest Service, that blow would cascade throughout the Northwest and ripple throughout the nation. A recharged Forest Service was thus worth scores of local and state reforms; the Baudette Burn remained, finally, a regional catastrophe, the Big Blowup a prod for national reform.

To put it bluntly, it seemed pointless to reserve lands if they burned. Moreover, as the year ended, the educated consensus held that they burned because of poor policy, feeble institutions, and lack of funds. The solution was to confirm fire control as fundamental, to create a powerful organ for directing fire protection on a national level, and to give it money. In its December issue *Everybody's Magazine* published what was becoming the prevailing wisdom: that "this national calamity is blamable to the petulance and vindictiveness of certain men," that it could have been "prevented," that "only the pique, the bias, the bull-headedness of a knot of men who have sulked and planted their hulks in the way of appropriations for the protection and improvement of the national reserves" made prevention impossible. Pinchot had insisted that his quarrel with Ballinger (and Taft) would be won in the court of public opinion. The Forest Service lost the Great Firefight in the field; it won the greater war for the public mind.[5]

In his report for 1911, Chief Forester Harry Graves noted that the influence of the Great Fires on public sentiment toward fire protection and on the Forest Service as a firefighting institution "would be hard to overestimate." Quick passage of the Weeks Act in February 1911 confirmed that judgment, and nothing in the following decades diminished its immense institutional weight. Forty years later William Greeley reviewed the fantastic progress that had made American fire control a marvel of the world and that seemed poised to abolish smoke in the woods forever. "All of this matter of protection," he said simply, "goes right back to the 1910 fire."[6]

•

ON 14 DECEMBER Louis R. Glavis, the prickly special agent who had sparked the charges that flared into the Ballinger-Pinchot controversy, found himself in court. He had avoided legal action for his innuendo regarding the harassed Ballinger, for he had never charged criminal misconduct, only the appearance of suspicious coincidence. There had been grueling congressional hearings, but no courtroom drama.

Now Glavis, the ember responsible for kindling the Big Brouhaha that had destroyed the Taft administration and split the Republican party, was charged with actual rather than political arson. The specific indictment stated that he had started a fire on his property that then escaped and rampaged outside White Salmon, Washington. The burn had originated from a scheme to convert wild forest to fruit orchards; the fires were set to expedite the clearings, and the drought rendered the flame both more effective and less controllable. According to the *Seattle Daily News,* among the group of investors in the White Salmon Fruit Company was Amos Pinchot, brother of Gifford. The jury acquitted Glavis, as public opinion had acquitted him and Amos's brother.[7]

On 6 March 1911 the once-proud Ballinger, who had fired Glavis eighteen months before, his public reputation in tatters, requested of Taft that he be allowed to resign.

# AFTER

AS THE YEAR ended, the American fire scene had crossed a political and ecological threshold. Some changes were obvious: There were burned patches where none had existed before. Some five million acres of national forest had burned, and heaven knows how much else. Vicious black swaths gouged the Northern Rocky Mountains. Yet even this was, on the scale of the American landscape, relatively minor. The larger story would continue to be one of fire's relentless recession. There was less fire than fifty years before or, for that matter, five hundred years earlier. The Great Fires, and the not-so-great fires, of 1910 hastened that trend.

They did what fires do best: They quickened; they forced; they tore down and opened to new growth. Their most powerful impact was not directly on the land but on the humans who held torch and shovel and who applied and withheld fire according to a cultural logic that often merged and sometimes collided with nature's. This year's burns redefined, wrenchingly, the relationship of Americans to fire. This year there were institutions, personalities, and ideas ready to absorb the blows and then return as good as they got. There was a toughening of the mind, a refusal to compromise, on the part of those who had passed through the flames. In particular, there was the U.S. Forest Service.

No single event changes history. No fire, however awesome, can imprint itself on a continent for decades. But a fire can catalyze change that becomes encoded into public sentiment and political bureaucracies, and that is what the Great Fires did. They prompted reforms that affected how fire would come and go on tens of millions of acres. They brought the Forest Service to a fork in the road and forced it to choose one path over another. That decision, so hasty and urgent, might have softened over the years except that the experience had so branded the organization and its bosses that when they came to other forks in the fire road, they consistently chose those that repeated the frantic choices made during the lethal chaos of the Big Blowup. Each decision moved the Forest Service, and American fire protection overall, further in one direction, a trajectory of fire exclusion, until there was no way to reverse its route or even to veer back to something nearer the original. By the end of the century options were nearly gone. The American tragedy was not that wildfires were fought but that controlled fires had ceased. No suite of complementary fire practices flourished. No alternative story existed. The fire season of 2000 showed how fully fire protection continued to be overwhelmed by the force of events—acting, reacting, overacting. The narrative ruts ran deep.

The Great Fires of 1910 shaped the American fire landscape more than any other fire in any other year throughout the twentieth century. For ninety years the United States never experienced another such conflagration. Possibly, it never will again.

•

LANDS RESPOND DIFFERENTLY to fire and recover from it at various rates and in assorted ways, and even the same lands can react differently to the fires that visit it. So it is also with people and with institutions. And so it happened that the Great Fires gave rise to a tangled succession of responses.

The regrowth began with the political fireweeds of congressional inquiries. Here the politics of assorted partisans sprouted in the deep ash bed of money. Many congressional Democrats and critics of conservation were already suspicious over Pinchot's use of Forest Service appropriations for self-promoting publicity well before the fires sent in their staggering bills. So while Taft's commission on efficiency lumbered through the mechanics of Forest Service clerical operations, and Secretary Wilson urged "strict economy," Congress lopped off a huge chunk of the Service's 1911 budget. In effect, it argued that 1910's gut-wrenching emergency expenditures were an advance against future appropriations and expected repayment in the fiscal year to come.

The Forest Service found that the emergency accounts were more scrambled than it wished. Some timekeepers (and their books) had burned in the fires. Others had begun the practice of shifting to the emergency fire fund costs that would otherwise have remained chargeable to their regular budget. The Senate expanded the investigation by passing an amendment that required the Forest Service to report on *all* moneys expended from 1900 to 1910. Then there were "irregularities," like those charged to the unfortunately named Ranger Debitt, which resulted in the request for his early resignation.[1]

The congressional ax threatened to destroy the whole master strategy by which steady capital improvements would reduce large fires. The 1911 budget slashed a quarter of a million from roads and trails and depleted the fire fund by $800,000. Despairing, Graves fought back and exclaimed to Pinchot that it was "unbelievable that the country will approve of the so-called economy which affects the protection of life and property." Worse, receipts from timber sales lagged behind projections, which made the budgetary "deficit" loom larger yet. Ultimately the Forest Service successfully rallied. Further inquiries, the salvage sales of the 1910 burns, and the dampening of the Pinchot protest not only restored but bolstered those funds for the following fiscal year. The recovery justified fully the enormous effort expended in forest-by-forest fire planning. It also confirmed that the prevailing interpretation of the Big Blowup would be one of "heroic" struggle, not of hopeless bungling.[2]

The other money matter involved claims pending under the provisions allowed by the General Deficiency Bill of 4 March 1911. The chair of the House Committee on Expenditures, Ralph Moss, planned hearings in July 1911. To that end he requested a "full report," to include the names not only of those who perished but the officers in charge, the "nature of their duties," and the "particular order of instructions which led to their deaths." In short, there would be a full rendering.[3]

The Washington office of the Forest Service pooled the various reports from the field and submitted a summary statement on 15 July. (Perhaps the Taft committee on efficiency was shrewder in its queries about correspondence than at first seems possible; the slag heap of paper threatened to bury field operations. Weigle complained that he, like all the other supervisors he knew, filled "in the blank spaces with figures, about which I knew very little"; not quite "the right method of procedure" for publicity campaigns, he suggested. Besides, not hiring enough clerks meant that rangers moved from the field into the office, not what the Service desired or claimed before Congress.) Larger than the preliminary briefs already issued, the July statement was less complete than those that would close the inquiry in March 1912. None was fully comprehensive. As Secretary Wilson explained in his final submission, "the small number of claims filed" undoubtedly testified to the "migratory class" that had supplied the labor.[4]

But as with nature, so with institutions. Fire's effects proved ephemeral. They were greatest in their first year and almost gone, at least on the surface, by their third. The dreaded reburn failed to appear. The weather proved favorable; no major outbreaks of fire occurred from 1911 to 1913. By 1914, a bad year with a drought as deep as 1910's, the Forest Service stubbornly held its lines. Meanwhile new politics and elections beckoned. New projects poked through the ash and covered the charred stumps. Congress moved on.

•

OF GREATER INSTITUTIONAL impact was the immense prod given cooperative fire protection. The long-suffering Weeks bill, voted down in June 1910, passed into law in February 1911.

Like most American legislative triumphs, the Weeks Act was a compromise, but one made possible only after a ferocious catalyst. The federal acquisition by purchase of lands for national forests had proved difficult. It offended those who wanted to see the Forest Service restrained, not enlarged; it upset others who fretted that the states should exercise primary responsibility; it placed the constitutional burden of proof on the slippery syllogism of forests and flooding. And it might prove bottomless. While preliminary surveys recommended 600,000 acres in the White Mountains and five million acres in the Southern Appalachians, the House Committee on Agriculture noted that the land recommended for watershed protection could reach seventy-five million acres, all of which "it might ultimately be necessary to purchase."[5]

Two changes moved the bill from failure to success. One was the addition of provisions that shifted the federal role from a focus on water alone to include fire protection as well and that shunned federal hegemony in favor of shared programs with the states. The second was a massive reversal of votes by western senators. This time only two westerners voted against it, Senator C. D. Clark from Wyoming and Heyburn from Idaho (who no doubt still had his blood up from Pinchot's accusations months earlier). The stick of dynamite that broke the legislative logjam was the Big Blowup.[6]

General stewardship over that program fell to Bill Greeley, called out of Missoula to the Washington office to direct timber sales and, now, to liaise with the states. Cooperative fire protection was already Greeley's passion; now it became his mission. Over and again, he told Congress, and anyone else willing to listen, that "the first and greatest commandment of American forestry is to keep fire out of the woods." The Forest Service could never achieve that end by itself, could do it only by merging with the goodwill and practical assistance of private timber owners and the states. The Weeks Act made that possible by appropriating $200,000 for grants to those states that had forestry bureaus, bona fide fire protection programs, and a willingness to accept some federal oversight. Those states that needed the most help and that invested the most on their own got the greatest dollop of federal moneys. The Forest Service could stimulate protection over far vaster landscapes by working through the states than it could by attempting to purchase all those lands for national forests or by unilaterally legislating practices.[7]

In 1913 the Service convened a special Weeks Law Forest Fire Conference, chaired by J. Girvin Peters, Greeley's special assistant for state cooperation. Graves opened the sessions by observing that the cooperative fire program was indeed a surrogate for outright federal ownership and that Congress considered it "an experiment to test the efficacy of this kind of federal aid." By then fourteen states belonged. The limiting factor was the nagging constitutional concern that just as with national forest purchases, the funds could apply only to forests clothing the headwaters of navigable streams. That changed in 1924, when the Clarke-McNary Act allowed for cooperative fire funds for virtually any watershed. The number of states participating shot up; by 1925 twenty-nine belonged to the club; by 1945, forty-one. The Weeks Act also provided for the states to band together on their own for fire protection. The Northeast States organized the first such compact in 1949, after the disastrous 1947 season and in the absence of a strong federal land establishment.[8]

The Weeks Act, in brief, unpacked the political gridlock about which level of authority, state or federal, would oversee forestry. Both would. What made that alliance work was that one issue existed, almost uniquely, about which all the competing parties of foresters, the timber industry, and Congress could concur. They agreed with Bill Greeley;

they agreed when he told them during the public hearings over Clarke-McNary that the single most important thing they could do to advance the cause of forestry and conservation was to "stop the fires." It was not simply that forestry brought fire control but that fire control carried forestry. Pinchot muttered in protest. Now shoved further to the fringe, he worried that the fire cause was a smoke screen for not legislating national control over logging. The corporatist mood of the nation was otherwise. The nation sided with the young forester who had masterminded the Great Firefight of 1910. Reminiscing, Greeley agreed. "With reason," he believed, one could argue that the whole "progression" of cooperative forestry, as based in the Weeks Act, was an institutional succession that rose out of the deep disturbance of the Great Fires.[9]

•

WHILE THE WEEKS ACT created a structure, the legislation said nothing about what that structure should house. Especially, it was—after all this time—not obvious to everyone that fire protection meant fire suppression or that fire control had any practical meaning on remote wildlands.

The fires hastened the first, daunting task of creating a firefighting force and an infrastructure to carry it into what the chief forester rightly called an "unoccupied and pathless wilderness." The immense planning exercise conjured out of the faulty data and narrative reports of the 1910 fire season stirred the imaginations of field officers, and proposals for just how to construct such a network spilled out. Virtually every figure of importance in the Service weighed in with schemes. And not only the Forest Service; even the WFCA published the first edition of the *Western Fire Fighters Manual,* the first practical field guide. From around the country foresters reported immediate successes: Burned areas decreased because of both favorable weather and improved access. Yet while the duBois model quickly became ascendant, it finessed around the most critical component. It failed to state an explicit objective, suitable across the nation. That became the second charge, and the two soon became inextricably entangled. The problem here was that fire control was not the only possible end. The more popular ambition was light burning.[10]

The two sides played against each other, like the two shears of a scissors. Before 1910 foresters had, if reluctantly, accepted that controlled burning might have a supportive role in forest protection. They were willing to burn off fuelbreaks and slash piles and even to broadcast-burn some sites under rigid conditions. Because they lacked the staffing to assault fire directly, many experimented with some protective burning on their own or burned sub rosa under the guise of "administrative experimentation." But mostly (save in the South) they deemed light burning as, at best, an expedient, an evil tolerated only because, with nothing else, the alternative might be no protection at all, which was worse. Foresters were willing to discuss light burning, as one might grudgingly welcome a wayward cousin to a family reunion.

After 1910 their position hardened. That *Sunset* had published its pro-burning screed even as the Army charged into the firefight seemed treasonous. Its register of supporters proved suspect: Secretary Ballinger; wealthy timber owners like Walker and railroads like the Southern Pacific; nonforestry engineers like William Hall and Joseph Kitts; populist writers like Joaquin Miller and Stewart Edward White. The thesis that controlled fire should be the defining practice of forest protection attacked not only foresters' competence but the very axioms of their academic training and science. From forestry's German heartland Professor E. Deckert lectured that "devastating conflagrations of an extent elsewhere unheard of have always been the order of the day in the United States." Worse, a tradition of broadcast burning survived that was nothing more than "vandalism." The scene offered, by contrast, a "brilliant vindication of the forestry system of middle Europe." While plenty agreed with Coert duBois that America had unique problems and had to seek its own solutions, they could not deny the shame of the comparison, and they understood, as the touring professor could not, its latent political ramifications.[11]

For more than a decade the Forest Service fought back, tooth and talon. Graves dismissed the light burning of Indians and settlers as a "fearful devastation." The doctrine, as promulgated in California, was "nothing less than the advocacy of forest destruction, and those who preach the doctrine have a large share of responsibility for fires which their influence has caused." For years "incendiarism" remained on the rise, the result not of "ill feeling" but of the fallacious and malicious "theory of light burning which is being preached by certain influential men." In fact, Graves knew better; his 1910 notes from Walker's estate testified that good light burning was neither random nor ruinous. (Fire control could also be done badly.) But tolerance seeped away; light burning became the undead of awful forest doctrines. In 1919 the matter resurfaced, and a weary Graves denounced the practice as "inherently destructive" and threatened lawsuits against *Sunset* if it ran a particular exposé. Then, exhausted, he turned over the campaign to Bill Greeley.[12]

Greeley led the Forest Service over the top. To approve western light burning was implicitly to sanction southern woods burning, and Greeley had no tolerance for either. The "Indian way" he condemned as mere "Paiute forestry." If light burning survived, forestry would fail. Certainly a national consensus for forest conservation on the Forest Service model would vanish without the strong nuclear attraction of fire control. Other federal agencies, notably those in Interior, would balk; the states without forestry bureaus might never push ahead to create them, and those with forestry bureaus might renege on what they had; and "public sentiment," which Graves considered the "greatest asset" to forest conservation, would lose its most powerful message, "to keep fire out of the woods." Particularly in the South, the state forestry bureaus, fledglings all, would never leave their meager nests. Everywhere light burning, Graves insisted, "tends to destroy the confidence of the public in real protection efforts." When the smoke cleared in the 1920s, professional forestry had succeeded in equating light burners with spoon-bending psychics and perpetual motion mechanics.[13]

Yet by the end of the twentieth century the Forest Service found itself agreeing almost line for line with the propositions outlined by George Hoxie for *Sunset* in August 1910 and desperately eager to reintroduce the fire that it had, at such immense struggle, successfully excluded, and it did so for exactly the reasons light burners had predicted. That realization, however, dawned with appalling slowness. Not until 1939 did the Service admit any validity to fire's useful role. Not for four more years did it accept as legitimate even a smidgen of controlled burning. In retrospect, its true Great Firefight was not against the conflagrations of the Coeur d'Alene, in which it failed, but against light burning, which it strove not merely to defeat but to humiliate, and then found that having achieved what it so strenuously sought was not what it really wanted after all.

•

THE TIMING OF that shift in attitude underscores a vital fact: Institutions do not act abstractly; they operate through people. The memory of the Great Fires became embedded in institutional fibers through statutes and manuals and bureaucratic records. But their memory animated the Forest Service through those members who championed the cause the Great Fires had represented. They breathed spirit into bureaucratic letters. The Big Blowup persisted in influencing the Forest Service because those who experienced it continually reminded the Service by waving, as it were, the bloody red shirt of 1910. For another twenty-nine years the Big Blowup personally affected every chief forester. Only after the last veteran had passed away did the Forest Service allow for even token controlled burning, and that in the inscrutable southern pineries.

Henry Graves found his shaky administration hounded and nearly consumed by fire. He was too much the bureaucrat, too securely the dean to allow even the Big Blowup to unhinge his assessment of forestry's place or to romanticize the task before him. He would beat back fire as he would other challenges, by steady application of organization. That he chose fire for his first official treatise was a public declaration that even fire—so bred into the bones of rural America, so ineffable, so pervasive—was amenable to methodical forestry. But fire did not behave like garrulous senators or trespassing homesteaders or conniving rivals from Interior. It understood neither the logic of texts nor the force of public good. It was the foremost challenge to field forestry, and its suppression a model for the administration of the public domain.

He found himself continually responding to those who claimed that fire control was impossible, that light burning was a superior doctrine, that the Great Firefight was in fact a blistering failure. As imperturbable as Joffre on the Marne, Graves dug in and fought back. When *American Forestry* revisited fire in a special issue in 1913, it spoke of major successes. The 1914 season was meteorologically rougher than 1910 but yielded far fewer losses. The 1919 season, however, was a horror in the Northern Rockies, suggesting that this empire, like Rome's, required more than steady road building to hold it in thrall. And then the light burning controversy rose once more from the dead. Suffering from Ménière's syndrome, Graves slumped into exhaustion and then resigned in March 1920. After a few years he returned to Yale, having lived long enough to witness fire control's triumph, yet not so long as to reckon the irony of that nominal victory.

William Greeley succeeded him. The man who had field-marshaled the Great Firefight, the man who had declared the tradition of rural woods burning the greatest risk to sound forestry, now oversaw the nation's primary institution for fire protection. The 1910 fires had burned deeply into his memory. From that summer onward, Greeley considered "smoke in the woods" his "yardstick of progress in American forestry." Light burning found no more severe critic.[14]

Quickly he convened the first all–Forest Service convocation, the Mather Field Conference, focused on fire and held in California in 1921. Cooperative fire protection became the signature of the Greeley years. He had indirectly supervised the Weeks Act, and its expansion into the Clarke-McNary program was not only his personal triumph but the linchpin of his philosophy of public forestry. He knew as only someone who had watched the bodies hauled out of the sour smoke of the Big Blowup could know that effective fire control was the rock on which to build forestry. If big fires could not be controlled in the West, the public forests would collapse. If light burning replaced systematic fire control, then the movement to reforest the South was doomed. If the timber industry had no point of agreement with the Forest Service, then both would sink into an exhausted stalemate and the woods would suffer. He had fought both monsters, the Grendel of the Big Blowup and the Grendel's mother of light burning.

When he resigned in 1928 to become the executive secretary of the West Coast Lumbermen's Association, critics denounced him as a sellout. Bill Greeley, however, believed he was only working the other half of cooperative forestry, that he could help reorganize industry as he had federal bureaucracy. Fire control now had a powerful lobbyist inside the private sector. To forestall the predicted timber famine, he helped found the tree farm movement, and along with it the Keep America Green campaign for fire prevention. The veteran of 1910 knew that America couldn't be black and green at the same time. There was no point in planting trees if they could immolate on any hot afternoon.

Rather, firefighting, Greeley argued in good Progressive fashion, was "a matter of scientific management, just as much as silviculture or range improvement." His vision complemented precisely that of duBois. When he resigned in 1928, he left the Forest Service with a story that deeply impressed his listeners. During his tour with the Tenth Forestry Engineering Corps in France, Greeley observed that every time the anchor on their transport ship was withdrawn, without exception, each link was tested. Even when only a few hours separated the act, the captain insisted on repeating the test. He explained to the curious forester that experience over the centuries had demonstrated to shipmasters that they could never take any chances with the anchor chain, on which the safety of the ship depended. What seemed like an indiscriminate obsession was in truth fundamental to a safe voyage. To Greeley it appeared that fire control was the anchor of forest management and that by attacking all fires, regardless of season or location, officials were merely testing the links of protection's chain. There could be no exceptions.[15]

His successor as chief was Robert Y. Stuart. Stuart had quietly worked the District One offices on night shift while Greeley field-managed the daily campaign. Now, as then, he continued the practices of his former boss until, mysteriously, on the morning of 23 October 1933, his body plunged seven stories out of the Washington office and onto the parking lot below. The cause of his fall was never determined.[16]

Briskly stepping into the administrative vacuum was none other than Ferdinand Augustus Silcox, Greeley's assistant during the Great Firefight. Gus Silcox had written the most detailed accounts of how the Forest Service had fought the Great Fires and, as Greeley's successor in District One, had implemented the reforms that made the droughty 1914 season seem a triumph of fire control. He had never doubted that the Service could fight those fires, and should, if only it had the stuff on hand to make it happen.

What mattered too was that Gus Silcox was an instinctive New Dealer. President Roosevelt had long fancied himself a gentleman forester, had in fact fought a fire on his own along the shores of the Bay of Fundy the afternoon before his legs sank into paralysis, and had a gut belief that people and land had to be revived together. He launched the greatest conservation programs in American history, spearheaded by the Civilian Conservation Corps, which enrolled hundreds of thousands of unemployed youths and sent them to work in labor camps. The Army ran the camps and oversaw logistics, while civilian agencies directed the work in the field. The Forest Service claimed half the camps. Instantly it had its long-coveted army for firefighting, and with its immense labors the CCC created almost overnight an infrastructure for fire protection.

Great heroes require great villains. These too appeared; the early

1930s, drought-plagued, were as full of towering smokes as of far-ranging dust storms. The best fire minds in the Forest Service, including Silcox, convened for a two-week pack trip through the Northern Rockies to debate how completely fire control should extend into the roadless backcountry. These were the lands that had spawned the Great Fires. The Service could not prevent a replay unless it pursued every fire, even those inconveniently remote. But the old caveats persisted: The justification remained abstract; the means, too feeble. The first changed when immense fires—the largest since 1910—burned over the Selway Mountains in Idaho. The second vanished with the advent of the CCC and other emergency conservation programs. In fact, the creation of a fire danger rating index (providentially in 1934) suggested that the Forest Service could tap the emergency fire fund for *pre*suppression activities, not simply for firefighting.

Gus Silcox could now do what he had claimed in 1910 he would have done if he could. He had the means—the men, the money. It remained only for the ends to expand to accommodate them. In 1935, flush with Civilian Conservation Corps camps and Emergency Conservation Work funds, he ordered a final assault on fire.

•

SILCOX CHARACTERIZED HIS command as "an experiment on a continental scale." But even as he promulgated his all-out-attack-every-fire policy, critics outside the Forest Service were voicing protests, while within its ranks, doubts bubbled to the surface. Some fretted that fire exclusion was the wrong goal; others, that its pursuit would inspire ruin, that even the *effort* to abolish fire would damage what the program claimed it sought to protect.

The biological critics—committed to controlled fire, southern, heirs of the light burning controversy—were the most familiar. For a decade the Forest Service had managed to contain the release of information that found a value to surface fires, particularly in longleaf pine. Yet because of the 1928 McNary-McSweeney Act (one of Greeley's last legislative triumphs), it claimed a virtual monopoly over federal research on fire. Few others had the money or incentive to study fire ecology. To question Service dogma was, as the redoubtable H. H. Chapman learned, to be labeled a "dangerous eccentric," perhaps a heretic.

The breakthrough finally came in 1935 at the annual convention of the Society of American Foresters in a session organized by Chapman, then SAF president. Critics spilled out their doubts. One participant, E. V. Komarek, spoke for them all when he muttered damningly that "this is the first time that censorship on the subject has been removed and we have been told the facts." More forgivingly, Chapman thought the problem lay with the Forest Service's disbelief that the public could understand anything beyond the simplest message. A few years earlier it had dispatched the Dixie Crusaders, modeled on traveling evangelists, to spread the gospel of fire prevention throughout the South and was soon to hire a psychologist, John Shea, to try to understand how woods-burning folk could be so wrongheaded. But the other explanation is that the Forest Service could not tolerate any effort that might whittle away or abrade its commitment to fire control. The specter of future fire problems in Georgia or North Carolina could not compete with the memory of the Big Blowup in Idaho and Montana. The last of the old guard of 1910 had to depart before that sentiment might waver.[17]

Which makes all the more striking the other critique and the man who gave it voice: that aggressive fire control was destroying the cultural value of the lands under protection; that no less a veteran of 1910 than Elers Koch should utter such a *cri de coeur.* The protest was uncannily similar to that made by Inman Eldredge in Florida. Fire exclusion could not work, and the effort to apply it only worsened conditions. In this instance the critique emerged out of cultural values rather than ecological studies.

The immediate cause for despair was the 1934 Selway fires. Koch had been sending fire crews over the Bitterroots since 1910 and had personally led the worst campaigns. He chronicled his life by those fire years. Yet he now regarded "the whole history of the Forest Service's attempt to control fire in the backcountry of the Selway and Clearwater" as "one of the saddest chapters in the history of a high-minded and efficient public service." Despite "heroic effort," the country remained "swept again and again by the most-uncontrollable conflagrations." In 1934, despite thousands of firefighters and unlimited dollars, crews had made no better progress than in 1910. Throw in the whole United States Army, Koch declared, and it could do nothing "but keep out of the way." After nearly thirty years of hard-core fire suppression, Elers Koch decided that the control of fire in such backcountry was "a practical impossibility." Rather, he "firmly" believed that "if the Forest Service had never expended a dollar in this country since 1900 there would have been no appreciable difference in the area burned over." Worse, it was possible that extinguishing surface fires during mild seasons had improved the likelihood of more damaging fires during extreme summers.[18]

Worse still, the reckless ripping open of the backcountry in the name of fire control was destroying what was most valuable about those lands. The Lolo Trail, Koch observed, "is no more." The fabled pass over the Rockies through which Lewis and Clark had boldly explored had shed completely its wilderness character. It was now a road, and roads were "such final and irretrievable facts." The Forest Service had built it, as it had developed the backcountry everywhere. All this was done "for one purpose only—to facilitate the suppression of forest fires." Koch dared ask if all this effort had "added anything to human good." Was it possible that "it was all a ghastly mistake"?[19]

The Selway fires had in truth stunned the Forest Service. Sustained by the great droughts of the early 1930s and by decades of excessive forest litter, the lightning-kindled fires had simply washed over the vaunted infrastructure of fire control like so much beach sand. On 12 to 13 September the Service convened a large board of review in Missoula. The head of fire control, Roy Headley, unblinkingly laid out the issue: that the "present status of fire control in Idaho is disconcerting." The Service was "never so well equipped and in certain ways, never so helpless as in 1934." The board outlined three possible strategies for the future: one, to "keep every acre green"; two, to continue incremental development as economically as possible; three, to accept Koch's proposal that it simply withdraw from aggressive fire control in areas like those blasted over the last summer.[20]

Headley elaborated on Koch's "heretical" proposal. The fires of the mild years would quell somewhat the fires of the bad years; before the Forest Service arrived, even with endless burning, the country was magnificent; the intangible benefits of "forest influence" were exaggerated; the cost of protection was exorbitant. Koch's summary argument was "the unquestionable fact that the country is in worse shape now than when we took charge of it." Headley admired Koch's "characteristic courage" and agreed on the last two points and was "sure" that others did as well but would "not ask them to brand themselves publicly as heretics." Yet Headley did not believe that the Service could withdraw; public opinion, which it had struggled so fiercely to shape, would not allow it. Besides, as a wily survivor of Washington bureaucracy Headley saw other difficulties. "I do not think any one regards Koch's proposal as practicable. Bureaus and professions do not voluntarily withdraw under such circumstances. It simply is not done."[21]

While Headley drafted his lengthy report to Silcox, Koch wrote up his ideas into an essay, "The Passing of the Lolo Trail," and sent it to the *Journal of Forestry.* The editor claimed the magazine was full and redirected it to *American Forests,* which agreed to publish it in January. Then Koch, on his own, worried that it was "indiscreet and might be quoted to the disadvantage of the Forest Service," withdrew the piece. Instead he sent it to Silcox. Headley was willing to see the Selway debate broadened and urged publication in the *Journal,* which printed it in February. Earl Loveridge, another participant in the Selway debates, drafted a vigorous reply. The failure of fire control, he argued, was the result of compromised policy and incomplete infrastructure; the Forest Service had simply not gone far enough. Withdrawal was inconceivable. Incremental measures would not work.[22]

The matter landed on Silcox's desk. The critics had stated their case; large fires had roamed, more or less untrammeled, in the backcountry, and light fires continued to dapple the piney woods like blue fungus. In April, Gus Silcox, the man who had outfitted the field campaign of 1910 and who had then overseen the construction program that had bulldozed over the Lolo Pass, announced what became known as the 10 A.M. Policy, which stipulated as the universal objective of fire control that every fire should be controlled by 10 A.M. the day following its report. If that effort failed, then fire officers should plan to control it by 10 A.M. the following day, and so on, for weeks if necessary, until the fire was out. Whether the fire was big or small, near or remote, kindled by lightning or by locomotives, burning through pine reproduction or Douglas-fir crowns, one standard applied with equal force everywhere. The best way to prevent big fires was to smash every fire while it was small. By the end of the Silcox regime, two specialty fire crews appeared: smokejumpers (smokechasers with parachutes) to attack fires in the backcountry and the forty-man crew, self-styled "shock troops" for campaign fires. The Forest Service committed itself to pursue every fire in every conceivable place. It would brook no sanctuary—not the Lochsa River, not the Carolina Piedmont, not California's once-open pineries. The response to the failed campaign of

1934 would be the same as the response to the failure of 1910: more trails, more roads, more men, more money. The New Deal largesse practically invited excess. A final surge—an absolute policy that brooked no interpretation or exceptions, all the resources any forest ranger could ask for—would finally wipe out the nation's fire menace.

The 10 A.M. Policy guided federal fire protection until the National Park Service broke ranks in 1968. Ten years later the Forest Service altered the old policy to allow for natural fires to burn in wilderness sites and for controlled burning to reduce fuels and improve habitat. In 1995 the federal agencies accepted a more or less common accord that sought to suppress "bad" fires and promote "good" ones. But little actually happened on the ground. The institutional culture of fire was—inevitably, perhaps—a culture of fire suppression. The land too had accommodated fire's exclusion to the point that it could not readily accept light fires, nor could air sheds easily accept the added effluent. Wildfires blew up; costs soared; prescribed burns careered out of control.

Wildland fire managers discovered they did not need a policy; they needed a poet. If they wished to rally public sentiment, if they wished to overcome the immense inertia of a near century of fire exclusion, they needed a story as compelling as that bequeathed by the Great Fires, and there was none on hand.

•

MEMORIALS TO THE Great Fires did not reside solely on the pages of professional journals or in the fine print of the *Federal Register.* As Greeley insisted, the dead deserved suitable burial.

Those near towns or those with relatives to claim them got it. The Bullion Mine and Placer Creek victims—eleven unclaimed bodies—were promptly reburied in two common graves at Wallace with wooden slabs for headstones. The others, fifty-three in all, lay in their "temporary" graves until the summer of 1912, when the Forest Service contracted with a local undertaker to exhume them from Setzer Creek and Big Creek and the rest and bury them, at a cost of $60.15 each, in Woodlawn Cemetery at St. Maries, Idaho. Meanwhile, Ed Pulaski took it upon himself, on his own time, to tend the shabby graves of the fallen firefighters, which contrasted so poignantly with the rest of the Wallace cemetery. And there the matter seemingly ended.[23]

Pulaski, however, continued to prod the bureaucracy to provide something more durable. In 1916 Meyer Wolff, then supervisor of the Coeur d'Alene, carried the cause to Silcox in the Missoula office to protest that "truly Government tendency to absolutely forget and discard." The Wallace graves were a "disgrace." He then offered one of the sanest judgments ever pronounced about the terrors of the Big Blowup. "These men had in the last analysis not at all a heroic death, but a violent death," yet one endured in government service. Some suitable memorial was, he confessed, "not a matter so much of reason as of sentiment, and for that reason action is not so much essential as it is desirable."[24]

District Forester Silcox asked for plans and estimates, then concluded that Congress would have to pass a specific appropriation. Wolff deferred to Pulaski, who proposed concrete coping, three blocks of granite with the names of the deceased, and grass, for a cost of $425. Another year passed. Wolff queried Pulaski again about progress. In despair Pulaski doubted that anything could be done, "[rules and regulations] in the way of my taking the matter up." He suggested some outsider who might shame the Forest Service, but even that, he suspected, would end with a personal reprimand. After all, his experiences in seeking compensation for medical expenses gave him little confidence in the bureaucratic process. The easiest solution was to care for the graves "on my own time and save trouble for myself." Still, other veterans (like Major Fenn, now in the district office, and Fred Morrell, now district forester, sensitive to criticism that the graves' condition was "unworthy of our Service") kept the pot simmering by sending appeals to the chief forester.[25]

In 1921, with Bill Greeley now firmly ensconced as chief and the country attuned to war memorials, Congress allocated $500 for the Wallace graves, much along the lines Pulaski had sketched. Three years later it allotted moneys for a memorial stone and plaque for the dead firefighters buried at St. Maries. The Wallace memorials consisted of two raised monuments, built of river stone, with a bronze plaque listing the names of the dead. Although there were originally eleven bodies, inexplicably only ten rest under the plaques. The St. Maries site assumed a more elaborate, circular design. In January 1933 a letter went out to all "forest officers" that the Forest Service would expand that special plot into "a central burial ground for forest workers killed in the line of duty."[26]

They are the first fire memorials for the public domain. Others rose to commemorate the fallen after the Blackwater fire (1937), the Mann Gulch fire (1949), the South Canyon fire (1994), eleven sites in all by the end of the century, with a general Wildland Firefighters Monument planned outside the National Interagency Fire Center in Boise. Most, unsurprisingly, declare the fallen as "heroes." Most appeal to military analogies, to the cemeteries of great combats, an iconography that merged readily into the prevailing firefight-as-battlefield metaphor that has never loosened its death grip on journalism. It remained the moral equivalent of war. Likely too one of the reasons the 1910 monuments appeared in 1921 is that the memorial captured some spillover from the flood of public memorializing over the Great War. *American Forestry,* for example, published photos of the completed Wallace monuments and explained that these men were "heroes of peace" who had died "as truly in the service of their country as did those on Flanders' poppy-covered fields." The Blackwater tragedy inspired a special firefighter medal for heroism. The South Canyon ceremony echoed military pomp. The proposed Wildland Firefighters Monument mimics the Vietnam War Memorial.[27]

All of which makes the St. Maries memorial so intriguing. Instead of crosses marking the spots where the men fell, or headstones spiked into rows as if they stood in rank, the graves of the fifty-three dead circle a plaque-bearing granite monolith and a flagpole as though around a campfire. A stone marker rests at the head of each grave, a final roster of the known and the unknown. "Gust Johansen, Died August 20, 1910, Big Creek." "L. Ustlo, Died August 20, 1910, Setser Creek." "Unknown, Died August 20, 1910, Setser Creek." The Woodlawn Cemetery has one other burial circle, sited on an opposing corner, this one for infants and very young children. The implied symmetry is unsettling, suggesting as it does a common innocence. No one who signed on for duty in the St. Joe Mountains in 1910 was an innocent. Yet both men and babies died from what seemed an ineffable act of God, or at least the tantrum of an inscrutable Nature, from forces outside their control and for purposes beyond their ken. The earliest firefighter memorial may be the truest.

•

THE OTHER MEMORIAL was inscribed in ink. Most stories never got written; those that did, as government reports, could expect short shelf lives. The only permanent written records might be those that, like compensation claims, had legal standing. The Great Fires deserved better. After he had secured funding for the Wallace graves, District Forester Fred Morrell turned his attention to protecting, or where necessary creating, the more perishable documentation.

His motives were several. Mostly, it seems he was simply curious. The Big Blowup predated his tenure at the Missoula office, yet it bulked large in regional folklore; he wanted to hear it full. He hoped as well to get it right: The news stories were inaccurate; the files, incomplete. It would be useful to have the documents on hand for publicity on behalf of better fire protection. He even nurtured some vague ambition of writing up the story himself. Regardless, he needed more material, and to that end he directed Mary E. Turrell to collect statements from as many participants as she could and to organize the documents for his inspection.[28]

Mrs. Turrell went briskly about her "little pilgrimage," collecting statements from Haun, Hillman, Wolff, Koch, Halm, Phillips, Breen, and others. Morrell first thought it enough to gather the accounts before he reluctantly recognized what a "time-consuming job" it would be for someone to "work out of it a new story or a consecutive history." Yet Mrs. Turrell had some literary aspirations and nursed the ambition that she might weave the various personal accounts together "after the fashion of the Canterbury Tales." The project lost its way, however, and by early 1926 it had sunk into bureaucratic lethargy. Some files were missing. Mrs. Turrell had transferred, could never find the time to pen properly her imagined narrative, and wrote to suggest to Morrell that he consider someone else to compose a manuscript.[29]

There was no one on hand, and Morrell, like many another fire aficionado, discovered that his enthusiasm outran his time and his talents. A few of the accounts found their way into print. Joe Halm published his in *American Forests;* others were gathered into mimeographed volumes, *Early Days in the Forest Service,* published by the Northern Region. Collectively, though, the files gathered dust until Elers Koch retired in 1943. Assembling the files became his final act as a federal forester, a fitting memorial to his own forty-year-long tenure in fire protection. There is scant reason to doubt his own explanation of purpose: that history if not written is "soon forgotten"; that the Great Fires had "much to do with shaping the fire policy" not only of the Northern Rockies but of the whole United States; that the men who had experienced the Big Blowup were dying and the fabled year of the fires would become "only a tradition." (He was right. By 1938 the Forest Service had discovered, to its chagrin, that it could no longer identify "Pulaski's tunnel.") The resulting compilation he titled *When the Mountains Roared: Stories of the 1910 Fire.* It was released in mimeographed format, not intended for formal publication, but "primarily as a record for the Forest Service, so that the story will not be lost."[30]

In the early 1950s Betty Spencer built on that documentary record, adding copious newspaper accounts and interviews with survivors, and arranged them into something approximating a narrative, a book published locally in 1956 as *The Big Blowup.* Perhaps it was the result of her researches—notably an interview with Pulaski's daughter, Elsie—that she inspired the doting daughter to request from the Forest Service a firefighting tool that her father had devised. Now married to Arthur Pabst, a compressor operator with the Federal Mine and Milling Company, Elsie visited personally the Coeur d'Alene headquarters with her petition in July 1955.[31]

The Forest Service immediately saw "a very good opportunity to gain some worthwhile publicity" if it was to present Mrs. Pabst with a tool on the occasion of the fiftieth anniversary of the Forest Service. But further discussion saw another grand opportunity or, as staff publicist J. K. Vessey put it, "a good stunt": to celebrate the fiftieth anniversary of the Great Fires. That would grant enough time (as the Forest Service commemoration would not) to establish a fund-raising campaign to erect a "suitable memorial," at which time both plaque and tool could be presented to Elsie Pabst outside her father's famous tunnel.[32]

A year later nothing had happened, and the scheme had fallen into comparative disarray. Carl Krueger, the new forest supervisor of the Coeur d'Alene, could find no record of any correspondence and had to write the Missoula office to see what, if anything, the Service had promised to do. The records were exhumed, and the institutional consensus argued for withholding any formal ceremony until 1960. It was also determined that the Forest Service could then present either a nickel-plated pulaski tool or a scale model suitable for mounting "as a mantal [*sic*] display." In November 1956 the Service found the $9.85 needed to purchase the tool and ship it from the True Temper Corporation and arranged to have it sent to Coeur d'Alene. The plans went back into manila folders.[33]

In 1959 the panic returned, threefold. First, a scale pulaski tool cost more than the office could afford. Second, the photographs that were so vital to any publicity campaign had "been removed from the forest's photographic album," and the forest had nothing to replace them. Staff members began a scramble for copies, wherever they might find any. Third, they faced the "rather remarkable fact" that once again, they could no longer locate "Pulaski's tunnel." Soil had slipped; trees had regrown; the hills along the West Fork were dotted with indistinguishable former mine shafts. They had no written record (or map) of where, precisely, the adit was located, and no one in the district could personally escort them to the site. As Koch had predicted, they had forgotten. Luckily Will Morris, then 80 and living in Wisconsin, explained precisely where the tunnel was. But the local population, not always sympathetic to the USFS, was sure to dispute whatever locale the Forest Service selected to honor. Moreover, some feeling existed that the "incident in question" had been the "result of ill chosen action" and did not deserve the attention lavished on it. The prodigious plans ended with an innocuous sign, planted alongside the highway near the junction of the West Fork with Placer Creek.[34]

The Forest Service was quick to compromise because modern publicity, not the old fire, was now the purpose of the exercise. Guidelines for forest officers instructed them that the "multiple-use theme should be integrated wherever possible." The climax of the anniversary year came on 30 May, Memorial Day, with a service at the Woodlawn Cemetery. Boy Scouts presented colors, the St. Maries High School band played patriotic songs, ministers prayed, the Veterans of Foreign Wars and American Legion cochaired, and W. W. Dresskell, assistant regional forester, placed a wreath on the firefighters' monument. Then arrived the extraordinary moment when "old-timers," those who had survived the Great Fires, were introduced. Most were local men who had been out on the firelines somewhere. But two of the rangers who had led them were on hand: Will Morris and Joe Halm. Morris, dapper and spry, had come from Madison; Halm, now retired, from Missoula.[35]

It was right that Morris should be there. He had been there, in the field, the whole horrible season, and no one had documented the summer more thoroughly or zestfully. Throughout that prodigious year he had told the story in letters home, all saved by the family for later transcription and then carefully archived. Whereas others, if they wrote accounts at all, had addressed the nightmare of the Big Blowup, young Will had recorded the winter forays into the woods, the snowslides, the companionship the foresters knew unstressed by the conflagrations, the routine of the lesser fires, the return to the firelines after the Blowup, the photographic tour of the blowdowns and burnouts, the costly campaign to replant. He was seemingly everywhere, the Little Big Man of the Big Burn. In what are probably the most famous photos of American fire history, the gutted entry to the Nicholson adit, Will Morris stands as witness. He remembered the location of Pulaski's tunnel. He described more closely than anyone else the life of the firefighters on the line. Because he was literate, he could preserve that record in writing, and because he had a family to listen to him, he did.

That education led him to contemplate the meaning of his long adventure. His years there were knotted strands in a vaster tapestry. Five years after the Great Fires he became a professor of forestry at the University of Nebraska. After another five years he transferred to the Forest Products Laboratory in Madison and then to the Wisconsin forestry department, at last returning to the countryside in which he felt most at home. By 1960 time had, for him, squeezed the Blowup into an event rather than a world-collapsing moment, the most spectacular of his handful of years on the Coeur d'Alene. He turned from flame to rock, looked to the ridgeline of the Rockies, and agreed with the westerners (with whom he never fully assimilated) that "the mountains do have an inspiring and uplifting effect on those within their environs." So they had affected him. But in what may be the most unusual mixed metaphor ever applied to the Rockies, he combined high peaks with higher mathematics. To its summit all the parts of the mountain relate. "It is the theory of limits over again; on one side approaching zero, on the other side infinity. Thus, a great mountain peak, lifting its massive head above the clouds, covered with eternal snows and reigning supreme over all times and civilization, may well typify the Infinite."[36]

His forester comrade Joe Halm had a different story to tell, for he was one of the few rangers who stayed on with the Forest Service. In the years after 1910, he worked in the field on assorted projects but gradually drifted into engineering, where he could transform his talent for drawing into drafting. He became deeply involved in all the vast task of "developing" the forests—roads, trails, bridges, culverts, lookout stations, nurseries, portable sawmills. In 1918 he passed the civil service exam for draftsman and assistant engineer. Two years later he became fire officer for the Missoula forest and undertook an ambitious scheme of "permanent improvements." He continued to study drawing, especially cartooning, through correspondence courses, and in 1922 he resigned for a year to attend the Art Institute of Chicago. When he returned, he became a senior draftsman, much of his labor invested in fixing a fire protection system on the ground. He took to writing articles for outdoor magazines, illustrating them himself. One, "The Great Fire," recounted his experiences in 1910. When the CCC arrived, he trained a group in drafting and found his time full as the thousands of enrollees, ready for work, began cracking open the backcountry. He retired on 31 August 1945, thirty-five years and eleven days after the Big Blowup had stranded him with a panicky crew in the St. Joe Mountains.[37]

Joe Halm carried the story of the Great Fires personally longer than anyone else in the Forest Service. That he remained in the region made him an enduring oracle of the 1910 season; the assembled throng at the Woodlawn commemoration turned naturally to him for inspiration. The Great Fires had stamped him and shaped his reputation. Yet more than many, he had grown. Thanks to collegiate sports, he had an education; the dropkicker became an accomplished cartoonist and draftsman, the hammer thrower a veteran fire boss, the athlete an administrator. The Great Fires had sculpted his career, for fire protection demanded development, and development demanded draftsmen. Unlike Will Morris, perhaps because he had stayed, he found his thoughts turning to matter rather than spirit. Joe Halm's real recollection of the Big Blowup was written not in words but in blueprints.

•

IN THE END the story belonged not to Joe Halm but to Ed Pulaski. It was Pulaski's account that, rightly or wrongly, the public first and most strongly remembered. It was he who lived most directly with the Great Fires' consequences. It was Pulaski who tended the graves and quietly insisted that the dead deserved better memorials; who stayed on the Wallace district, near ground zero of the Big Blowup, for an additional twenty years; who oversaw the salvage of the burned timber, the replanting of seedlings, the reconstruction of the trails and telephone lines, the eventual, hard-slogged suppression of fire. His doting daughter had prompted the bureaucratic lurch to a fiftieth-anniversary commemoration. The Forest Service's inability to locate the Nicholson adit, universally known as Pulaski's tunnel, measures both the self-serving limitations of that exercise and the degree to which, perhaps unrivaled by any wildland fire before or since, the quest mattered. The last word on the Great Fires was Pulaski's.

He was, however, a man of few words. He wrote no account in the days and months after the Big Blowup. The story of his exploits came initially from others. His written comments are limited to replies to queries regarding the compensation claims of those who were under his general direction. He expressed himself, as C. K. McHarg recalled, "simply and with few words." He directed workers "with simple, definite instructions." He was frank, almost naive in speech. Silcox, who knew him in the field, described him as "quiet and fearless, very even tempered and very modest," and asserted that for him "to use force in a spirit of braggadocio would be wholly incongruous with the man's whole makeup." Probably his relative silence cost him official compensation. Over and again he declined to tell his story, to play it into celebrity, to live out his years as "the hero of 1910." He no more claimed heroic status than he claimed descent from Count Pulaski; others said that about him until the one seemed to depend on the other. Uniquely Mrs. Turrell could "get nothing from" him on her pilgrimage. "I think he felt his story had been told a good many times," she concluded. Yet "he really has much to say . . . if it could be gotten out." Instead she sensed that he nursed "a sort of spiritual hurt," or perhaps she was searching for a way to place him into her projected *Canterbury Tales* of the Coeur d'Alene.[38]

Once, however, he did speak. In 1923 *American Forests* advertised an essay contest, "My Most Exciting Experience as a Forest Ranger." Friends urged Ed Pulaski to enter. There was a $500 prize that he could use to help cover the medical costs that still lingered after his ordeal. He dictated his story to Emma, who helped write it. "Surrounded by Forest Fires," which dramatically describes their flight and survival in the tunnel in some 1,400 words, won easily. Big Ed Pulaski never wrote another word about the Great Fires or, for that matter, spoke of them further in any formal way. Their aftermath he dismissed as one of "poor eyes, weak lungs and throat," but he thanked God "I am not now blind." Older than most of his comrades, he was less prone to their enthusiasms; the fires were not for him, as for so many, a coming-of-age story. When he retired in 1930, Chief Forester Robert Stuart drafted a personal letter of congratulations that he urged the secretary of agriculture to send. Pulaski had first refused retirement, then suffered injuries in an automobile accident while on duty, retired soon afterward, and moved to Coeur d'Alene. A year later he died.[39]

He spoke instead with his hands. He had led his crew with acts, not words, and he embedded his story into institutional lore by his talent as a craftsman. The man who took pride in the things he could make with his hands made a tool. The origins of what became known as the pulaski tool are murky. Devising combination tools had become a rage; only a handful survived. The Macleod tool resulted when Ranger Malcolm Macleod welded a rake to a sharpened scraper in California. The Koch tool never traveled beyond Missoula. What became the pulaski tool apparently originated with W. G. Weigle, or so Joe Halm believed. Initially it combined an ax and a mattock with a detachable shovel. In one version the prototype emerged from the labors of Joe Halm, Ed Holcomb, and Ed Pulaski, working in Pulaski's blacksmith shop prior to the 1910 fire season. In another, Weigle wanted it for use in the massive replanting program, and still other variants claim Will Morris first sparked the design. Regardless, the 1911 supervisors' meeting greeted the prototype "without enthusiasm."[40]

But Pulaski continued to tinker. He discarded the shovel and balanced the ax and mattock better and in 1913 broached the new version to the hierarchy. He found a champion of sorts in Meyer Wolff, at the time the supervisor of the Coeur d'Alene. He also urged that the Forest Service patent the tool, fearing otherwise that "some private person will take advantage" of his invention. The Service had no intention, however, of pursuing the matter, and Pulaski, as a private person, would have to submit a detailed application along with fees. Since his purpose was to preserve the invention for the public, he let the matter drop, as he had with the gravestones. Still, he admitted that "the tool it is true has not been demonstrated to show it has any value and the only way to prove its worth is take it out and try it as I have done."[41]

That he did. He made more copies and sent them into the field. Further tinkering lengthened the shank and narrowed the mattock. Firefighters began to use pulaskis fitfully, then in a flood. By 1920 the Northern Rockies had adopted the tool as its own. The Forest Service requested commercial tool companies to manufacture it out of steel in industrial quantities. The pulaski and the shovel became the dominant, defining tools of fire control. Within a decade pulaskis lined fire caches and firelines by the tens of thousands. The deed had triumphed over legal qualms and bureaucratic squirming, over the lost and found memorials, over the written and mislaid word.

•

THE STORY MIGHT end here, except that fire transcends history, as it does art. Fires come without regard to agency budgets or national politics, and their enforced absence can affect the land with every bit as much ecological power as their presence.

By the end of the twentieth century, the triumph of fire exclusion had proved as fleeting as its critics had claimed it would be. Many of the public lands suffered fire famine; forests were diseased and dying and prone to catastrophic fires. Then came that *annus horribilis,* 1994, in which thirty-four firefighters died, two million acres burned, and emergency fire costs reached a ballistic $965 million. Everyone admitted the system was broken. The policy that had boiled out of the Great Fires had, like the conflagrations themselves, at last ended its colossal run. The federal agencies sought to salvage what they could, and they intended to do so by reintroducing some species of controlled (or prescribed) burning.

That proved vexing. Fire removed had shown itself as powerful as fire applied. The land had changed and often could accept only grudgingly fire's sudden reintroduction. The agencies had long aligned themselves around fire control like iron filings within a magnetic field and could not easily switch polarities. American society, no longer rural, had shed its familiarity with fire and now feared it. Other environmental values competed with fire, which, unlike condors and black-footed ferrets, had no group to adopt it as a poster child, slogan, or cuddly toy. Clean air, clean water, endangered species, greenhouse gases—free-burning fire challenged them all. Prescribed fire, moreover, also had its costs: fires that escaped, fires that failed to do the job demanded, fires that cost millions, fires that killed firefighters.

Then, as the agencies, penitential, enlightened, resolute, began to ramp up their burning programs, prescribed fire crashed. What the summer of 1994 did for fire suppression, the spring of 2000 threatened to do for controlled burning. The National Park Service lost two fires simultaneously. The nearly 15,000-acre Outlet fire forced the evacuation of the North Rim of the Grand Canyon. The 46,475-acre Frijoles

#1 fire blasted out of Bandelier National Monument and scoured Los Alamos, New Mexico, like the cutbank of a river. West of the 100th meridian, prescribed fire stalled under a thirty-day stand-down; the Park Service faced an indefinite moratorium. Before the summer ended, wildfire of all provenances broke out across the West, particularly in the Northern Rockies, where it was sparked by wave upon wave of dry lightning, on a scale comparable to that of 1910. The fires were doing what fire had always done. They were synthesizing their surroundings, and until their context changed, both environmentally and culturally, wildfires would continue to roar out of the woods.

No one argued over the prevailing policy, which accepted a pluralistic strategy toward fire. What broke down was the false dichotomy that forced one to choose between suppressing and starting. What failed, by omission or commission both, was that moment when flame hit forest. National policy was just that, a policy, lacking both the poetry to inspire and the practices needed to put it on the ground. The nation's fire mission lost its beguiling, if quixotic, simplicity. It was clear that wildland fire management must involve awkward mixes of firefighting and fire lighting and, somehow, of fire storytelling, and it languished for want of a contemporary event, as catalytic as the Big Blowup, to fuse them into a new compound. All in all, wildland fire management was proving itself a hybrid as unwieldy as the roughly wrought iron Ed Pulaski first forged in his backyard.

Yet whatever the mix, those in the field would almost certainly reach for a pulaski to make it happen. It remained the supreme fire tool, and it embedded the legend of 1910 more firmly than any agency stunt, congressional memorial, or recovered memory. Every time a firefighter grasped its shaft—each instant a smokechaser, hotshot, EFFer, helitacker, volunteer, or prescribed fire specialist hefted a pulaski to dig, cut, roll, gouge, fell, or scrape—he or she would be retelling the story of Big Ed and the Big Blowup, the saga of the Great Fires and the year that tried to contain them.

# AFTERWORD

THE INSTITUTIONAL IMPACT of the Great Fires on a national scale was unusually powerful. To date, however, the published histories have emphasized the fires' regional character or their impact on Forest Service folklore. When combined with the fuller historical geography of a year that overflowed with fires, however, the Big Blowup becomes both much more extensive and much more decisive. It had national consequences, and by shaping America's wildland fire establishment, it has influenced the world. Bushfire protection in Australia, wildfire fighting in Canada, proposals to contain folk burning in Brazil all reflect the impact of the Great Fires. That is the scholarly justification for a new book about them: to re-create their cultural context.

A wide-angle lens, however, requires a platform larger than the lean and often self-serving reports of the Forest Service. I needed other (preferably several) experiences to triangulate with the official record. These appeared with the voluminous reports of the U.S. Army as it was called into action; with the marvelous letters of William W. Morris; with personnel files of major characters like Edward Pulaski; with a fuller sifting of the claim reports filed for damages; and with some miscellaneous letters from observers at the time. All these are new, at least as brought to bear on the 1910 fires.

Not least, I wanted to assemble those parts into a more purely narrative history than I have attempted previously. Never have I had the opportunity to write a true story, a tale with a clear beginning, middle, and end. *Year of the Fires* invited such a narrative, and the opportunity to indulge in that style became, for me, much of the appeal of the subject.

But to hold to the story line and to keep the text brief (which I thought important), there was little chance for scholarly exegesis. My hope is that the style does that by itself, that the swell of the narrative demonstrates the surge of the fires. The book is what it is. The Great Fires are a magnificent saga. I hope my retelling can do them justice.

•

SINCE, IN ITS raw collecting, the book began twenty-three years ago, there are many people who have contributed. But let me acknowledge, here, those who directly assisted in this most recent round. Mostly, they are folks who helped access sources. Among them are: Cort Sims, Idaho Panhandle National Forests; Carl Ritchie, Wallace District, Silverton, Idaho; Candace Lein-Hayes and Joyce Justice at the National Archives, Seattle; Joe Schwartz, National Archives, College Park; Mitchell Yokelson, National Archives, Washington, D.C.; and Rob Staunton and Joshua Hagelgans, Region One, Forest Service, Missoula. A cavalcade of clerks and correspondents helped at the Lolo National Forest, Wallace Public Library, and Missoula Public Library. Extra thanks go to Maren R. Wilm, Washington State University Alumni Association; Dorothy Dahlgren, of the Museum of North Idaho; Susan Seyl, of the Oregon Historical Society; Barry Carver, of the Historic Nine Mile Cemetery; Barbara Tokmakian; and Henry Logsdon, of the St. Maries Forest Service office. Notable nods to Gerry McCauley, whose astute negotiating forced me to consider actually moving this text out of my head and onto paper, and to Wendy Wolf, shrewd reader and skeptical editor, who arrived too late to trench around my small manuscript and keep it from becoming big but did contain it from undergoing the literary equivalent of a blowup. My thanks to all of you.

Not least to Sonja, who knows only too well how the story of the writing had its long summer of creeping and sweeping and who knew how to let it run. To Lydia, ever the skeptic of rhetoric-drenched history, who cheerfully read it nonetheless. And to Molly, who managed to grow up despite my best efforts.

# NOTES

## *Abbreviations*

1910 Claims—National Archives at College Park, RG 95, Records of the Forest Service, Division of Fire Control, General Correspondence—Claims.

AGO—National Archives at Washington, D.C., RG 94, Records of the Adjutant General's Office, file citation no. 1681570.

Ballinger Papers—Richard A. Ballinger Papers, University of Washington Libraries, Manuscripts and University Archives Division.

Graves Papers—Henry Solon Graves Papers, Manuscript Group Number 249, Yale University, Sterling Memorial Library, Manuscripts and Archives.

IPNF—1910 Fire National Register Information, Supervisor's Office, Idaho Panhandle National Forests, Coeur d'Alene, Idaho.

Morris Letters—William W. Morris, "Letters from the Coeur d'Alene National Forest, 1908–1914," University of Washington Libraries, Manuscripts and University Archives Division, acc. no. 4828-001.

NACP—National Archives at College Park, Record Group 95, Records of the Forest Service.

NAPAR—National Archives, Pacific Alaska Region, Record Group 95, Records of the Forest Service, Seattle, Washington.

USFS R1—Forest Service Records, Region One Office, Missoula, Montana, Historic Files.

## *Before*

1. John Muir, "The American Forests," *Atlantic Monthly* LXXX (August 1897), p. 154; Gifford Pinchot, *Breaking New Ground* (Seattle: University of Washington Press, 1972; reprint of 1947 edition), p. 29.
2. Franklin Hough, *Report on Forestry,* vol. 3 (Washington, D.C.: Government Printing Office, 1882), pp. 129–30; Plumas references from "Plumas Boundary Report of 1904," quoted in Louis Barrett, "A Record of Forest and Field Fires in California

from the Days of the Early Explorers to the Creation of the Forest Reserves" (U.S. Forest Service, 1935), p. 48.

3. Fernow quoted in Andrew Denny Rodgers III, *Bernhard Eduard Fernow: A Story of North American Forestry* (New York: Hafner, 1968), p. 167; Henry Gannett, "Forest Fires," *Forum* (December 1898), p. 412; Gifford Pinchot, "Study of Forest Fires and Wood Protection in Southern New Jersey," *Annual Report of Geological Survey of New Jersey* (Trenton, 1898), Appendix, p. 11.
4. John Wesley Powell, *Report on the Lands of the Arid Region of the United States* (Washington, D.C.: Government Printing Office, 1878), pp. 25–26.
5. Quote from Andrew Denny Rodgers III, *Bernhard Eduard Fernow: A Story of North American Forestry* (Princeton: Princeton University Press, 1951), p. 154.
6. Gifford Pinchot, *Breaking New Ground,* p. 36; *Report of the National Forestry Committee upon the Inauguration of a Forest Policy for the Forested Lands of the United States to the Secretary of the Interior, May 1, 1897* (Washington, D.C.: Government Printing Office, 1897), pp. 17–18.
7. Henry Gannett, ed., *Twentieth Annual Report of the United States Geological Survey* (Washington, D.C.: Government Printing Office, 1900), Part V—Forest Reserves, "Forests of Washington," pp. 40–41; H. B. Ayres, "Washington Forest Reserve," ibid., pp. 306, 309; Martin W. Gorman, "Washington Forest Reserve," ibid., p. 344; John B. Leiberg, "Priest River Forest Reserve," ibid., p. 233; Leiberg, "Bitterroot Forest Reserve," ibid., p. 373; Leiberg, "Bitterroot Basin," ibid., p. 275; H. B. Ayres, "Flathead Forest Reserve," *Nineteenth Annual Report of the United States Geological Survey* (Washington, D.C.: Government Printing Office, 1899), Part V—Forest Reserves, p. 283; F. E. Town, "Bighorn Reserve," *Twentieth Annual Report,* pp. 177–78; Henry Graves, "Black Hills Forest Reserve," ibid., pp. 50, 80.
8. Leiberg, "Bitterroot Forest Reserve," loc. cit., p. 388; Gifford Pinchot, *The Fight for Conservation* (Seattle: University of Washington Press, 1967; reprint of 1910 edition), p. 45.
9. For the story of the midnight reserves, see Harold K. Steen, *The U.S. Forest Service: A History* (Seattle: University of Washington Press, 1976), p. 84.
10. Eldredge quoted in Elwood R. Maunder, ed., *Voices from the South: Recollections of Four Foresters* (Santa Cruz, Calif.: Forest History Society, 1977), p. 35; Inman Eldredge, "Fire Problems on the Florida National Forest," in *Society of American Foresters Proceedings* 6 (1911), pp. 166–68.
11. William Greeley, *Forests and Men* (Garden City, N.Y.: Doubleday, 1951), p. 23.
12. Pinchot, *The Fight for Conservation,* pp. 44–45; Pinchot quoted in Roy Headley, "Beating Fire," *American Forests* 36 (July 1930), p. 449.
13. Harlem: *New York Times,* 23 January 1908, 1:5; California: *New York Times,* 9 August 1908, pt. 2, 5:2; 11 August 1908, 1:5; 3 September 1908, 6:5, 7:5; New York: *New York Times,* 23 October 1908, 1:2.
14. Michigan: *New York Times,* 21 June 1908, pt. 2, 5:5; New York: *New York Times,* 29 June 1908, 3:6; Maine: *New York Times,* 13 July 1908, 1:2; Massachusetts: *New York Times,* 14 July 1908, 3:2; New York, New Jersey: *New York Times,* 11 July 1908, 14:4.
15. Canada: *New York Times,* 9 August 1908, pt. 2, 5:2, and 27 August 1908, 4:4; Northern Rockies: *New York Times,* 10 August 1908, 3:4; Canada: *New York*

*Times,* 3 August 1908, 1:5; 4 August 1908, 1:1, 2:2, 2:3; 5 August 1908, 12:3; 6 August 1908, 12:6; 12 August 1908, 2:5; 16 August 1908, pt. 2, 1:6.

16. Canada: *New York Times,* 3 September 1908, 7:2; Minnesota: *New York Times,* 6 September 1908, pt. 1, 1:5; 7 September 1908, 1:3; Forest Service: *New York Times,* 12 September 1908, 5:5; New York: *New York Times,* 20 September 1908, pt. 2, 5:1; Pennsylvania: *New York Times,* 21 September 1908, 3:4.
17. *New York Times,* 17 October 1908, 2:5. For lengthy feature on Adirondacks fires, see *New York Times,* "With the Fire-Fighters of the Adirondacks," pt. 5, 4 October 1908, 4:1.
18. Forest Service quoted in *New York Times,* 12 September 1908, 5:5.
19. Pinchot quoted in *New York Times,* 25 October 1908, pt. 2, 10:2.
20. For the organizational setup and the 1908 fire record, see Elers Koch, *When the Mountains Roared: Stories of the 1910 Fire,* R1-78-30 (Coeur d'Alene: Idaho Panhandle Forests, 1978; many editions), pp. 1–2.
21. Clyde Leavitt, "Forest Fires," in *Report of the National Commission* (New York: Arno Press, 1972, reprint), vol. 2, pp. 390, 391, 446.

## *January*

1. Gifford Pinchot, *Breaking New Ground* (Seattle: University of Washington Press, 1972; reprint of 1947 edition), p. 451; Harold K. Steen, *The U.S. Forest Service: A History* (Seattle: University of Washington Press, 1976), p. 102. Steen cites other details from Thornton Munger.

   The Ballinger-Pinchot controversy has spawned a large, and largely partisan, literature. A useful introduction is James Penick, Jr., *Progressive Politics and Conservation: The Ballinger-Pinchot Affair* (Chicago: University of Chicago Press, 1968). For a distillation, see Winifred McCulloch, *The Glavis-Ballinger Dispute* (New York: Harcourt, Brace, 1952), and for the general context, Samuel Hays, *The Gospel of Efficiency: The Progressive Conservation Movement, 1890–1920* (New York: Atheneum, 1969).
2. Pinchot, *Breaking New Ground,* p. 453.
3. Morris Letters, 18 June 1909, p. 4. Education quotes from William W. Morris, "Experiences on a National Forest," in *Early Days in the Forest Service,* vol. 1 (Missoula, Mont.: U.S. Forest Service, n.d.), p. 157.
4. Morris Letters, n.d. (1910), pp. 80, 76.
5. Elers Koch, "Early Ranger Examinations in Montana," in *Early Days in the Forest Service,* vol. 1 (Missoula, Mont.: U.S. Forest Service, 1944), pp. 109–10.
6. Ibid., pp. 26–34, 44.

## *February*

1. Harold K. Steen, *The U.S. Forest Service: A History* (Seattle: University of Washington Press, 1976), pp. 103–4; Gifford Pinchot, *Breaking New Ground* (Seattle: University of Washington Press, 1974; reprint of 1947 edition), p. 72; Graves Pa-

pers, Series. II, Box 17, Folder 210, "Biographical Notes of Henry S. Graves," p. 22.

2. Gifford Pinchot, *Breaking New Ground* (Seattle: University of Washington Press, 1972; reprint of 1947 edition), pp. 5–9, quotes from pp. 5 and 9.
3. Graves biography from *Yale Forest School News* XXXIX, No. 2 (April 1951), pp. 22–24.
4. Graves quoted in Henry Clepper, *Professional Forestry in the United States* (Baltimore: Johns Hopkins University Press, 1971), p. 125.
5. Quotes from Steen, *U.S. Forest Service,* p. 104.
6. Graves on Black Hills: Henry Graves, "Black Hills Forest Reserve," in Henry Gannett, ed., *Twentieth Annual Report of the United States Geological Survey,* Part V—Forest Reserves, pp. 79–86; on Philippines: Graves Papers, Series I, Box 10, Folder 122, Notes on early career; on India: Graves Papers, Series II, Box 17, Folders 208–11, "Reflections of an Old Time Forester" and Box 20, Folder 241, pp. 19, 37–38.
7. Henry S. Graves, *Protection of Forests from Fire,* U.S. Forest Service Bulletin 82 (Washington, D.C.: Government Printing Office, 1910), p. 7; see also, Henry S. Graves, "Fundamentals of the Fire Problem," *American Forestry* XVI, No. 11 (November 1910), p. 629.
8. Graves quoted in Clepper, *Professional Forestry in the United States,* p. 56.
9. Logging statistics from Bureau of the Census, *Historical Statistics of the United States* (Washington, D.C.: Government Printing Office, 1975), Part 1, Series L 56-71, Forest Product Raw Materials, p. 538; Treadwell Cleveland, Jr., "The Status of Forestry in the United States," *Forest Service Circular 167* (Washington, D.C.: Government Printing Office, 1909), pp. 4–5; Gifford Pinchot, *Fight for Conservation* (Seattle: University of Washington Press, 1967; reprint of 1910 edition), p. 15.
10. Pinchot quoted in Gordon B. Dodds, *Hiram Martin Chittenden: His Public Career* (Lexington: University Press of Kentucky, 1973), p. 157. Story of water demonstrations in Steen, *U.S. Forest Service,* p. 126, and a scathing description by Chittenden is given in Ashley L. Schiff, *Fire and Water: Scientific Heresy in the Forest Service* (Cambridge, Mass.: Harvard University Press, 1962), p. 121; Pinchot on "little rioting" quoted in Charles D. Smith, "The Movement for Eastern National Forests, 1899–1911," Ph.D. dissertation, Harvard University, 1956, p. 242.

    The best expressions of the history of the deforestation-desiccation thesis is found in Richard Grove, *Green Imperialism: Colonial Expansion, Tropical Island Edens, and the Origins of Environmentalism, 1600–1860* (Cambridge, U.K.: Cambridge University Press, 1995), and *Ecology, Climate, and Empire: Colonialism and Global Environmental History* (Cambridge, U.K.: White Horse Press, 1997). For a summary of the field, less warped than Pinchot's, see Bernhard E. Fernow et al., *Forest Influences* (New York: Arno Press, 1977; reprint).
11. Biographical and professional information on Chittenden from Dodds, *Chittenden;* H. M. Chittenden, "Forests and Reservoirs in Their Relation to Stream Flow with Particular Reference to Navigable Rivers," *Proceedings of the American Society of Civil Engineers* 34 (1908), pp. 281–82.
12. Dodds, *Chittenden,* p. 154.
13. On the Wagon Wheel Gap experiments, see Schiff, *Fire and Water,* pp. 128–34.
14. Pinchot, *Breaking New Ground,* p. 123.

15. Henry Gannett, ed., *Nineteenth Annual Report of the United States Geological Survey,* Part 5—Forest Reserves, pp. 1–22; Gannett, "Do Forests Influence Rainfall?," *Science* 11 (6 January 1888), pp. 3–5, and idem, "The Influence of Forests on the Quantity and Frequency of Rainfall," *Science* 12 (23 November 1888), pp. 242–44.

    For Powell's critiques, see Donald J. Pisani, "Forests and Reclamation, 1891–1911," p. 238, in Harold K. Steen, ed., *The Origins of the National Forests* (Durham, N.C.: Forest History Society, 1992); and John Wesley Powell, *Report on the Lands of the Arid Regions of the United States* (Washington, D.C.: Government Printing Office, 1878), pp. 25–26.
16. Pinchot, *Breaking New Ground,* pp. 123–24; Henry Gannett, "Forest Fires," *Forum* (December 1898), pp. 406–7, 411.
17. See Letter, Charles D. Walcott to Secretary of Agriculture, January 11, 1927, Smithsonian Institution Archives, Record Group 7004-2-3. My thanks to Ellis Yochelson for bringing this item to my attention. See Yochelson's fine biography, *Charles Doolittle Walcott, Paleontologist* (Kent, Ohio: Kent State University Press, 1998) for a rendition of early government forestry without Pinchot as self-appointed ringmaster.
18. Morris Letters, 13 February 1910, pp. 48, 50.
19. Morris Letters, 20 March 1910, pp. 62–66.
20. Morris Letters, 20 March 1910, p. 68. Much of the genealogical work and a reconstruction of Pulaski's life outside the Forest Service I owe to the labors of Sonja S. Pyne.
21. The single richest source of Pulaski materials are personnel files in USFS R1. "Quit school" remark from Pulaski given in reply to Forest Service circular letter, 22 April 1914.
22. The itinerary of Pulaski's career is best summarized in a letter by C. K. McHarg, 7 November 1941, included with Pulaski's personnel file in USFS R1; occupations quote from "Edward C. Pulaski, Pioneer Forest Ranger, Retires," press release by the Forest Service on the occasion of Pulaski's retirement (February 1930); "pride in hands" quote from McHarg letter; "thrifty" and "no desire" quotes also from McHarg letter, p. 2.
23. Morris Letters, 20 March 1910, p. 64.

## *March*

1. William W. Morris, "Experiences on a National Forest," in *Early Days in the Forest Service,* vol. 1 (Missoula, Mont.: U.S. Forest Service, n.d.), pp. 161–62.
2. My account follows closely from Ruby El Hult, *Northwest Disaster: Avalanche and Fire* (Portland, Ore.: Binfords & Mort, 1960).
3. Morris Letters, n.d. (ca. March–April 1910), p. 74.
4. For the Milwaukee Way story, I relied on Sandra A. Crowell and David O. Asleson, *Up the Swiftwater: A Pictorial History of the Colorful Upper St. Joe River Country* (Coeur d'Alene: Museum of Northern Idaho, 1995), pp. 52–59.
5. A copy of the cooperative agreement exists in the Graves Papers, II, Box 24, Folder

280. Fire statistics from "Supervisor W. G. Weigle's Report on the 1910 Fires. Wallace, Idaho, June 24, 1911," NAPAR, Box 19, Misc. Reports, 1910 Fires, p. 2. Numerous copies of this report—the most oft-cited source for the Great Fires—exist.

6. William B. Greeley, *Forests and Men* (Garden City, N.Y.: Doubleday & Co., 1951), p. 242; Graves, in Harold K. Steen, *The U.S. Forest Service: A History* (Seattle: University of Washington Press, 1976), p. 145. For a thumbnail biography of Greeley, see George T. Morgan, Jr., "The Fight Against Fire: Development of Cooperative Forestry in the Pacific Northwest, 1900–1950," Ph.D. dissertation, University of Oregon, 1964, p. 90, and for a fuller rendition, Morgan, *William B. Greeley, Practical Forester, 1879–1955* (St. Paul: Forest History Society, 1961).
7. Greeley, *Forests and Men,* pp. 81–82.
8. Ibid., p. 31.
9. Ibid., p. 76.
10. Ibid., p. 23.
11. For a good summary, see Morgan, "Fight Against Fire," especially p. 73 fn; for an in-house history, Eloise Hamilton, *Forty Years of Western Forestry* (Portland, Ore.: Western Forestry and Conservation Association, 1949); and Stephen J. Pyne, *Fire in America* (Seattle: University of Washington Press, 1995), pp. 233–34. On the origins of the idea (always murky), A. B. Curtis, *White Pines and Fires: Cooperative Forestry in Idaho* (Moscow, Ida.: University Press of Idaho, 1983), p. 12, gives a somewhat different version.
12. Morgan, "Fight Against Fire," pp. 80–87.
13. George Long quote from Hamilton, *Forty Years of Western Forestry*, p. 3.
14. Morgan, "Fight Against Fire," pp. 92–96; Pinchot quote from *The Use of the National Forests,* rev. ed. (Washington, D.C.: Government Printing Office, 1907), p. 31; on responsibilities, see Betty G. Spencer, *The Big Blowup* (Caldwell, Ida.: Caxton Printers, 1956), p. 30.
15. W. B. Greeley, "Annual Report, September 3, 1910," NAPAR, Historical Collection, 1905–73, Box 42, Folder S+PF Fire Protection.
16. "Forest Fires Still Raging," *New York Times,* 27 March 1910, 2:5.
17. Alfred Gaskill, *Report for 1910, Sixth Annual Report of the Forest Park Reservation Commission of New Jersey* (Paterson, N.J.: News Printing Co., 1911), pp. 16–17.
18. Ibid., p. 3.
19. Ibid., p. 19; *New York Times,* "Caring for Jersey Forests," 15 May 1910, 20:4.
20. For a survey of early North Carolina forestry, see Ralph R. Widner, ed., *Forests and Forestry in the American States: A Reference Anthology* (Association of State Foresters, 1968), pp. 201–5.
21. J. S. Holmes, "Forest Fires and Their Prevention, Including Forest Fires in North Carolina During 1910," Economic Paper No. 22, North Carolina Geological and Economic Survey, Raleigh, 1911, pp. 17, 22, 19.
22. Morris Letters, 20 March 1910, p. 66.

## April

1. Statistics from Charles A. Donnel, "Dry Season in Idaho," *Monthly Weather Review* (September 1910), pp. 1279–80.
2. Henry Gannett, "Forest Fires," *Forum* (December 1898), p. 407.
3. William W. Morris, "The Great Fires of 1910," unpublished ms, NAPAR, RG 95, and Region One headquarters, U.S. Forest Service. Later Morris wrote a fuller version of his career on the Coeur d'Alene titled "Experiences on a National Forest" which absorbs the earlier draft and which was published in *Early Days in the Forest Service,* vol. 1 (Missoula, Mont.: U.S. Forest Service, 1944), p. 166.
4. Morris Letters, n.d., p. 78. For excellent background on homesteading in the region, refer to Sandra A. Crowell and David O. Asleson, *Up the Swiftwater: A Pictorial History of the Colorful Upper St. Joe River Country* (Coeur d'Alene: Museum of Northern Idaho, 1995), pp. 16–30.
5. Morris Letters, n.d., p. 78.
6. John B. Leiberg, "Priest River Reserve," in Part V—Forest Reserves, *Twentieth Annual Report of the United States Geological Survey* (Washington, D.C.: Government Printing Office, 1900), p. 235; William B. Greeley, *Forests and Men* (Garden City, N.Y.: Doubleday and Co., 1951), p. 23.
7. Martin W. Gorman, "Eastern Part of Washington Forest Reserve," *Twentieth Annual Report of the United States Geological Survey,* Part V—Forest Reserves (Washington, D.C.: Government Printing Office, 1900), p. 347.
8. Halm quoted in Crowell and Asleson, *Up the Swiftwater,* p. 66; Morris Letters, 26 September 1909, p. 10.
9. C. K. McHarg letter, 7 November 1941, Personnel File for Edward C. Pulaski, Region One, U.S. Forest Service, Missoula, Montana.
10. Morris Letters, 12 October 1910, p. 132. Letter from end of season but conveys feelings arrayed against rangers; Morris later wrote: "Many of our recent fires I believe can be attributed to this cause."
11. See J. P. Kinney, *A Continent Lost—A Civilization Won: Indian Land Tenure in America* (Baltimore: Johns Hopkins University Press, 1937), pp. 265–66, and *Guide to the National Archives of the United States* (Washington, D.C.: Government Printing Office, 1974), pp. 192–93. A good summary exists in Division of Forestry and Grazing, *Forestry on Indian Lands,* Part II of a report submitted in January 1940 by the Department of the Interior to a congressional committee studying forest conditions throughout the nation: untitled copy from U.S. Forest Service; statistics on burned area on p. 98.
12. Kinney, *Continent Lost,* p. 265.
13. John Wesley Powell, *Report on the Lands of the Arid Region of the United States* (Washington, D.C.: Government Printing Office, 1878), p. 28.

## *May*

1. Quoted in H. Duane Hampton, *How the U.S. Cavalry Saved Our National Parks* (Bloomington: Indiana University Press, 1971), pp. 82–83.
2. Captain Moses Harris, "Report of Capt. Moses Harris, First Cavalry, Acting Superintendent, 1886," *Annual Reports of the Superintendents, Yellowstone National Park,* vol. 3 (Washington, D.C.: Government Printing Office, 1886–1890), Yellowstone National Park Library.
3. J. B. Leiberg, "Forest Conditions in the Absaroka Division of the Yellowstone Forest Reserve, Montana," *USGS Professional Paper 29*, Series H, Forestry 9 (Washington, D.C.: Government Printing Office, 1904), p. 27; Harris, "Report of Capt. Moses Harris," loc. cit.
4. On Logan, see Mel Ruder, "Memory of First Superintendent," *Hungry Horse News* (7 February 1985), Columbia Falls, Montana, copy in NAPAR, Historical Collection 1905–73, Box 14, Folder 1680.
5. *Report of the Committee Appointed by the National Academy of Sciences upon the Inauguration of a Forest Policy for the Forested Lands of the United States to the Secretary of the Interior, May 1, 1897* (Washington, D.C.: Government Printing Office, 1897), pp. 17–18, 21, 23, 25.
6. "Glacier Park Fire Serious," *Daily Missoulian,* 17 July 1910; *Report of the Committee,* p. 22.
7. "Snowfall," *New York Times,* 21 April 1910, 1:6. For background on the regional fire geography, see J. A. Mitchell and Neil LeMay, *Forest Fires and Forest-Fire Control in Wisconsin* (Wisconsin State Conservation Commission and U.S. Forest Service, 1952), pp. 12–14, and for interesting graphs on fire season for Minnesota, J. A. Mitchell and G. M. Conzet, *Forest Fires in Minnesota* (Minnesota Forest Service and U.S. Forest Service, c. 1927).
8. "Forest Fires Doom Town," *New York Times,* 1 May 1910, 1:6; 11 May 1910, 1:2; 13 May 1910, 6:5.
9. "Forest Fire Casts Embers over Town," *New York Times,* 15 May 1910, 18:3.
10. To place into the context of regional fire history, see Stephen Pyne, *Fire in America* (Seattle: University of Washington Press, 1996), pp. 199–218.
11. "Fighting Costly Forest Fires," *New York Times,* 5 June 1910, pt. 5, 3:5.

## *June*

1. F. E. Clements, *The Life History of Lodgepole Burn Forests,* Forest Service Bulletin 79 (Washington, D.C.: Government Printing Office, 1910).
2. Gifford Pinchot, "The Relation of Forests and Forest Fires," *National Geographic* X (1899), pp. 393, 403; *Report of the Forester for 1899* (Washington, D.C.: Government Printing Office, 1900), p. 98; *Report of the Forester for 1902* (Washington, D.C.: Government Printing Office, 1903), p. 124; *Report of the Forester for 1903* (Washington, D.C.: Government Printing Office, 1904), pp. 524–25; Henry S. Graves, *Protection of Forests from Fire,* Forest Service Bulletin 82 (Washington, D.C.: Government Printing Office, 1910), pp. 12–17, 28.

3. H. H. Chapman, "A Method of Studying Growth and Yield of Longleaf Pine Applied in Tyler County, Texas," *Proceedings, Society of American Foresters* 4 (1909), pp. 217–18.
4. Clements, *Life History,* pp. 61–63; John B. Leiberg, "Forest Conditions in the Absaroka Division of the Yellowstone Forest Reserve, Montana," U.S. Geological Survey, *Professional Paper 29,* Series H, Forestry 9 (Washington, D.C.: Government Printing Office, 1904), p. 27.
5. Gifford Pinchot, "A Study of Forest Fires and Wood Production in Southern New Jersey," appendix to *Annual Report for 1898 of State Geologist of New Jersey* (Trenton, N.J.: Geological Survey of New Jersey, 1898), pp. 19–21.
6. Morris Letters, 2 June 1910, pp. 82–84; 22 June 1910, p. 92 (letter by Aubrey Morris to his mother).
7. Elers Koch, *Forty Years a Forester,* ed. Peter Koch (Missoula, Mont.: Mountain Press Publishing Co., 1998), p. 91.
8. Prisoners reference: Sandra A. Crowell and David O. Asleson, *Up the Swiftwater* (Coeur d'Alene: Museum of Northern Idaho, 1995), p. 79; J. E. Kirkwood, "Notes on Observations in National Forests and Elsewhere During the Summer of 1910," unpublished report (1910), Historic Files, USFS R1, p. 15.
9. Koch, *Forty Years,* pp. 100–101.
10. Lieutenant Horace Sykes, Report to Adjutant, Fort George Wright, 6 September 1910, p. 3, and Captain Charles Bates, Report to Adjutant, Fort George Wright, 5 September 1910, p. 3, AGO.
11. E. I. Kotok and R. F. Hammatt, "Ferdinand Augustus Silcox," *Public Administration Review* 2 (Summer 1942), pp. 240–53.
12. Koch, *Forty Years,* p. 102.
13. Ibid., pp. 102-3.
14. Greeley episode cited in Betty G. Spencer, *The Big Blowup* (Caldwell, Ida.: Caxton Printers, 1956), p. 51; Koch, *Forty Years,* pp. 102–3.
15. "Ranger Robinson Is Condemned," *Daily Missoulian,* 28 September 1910, copy in NARA Seattle [F Control Suppression 1910 Fires].
16. "House for Forest Reserves," *New York Times,* 25 June 1910, 3:3; "Flames Sweep Forests," *New York Times,* 2 July 1910, 1:6; William W. Morris, "Experiences on a National Forest," *Early Days in the Forest Service,* vol. 1 (Missoula, Mont.: U.S. Forest Service, 1944), p. 165.

## *July*

1. Morris Letters, 11 July 1910, p. 94.
2. Ibid., p. 96.
3. An excellent summary is of course Henry S. Graves, *Protection of Forests from Fire,* USFS Bulletin 82 (Washington, D.C.: Government Printing Office, 1910).
4. From a letter quoted by Betty G. Spencer, *The Big Blowup* (Caldwell, Ida.: Caxton Printers, 1956), p. 192.

5. Roy A. Phillips, "Recollections," in *Early Days in the Forest Service* (Missoula, Mont.: U.S. Forest Service, 1944), vol. 2, p. 21.
6. Halm information from Spencer, *Big Blowup,* pp. 70–72, quote from p. 70. Other sources: Washington State Alumni Association (I thank Maren R. Wilm for help); Richard Fry, *The Crimson and the Gray: 100 Years with the WSU Cougars* (Pullman: Washington State University Press, 1989); and Washington State College yearbooks; Personnel Files, USFS R1; and census records.
7. Morris Letters, 6 August 1910, p. 100.
8. "Forest Fires Menace Town," *New York Times,* 11 July 1910, 2:5; "Smoke Pall over State," *Daily Missoulian,* 13 July 1910, 1:1, and 14 July 1910.
9. William W. Morris, "The Great Fires of 1910," NAPAR, Box 20, p. 1.
10. *New York Times,* 10 July 1910, 16:4, and 20 July 1910, 1:4. Oregon: *Daily Missoulian,* 21 July 1910, 1:1. Washington: *Daily Missoulian,* 21 July 1910, 1:1, 3:2; Polleys death: Roy A. Phillips, Narrative, NAPAR, Box 19, Misc. Reports, "Phillips."
11. *New York Times,* 22 July 1910, 1:3; 23 July 1910, 2:4; 24 July 1910, pt. 4, 15:1.
12. Morris, "The Great Fires," pp. 2–3; references on county support from *Daily Missoulian,* 21 July 1910, 1:1.
13. Frances Bogert Eaton, " 'The Sun Rises in a Bank of Smoke and Sets in a Bank of Smoke': Letters from the 1910 Fire," *Idaho Yesterdays* (Fall 1995), pp. 14–21; quote from p. 17.
14. H. H. Chapman, "Fires on the Flathead Forest in Montana," *American Forestry* XVI, No. 11 (November 1910), p. 657.
15. Ibid., p. 658. Statistics from Jack S. Barrows et al., "Lightning Fires in Northern Rocky Mountain Forests," Final Report for Cooperative Agreement 16-440-CA, Intermountain Forest and Range Experiment Station, April 1977.
16. Chapman, "Fires on the Flathead Forest," p. 658.
17. "Secretary Wilson Reaches Missoula," *Daily Missoulian,* 16 July 1910, 1:2–3 and "Friendly Exchange on Conservation," 1:5. See also *New York Times,* 16 July 1910, 1:5.
18. "Forest Fires Burning Fiercely," *Daily Missoulian,* 16 July 1910, 1:1.
19. James Wilson, "Protecting Our Forests from Fire," *National Geographic Magazine* XXII, No. 1 (January 1911), p. 99. Reprinted from the *Secretary of Agriculture's Report for 1910.*
20. Elers Koch, *Forty Years a Forester* (Missoula, Mont.: Mountain Press, 1998), p. 101; "Forest Conditions Much Improved," *Daily Missoulian,* 21 July 1910.
21. "Forest Fires Contained," *Daily Missoulian,* 22 July 1910; William Greeley, circular letter to Forest Supervisors, 27 July 1910, NAPAR, Box 20, Fire—Misc. Correspondence.
22. Morris, "The Great Fires of 1910," pp. 2–3; Morris Letters, 6 August 1910, Graham Creek Ranger Station, p. 100.

## *August*

1. John C. Scoffield, Assistant and Chief Clerk for Secretary of War to Charles D. Norton, Secretary to the President, 6 August 1910, AGO.

2. Telegram, 7 August 1910, AGO.
3. Letter, Silcox to Commanding Officer, Fort Harrison, 8 August 1910, NAPAR, Box 20; Letter, Captain James Hanson to District Forester, 10 August 1910, NAPAR, Box 20, Fire—Misc. Correspondence.
4. Special Orders, No. 200, The Presidio of San Francisco, 22 August 1910, Extract, AGO; *New York Times,* 7 August 1910, 16:6; "Troops for Forest Fires," *New York Times,* 9 August 1910, 4:5.
5. Quoted in Betty G. Spencer, *The Big Blowup* (Caldwell, Ida.: Caxton Printers, 1956), p. 64.
6. "Fail to Stop Fires in Western Forests," *New York Times,* 14 August 1910, 4:3.
7. Letter of Clement Ucker to Richard Ballinger, 12 August 1910, Ballinger Papers, Box 13, Folder 28.
8. Ibid.
9. Ibid.
10. Gifford Pinchot, *The Fight for Conservation* (Seattle: University of Washington Press, 1967; reprint of 1910 edition), p. 46; Elers Koch, *Forty Years a Forester* (Missoula, Mont.: Mountain Press, 1998), p. 91; Ballinger quoted in *New York Times,* 26 August 1910, 4:1.2.
11. George L. Hoxie, "How Fire Helps Forestry," *Sunset* 25 (August 1910), p. 145.
12. Ibid., pp. 146–48.
13. Ibid., pp. 148–49.
14. Graves, *Protection of Forests from Fire,* Forest Service Bulletin 82 (Washington, D.C.: Government Printing Office, 1910), pp. 27–28.
15. H. H. Chapman, "Prescribed Burning Versus Public Forest Fire Services," *Journal of Forestry* 45, No. 11 (November 1947), p. 804.
16. "Yellowstone Park Ablaze," *New York Times,* 11 August 1910, 14:3; H. C. Benson, "Report of the Superintendent of Yellowstone National Park for 1910," *Annual Reports of the Superintendents, Yellowstone National Park* (Washington, D.C.: Government Printing Office, 1910), Yellowstone Park Library, pp. 11–12.
17. Letter from Captain Alfred Aloe to Adjutant General, Department of the Columbia, 6 September 1910, AGO.
18. Ibid.
19. Letter from Lieutenant Ralph Lister to Adjutant General, Department of the Columbia, 10 September 1910, pp. 1–2, AGO.
20. Ibid.
21. Letter from Boise Barracks to Adjutant General, Department of the Columbia, 2 September 1910, AGO.
22. Letter from Captain Charles Bates to Adjutant, Fort George Wright, 5 September 1910, AGO.
23. Ibid.
24. Letter from Captain E. A. Lewis to Adjutant, Fort George Wright, 14 September 1910, AGO.
25. Letter from W. R. Logan to Secretary of the Interior, 9 October 1910, AGO; Letter from Lieutenant W. S. Mapes to Adjutant, Fort George Wright, 17 September 1910, AGO.

26. Ibid.
27. Letter from W. R. Logan to Secretary of the Interior, 9 October 1910, and Letter from R. A. Ballinger to Secretary of War, 24 December 1910, AGO.
28. Lieutenant L. B. Chandler to Adjutant, Fort George Wright, 6 September 1910, AGO. His report includes copies of daily telegrams. On firebrands, see Elers Koch, *When the Mountains Roared: Stories of the 1910 Fire* (Coeur d'Alene: U.S. Forest Service, Idaho Panhandle Forests), p. 4. See also Frances Bogert Eaton, "'The Sun Rises in a Bank of Smoke and Sets in a Bank of Smoke': Letters from the 1910 Fire," *Idaho Yesterdays* (Fall 1995), p. 17.
29. Copy of diary of A. H. Abbott, 1 August to 2 September 1910. NAPAR, Box 20, Fire—Misc. Correspondence.
30. Thenon story and quotes from Spencer, *Big Blowup,* pp. 47–48, 50–51.
31. Quoted from ibid., pp. 46–47, 52–54.
32. Morris Letters, 6 August 1910, pp. 100–102; Morris, "The Great Fires of 1910," NAPAR, Box 20, p. 3.
33. Morris, "Great Fires," pp. 3–4; Morris Letters, 6 August 1910, p. 102.
34. Morris, "Great Fires," p. 4; Morris Letters, 6 August 1910, p. 102.
35. Morris, "Great Fires," pp. 4-5; Morris Letters, 19 August 1910, p. 106.
36. Morris, "Great Fires," p. 5.
37. Letter, George H. Cecil to the Forester, Washington, D.C., 19 August 1910, copy in AGO.
38. Telegraphs quoted in letter, Frank Pierce to Secretary of War, 19 August 1910, AGO; Greeley quoted in Spencer, *Big Blowup,* p. 81; Koch, in *When the Mountains Roared,* p. 3.
39. "Supervisor W. G. Weigle's Report on the 1910 Fires, Wallace, Idaho, June 24, 1911," NAPAR, Box 19, Misc. Reports—1910 Fires, pp. 2–3; Halm, quoted in Spencer, *Big Blowup,* p. 96; Morris Letters, 19 August 1910, p. 108.
40. The best review of the fire dynamics associated with the Big Blowup is Stephen J. Pyne and Philip N. Omi, *Wildland Fires and Nuclear Winters: Selected Reconstructions of Historic Large Fires,* Technical Report, Defense Nuclear Agency, DNA-TR-85-396 (1986). Edward A. Beals, "The Value of Weather Forecasts in the Problem of Protecting Forests from Fire," *Monthly Weather Review* (February 1914), pp. 111–19; quote from p. 116.
41. Beals, "Value of Weather Forecasts," pp. 116–17, for synoptic charts. For smoke, see Fred G. Plummer, *Forest Fires: Their Causes, Extent and Effects, with a Summary of Recorded Destruction and Loss,* U.S. Forest Service Bulletin 117 (Washington, D.C.: Government Printing Office, 1912), p. 20.
42. Morris, "Great Fires," p. 6.
43. Ibid.; Morris Letters, 23 August 1910, p. 112, and 28 August 1910, pp. 114–18.
44. Morris, "Great Fires," p. 6.
45. Greeley quoted, apparently from interviews with the author, in Spencer, *Big Blowup,* p. 81.
46. Koch, *When the Mountains Roared,* pp. 24, 23, 20.
47. M. H. Wolff, Memorandum for Mrs. Turrell, 23 August 1923, NAPAR, Box 20, Fire—Misc. Correspondence, p. 1.

48. Ibid., pp. 4–5.
49. Letter from J. E. Barton to District Forester, 3 July 1911, forwarded by F. A. Silcox to Forester, 5 July 1911, NAPAR, Box 20, Fire—Misc. Correspondence; also in Koch, *When the Mountains Roared,* pp. 19–20.
50. Koch, *When the Mountains Roared,* pp. 19–20, quoting from official report; W. P. Hillman, statement on file, NAPAR, Box 19, Fire—Misc. Reports, W. P. Hillman.
51. Several publications have reprinted Thenon's account. See Koch, *When the Mountains Roared,* pp. 21–23; Spencer, *Big Blowup,* pp. 83–89; Ed Thenon, "Forest Fires. The Adventures of Three Men in the Great Forest Fires of 1910," NAPAR, Box 19, untitled folder.
52. Thenon, in Koch, *When the Mountains Roared,* p. 21.
53. Ibid., p. 22.
54. Ibid., p. 23.
55. Thenon, "Forest Fires," pp. 32–35; another version of Ray Fitting's story in Koch, *When the Mountains Roared,* p. 23.
56. Story and quotes from official report, reproduced in Koch, *When the Mountains Roared,* pp. 18–19.
57. Dixon accounts in 1910 Claims—Dixon; Haney letter, 23 June 1911, to Secretary Wilson, in 1910 Claims—Strong, George.
58. Koch, *When the Mountains Roared,* p. 15; Abbott field diary, loc. cit.
59. H. P. Barringer, Grave Creek–Trout Creek Fire Report, Clearwater and Lolo Forests, 8 November 1910, NAPAR, Box 19, Fire—Misc. Reports.
60. Letters, Elers Koch to District Forester, 9 September 1910, p. 2, NAPAR, Box 20, Fire—Misc. Correspondence.
61. William J. McPherson, "The Iron Mountain Fire, August 1910," NAPAR, Box 20, Recollections and Narrated Accounts, Iron Mountain Fire.
62. Ibid., p. 2.
63. Koch, *When the Mountains Roared,* p. 15; Grand Forks story related in Sandra A. Crowell and David O. Asleson, *Up the Swiftwater* (Coeur d'Alene: Museum of Northern Idaho, 1995), p. 67.
64. Frank Haun, Report, NAPAR, Box 19, Fire—Misc. Reports, p. 1.
65. Ibid., p. 2.
66. Ibid.
67. Taft story, from Crowell and Asleson, *Up the Swiftwater,* p. 65; Haun, Report, p. 3; also told in Koch, *When the Mountains Roared,* p. 15.
68. Haun, Report, pp. 3–4.
69. Koch quoted in Spencer, *Big Blowup,* p. 164.
70. Mr. Swaine, "Our Experience with the Forest Fires," in Koch, *When the Mountains Roared,* p. 35.
71. Ibid., pp. 36–37.
72. Letter, Roy A. Phillips to Elers Koch, 29 July 1942, NAPAR, Box 20, Information—Nezperce.
73. Phillips, Narrative, NAPAR, Box 19, Misc. Reports, 1910 Fires, pp. 1–2.
74. Ibid., pp. 2–3. The entire account is also reproduced in Spencer, *Big Blowup,* pp. 166–69, and Koch, *When the Mountains Roared,* pp. 16–18.

75. Phillips, Narrative, p. 3.
76. Ibid., p. 4; Letter, Phillips to Koch, 29 July 1942, loc. cit., p. 2.
77. Phillips, Narrative, pp. 4, 6–7. Letter, Roscoe Haines to District Forester, 25 November 1910, regarding claims of S. D. Adams, NAPAR, Box 19, Fire on Coeur d'Alene Forest.
78. Phillips, Narrative, p. 5; Baird story in Letter, Phillips to Koch, 29 July 1942, loc. cit., p. 2.
79. Robert Stewart, "'The Fire Was on All Sides of Us,' A Ranger's Reminiscence," *Idaho Yesterdays* (Fall 1995), pp. 22–23. Pulaski gives his account of the meeting in a response to a claims letter from the relatives of Beauchamp; see Letter, Edward C. Pulaski to Roscoe Haines, 30 March 1912, 1910 Claims—Beauchamp, Joseph.
80. Stewart, "Fire on All Sides," pp. 22–23. But see Ritchie, "Two Days in August, 1910," pp. 4–5, for a more complex synthesis of the disintegration of the crew and its reconnection with Pulaski, in which no one mentions Stewart's role at all.
81. "Supervisor W. G. Weigle's Report on the 1910 Fires," Coeur d'Alene National Forest, 24 June 1911, NAPAR, Box 19, Misc. Reports, 1910 Fires, pp. 6–7, but often reproduced, including *Big Blowup,* pp. 105–7, and Koch, *When the Mountains Roared,* pp. 8–9.
82. "Weigle's Report," p. 9; Koch, *When the Mountains Roared,* p. 9.
83. Letter of Arthur Hogue, cited in Spencer, *Big Blowup,* pp. 193–94.
84. Ibid., pp. 195–96.
85. Joe B. Halm, "The Great Fire of 1910," *American Forests and Forest Life* (July 1930), p. 425. The article is also reproduced in Spencer, *Big Blowup,* pp. 96–101, and Koch, *When the Mountains Roared,* pp. 29–34.
86. Halm, "Great Fire," p. 425.
87. "Weigle's Report," p. 10; Spencer, *Big Blowup,* p. 137; Koch, *When the Mountains Roared,* p. 10.
88. "Weigle's Report," p. 11; Phillips, Narrative, p. 3, reprinted in Koch, *When the Mountains Roared,* p. 17.
89. General accounts of Avery fire: "Weigle's Report," pp. 8–9; Roe's account, mostly reprinted in Spencer, *Big Blowup,* pp. 152–57. By far the richest source is Lieutenant Lewis, "Report to Adjutant, Fort George Wright, September 7, 1910," complete with telegrams as an appendix, AGO. Quotes from Lewis, "Report," Exhibit C and D (telegrams).
90. Lewis, "Report," Exhibits E, F, G (telegrams).
91. "Weigle's Report," p. 8.
92. Roe quoted in Spencer, *Big Blowup,* pp. 153–54.
93. Roe story appears as "Avery man tells his experiences in hell of fire," *Seattle Sunday Times,* 28 August 1910. The feature ends with Roe lavishing high praise on the paper for its "marvelous" coverage and "absolutely accurate" reports on the fires. See also Letter, Roscoe Haines to Weigle, April 8, 1918, IPNF, which lists the names of forest officers. Roe is not among them, but then neither is Pulaski. Debitt problems cited in C. W. Griffin to District Forester, 7 March 1912, 1910, 1910 Claims—Stump, Reese. Lieutenant Lewis, it should be noted, had high praise for Debitt.
94. Lewis, "Report," pp. 3–4.

95. Ibid., p. 4. Other railroad stories from Spencer, *Big Blowup,* pp. 151–52, which seem to derive from Koch, *When the Mountains Roared,* p. 11.
96. Lewis, "Report," pp. 4–7.
97. Ibid., pp. 7, 9; Captain George Holden, "Report to Adjutant, Fort George Wright, September 5th, 1910," p. 9, AGO. Roe also gives a detailed account of the backfire operations, though he claims the troops were involved while my reading of Lewis's report is that Company G did not return to Avery until the next morning.
98. "Weigle's Report," pp. 7–8; quotes from Captain George Chandler, "Report to Adjutant, Fort George Wright, September 5th, 1910," p. 8, AGO.
99. Stories in Koch, *When the Mountains Roared,* pp. 11–14. The section includes original newspaper accounts, not always reliable but indicative of the experiences of those who were not on the fireline.
100. Insurance information from Spencer, *Big Blowup,* p. 115; "sound at sea," from Mr. Swaine, "Our Experience with the Forest Fires," op. cit., p. 35; the timing of the wind shift, from Lieutenant L. B. Chandler, "Report," 6 September 1910, p. 3.
101. The most extensive summary of Wallace fires in Spencer, *Big Blowup,* pp. 114–36; Getz quote from p. 123. "Big Burn," NAPAR, Box 19, has complete (retyped) cuttings of all the Wallace newspapers during the fire crisis.
102. Mildred Hord Mellinger, "Two Nights on a Tailing Pile," *North Idaho Press,* 7 August 1970, clipping in NAPAR, Box 19, Fire—Misc. Reports.
103. Letter, Marie S. Alger, Osburn, Idaho, 24 August 1910, Museum of North Idaho, Coeur d'Alene.
104. Many newspaper accounts exist. A full rendering of those on Wallace is available in the Forest Service records, NAPAR. Sober personal reminiscence in L. Worstell, "The 1910 Forest Fire in Wallace, Idaho," 11 April 1953, NAPAR.
105. Telegram, Adjutant General's Office, 25 August 1910, to Commanding General, Department Dakota, AGO Records.
106. Telegrams with orders for Second Infantry, Idaho National Guard, 23 August 1910, RG 94.
107. Emma Pulaski, "My Experience as a Forest Ranger's Wife," manuscript, Wallace District, Idaho Panhandle National Forest, pp. 1, 3.
108. Ibid., pp. 4–5.
109. Ibid., pp. 5–6.
110. Ibid., p. 6.
111. See Letter from W. G. Weigle to L. A. Campbell, 30 June 1938, NAPAR; Koch, *When the Mountains Roared,* p. 5; and, richer with detail, Joe Halm, "The Big Fire," reproduced in Koch, *When the Mountains Roared,* p. 33.
112. Pulaski quote from F. R. Foltz, Statement (1951), p. 3, Wallace Ranger Station.
113. The two best compilations of Pulaski sources are: Carl Ritchie, "Pulaski, Two Days in August, 1910," Cultural Resource Inventory, Wallace Ranger District, Idaho Panhandle National Forests (1984), and various documents gathered by Cort Sims, forest archaeologist, Idaho Panhandle National Forests, in support of the case for admitting the Nicholson adit to the register of national historic sites. Other useful materials are found in the personnel files at Forest Service Region

One headquarters and an account, apparently the result of interviews with Elsie Pulaski, in Spencer, *Big Blowup,* pp. 111–13.

Perhaps most provocative is Stewart, "Fire on All Sides," pp. 22–25, which (alone) suggests Pulaski had the idea to sprint home after he had the crew safely secreted in the first cave. It has the merit that it was written very soon after the fire. Many other accounts did not appear until twenty-eight or forty-one years later.

All in all, it makes a very confusing body of information, not helped by Pulaski's reluctance to retell or amplify his role but on the contrary to dampen it.

114. Stewart, "Fire on All Sides," p. 23.
115. Not surprisingly, several accounts exist. One claims he had gotten into the Nicholson adit and then managed to squeeze through before meeting his death. Such confusion is typical of the sources.
116. Morris Letters, Telegram, 21 August 1910, p. 110.
117. Halm, "The Big Fire," in Koch, *When the Mountains Roared,* p. 30.
118. Ibid., pp. 30–31; Halm motto from 1910 *Washington State College Yearbook,* p. 176.
119. "Weigle's Report," pp. 6–7; also, newspaper accounts cited in Spencer, *Big Blowup,* pp. 107–98.
120. "Weigle's Report," p. 11.
121. Ibid., pp. 9–10; Spencer, *Big Blowup,* pp. 104–5; statement by Peter Kinsley, 1910 Claims—Kinsley, Peter.
122. Hollingshead quote, telegram from Debitt to Weigle, cited in Spencer, *Big Blowup,* p. 135; statement by Reese Stump, 1910 Claims—Stump, Reese.
123. Hogue letter, quoted in Spencer, *Big Blowup,* pp. 196–97.
124. "Weigle's Report," p. 8.
125. Ibid., pp. 10–12; see Letter, Roscoe Haines to District Forester, April 3, 1912, 1910 Claims—Fanning, Claude, pp. 2–4.
126. Morris Letters, 6 September 1910, p. 121; see also 18 September 1910, p. 126.
127. Danielson quoted in Letter from C. W. Griffin to District Forester, Missoula, Montana, 14 March 1912, 1910 Claims—Danilson, James, pp. 2–3. See also claims by other survivors, e.g., Claude Fanning.
128. Lewis, "Report," pp. 7–8, Exhibit I, telegram received, 22 August 1910.
129. Ibid., pp. 7–8; Holden, "Report," p. 2.
130. Halm, "The Big Fire," in Koch, *When the Mountains Roared,* pp. 32–33.
131. "Weigle's Report," p. 9; Roe's account of the search is given in Spencer, *Big Blowup,* p. 155. On funerals, see also Holden, "Report," p. 4.
132. Pulaski's story exists in various versions. Here I follow that recorded by his daughter, reproduced in Spencer, *Big Blowup,* pp. 112–13; Webb from Letter to Forest Supervisor, 14 April 1912, 1910 Claims—Webb.
133. Spencer, *Big Blowup,* pp. 112–13.
134. Emma Pulaski, "My Experience," p. 6.
135. Henry James, ed., *The Letters of William James,* vol. II (Boston: Atlantic Monthly Press, 1920), p. 350.
136. William James, "What Makes a Life Significant," in John J. McDermott, ed., *The Writings of William James* (New York: Modern Library, 1967), pp. 648–49.

137. Ibid., pp. 658, 656.
138. Norman Angell, *The Great Illusion* (New York: G. P. Putnam's Sons, 1910), p. 147.
139. James, "The Moral Equivalent of War," in McDermott, ed., *The Writings of William James,* pp. 668–70.
140. Ibid., p. 669.
141. Koch, *Forty Years a Forester,* p. 108.
142. Minutes of the Service Committee, Minutes for 24 August 1910, pp. 4–5, NACP, General Records, Minutes of the Service Committee, 1903–1935.
143. Abbott diary, loc. cit.
144. Circular letter, J. E. Barton to Forest Officers, Pend Oreille, 25 August 1910, 1910 Claims.
145. Abbott diary, loc. cit.
146. Morris, "The Great Fires of 1910," pp. 6–7; Morris Letters, 6 September 1910, p. 120.
147. Morris, "Great Fires," p. 7.
148. Morris Letters, 23 August 1910, p. 112; Morris, "Great Fires," p. 7.
149. Greeley memo, 29 August 1910, quoted in Spencer, *Big Blowup,* pp. 214–15.
150. Roscoe Haines, "Fire Report on the Coeur d'Alene National Forest," 9 November 1910, NAPAR, Box 19, Folder: "Fire on Coeur d'Alene." Quote from telegram, 24 August 1910, from Captain Holden to Adjutant General, in Holden, "Report," p. 4, AGO; Utah references: *New York Times,* 25 August 1910, 3:3; Sharlot Hall, *Sharlot Hall on the Arizona Strip,* ed. C. Gregory Crampton (Flagstaff: Northland Press, 1978), p. 69; Morris Letters, 6 September 1910, p. 120.
151. Telegram, 23 August 1910, from Captain Holden to Adjutant General, in Holden, "Report," p. 3.
152. Ibid., p. 4.
153. Telegram, 25 August 1910, from Captain Holden to Adjutant General, Vancouver Barracks, ibid.
154. Letter, Roy Phillips to Elers Koch, 29 July 1942, NAPAR, Box 20, unmarked folder.
155. Letter, Phillips to Koch, ibid.; Telegram, Captain Holden to Adjutant General, 25 August 1910, in Holden, Report to Adjutant General, 5 September 1910, p. 5.
156. "Rushing More Fire Fighters," and Taft and Brady telegrams reproduced in *New York Times,* 24 August 1910, 4:1.
157. Ibid. The whole episode—telegrams, Fales's report, and Maus's endorsement—is in AGO. See especially Maus's report dated 12 September 1910.
158. Lieutenant H. M. Fales, Report to Adjutant General, Vancouver Barracks, 31 August 1910, p. 2, included with Maus's report (Note 6), AGO.
159. Whole episode documented in detail with telegrams and reports in AGO. See also *New York Times,* 27 August 1910, 3:1.
160. See Letter from Willis L. Moore to Major General F. C. Ainsworth, 27 August 1910, with files (Note 8), AGO.
161. Greeley to the Forester, 24 August 1910, USFS R1.
162. Telegram, Smith to Adjutant General, Washington, D.C., 30 August 1910, AGO.
163. Major C. N. Martin, "Report to Adjutant General, Department of the Columbia, September 24, 1910," p. 4, RG 94; statistics from Lieutenant A. N. Budd,

"Report to Adjutant, 2nd Battalion, First Infantry, September 22, 1910," which includes photos, AGO.

164. Richard L. P. Bigelow to District Forester, San Francisco, California, 8 September 1910, NAPAR, Box 20, Fire—Misc. Correspondence.

165. Major General Chief of Staff Leonard Wood and Major General Chief of Staff Ainsworth, Memorandum for the Acting Secretary of War, 26 October 1910, AGO.

166. Martin, "Report," p. 17.

167. Brigadier General Tasker Bliss, "Report to Adjutant General, November 30, 1910," p. 4; Letter, Major General Leonard Wood to Charles D. Norton, Secretary to the President, 17 August 1910, both in AGO.

168. *New York Times,* 23 August 1910, 1:1 and 2:2–2:6; *New York Times,* 28 August 1910, pt. 5, p. 7.

169. *New York Times,* editorial, 23 August 1910, 8:2; Ballinger quoted, *New York Times,* 25 August 1910, 1:2; Pinchot, *New York Times,* 27 August 1910, 3:1.

170. Pinchot quoted in *New York Times,* 27 August 1910, 6:1.

171. All quotes are included in Spencer, *Big Blowup,* pp. 211–12; Carter quoted in *New York Times,* 31 August 1910, 1:2.

172. *New York Times,* 28 August 1910, pt. 5, p. 7.

## *September*

1. Potter quoted in *New York Times,* 26 August 1910, 4:1; Morris Letters, 28 August 1910, p. 118; William W. Morris, "The Great Fires of 1910," NAPAR, Box 20, "The Great Fires of 1910," p. 8.

2. Morris, "Great Fires," p. 8; M. H. Wolff, Memorandum for Mrs. Turrell, 23 August 1923, NAPAR, Box 20, Fire—Misc. Correspondence, p. 5.

3. Wolff, Memorandum for Mrs. Turrell, pp. 5–6.

4. Ibid., p. 5; Mrs. Swaine, in "Our Experience with the Forest Fires by Mr. Swaine," in Elers Koch, *When the Mountains Roared: Stories from the 1910 Fire* (U.S. Forest Service: Idaho Panhandle Forests, n.d.), p. 37; Mrs. Frances Bogert Eaton, "'The Sun Rises in a Bank of Smoke and Sets in a Bank of Smoke,' Letters from the 1910 Fire," *Idaho Yesterdays* (Fall 1995), p. 21; William B. Greeley, *Forests and Men* (Garden City, N.Y.: Doubleday & Co., 1951), p. 18; Koch, *When the Mountains Roared,* p. 1; Pulaski, quoted in Robert Percy Stewart, "'The Fire Was on All Sides of Us.' A Ranger's Reminiscence," *Idaho Yesterdays* (Fall 1995), p. 25; Morris Letters, 6 September 1910, p. 124, and Morris, "Great Fires," pp. 7–8.

5. Roscoe Haines, "Annual Fire Report for Coeur d'Alene Forest, January 5th, 1911," NAPAR, Box 19, untitled folder, pp. 1–3.

6. Koch, *When the Mountains Roared,* p. 26.

7. Ibid.

8. Morris Letters, 12 October 1910, p. 134.

9. See Minutes of the Service Committee, 24 August 1910, p. 1, NACP, General Records, Minutes of the Service Committee, 1903–1935.

10. Quoted in M. Nelson McGeary, *Gifford Pinchot: Forester-Politician* (Princeton, N.J.: Princeton University Press, 1960), pp. 193–94.
11. Samuel P. Hays, *Conservation and the Gospel of Efficiency: The Progressive Conservation Movement 1890–1920* (New York: Atheneum, 1969), pp. 180, 182; Gifford Pinchot, *The Fight for Conservation* (Seattle: University of Washington Press, 1967; reprint of 1910 edition), pp. 132–33.
12. Quotes from McGeary, *Gifford Pinchot,* p. 194.
13. Henry S. Graves, "The Forest and the Nation," manuscript of address delivered at Conservation Congress, 8 September 1910, Graves Papers, II, Box 49, Folder 533, pp. 1, 11.
14. Ibid., p. 13.
15. Henry S. Graves, "The Forestry Problem of Today," address delivered to American Forestry Association, 12 January 1911, reproduced in *American Forestry* XVII (February 1911), pp. 111–12; Roosevelt quoted in Circular Letter, W. B. Greeley to Forest Supervisors, 15 September 1910, NAPAR, Box 20, Fire—Misc. Correspondence.
16. Pinchot, *Fight for Conservation,* p. 147.
17. Minutes of the Service Committee, 14 September 1910, p. 2, NACP, General Records, Minutes of the Service Committee, 1903–1935.
18. Ibid., pp. 2–3.
19. Morris Letters, 18 September 1910, p. 126. No official report of the photography expedition was ever submitted (that I could find), but the many photos with their lengthy captions speak for themselves. Presently in National Archives Still Photo Collection.
20. Graves, Minutes of the Service Committee, 14 September 1910, NACP, General Records, Minutes of the Service Committee, 1903–1935.
21. See W. B. Greeley, "Progress in Sales of Fire-killed Timber in Idaho and Montana," *Forestry Quarterly* X, No. 1 (1912), p. 24. See also Letter, W. G. Weigle, to A. W. Cooper, Secretary, Western Pine Manufacturers Association, Spokane, 20 September 1910, NAPAR, Box 19, Fire—Misc. Reports, which conveys both the dismay of those timber concerns that had been burned out and the desperation of the Forest Service to unload as much of the loss as possible. On the area burned, estimates vary. The earliest suggest 1.25 million acres. The Forest Service eventually settled on 3.25 million acres in the Northern Rockies and 5 million in the national forest system overall. See "Forest Fire Loss Put at $15,000,000," *New York Times,* 25 October 1910, 8:3.
22. Wilson, in press release, "National Forest Fire Damage in Montana and Northern Idaho, October 9, 1910," NAPAR, Box 19, Fire—Misc. Reports, p. 4; Letter, Weigle to A. W. Cooper, 20 September 1910; Greeley, "Progress in Sales," USFS R1, p. 25.
23. Koch, *When the Mountains Roared,* pp. 24–25.
24. For a good introduction to the replanting, see William W. Morris, "Experiences on a National Forest," *Early Days in the Forest Service,* vol. 1 (Missoula, Mont.: U.S. Forest Service, 1944), pp. 174–76; *History of the Savenac Nursery,* brochure published by Region One, U.S. Forest Service, n.d.
25. Greeley, "Progress in Sales," p. 26.

26. "Relief for Fire Fighters," *New York Times,* 19 September 1910, 18:2; Morris Letters, 18 September 1910, p. 126.
27. Letter from Greeley to Forest Supervisors, 6 September 1910, NAPAR (reproduced in Spencer, *Big Blowup,* pp. 229–31); Letter, Paul Redington to District Forester, Missoula, Montana, 8 September 1910, NAPAR, Box 19, Fire—Misc. Reports. For the final tally of claims, see James Wilson, "Persons Injured Fighting Forest Fires," Senate Document No. 339, Sixty-second Congress, Second Session (1912), included with 1910 Claims—General.
28. James Wilson, Letter of 4 January 1911 to Secretary of the Treasury, House Document No. 1271, Sixty-first Congress, Third Session (1911), p. 2. Available in 1910 Claims—General. Each forest had submitted a separate report on fatalities and claims; some several, each typically giving different figures.
29. See letters from C. S. Chapman to General M. P. Maus, 14 September 1910; Chapman to Graves, 17 September 1910; Graves to Greeley, 7 October 1910; Greeley to Graves, 15 October 1910; Graves to Wilson, 30 September 1910; Wilson to Graves, 3 October 1910, all in 1910 Claims—General. Greeley quotes come from Letter to Graves, 15 October 1910.
30. Letter from James Denton to Thomas Butler, 31 October 1910, 1910 Claims; Letter from C. S. Chapman to the Forester, 6 October 1910, 1910 Claims.
31. Correspondence relating to Ruzic claim, 1910 Claims—Ruzic, Josef.
32. See 1910 Claims, with each source listed alphabetically by last name of claimant.
33. Correspondence in 1910 Claims—Adams, Salvar.
34. Ibid.—Schmidt, Peter.
35. Ibid.—Adsit, William; see especially William Adams, Letter of 10 November 1913.
36. Ibid.—Ames, Roderick; Beauchamp, Joseph; and Robicheau, Joe.
37. Ibid.—Anderson, W. M., especially statement by Anderson.
38. Ibid.—Beaman, Justus.
39. Ibid.—Omerza, Josef.
40. Ibid.—Polic, Vika.
41. Ibid.—Polleys, William.
42. Ibid.—Siphers, J. W.
43. Ibid.—Lalor, Jason.
44. Ibid.—Carnahan, M. J.
45. Ibid.—Mason, T. R., and Knudson, Albert. Quotes from Dr. Mason. Letter from T. R. Mason to Roscoe Haines, 22 June 1912, and Letter from W. G. Weigle to W. B. Greeley, 19 October 1910.
46. Correspondence in 1910 Claims—Early, Maude, and Haines, Roscoe.
47. Ibid.—Bratton, Charles.
48. Ibid.—Nicholson, Val. In fact, father and son were eventually interred together in a common grave at Wallace's Nine Mile Cemetery. The inscription reads: "Died fighting forest fire on Coeur d'Alene Forest." Who paid for the headstone is unknown.
49. Correspondence in 1910 Claims—Noonan, Thomas, especially Letter, Roscoe Haines to District Forester, 2 April 1912.
50. Correspondence in 1910 Claims—Weigert, Oscar.

51. Ibid.—Hansen, Catherine.
52. James Wilson to Senate, 26 February 1912, Response to Resolution of February 5, 1912, 1910 Claims—General; McCabe quote, from Letter from George McCabe to the Forester, 25 May 1912, and Letter from W. P. Jones to the Forester, 6 April 1912, both in 1910 Claims—Danilson, James.
53. James Wilson to Hon. W. B. Heyburn, United States Senate, 6 July 1912, 1910 Claims—General.
54. Letter, Roscoe Haines to District Forester, 28 November 1911, 1910 Claims—Pulaski, Edward.
55. Letter, F. W. Reed to District Forester, 26 February 1912, and R. H. Rutledge to the Forester, 5 March 1912, both in 1910 Claims—Pulaski, Edward.
56. Letter, R. H. Rutledge to Forester, 5 March 1912; Letter, J. D. Jones to Forest Supervisor, Coeur d'Alene, 23 October 1911; F. W. Reed to District Forester, 24 March 1912, 1910 Claims—Pulaski, Edward.
57. Letter from Richard Eggleston to Meyer Wolff, 21 November 1949, IPNF, Historic Files; Carnegie correspondence, F. M. Wilmot to Roscoe Haines, 26 July 1912, and Haines to E. C. Pulaski, 8 August 1912, USFS R1, personnel files—Pulaski, Edward.
58. Letter from U.S. Department of Agriculture Committee on Economy and Efficiency to Chief of the Forest Service, 8 February 1911, and Letter from Carroll to Forest Service, 22 July 1912, both in NAPC, Gen. Records, Records of Office of the Chief, 1908–47, Box 3, Reports, Presidential Commission on Economy and Efficiency (1911–13).
59. Letter, John D. Jones to George P. McCabe, Solicitor, 2 November 1911, p. 13, in 1910 Claims—Weigert, Oscar.
60. Captain George Holden, "Report to Adjutant, Fort George Wright, September 5th, 1910," AGO; Morris Letters, 6 September 1910, p. 121; Letter, Greeley to Forest Supervisor, Wallace, Idaho, 29 August 1910, cited in Spencer, *Big Blowup,* pp. 214–15.
61. Letter, Roscoe Haines to the District Forester, Missoula, Montana, 31 May 1912, p. 2, in 1910 Claims—Johansen, Gust.
62. "Supervisor W. G. Weigle's Report on the 1910 Fires. June 24, 1911," NAPAR, Box 19, Misc. Reports, 1910 Fires, pp. 11–12.
63. Information in Spencer, *Big Blowup,* p. 231. As with everything connected with this story, discrepancies abound. Forest Service historic files at Idaho Panhandle National Forest include a photocopy of a newspaper article, dated 26 August 1962 but otherwise unattributed as to writer or journal, titled "Graves of Firefighters Still Are Cared For After 52 Years." This article claims ten of the dead were buried in Wallace in two graves, one in the old Miners Union plot, and another in the Worstell section, both at Nine Mile.
64. "Idaho's Thirty Days' War," *Collier's* (24 September 1910), pp. 24–28.
65. Ballinger speech, 21 September 1910, in Ballinger Papers, Box 17, Folder 16, Speeches.
66. Theodore Roosevelt, *Addresses and Proceedings of the Second National Conservation Congress held at St. Paul, Minnesota, Sept. 5–8, 1910* (Washington, D.C.: National Conservation Congress, 1911), p. 86; *New York Times* editorial, 26 October 1910.

## October

1. Morris Letters, 12 October 1910, p. 134.
2. Best accounts of the fires are: General C. C. Andrews, "Special Report," *Sixteenth Annual Report of the Forestry Commissioner of Minnesota for the Year 1910* (St. Paul: Pioneer Co., 1911); General C. C. Andrews, "Two Million Dollars Worth Burned in One Day," *American Forestry* XVI, No. 11 (November 1910), pp. 655–56; Carrington A. Phelps, "A Great Fire and Its Heroes," *Metropolitan Magazine* (January 1911), pp. 435–45; Esther E. Larson, *Tales from the Minnesota Forest Fires: A Personal Experience of a Rural School Teacher* (St. Paul: Webb Publ. Co., 1912). Also, *New York Times,* 9 October 1910, pt. 3, 1:4; 10 October, 1:1; 11 October, 11:3; 13 October, 2:3.
3. See *New York Times,* 9 October 1910, pt. 3, 1:4; 10 October, 1:1; 11 October, 11:3. For some individual accounts, see Phelps, "A Great Fire," pp. 444–46.
4. See *New York Times,* 13 October 1910, 2:3; Chapin story, in Phelps, "Great Fire," p. 438; Roulin story, ibid., p. 441.
5. Quotes: *New York Times,* 13 October 1910, 2:3; Donaghue quote, in Phelps, "Great Fire," p. 445.
6. Andrews, "Special Report," pp. 3–4.
7. Ibid., passim; quote from p. 18.
8. Alice E. Andrews, ed., *Christopher C. Andrews: Recollections, 1829–1922* (Cleveland: Arthur H. Clark Co., 1928).
9. Ibid., pp. 283, 275, 280–82.
10. Ibid., p. 284.
11. Andrews, "Special Report," p. 3.
12. Gifford Pinchot, *The Use of the National Forests* (Washington, D.C.: Government Printing Office, 1905), pp. 17–18.
13. Graves Papers, Sec. II, Box 20, Folder 237, Field Notes, 1910.
14. Ibid., on Walker lands; on the possible Graves-sponsored link between Walker and Yale, see Harold K. Steens, *The U.S. Forest Service: A History* (Seattle: University of Washington Press, 1976), p. 135.
15. Graves Papers, Field Notes, Walker lands.
16. Graves Papers, Series II, Box 20, Folder 241, India diaries, p. 19.
17. Elers Koch, *Forty Years a Forester* (Missoula, Mont.: Mountain Press, 1998), p. 99; James Wilson, "Protecting Our Forests from Fire," *National Geographic Magazine* XXII, No. 1 (January 1911), p. 102; Morris Letters, 12 October 1910, p. 132; Major C. H. Martin, "Summary Report of Department of the Columbia, to Adjutant General of the Army, October 12, 1910," p. 12, AGO.
18. *New York Times,* 24 August 1910, 8:4.
19. Lieutenant W. S. Mapes, Report to Adjutant, Fort George Wright, 17 September 1910, p. 2; Captain Charles Bates, Report to Adjutant, Fort George Wright, 5 September 1910, p. 2.
20. "Soldier Fire-Bugs Found Guilty," *Daily Missoulian,* 25 September 1910.
21. Bates, "Report to Adjutant," p. 3.
22. Letter, E. T. Abbott to R. A. Ballinger, 6 November 1910, and Ballinger to Ab-

bott, 31 October 1910, Ballinger Papers, Accession No. 15, Box 3, Folder 1. See also E. T. Abbott, "Some Words on the Forest Fires," *Engineering News* 64, No. 13, p. 340.

## November

1. Henry S. Graves, "Fundamentals of the Fire Problem," *American Forestry* XVI, No. 11 (November 1910), pp. 629–30.
2. E. T. Allen, "What Protective Co-operation Did," ibid., p. 642.
3. "Random Talk on Forest Fires," ibid., pp. 668–69.
4. Ibid., pp. 667–68.
5. "Forest Fires," *Outlook* (19 November 1910), p. 616.
6. C. J. Buck, "How Telephones Saved Lives," *American Forestry* XVI, No. 11 (November 1910), pp. 648, 650–51.
7. F. A. Silcox, "How the Fires Were Fought," ibid., p. 638.
8. A reply to the questionnaire for Region One is preserved in Roscoe Haines, "Fire Report on the Coeur d'Alene National Forest," 9 November 1910, which includes the mandatory outline, NAPAR, Box 19, untitled folder.
9. For national fire planning effort, see *Report of the Forester for 1911* (Washington, D.C.: Government Printing Office, 1912), p. 29.
10. Coert duBois, *Trailblazers* (Stonington, Conn.: 1957), pp. 61, 69.
11. Ibid., pp. 69, 76, 79.
12. Coert duBois, *Systematic Fire Protection in the California Forests,* U.S. Forest Service, for Forest Officers in District 5 (Washington, D.C.: Government Printing Office, 1914), p. 7.

## December

1. *Lake States Forest Fire Conference* (The American Lumberman, 1911). See pp. 5 and 38 for the circumstances of its origins.
2. Ibid., p. 25.
3. O'Neill quotes, *Lake States Forest Fire Conference,* pp. 149–50.
4. Graves, "Fire Protection on the National Forests," *Lake States Forest Fire Conference,* pp. 25–27.
5. G. W. Ogden, "A World Afire. Heroes in the Burning of the Northwestern Forests," *Everybody's Magazine* 23 (December 1910), pp. 754–66.
6. Henry Graves, *Report of the Forester for the Year 1911* (Washington, D.C.: Government Printing Office, 1912), p. 32; Greeley quoted in Betty G. Spencer, *The Big Blowup* (Caldwell, Ida.: Caxton Printers, 1956), p. 268.
7. *New York Times,* 15 December 1910, 1:2; information on the White Salmon Fruit Company from *Seattle Daily News,* 21 August 1910, p. 1. I am unable to verify the charge that Amos Pinchot was in fact a business partner. The Seattle papers tended to side with Ballinger.

## *After*

1. On Taft and Wilson, see Harold K. Steen, *The Forest Service: A History* (Seattle: University of Washington Press, 1976), p. 107; on the Presidential Commission on Economy and Efficiency, see NACP, RG 95, Records of the Forest Service, General Records, Records of Office of the Chief, 1908–47, Box 3, Reports, and Minutes, Service Committee, 8 March 1911; on Debitt, Letter, C. W. Griffin to District Forester, 7 March 1912, 1910 Claims—Stump, Reese.
2. Letter, Henry S. Graves to Gifford Pinchot, 16 February 1912, Graves Papers, Group 249, Unit I, Box 10, Folder 126.
3. Letter, Ralph Moss to Henry S. Graves, 21 June 1911, 1910 Claims—1910.
4. Letter from Secretary James Wilson to Senate, 17 February 1912, Senate Document No. 339, Sixty-second Congress, Second Session, p. 11; Weigle, Letter from W. G. Weigle to District Forester, 9 February 1911, NAPAR, RG 95, Region One, Historical Collection, 1905–73, Box 7, Folder, 1300, Management—Historical Material Relating to District 1 Activities 1910–1911.
5. See Earl Pierce and William Stahl, "Cooperative Forest Fire Control: A History of Its Origin and Development Under the Weeks and Clarke-McNary Acts" (Washington, D.C.: U.S. Forest Service, 1964), p. 4.
6. See G. T. Morgan, Jr., "The Fight Against Fire: Development of Cooperative Forestry in the Pacfic Northwest, 1900–1950," Ph.D. dissertation, University of Oregon, 1964; John James Little, "The 1910 Forest Fires in Montana and Idaho: Their Impact on Federal and State Legislation," M.A. Thesis, University of Montana, 1968; and Pierce and Stahl, "Cooperative Forest Fire Control." Also, quote from Greeley, in Betty G. Spencer, *The Big Blowup* (Caldwell, Ida.: Caxton Printers, 1956), p. 266.
7. William B. Greeley, *Forests and Men* (Garden City, N.Y.: Doubleday & Co., 1951), p. 26.
8. H. S. Graves, "The Policy of the Federal Government in Assisting States to Protect the Forested Watersheds of Navigable Streams," in J. Girvin Peters, ed., *Forest Fire Protection by the States* (Washington, D.C.: Government Printing Office, 1913), p. 2.
9. Greeley quote from Spencer, *Big Blowup*, p. 267.
10. A good summary of sentiment and success is contained in Earle H. Clapp, "Fire Protection in the National Forests," *American Forestry* XVII, No. 10 (October 1911), pp. 573–84, and No. 11 (November 1911), pp. 678–80.
11. Professor Dr. E. Deckert, "Forest Fires in North America. A German View," *American Forestry* XVII, No. 5 (May 1911), pp. 272, 275.
12. Henry S. Graves, "The Forest Service and Light-Burning Experiments," *American Lumberman* (28 February 1920), p. 76, and idem, *Report of the Forester for 1912* (Washington, D.C.: Government Printing Office, 1913), p. 43. For a survey history of the light burning controversy, see Stephen Pyne, *Fire in America* (Seattle: University of Washington Press, 1995), pp. 100–112.
13. Graves, "Forest Service," p. 76.
14. Greeley, *Forests and Men,* p. 18.
15. W. B. Greeley, "Better Methods of Fire Control," *Proceedings of the Society of American Foresters* VI, No. 2 (1911), p. 165; Pyne, *Fire in America,* p. 272.

16. On Stuart, see Herbert Smith, "Robert Young Stuart," *Journal of Forestry* 31, No. 12 (December 1933), pp. 885–90.
17. For good surveys of the controversy, see Ashley L. Schiff, *Fire and Water: Scientific Heresy in the Forest Service* (Cambridge, Mass.: Harvard University Press, 1961). Quotes from Inman Eldredge, "Administrative Problems in Fire Control in the Longleaf-Slash Pine Region of the South," *Journal of Forestry* 33, No. 3 (March 1935), p. 344, and Komarek, *Journal of Forestry* 33, No. 3 (March 1935), p. 360.
18. Elers Koch, "The Passing of the Lolo Trail," *Journal of Forestry* 33, No. 2 (1935), pp. 98–104, reprinted in Elers Koch, *Forty Years a Forester* (Missoula, Mont.: Mountain Press, 1998); quotes from pp. 191–92.
19. Ibid., pp. 189–91.
20. Roy Headley, "Memorandum for Mr. Silcox, September 17, 1934," NACP, RG 95, Records of the Forest Service, Division of Fire Control, General Correspondence—Fire—Back Country Fire Policy, pp. 4, 6.
21. Ibid., p. 7.
22. Earl W. Loveridge, "Is Back Country Fire Protection a 'Practical Impossibility'?," undated report, and Letter, Elers Koch to F. A. Silcox, 20 November 1934, both in NA, RG 95, Records of the Forest Service, Division of Fire Control, General Correspondence, Fire—Back Country Fire Policy.
23. Letter, Ed. C. Pulaski to Forest Supervisor, Coeur d'Alene, 30 April 1917, NAPAR; reburial, Spencer, *Big Blowup,* p. 235.
24. Quoted in Spencer, *Big Blowup,* pp. 231–32. Correspondence between Wolff, Pulaski, and Fenn in Idaho Panhandle National Forests, Historic Files, and in collections of the Wallace District Office.
25. Letter, Ed. Pulaski to Forest Supervisor, Coeur d'Alene, 30 April 1917, NAPAR (reproduced in Spencer, *Big Blowup,* pp. 232–33); Fred Morrell, Letter to Forest Supervisor, Coeur d'Alene, 3 January 1921, NAPAR.
26. Most of the correspondence relating to designs is contained in IPNF and in Wallace District Office historic files; L. C. Stockdale, Circular Letter to Forest Officers, 27 January 1933, IPNF. For the Woodlawn Cemetery story, see Dorothy Clanton, "Memorial to a Tragedy," manuscript on file, Woodlawn Cemetery, St. Maries, Idaho.
27. Quote from "A Monument to Bravery," *American Forestry* 29 (August 1923), p. 486. For a survey of fire memorials (which, incredibly, manages to overlook the 1910 story), see Andrew Gulliford, "Fire on the Mountain," *Montana* 47, No. 2 (Summer 1997), pp. 44–57.
28. See correspondence between Turrell and Morrell, NAPAR, RG 95, Box 20, Fd. Fire—Misc. Corresp. Circulars, and Other Material, 1910 Fire Season; esp. letters 1 February, 5 February, 1 April 1926.
29. Letter, Turrell to Morrell, 1 April 1926, NAPAR, loc. cit.
30. Elers Koch, "Introduction," *When the Mountains Roared* (U.S. Forest Service, many editions, n.d.); the most recent comes from the Idaho Panhandle National Forests. On the Pulaski tunnel fiasco, see G. S. Haynes, Memorandum for Ranger Puphal, 6 November 1938, Wallace District, U.S. Forest Service, Silverton Office.

31. Memorandum, E. F. Barry to Forest Supervisor, 29 July 1955, Region One, U.S. Forest Service, Historic Files.
32. Memorandum, J. K. Vessey to Forest Supervisor, Coeur d'Alene National Forest, 2 September 1955, USFS R1 and Silverton [Wallace] Office files.
33. Memorandum, Robert A. Cook to Forest Supervisor, 13 July 1956, USFS R1 and Silverton [Wallace] Office files; Letter, L. E. Noel to True Temper Corporation, 15 November 1956, Silverton Office historic files.
34. Memorandum, Carl G. Krueger to Regional Forester, 28 September 1959, USFS R1; on local objections, see Memorandum, L. R. Fulton to Forest Supervisor, 15 January 1960, USFS R1.
35. K. A. Keeney, "Memorandum for Division Chiefs, Supervisors of Colville, Lolo, St. Joe, Coeur d'Alene, Kaniksu, Clearwater, and Nezperce National Forests," 15 February 1960, and "Memorial Day Services, Woodlawn Cemetery, St. Maries, Idaho, Commemorating the 50th Anniversary of the 1910 Fire," both in NAPAR, RG 95, Box 19, Folder: 50th Anniversary of the 1910 fire.
36. William W. Morris, "Experiences on a National Forest," *Early Days in the Forest Service,* vol. 1 (Missoula, Mont.: U.S. Forest Service, 1944), p. 176.
37. See "Joseph B. Halm," Region One, U.S. Forest Service. Personnel Files—Halm. His "Great Fire" account was published in *American Forests* (July 1930) and reprinted in Ovid Butler, ed., *Rangers of the Shield: A Collection of Stories Written by Men of the National Forests of the West* (Washington, D.C.: American Forestry Association, 1934).
38. C. K. McHarg, "Edward C. Pulaski 1868–1931," Region One, U.S. Forest Service, Personnel Files—Pulaski; Letter, Mrs. Mary Turrell to Fred Morrell, 1 April 1926, NAPAR, RG 95, Box 20, Folder: Fire—Misc. Correspondence, Circulars, and other Material, 1910 Fire Season; Letter, F. A. Silcox to the Forester, 26 June 1911, cover letter to Supervisor Weigle's Report, 1910 Claims—General.
39. Edward C. Pulaski, "Surrounded by Forest Fires," *American Forests and Forest Life* (August 1923), pp. 485–86; Letter, R. Y. Stuart to Secretary of Agriculture, 14 March 1930, Region One, U.S. Forest Service, Personnel Files—Pulaski.
40. Many versions exist purporting to tell how the pulaski tool was invented, almost as many as there are claimants to Smokey the Bear. I rely here on Letter, Evan W. Kelley to Fred W. Funke, 30 May 1944, Region One, U.S. Forest Service, Historic Files.
41. Letter, Meyer Wolff to District Forester, Missoula, 16 February 1914; Letter, W. W. Morris to E. C. Pulaski, 13 March 1914; Letter, E. C. Pulaski to Forest Supervisor, Coeur d'Alene, 27 March 1914, all in Region One, U.S. Forest Service, Personnel Files—Pulaski.

After Pulaski's death his daughter tried to patent the tool. But it was too late; two years of public use without a patent application had placed the invention beyond private royalties. There was, however, a provision in patent law that allowed government workers to patent inventions created during public service. There was no royalty, but the device could bear his name, as it does. A summary of the original correspondence is given in Terry Brenner, "Pulaski: The Man, the Tool," *American Forests* 90 (July 1984), pp. 36–38, 49–51.

# SOURCES

## *Written Sources*

Among forest fires, the Big Blowup is unusually blessed with documentary sources. These fall into three groups.

One, the smallest and most scattered, consists of personal letters or accounts. Mostly these derive from persons who were not hired firefighters, for example, the letters of Marie Alger or Frances Eaton. These are not gathered into any common pool; some have been published from time to time, and their full citations appear in the notes, as they are referenced. Several such sources belong with larger collections. The most significant is that from William W. Morris.

Morris regularly wrote to his family in Chicago. This correspondence he later retyped into a composite manuscript titled "Letters from the Coeur d'Alene National Forest, 1908–1914," and deposited at the University of Washington Libraries, Manuscripts and University Archives Division (accession number 4828–001). These in turn became the source for a fuller account of the fire season that he later wrote, which he titled "The Great Fires of 1910" and which exists in mimeographed form in several Forest Service archival sites. Still later he expanded that account into a general description of his first years as a forester, "Experiences on a National Forest," published by Forest Service Region One in *Early Days in the Forest Service,* vol. 1 (1944). While much overlaps, each of the accounts includes material not present in the others. Together they form the most comprehensive single source of what the fire season was like for someone on the ground, and they have the advantage of tracking the season as it evolved.

Additionally I have relied on the papers of Henry Solon Graves, lodged at the Yale University Library, Manuscripts and Archives, Group Number 249. I found Graves's unpublished autobiography and the field diary for 1910 particularly informative. Also useful, if spotty, were the Richard Ballinger Papers, University of Washington Libraries, Manuscripts and University Archives Division (accession number 15).

The second and most coherent source of on-hand accounts consists of those stories written by Army officers after their tour to the fires. The adjutant general's office prepared a questionnaire to which each officer replied, item by item. Some officers elaborated; some did not. Some included copies of telegrams sent and received; others didn't. Some commanding officers drafted summary overviews of the involvement of the units under their direction; others did not. In addition, the files include virtually all correspondence (and telegrams) between the White House and the War Department and between field units. The records contain also some maps, tables, and photos. This marvelous cache is located in the National Archives, Record Group 94, Records of the Adjutant General's Office, file citation no. 1681570.

The third, and largest, group is made up of official records of the Forest Service. These take several forms. There are records stored on the Silverton (Wallace) District of the Idaho Panhandle National Forests. These have been orchestrated into a detailed study of the Pulaski narrative by Carl Ritchie, "Pulaski, Two Days in August, 1910. A Cultural Resource Inventory" (1984), prepared for the district and published by the Idaho Panhandle National Forests in conjunction with the 10 August 1984 ceremonies for the Memorial to the 1910 Fire.

There is an impressive compilation of documents at the headquarters of the Idaho Panhandle National Forests, Coeur d'Alene, Idaho. These were also gathered in the early 1980s, when the forest applied to have the Nicholson adit named to the National Register of Historic Places, and they survive under the care of the forest archaeologist. There also remain several caches at the Forest Service Region One headquarters in Missoula, Montana. Some of these exist among the historic files collection (part of which has been shipped to the Seattle branch of the National Archives). Others, a surprising find (to me), belonged in the personnel files. Only a handful of participants in the Great Fires had their files retained, but among them were Edward Pulaski and Joseph Halm.

From the early 1920s there was some ambition to collect (or where necessary, to solicit) accounts of the Great Fires. These were subsequently published (along with many other personal experience statements not related to fire) by the Missoula office as *Early Days in the Forest Service,* eventually swelling to four volumes. These have, in turn, been selectively edited and republished by Hal K. Rothman, ed., *"I'll Never Fight Fire with My Bare Hands Again": Recollections of the First Forest Rangers of the Inland Northwest* (Lawrence: University Press of Kansas, 1994). The more powerful source, however, remains Elers Koch, *When the Mountains Roared: Stories of the 1910 Fires* (Missoula, Mont.: U.S. Forest Service, 1944), variously republished, most recently by the Idaho Panhandle National Forests. Koch includes excerpts from all the forest supervisors' reports, other episodes (derived from the accounts in *Early Days*), and some material from newspapers and settler letters. Of special merit too are Koch's own account, now safely embedded in the story of his career, as Elers Koch, *Forty Years a Forester, 1903–1943* (Missoula, Mont.: Mountain Press, 1998), and the chapter devoted to the fires in William B. Greeley, *Forests and Men* (Garden City, N.Y.: Doubleday & Co., 1951).

Over the years documents have moved (selectively) up the bureaucratic ziggurat. Many of the historic files pertaining to the 1910 fire season have been transferred to the regional branch of the National Archives in Seattle, as Record Group 95, Records of the Forest Service. Others remain in Missoula, although it is likely that they too will be tranferred over the coming years. The other major source is the National Archives at College Park, Maryland, which houses Record Group 95, Records of the Forest Service, as those records were generated by the Washington office. There are many points of contact here, but the two dominant documents relate to congressional requests for information about deaths and injuries and, subsequently, to the applications filed by those claiming compensation. All the forests wrote accounts of the season, emphasizing the circumstances under which fatalities occurred. Virtually everyone who suffered injury, the loss of a dependent relative, or damage to horses or equipment filed for compensation. Forest officers were in turn required to evaluate and pass judgment on these applications. The outcome, while chaotic, is a rich compost of original reports. Unsurprisingly, many documents are housed, in copies, in several Forest Service sites. Thus Supervisor W. G. Weigle's "Report on the 1910 Fires" can be found in Silverton, Coeur d'Alene, Missoula, Seattle, and College Park, and probably elsewhere.

The fires have entered into several books. The most important is Betty G. Spencer, *The Big Blowup* (Caldwell, Ida.: Caxton Printers, 1956), reissued in a limited edition by the International Association of Wildland Fire in 1994. Spencer was able to interview some original participants, including Elsie Pabst, and her book thus becomes an original source in its own right. Unfortunately she depends rather uncritically on local newspapers, which I have found almost wholly unreliable, save when they quote from written sources such as a telegram or press release. The story was recycled as a picture book by Stan Cohen and Don Miller, *The Big Burn: The Northwest's Forest Fire of 1910* (Missoula, Mont.: Pictorial Histories Publishing Co., 1974) and revised and reissued in 1993. The fires figure prominently too in Ruby El Hult, *Northwest Disaster: Avalanche and Fire* (Portland, Ore.: Binsfords & Mort, 1960). Also worth mentioning is Sandra A. Crowell and David O. Asleson, *Up the Swiftwater: A Pictorial History of the Colorful Upper St. Joe River Country* (Coeur d'Alene: Museum of North Idaho, 1980). While the fires constitute only one chapter, the account is particularly sensible, rich in local detail and framed nicely within the larger setting.

On the general history of fire, see Stephen J. Pyne, *Fire in America: A Cultural History of Wildland and Rural Fire* (Princeton, N.J.: Princeton University Press, 1982; reprinted, Seattle: University of Washington Press, 1995) and, of steadily decreasing value, Stewart Holbrook, *Burning an Empire: The Story of American Forest Fires* (New York: Macmillan, 1943), whose chapter on the Great Fires basically recycles the Pulaski narrative.

There are many, many other fine studies on forestry, conservation, and politics. Most I will leave in the notes since my purpose is really specific to the 1910 fire season and to creating, in something like a popular narrative, the meaning of the Great Fires as that derives from their context. A few works, however, qualify for special note: Harold K. Steen, *The U.S. Forest Service: A History* (Seattle: University of Washington Press, 1976); Samuel P. Hays, *Conservation and the Gospel of Efficiency: The Progressive Conservation Movement 1890–1920* (New York: Atheneum, 1969); and G. T. Morgan, Jr., "The Fight Against Fire: Development of Cooperative Forestry in the Pacific Northwest, 1900–1950," Ph.D. dissertation, University of Oregon, 1964.

## *Photographic Sources*

The 1910 fires are unusually well captured in photographs. In general the sources for photos parallel those of the written record, with a few exceptions. Also, like the written records, several sites have copies of the same photos.

Begin with Wallace, Idaho. The Wallace District Office of the Forest Service (in Silverton) holds prints of many official photos. The Wallace Public Library has several photos of the town after the fire, and the Historic Wallace Preservation Society has a fine suite taken by H. English in the mountains during and after the burns. Useful too are the photos taken by Thomas Barnard and Nellie Jane Stockbridge, who had a studio in Wallace and photographed the smoke over the town, the burned sections of Wallace, and fire victims (bandaged); these are now deposited with the Special Collections and Archives at the University of Idaho.

The Idaho Panhandle National Forests headquarters at Coeur d'Alene has a good selection of official photos. Several fascinating photos taken by others are housed elsewhere in Coeur d'Alene at the Museum of North Idaho, which has an exhibit on fire control and the 1910 fires. Likely every forest has a handful of historic pictures somewhere in its files.

The best single collection, though, seems to remain at Forest Service Region One offices in Missoula. An inventory was done in 1959, preparatory to the 1960 commemoration (the list is still available). By then some original photos had already been lost. The originals, or duplicate negatives, eventually moved to the Historic Photo Collection in the Washington offices. These have in turn been relocated to the Still Photographs Section of the National Archives at College Park, with a partial duplicate set for agency use housed at the National Agricultural Library in Beltsville, Maryland. There is no ready guide into these collections. The photos were taken in sequences, however, and the fact that many numbers of these sequences no longer have images attached to them suggests the degree of attrition.

The Oregon Historical Society has a duplicate set of some of the major Forest Service images. Another source, unofficial but revealing because they occur during the fires, not afterward, are the photos reproduced in the special fire issue of *American Forestry* in November 1910. The *Seattle Daily News* also published a series of photos during August. And Barbara Tokmakian, daughter of Roscoe Haines, possesses her father's photograph album, full of images he took or collected.

# INDEX